GENEALOGY *of* EARLY SETTLERS *in* TRENTON and EWING *"Old Hunterdon County,"* NEW JERSEY

by

ELI F. COOLEY and WILLIAM S. COOLEY

Prepared for Publication by

HANNAH L. COOLEY

GENEALOGICAL PUBLISHING CO., INC.

BALTIMORE **1977**

Originally Published
Trenton, New Jersey
1883

Reprinted
Genealogical Publishing Co., Inc.
Baltimore, 1977

Library of Congress Cataloging in Publication Data

Cooley, Eli Field, 1781-1860.
Genealogy of early settlers in Trenton and Ewing, "old Hunterdon County," New Jersey.
Reprint of the 1883 ed. published by W. S. Sharp Print. Co., Trenton.
Includes index.
1. Trenton—Genealogy. 2. Ewing, N. J.—Genealogy. 3. Mercer Co., N. J.—Genealogy. I. Cooley, William Scudder, d. 1882, joint author. II. Title.

F144.T7C62 1977 929'.2'0973 76-45636
ISBN 0-8063-0744-7

Made in the United States of America

Preface.

At the re-opening of the First Presbyterian Church of Trenton—now the Presbyterian Church of Ewing—after the edifice had been remodeled, the Rev. Dr. Eli F. Cooley preached a sermon, Sabbath morning, December 1st, 1839, on the text, "Your Fathers: where are they? and the Prophets: do they live forever?"—*Zechariah*, 1: 5. In the preparation of this discourse, he gathered a large amount of genealogical information concerning the families of his congregation. This led him to engage in further research into the history of that section of the county and of families under his pastoral care. In 1842, he wrote for the "State Gazette," at Trenton, a series of papers relative to the first settlement of Hopewell, and in 1844, Barber and Howe's "Historical Collections of the State of New Jersey" was published, with much of the article on Mercer county known to have been prepared by Dr. Cooley. His information, he said, was collected from the examination of deeds and wills, from surveys and family Bibles, and from daily conversation with aged persons of his acquaintance. During the latter part of his life, it was his intention to publish the result of his labors, but this pleasure was denied him. At his death, his papers came into the hands of his son, Prof. William S. Cooley, of Philadelphia, a gentleman eminently fitted to continue the researches made by his father. For many years, he devoted much time to verifying and amplifying these family records. Among his papers, we find a quotation from Dr. De Witt's journal, "Though every one ought to rest on his own merits, yet it is pleasant to trace one's lineage over a line of honest and honorable ancestors, with here and there one, perhaps, overtopping the rest and shedding the lustre of his character on the whole line." And in another place, we find he noted such sentiments as "The honorable life of a parent operates as a perpetual stimulant to a similar career;" "It is our duty to keep alive the memory of distinguished worth, that others may derive from it an impulse to a nobler and higher life." Imbued with this feeling, Prof. Cooley did what he could to perpetuate the good lives of the men and women among whom he passed his boyhood, and whom his father loved. He, too, in the last years of his life, had begun to copy, for publication, the result of his own and his father's researches. He died February 7th, 1882, and the manuscript notes of both grandfather and uncle came into possession of MISS HANNAH L. COOLEY, of Ewing, Mercer county, New Jersey. Many efforts have since been made by persons interested in these records, to have them printed, and, at their urgent solicitation, Miss Cooley has prepared them for the press. Without any previously-acquired skill in the ordinary compilation of family lineage, eschewing any responsibility for facts herein related, other than that, perhaps, of an accurate copyist, but actuated by an earnest desire that the many hours of pleasant labor given by her ancestors should not forever be lost, she has, with much care and patience, placed these notes of history and tradition in such a shape that they are now ready for the use of the public.

THE PUBLISHERS.

The Anderson Family.

As the name of this family was originally written Andris, and Andrus, it probably came from Holland. Joshua Anderson (1), the ancestor of one of the Trenton families of this name, who died 1810, aged 89, lived in Monmouth county, and married Hannah Smith, who died 1790, aged 54. Their children were John, born 1759; Anna, born 1762, married Mr. Clayton, of Schenectady, had a son, Anderson, a Presbyterian clergyman; Hannah, born 1764, married Solomon Combs; Sarah, born 1766, not married; Eleanor, born 1771, married Samuel Reading, (see Reading family, No. 18); Cyreneus Vanmarter (2), born 1773; Catharine, married Mr. Cozens, and had children, John and Sarah Ann; Joshua (3), born 1781.

Cyreneus (2), son of Joshua (1), married Julia Hoppock, and by her had children: George H. (4); John B. (5); Hannah S.; Clotilda; Margaret, married Joseph H. Hough, of Trenton, their children are Julia, Rebecca, John, Joseph, and William; Catharine, married Farley Shephard, merchant, of Sergeantsville, whose children are Cyreneus, Edward, Poueson, Jessie F., and Elizabeth; Elizabeth married Joseph Dean, and had children, Julia and Rebecca; Cornelius H., married Prudence, daughter of Benjamin Jones, they had children, William, Benjamin, Caroline, and Catharine.

George H. (4), son of Cyreneus (2), married Caroline Robbins, and had children: Lemuel, married Eliza, daughter of Benjamin Vancleve, (see Vancleve family, No. 16); Cyreneus, married Rebecca, daughter of Henry Stevenson, of Lambertville; Joseph, married Frances, daughter of the same; Rebecca, married Sylvester Phillips, son of John Phillips; John N., married Sarah Clark; and Alexander.

John B. (5), son of Cyreneus (2), married Rebecca Ann, daughter of Peter Forman, sheriff of Trenton, who died November 9th, 1873, aged 68, having had children: Julia, died in childhood;

Peter Forman; Edward MacIlvaine; Alfred H.; John L. T.; and Margaret L.

Hannah S. Anderson, daughter of Cyreneus (2), who married Solomon Wambaugh, had children: Cyreneus; John; Alonzo; Elizabeth; Emily; Caroline; Cornelia; Christiana J.; and Matilda.

Clotilda Anderson, daughter of Cyreneus (2), married John P. Combs, of Trenton, by whom she had Frances; Elizabeth; Hannah; Deborah; John; Herbert; Charles; and others died young.

Joshua (3), son of Joshua (1), who died June 13th, 1840, in his 60th year, was for many years an elder in the First Presbyterian Church, Trenton. He married Jemima Broadhurst, who died December 10th, 1839, in her 58th year, leaving children: Joseph B. (6); Keziah, married Thomas Broadhurst, her children are Winfield Scott and Anna; Phebe C.; Rebecca, married Nelson Large, and had children, Emma and Caroline; Hannah, married, first, Samuel Hart, having a son, George; second, Ebenezer Large, by whom she had a son, Nelson; John F., died 1840, aged 19.

Joseph B. (6), son of Joshua (3), died January 6th, 1875, in his 68th year. He had by his first wife, Eliza, daughter of Maj. Edward MacIlvaine, who died August 14th, 1831, aged 20, a daughter, Anna; she died 1834. By his second wife, Sarah, daughter of Benjamin Hendrickson, (see Hendrickson family, No. 7,) Eliza, who married Titus Scudder, son of Charles. His third wife is Matilda Hendrickson, sister of his former wife; no children.

Phebe E. Anderson, daughter of Joshua (3), married, first, Benjamin Franklin Vancleve, (see Vancleve family, No. 20,) a lawyer of Trenton, whose children are Frederic, Henry, Benjamin F.; second, Francis Breggy, Professor of French in the University of Pennsylvania, and had by him Amadie, a lawyer of Philadelphia; Louis Napoleon; and Clara, married George Hill. Mrs. Breggy died 1878.

The Anthony Family.

George Anthony (1), a native of Strasburg, Germany, settled, at an early period, in Pennsylvania, with his wife, Catharine, whose children were William (2) ; Mary, married John Paradise ; Catharine, married Henry Simmons ; Sarah, married John Ballum ; and Susannah, died unmarried.

William (2), who died 1831, aged 66, son of George (1), married Martha, daughter of Alexander Biles, of Maidenhead. She died 1848, aged 81. By her he had children : Catharine, married James B. Green, (see Green family, No. 17) ; Mary, married Elijah Green, her first husband, (see Green family, No. 59,) and Jacob Graffies, a merchant of Williamsport, Pa., for her second ; George, married Mary Crone ; Joseph (3); Rachel, became the second wife of Asa Fish, without issue.

Joseph (3), son of William (2), by profession a lawyer, settled in Williamsport, Pa., was appointed judge, and represented, from 1833 to 1838, his district in congress. He married Catharine Graffies, of that place, and had by her : Elizabeth, married John R. Campbell, a merchant ; Martha, married Hepburn McClure, a lawyer of Williamsport ; Daniel, a graduate of Princeton, and member of the bar ; Catharine, married Mr. White ; Mary, married Dr. Lyon ; Rachel, married James Montgomery ; and Emily, married John Morgan.

The Beatty Family.

John Beatty (1), the ancestor of the Beatty family of this region, was an officer of the British army, a native of county Antrim, Ireland, of Scotch-Irish descent and Presbyterian creed. He married a lady of English origin, whose family had removed to Ireland during the Rebellion—Christiana, daughter of James Clinton and sister of Charles Clinton, whose son George was successively general in the army of the Revolution, governor of New York, and vice-president of the United States. Mrs. Beatty, after the early death of her husband, emigrated, in company with her brother, Charles Clinton, and her four children, to America. After a protracted voyage of nearly twenty-four weeks, they landed at Cape Cod, in 1729, having suffered greatly from the want of both food and water, which cost the lives of many passengers. They settled, finally, at Orange, N. J. Her children were Elizabeth, married Mr. Denniston, and died on the voyage; Charles (2); Mary, married James Gregg; and Martha, married Mr. McMillan.

Charles (2), son of John (1), having received a classical education, partly in Ireland and partly in this country, entered the Log College as a student of divinity, and after having been licensed, was settled, in 1743, at Neshaminy, Pa., as the successor of his instructor, Rev. William Tennent, Sr., but he, by a permitted absence from his congregation, engaged in the public service as chaplain to the army, on several expeditions against the French and Indians. In 1763, he was appointed trustee of the College of New Jersey, and to raise funds in its behalf, went, in the place of Dr. Witherspoon, to Barbadoes, where he took the fever and died, 1772, aged 57. He married, in 1746, Ann, daughter of Gov. John Reading, (see Reading family, No. 2.) She died at Greenock, Scotland, whither she had gone with her husband, for medical advice, having borne him eleven children, nine of whom reached maturity: Mary, born April 21st, 1747, married Rev.

Enoch Green, (see Green family, No. 40); Christiana, born June 17th, 1748, died about 16; John (3), born December 10th, 1749; Elizabeth, born March 26th, 1752, married Rev. Philip Vicars Fithian, son of Joseph Fithian, of Greenwich, a Presbyterian clergyman, who, having been appointed to a chaplaincy in the army, in 1776, was at the battle of White Plains, and soon after died from exposure, in camp. Her second husband was a cousin of her former one—Joel Fithian, brother of Dr. Enoch Fithian and grandson of Samuel, an emigrant from Long Island, in 1700, and first of the name in Cumberland county. Mr. Joel Fithian represented the county in the legislature, and was an elder in the Presbyterian Church. He died 1821, his widow in 1825, having had nine children: Martha, died in early childhood; Charles Clinton, born February 10th, 1756, was graduated at Princeton, soon after received a captain's commission in the army, was with Wayne on his expedition into Canada, and being accidentally shot by a brother officer, died in 1776, aged 21; Reading (4), born December 23d, 1757; Erkuries (5), born October 9th, 1759; George, born June 28th, 1763, supposed to have been lost at sea; William P. (6), born March 31st, 1766; Ann, born 1768, in Greenock, Scotland, and is buried there with her mother.

Gen. John (3), son of Rev. Charles (2), was a graduate of Princeton, and adopted the profession of medicine, which he had not practiced long before the commencement of hostilities with Great Britain, when, in 1775, he received a captain's commission in the Fifth Pennsylvania Battalion, and after active participation in the service, and having attained the rank of major, he was taken prisoner, at the surrender of Fort Washington, November, 1776. On his exchange, May 28th, 1778, he was appointed, on the resignation of Dr. Elias Boudinot, commissary-general of prisoners, which office he held until his retirement in 1780, when he resumed his practice in Princeton. During his residence there, he represented his state in congress, in the years 1783–1785 and 1793–1795. He was also made brigadier-general of militia. In 1795, he was elected by the legislature, of which he had been speaker, secretary of state, and from that time till his death, May 31st, 1826, aged 77, resided in Trenton. He was president of the Trenton Delaware Bridge Company, and actively superintended the building of that structure. Gen. Beatty was also, for twenty years, a trustee of Princeton College, was president of the Trenton Banking Company, and an elder in the First

Presbyterian Church of Trenton till his death. He married, in 1756, Mary, daughter of Richard Longstreet, of Princeton, by whom he had children: Anna, died an infant, and Richard (7). She died 1815, aged 59. He married, second, Mrs. Catharine Lalor, daughter of Barnt De Klyn Lalor, of Trenton, who, without children by him, died January 27th, 1861, aged 88, having left to the First Presbyterian Church, for the communion table, a valuable silver flagon, which she had inherited.

Richard (7), son of Gen. John (3), was a graduate of Princeton, studied law, in the practice of which he engaged at Allentown, where he married Isabella Imlay, by whom he had children: Mary Elizabeth; John Imlay, married Susan McKean, and lives, a merchant, in Allentown; Isabella and Richard, both died in infancy; Anna C., married Lemuel S. Fithian, a merchant of Philadelphia; Christiana S., married George Robbins, of Allentown; Isabella, married Dr. A. Alexander Howell, (see Howell family, No. 34); Emily C., married E. H. Holmes, whose only son, James, is a physician of Allentown; Catharine Louisa, became a missionary to India, from whence she returned in 1869, and died 1870.

Dr. Reading (4), son of Rev. Charles (2), was a student of medicine when the war broke out, but at once entered the army, and soon was made lieutenant in his brother John's company; was, with his brother, taken prisoner at Fort Washington, and for a while treated with great severity, being confined in a prison-ship. He was released upon parole. While a captive, he continued his studies, and was ultimately commissioned by congress a surgeon in the army, which office he continued to discharge till the close of the war. He was a ruling elder in the Presbyterian Church at Newtown, Pa., till his death, in 1834. By his wife, Christiana, daughter of Judge Henry Wynkoop, of Bucks county, Pa., he had Ann, died in infancy; Ann, married Rev. Alexander Boyd, of the Presbyterian Church of Newtown, Pa.; Henry, died young; Charles C., a physician of Abington, Pa., married Rebecca Vanuxen, of Philadelphia; Susan; Mary, married Rev. Robert Steele, pastor of the Presbyterian Church at Abington, Pa.; John, married, first, Emily P., daughter of Dr. Samuel Moore, director of the Philadelphia mint, second, Mary Ashton Henry, of Evansburg, Pa., niece of Alexander Henry, of Philadelphia; and Sarah, married Rev. Henry Wilson, died as a missionary, in Arkansas.

Col. Erkuries Beatty (5), son of Rev. Charles, was preparing for Princeton College when the war between Great Britain and her colonies broke out. His patriotism, at the early age of 16, prompted him to enter the army under Lord Stirling. He was in the action on Long Island and at White Plains, having obtained an ensign's commission in the Fourth Pennsylvania Battalion. He was engaged in the battle of Brandywine, May, 1777, and also, in October, 1877, in that of Germantown, in which he was severely wounded. During the next campaign, he fought at Monmouth, June 28th, 1778, under Wayne, and after being in active service, in the meantime marched with him south, joined La Fayette, and was present at the capture of Yorktown, October, 1781, and continued with the army until its disbandment, November, 1783. He was, for several years, paymaster of the western army, under Gen. Harmar; for two years, was commandant of the Fort St. Vincents (Vincennes); promoted to the rank of major; in 1793, he resigned his position and retired to Princeton, where he resided till his death, 1823, aged 64, and is buried in the cemetery of that place. While living at Princeton, he was elected colonel of a regiment of militia. In addition to his military honors, he filled many civil offices and appointments—was a judge of the county court, a member, for several years, of either the assembly or council, was mayor of the borough, and for a time, a trustee of the Presbyterian Church. In 1799, he married Mrs. Susanna Ferguson (Ewing), widow of Maj. Ferguson. Their children were Charles Clinton (8); Susan, died at 16; Erkuries E., entered the army and died at Baton Rouge, 1827, aged 23.

Dr. Charles Clinton (8), son of Erkuries (5), was graduated at Princeton, and studied theology there. He settled at Steubenville, Ohio, over the First Church, where he was pastor for nearly fourteen years. He established there one of the largest and most eminent seminaries in the land, for the education of young ladies. He was vice-president of the New Jersey branch of the Society of the Cincinnati. His power in the church was great. He represented his presbytery in general assembly many times; was moderator of the one at Columbus, Ohio, in 1862; received the title both of D. D. and LL. D. He gave largely of his means to the church and many institutions of our land. He died October 30th, 1882, aged 82, having married, first, in 1824, Lydia Moore, of Bridge Point, who, with her infant child, died the next year;

second, Hetty Elizabeth Davis, of Maysville, Ky.; third, Mary Inskipt, widow of Dr. Crittendon, of Pittsburg.

William P. (6), son of Rev. Charles (2), after filling various civil offices, became a merchant of Columbia, Pa., of which he was, for several years, chief burgess, and was also a ruling elder in the Presbyterian Church there. He died 1848, aged 48, having married Eleanor, daughter of John Polk, of Neshaminy, Pa., by whom he had, besides several offspring who died in childhood, George (9); William P., who lived at Harrisburg till his death, 1860, having married Mary S. Clendenin; Ann Eliza, married Thomas H. Pearce, of Columbia; John R.; and Erkuries, who was proprietor and publisher of the Carlisle "Herald." At the outbreak of the late war, he volunteered and joined the Thirty-sixth Pennsylvania Regiment of the line under Gen. McCall; was present as a member of his staff, at the battle of Drainesville; was twice wounded in the battle of New Market. As captain, under Gen. Burnside, he participated in the bloody battle of Fredericksburg; was assistant adjutant-general at Washington, and in 1864, after an honorable discharge, he was honored by the war department for bravery and meritorious services in the field, with the brevet commissions of major and of lieutenant-colonel. He was an elder of the Presbyterian Church of Carlisle. He married Margaret E. Piper, of Harrisburg, and has children: William, Alexander P., Annie E., Fannie, and Helen.

Dr. George (9), son of William (6), a physician, resided for a time in Iowa, of which state he was auditor-general and treasurer. He afterward was proprietor and editor of "Niles' Register," of Philadelphia. He married, at Felicity, Ohio, Mrs. Eliza Salter, daughter of Rev. Thomas Ansley, of Nova Scotia.

The Brearley Family.

Two brothers Brearley, or, as originally spelled, Bryerley, younger members of a family of distinction in England, came to this country and settled—one of them ultimately at the South, where the name still retains its original spelling. The other, John (1), settled in the town of Lawrenceville, where he purchased, in 1695, of Mahlon Stacy, of Ballifield (the name of his place), a tract of land on the Shabakonk. He was also the owner of a large body of land near Philadelphia. He died, leaving a widow, Sarah, who survived till 1731, date of will. Their children were John (2), who had sons, John (5) and David; Benjamin (3); David (4); Joseph, died intestate, leaving an only son, John, who lived in Harding, Sussex county; Mary, married John Olden; Ruth, married George Rozell.

John (5), son of John (2), had children: James (6); a daughter, married Mr. Anderson; and Sarah, married Maj. Thomas Stockton, of Princeton, who died 1799, aged 69. She survived till 1814, aged 79.

James (6), son of John (5), married, first, Esther Johnes; had issue: Samuel (7); Isaac (8); James died 1851, aged 86, not married; John died 1846, aged 78, married Matilda, daughter of Joseph Baker, and have children: Randall, a physician, removed to the West, Joseph Baker, Susan, and Mary; George (9); Esther, not married; Stephen; Ellet died in Ohio. By his second wife, Penelope Cook, he had Sarah, not married; William died at the South; and Jonathan married Martha, daughter of Joseph Baker.

Samuel (7), son of James (6), died 1841, aged 80, having married Rhoda, daughter of Benjamin Mershon, whose children were Margaret, married Mr. Knot in the West; Mary, married Capt. Wells, and lives in the West; and Lewis, who is married, and resides in the West.

Isaac (8), son of James (6), born June 21st, 1763, married Sarah Bellerjeau, and had children: Eliza, died 1869, aged 75; Johnes, married, no children, died 1867, aged 71; Achsa, died 1869, aged 70; and James, married Frances, daughter of Joseph Baker, of Lawrence.

George (9), son of James (6), died 1857, aged 87, having married Nancy Gillingham, of Pennsylvania; she died 1843, aged 71, having had children: Samuel (10); James (11); Esther; Harvey (12); William, a Presbyterian clergyman, of South Carolina, married Miss English; Mary Ann; Joseph Gillingham (13); Stephen (14); Juliet; and Elizabeth.

Samuel (10), son of George (9), married, first, Elizabeth, daughter of Israel Smith, by whom he had Eliza, married Thomas R. English, lives in the South; second, Sarah Smith, who had a son, William Armstrong (15); third, Mary Ann Smith.

William Armstrong (15), son of Samuel (10), married, first, Mary M. Rue, whose children are Samuel; Joseph, whose first wife was Jennie Ray, of Brooklyn, second, Kate, daughter of Alfred Perrine. He married, second, Henrietta A. Moore, had children by her; William Henry, married Emily, daughter of Mathew Rue; Helen and Anna, both died in infancy.

James (11), son of George (9), died 1855, aged 60, having married Mehitable, daughter of Asher Smith; had children: Elizabeth, wife of William F. Rouse; Charles, married, first, Sarah, daughter of William Burke, had Lillie, who married Robert Kennedy—his second wife was Miss Sloane; Caroline, wife of David Lanning; George (16); and Sarah.

George (16), son of James (11), married Jane, daughter of James A. Phillips; have children: Joseph G.; Mabel, wife of George Hottel; Ellen, wife of Roland Loyd; Julia; Mary; and Angie.

Harvey (12), son of George (9), married Ann, daughter of John Moore, of Lawrence, and had by her; Edward, married Louisa Mershon; Harvey, married Hannah Shreves; Mary, married Garret Smith; Louisa, wife of Isaac Hutchinson; and Anna.

Joseph Gillingham (13), son of George (9), was for several years president of the Mechanics' and Manufacturers' Bank of Trenton, and also an elder in the First Presbyterian Church there. He married Catharine Lalor, by whom he had Anderson Lalor, married Annie Gardener; and Alice, married Mr. Moulton.

Stephen (14), son of George (9), died 1866, aged 55, having married Cornelia Conover; she died 1859, aged 45; had children: Emeline, married John L. Hendrickson; Conover, married Caroline Shultz; Sarah, married Henry Williams; and Catharine, married Mr. Mount.

Benjamin (3), son of John (1), left his property, by his will, dated 1756, recorded in 1757, of which Benjamin, his son, and George Rozell, his brother-in-law, were his executors, to his wife, Elizabeth, who died 1759, and to his children, Benjamin; Rachel; Sarah; Rebecca; and Elizabeth.

David (4), son of John (1), married Mary Clark, and by her had Joseph (17); David (18); Esther, not married; Abijah, not married; and Jerusha, was the second wife of Mr. Pierson.

Gen. Joseph (17), son of David (4), was actively engaged in the military service of his country. He was major of the Second New Jersey Battalion, engaged before Quebec, 1776, and major of the First Hunterdon Regiment, and captain in the Continental Army. He afterward held the rank of general. He married Rachel McClarey, and had by her: Charles, died unmarried, in Cincinnati; David (19); Joseph (20); Benjamin (21); Eliza, married Ezekiel Smith, of Lawrence, and had children: John, Ezekiel, and Robinson; Hetty; Pierson; and Maria; last three not married.

Col. David (19), son of Gen. Joseph (17), was actively engaged in the war of 1812, and associated with Gen. Scott. He married Hannah Jones and moved to Arkansas, where he died, leaving children: Joseph, who lives at Norristown, Ark., married, and has two sons; Eleanor, married William Lewis Wharton, surgeon in the army, and has children: David Brearley, Clifton Tucker, Amanda J., wife of Frederick H. Gibson, of Virginia, and William Lewis, married Jane A. Cavanna; and Mary, married Rev. William Smallwood, of Washington, D. C., an Episcopal clergyman; her children are Agnes, wife of Mr. Cassel, and Mary E.

Joseph (20), son of Joseph (17), married Joanna, daughter of Philip Hendrickson, (see Hendrickson family, No. 5,) whose children are Caroline, wife of Simon Sill, and resided in St. Louis; Henrietta, died unmarried; and Charity, died young.

Benjamin (21), son of Joseph (17), was, in 1812, a lieutenant of artillery in the regular army, and fought in the battle of Lundy's Lane. He married Susan, daughter of Thomas Riall, of Trenton, father of Hon. Daniel Riall, member of congress from Monmouth, by whom he had Rebecca, second wife of Imlah Moore, of Trenton; and Louisa.

Judge David (18), son of David (4), was colonel of Second

Regiment of Monmouth and lieutenant-colonel in the Continental Army, of the Fourth Battalion, and of the First Regiment, in 1780. He was a member of several state and federal conventions. He participated in the deliberations of the one which formed the constitution of the United States, and signed the document, and of the convention which ratified it. He resigned his military rank when appointed Chief Justice of New Jersey, an office he held for eleven years, when he was made judge of the United States District Court. He died August 16th, 1790, aged 45, having married, first, Elizabeth Mullen ; second, Elizabeth, daughter of Joseph and Rachel Higbee, who died August 20th, 1832, aged 81, by whom he had David, died 1820, aged 34, in Blakely, Ala., not married ; George, died before maturity ; and Joseph Higbee, died 1805, aged 20.

The Burroughs Family.

Jeremiah Burroughs, one of the Westminster divines, was the preacher of two of the largest congregations near London—Stepney and Cripplegate. He was a graduate of Cambridge, an excellent scholar, a popular preacher, and an ornament of the pulpit. Dr. Wilkins reckons him among the most eminent of English divines. Fuller enrols him among the learned writers of Emanuel's College, Cambridge. He was the author of twenty-five works. He died of pulmonary complaint, November 14th, 1646, aged 47.

John Burroughs (1), the ancestor of the families of that name in this part of the country, being of English birth, is most probably of the same family. He came to Massachusetts near the period of its settlement, as he is found living in Salem in 1637. Thence he removed to Newtown, Long Island, where he became a leading man, and died 1678, aged 61, leaving, by his first marriage, children: Jeremiah, who had a son Jeremiah, married to Cornelia Eckerson, and settled in Hunterdon county, N. J.; Joseph, a liberal supporter of the Presbyterian Church, whose son John owned land at Trenton, and some of whose descendants became prominent citizens of Georgia; Joanna, married Jacob Reeder; and Mary. His second wife was the widow Elizabeth Reed, whose only son was John (2).

John (2), son of John (1), was born 1665, married Margaret, daughter of Lambert Woodward, and died in 1699, leaving a son, John (3), and other children.

John (3), son of John (2), came to Ewing township at about the age of 21, and purchased a farm, on which he lived, not far from the church, and adjoining Judge William R. McIlvaine's. His name is signed to an agreement dated August 26th, 1703. He died 1772, aged 88, the date of his recorded will, leaving children: James (4); Isaac; and Benjamin; the two latter settled in Salem county, N. J.; Joseph (5); Jemima, born 1725, died

1825, married, successively, Mr. Barber and Joseph Howell; Henry lived in Bucks county, Pa., married Ann Palmer; Cornelius lived in Salem; Jeremiah—this is probably the one whose grave-stone, in Ewing church-yard, represents to have died 177–, aged 38; Philip; Sarah, married Mr. Moore; Mary, married, successively, Mathew and Henry Baker; John, married Lydia, daughter of Samuel Baker, of Bucks county; Hannah; Martha; and Elizabeth, married Mr. Rose and Samuel Baker.

James (4), son of John (3), who died 1784, aged 49, married Mary Jones. She died 1798, aged 63. Their children were John (6); Joseph (7); Elizabeth, born January 12th, 1758, married William Green, (see Green family, No. 8); Sarah, born June 20th, 1760, died young; Philip (8); Mary, born January 31st, 1765, married Henry Cook, and died 1798; Hulda, born May 5th, 1767, married Garret Johnson, died 1821; Jeremiah (9); Mercy, born October 26th, 1772, married Richard Scudder, (see Scudder family, No. 29); and Jemima, born December 9th, 1775, married Richard Scudder, (see Scudder family, No. 24,) and died June 27th, 1838.

John (6), son of James (4), who died April 28th, 1842, aged 89, married Rhoda, daughter of John Hendrickson, (see Hendrickson family, No. 3.) She died November 14th, 1844, aged 84. Their children were Enoch (10); Timothy (11); Joseph (12); Charles (13); Mary, married Elijah Lanning, (see Lanning family, No. 17); and Susan, born March 13th, 1793, married John Smith, of Lawrence, by whom she had Catharine, wife of John S. Cook, Charles, married Elizabeth, daughter of John Hazard, Garret, married Miss Brearley, Joseph, married Miss Tiffany, and John.

Enoch (10), son of John (6), married Phebe, daughter of John Smith, of Lawrence, whose children are John Stephens; David, married Miss Vanzant; Catharine, married William Phillips; Mary; Asa, married Miss Golder; Elizabeth, married John Cook; and Jane, married John V. Raum.

Timothy (11), son of John (6), born August 28th, 1782, married Phebe, daughter of Joseph Green, (see Green family, No. 47,) whose children are Jeremiah; Deborah; Elizabeth, married Mr. Smith, lived in Hackettstown; Rhoda, married Samuel Salter; and Isaac.

Joseph (12), son of John (6), born May 27, 1785, married Jemima, daughter of Thomas Hendrickson, (see Hendrickson family, No. 16.) Their children are Isaac; Charles; Elnathan; Sarah Ann, married Thomas Crosley; and Joseph.

Charles (13), son of John (6), born January 27th, 1788, was, for many years in succession, elected mayor of Trenton, and was also a trustee of the First Presbyterian Church. He died 1864, having married, in succession, Elizabeth and Lydia Ann, daughters of John Morris, of Trenton. By the first, who died 1838, aged 48, he had issue: Margaret Ann, wife of Henry C. Boswell, son of Rev. William Boswell, of Trenton; George W. (14); Elizabeth, wife of Benjamin S. Holt, of New Haven; James E.; John; Charles C., married Sarah, daughter of Maj. Hutchinson; Mary F.; Caroline; and Virginia. By his second wife, who died 1864, he had James Edward; Cornelia; Henry B.; and John H.

George (14), son of Charles (13), a graduate of Lafayette College and Princeton Theological Seminary, married, first, Angeline, daughter of Hezekiah Smith, of Connecticut; for his second wife, Olivia, daughter of Rev. Benjamin B. Stockton, of Rochester, N. Y., whose children are George, a graduate of Princeton College and Theological Seminary; and Olivia.

Joseph (7), son of James (4), born January 12th, 1756, and died 1784, having married Anna Kellum, and had issue: Sarah, married Benjamin Burroughs (22); and Mary, married Henry Simmons.

Philip (8), son of James (4), born July 4th, 1762, married Kesiah, daughter of Thomas Hendrickson, (see Hendrickson family, No. 16); had children: James (15); Ralph (16); Richard (17); Eliza, wife of John R. Hart, and had children: Eliza, Josiah, and Amos; Moses (18); Harriet; Hulda; and Mary.

James (15), son of Philip (8), married, first, Charity Drake, by whom he had George; Mary; Catharine; Kesiah; John; Louisa; and Sarah. His second wife was Lydia Pearson.

Ralph (16), son of Philip (8), married Deborah Golden, and had children: David; Philip; and Sarah.

Richard (17), son of Philip (8), married Penelope Labaw, and had children: John L., married Charity Golden; and Ralph, married Caroline Cook.

Moses (18), son of Philip (8), married, first, Jerusha, daughter of Richard Hart, (see Hart family, No. 13.) His second wife was Maria Mathews. His children are Richard; Hulda; and William.

Jeremiah (9), son of James (4), died 1843, aged 74, having

married Jemima, daughter of Jedediah Scudder, (see Scudder family, No. 14,) by whom he had Sarah, wife of Aaron Moore, (see Moore family, No. 13,) and Eliza, wife of Joseph Titus; (see Titus family, No. 14.)

Joseph (5), son of John (3), who died October 29th, 1798, aged 73, is, with his wife, buried in the Ewing church-yard. He resided in Hopewell, and by his marriage with Martha Willets, who died November 7th, 1808, aged 76, had issue: Joseph, died 1776, aged 22; James (19); John (20); Edmund (21); Elizabeth, married Philip Burroughs and moved to Goshen; Martha, married James Hill; Phebe, died January 3d, 1841, aged 85; Anna, married Peter Lott and moved to Ohio; and Jerusha, married William Burroughs.

James (19), son of Joseph (5), married Elizabeth Baldwin, and had issue: Benjamin (22); Elizabeth, married, first, Rev. William Mills; had a daughter, Martha, wife of John W. Snyder; second, Rev. William McClenahan, by whom she had Dr. Robert Mills, who married Christiana Sickles, James B., and Gertrude, wife of Daniel Titus; Martha, married Joseph B. Tomlinson; and Kesiah, married John Lambert. His second wife was Anna, daughter of Samuel Kellum, then the widow of Joseph Burroughs (7). Their children were James (23); Susan, married Elias Atchley; Phebe, married George D. Abrahams, of Londonderry; and Joseph, married Rachel, daughter of Elnathan Stevenson, whose children are Henry S. and Anna Maria.

Benjamin (22), son of James (19), married Sarah, daughter of Joseph Burroughs (7). Their children are John Wesley (24); Jedediah (25); William Mills, a Methodist clergyman, married Mary Thrawl, of Milford; Nancy, married Joseph Mathews; Theodosia, married John Atchley, had one son, Daniel, married Frances J., daughter of William B. Blackwell; and Mary.

John Wesley (24), son of Benjamin (22), married Ellen Hunt, whose children are Mary Elizabeth, wife of William Jones, (see Jones family, No. 6); Emma, wife of John Guild Titus; and Sarah, wife of Dr. Measer, of Philadelphia.

Jedediah (25), son of Benjamin (22), married Eliza Moore; had a son, Benjamin, who married Fanny Loos, and has children, Henry and Elmer.

James (23), son of James (19), who died 1869, aged 78, married Ann, daughter of Aaron Hart, (see Hart family, No. 17,) who died 1868, aged 78. Their children were Aaron H. (26); Stephen, married Sarah, daughter of Garret Schenck; Amos, died unmarried; Rebecca Ann, married Wilson Atchley; and Mary Frances.

Aaron (26), son of James (23), married Cornelia, daughter of Benjamin Hendrickson, (see Hendrickson family, No. 7.) Their children are: Edward M., married Cornelia, daughter of Elijah L. Hendrickson, (see Hendrickson family, No. 18); George, married Mary Catharine, daughter of Gershom Moore; and Sarah, wife of William Yardley.

John (20), son of Joseph (5), who died October 13th, 1817, aged 58, by his marriage with Mary, daughter of John Howell, (see Howell family, No. 7,) who died March 2d, 1832, aged 58, had children: Joseph, married Elizabeth Phillips, widow of Noah Hart; his children are Joseph and Ellen; John Howell (27); Aaron, married Sarah Ann Dilts; James Willis, married Elizabeth Blackwell; Horatio Nelson (28); Naomi, died February 17th, 1877, aged 77; and Mary, married William Farlie.

John Howell (27), son of John (20), married Francina, daughter of James Slack (see Slack family, No. 3,) who died April 9th, 1836, aged 27, leaving children: Horatio Nelson, married Julia Vandyke; John, married Hannah, daughter of Simeon Bainbridge; Amos Slack, married Sarah Elizabeth Craft. By his second wife, Lucretia, daughter of Holmes Large, he has Andrew; Edward; Aaron; and Francina.

Horatio Nelson (28), son of John (20), is a prominent business man, residing in Philadelphia; is president of the Commonwealth Bank. By his first wife, Ellen Douglass, daughter of Samuel Augustus Mitchell, of Philadelphia, he has children: Mary Elena; Annie; Joseph Howell; and Ellen D. By his second wife, Caroline, sister of the former, Henry Augustus.

Edmund (21), son of Joseph (5), married, first, Susan, daughter of Joseph Howell, of Pennsylvania, (see Howell family, No. 10,) and had children: Joseph Rue (29); Samuel H. (30); John, married; Anna, married Abner Howell, (see Howell family, No. 19); Sarah, married Andrew, son of Stephen Titus; and Eliza, married Abner Hunt. His second wife was Phebe Blatchley.

Joseph Rue (29), son of Edmund (21), married Asenath Mathews, whose children are: Edmund, married Mary, daughter of Andrew Hart; Alexander, married Hannah Tomlinson; Wesley; Pearson, married Miss Bainbridge; Kate, married William Lanning; Harriet; and Emma, married Theodore Hutchinson.

Samuel (30), son of Edmund (21), married, first, Adeline, daughter of Enos Titus, (see Titus family, No. 23.) His second wife was Emily Nelson, whose children are: Clark; Anna; Elizabeth; Theodocia, wife of George Pine; and Wesley, married Mary Baldwin.

The Cadwalader Family.

John Cadwalader (1), a native of Wales, a convert to the religious faith of George Fox and William Penn, came, at the age of 20, with the latter, in 1699, on the occasion of his second visit to Philadelphia, where he established himself, and became, from 1718 to 1733, one of its councilmen. He died in 1746, aged 67, having married, in 1702, Martha, daughter of Dr. Edward Jones, also of Wales, and Mary, daughter of Dr. Thomas Wynne, by whom he had issue: Thomas (2); Mary, second wife of Judge Samuel Dickinson, (see Dickinson family, No. 1); Hannah, wife of Samuel Morris, of Philadelphia; and Rebecca, wife of William Morris, of the island of Barbadoes. who settled in Trenton.

Thomas (2), son of John (1), received his classical education at the Friends' Academy, Philadelphia, and his medical and surgical at London. On his return from England, he soon acquired a large practice, and was one of the founders of the Philadelphia Library. He afterwards settled in Trenton, and when, in 1746, it was organized as a borough, he was elected its first chief burgess, his brother-in-law, Morris, being one of the councilmen. In 1750, he gave £500 to found a public library for Trenton. Dr. Cadwalader lectured on anatomy, in Philadelphia, in 1751, and was, in 1755, appointed, by Governor Robert Hunter Morris, a member of the provincial council of Pennsylvania, which office he held continuously till 1774. He attended the meetings in Philadelphia, in opposition to the stamp act, and signed, with his sons, Lambert and John, the celebrated "non-importation resolution," adopted by the citizens of that city. He was one of the founders of the Pennsylvania Hospital, from which sprang the medical department of the University of Pennsylvania. He was a member of many societies, among them, of the Royal Medical Society of Edinburgh and London. He was a large land-holder, as we may judge from his offering for sale, at one time, nine hundred acres of woodland, seven hundred acres on the Delaware, and twenty-five acres of meadow-land, all about two miles above Trenton. He died November 18th, 1779, in the 73d year of his age, having married Hannah, daughter of Thomas Lambert, Jr., of Trenton. He had issue: Martha, wife of Brig.-Gen. John Dagworthy, member of the Delaware assembly; Lambert (3); John (4); Mary, first wife of Maj.-Gen. Philemon Dickinson; Rebecca, second wife of the same, (see Dickinson family, No. 3); Elizabeth, died unmarried, 1799; and Margaret, wife of Brig.-Gen. Samuel Meredith, major of the Third Philadelphia Battalion of Associators, who was in the battle of Princeton, was a member of the Pennsylvania assembly from 1778 to 1783, a member of the continental congress, and treasurer of the United States from 1789 to 1801.

Lambert (3), son of Dr. Thomas (2), received his classical training in Dr. Allison's Academy, Philadelphia; was appointed colonel of the Third Pennsylvania Battalion, in the continental army, October 25th, 1776, and served with effect under Col. Magaw, commander of Fort Washington. He, with Col. Ramsey, of Maryland, made a gallant resistance to the assault of the British, but, being overpowered by a greatly superior force, the fort was obliged to surrender. Col. Cadwalader was paroled, and retired to his estate at Trenton. He represented New Jersey in the continental congress from 1784 to 1787. He was also a member of the federal house of representatives from 1789 to 1791, and again from 1793 to 1795. He died September 13th, 1823, aged 82, and is buried in the Friends' burying-ground, Trenton, N. J., leaving issue: John, died in infancy; and Thomas (5)—by his wife, Mary, daughter of Archibald McCall,* of Philadelphia, and Judith Kemble, who was the daughter of Hon. Peter Kemble, president of the New Jersey provincial council.

Thomas (5), son of Col. Lambert (3), who died October 22d, 1873, aged 79, and is buried in the Friends' burying-ground, Trenton, as is also his wife, was graduated by the College of New Jersey, was appointed adjutant-general of the state militia, by Gov. Pennington, July 13th, 1842, and breveted major-general during the administration of Gov. Newell. He owned and resided on the paternal estate, above the city of Trenton, on the River road, which he greatly improved, and occupied as a

*Archibald McCall was the son of George McCall, of Glasgow, Scotland, who married a daughter of Jasper Yeates, of Philadelphia, and his wife, Catharine Sanderland, who was a granddaughter of Joran Kyn (Keen), founder of the Swedish colony of Upland, Pa., and ancestor of Jacob Keen, of Trenton.

country seat, passing the winter months in Philadelphia. He married Maria, daughter of Nicholas Gouverneur, of New York, whose aunt, Eliza Kortright, was the wife of President Monroe. His children are: Emily, second wife of William Henry Rawle, LL. D., a distinguished member of the Philadelphia bar, the son and grandson of men eminent in the same profession; Mary, wife of Dr. Silas Weir Mitchell, of Philadelphia, a physician of distinguished reputation, has one daughter, Maria Gouverneur; John Lambert, was graduated at Princeton; received the degree of LL. B. from Harvard University, where he studied his profession, gained a lucrative practice in New York, and was appointed, in 1874, the assistant secretary of state of the United States under the Hon. Hamilton Fish, which office he filled until 1877; Richard (6); and Maria, wife of John Hone, Jr., of New York, has one daughter, Hester Gouverneur.

Richard McCall (6), son of Thomas (5), was a graduate of Princeton and of the legal department of Harvard, from which he received his LL. B., and practices his profession in Philadelphia. He married Christine, daughter of I. Williams Biddle. Their children are: Thomas; Williams Biddle; Richard McCall; Gouverneur; and Lambert.

John (4), son of Dr. Thomas (2), who died at Shrewsbury, Maryland, in 1796, aged 44, received his education at Dr. Allison's Academy, Philadelphia, where he continued to reside; was one of the original members of the committee of safety; was appointed, at the outset of the war, colonel of the Third Battalion of Associators; was promoted brigadier-general of militia, and was in command of the division of Washington's army stationed at Bristol, with the design of crossing there, and co-operating with Washington in his attack on the British at Trenton, December 26th, 1776. This, the ice prevented his doing, but he crossed the next day, and was with Washington when, a week afterward, he retreated before the superior numbers of Lord Cornwallis, across the Assanpink, where, eluding the vigilance of his enemy, turning his left flank and reaching his rear, he achieved the brilliant victory of Princeton. He was also in the battles of Brandywine, Germantown, and Monmouth. Gen. Cadwalader was a warm and devoted friend of Gen. Washington, so that when, in 1780, Gen. Conway, an English officer in the service of the United States, who was intriguing with the Gates cabal to supplant Washington, took occasion to speak disparagingly of the commander-in-chief in the presence of Gen. Cadwalader, he promptly took up the matter, and, with Gen. Dickinson as his second, challenged Gen. Conway, who accepted the challenge. The regulation agreed on was that, after the signal, each should fire, when ready. Gen. Conway fired first, and missed, and, as Gen. Cadwalader was about to fire, a strong gust of wind rendered his aim unsteady, and he lowered his pistol a moment, till it should pass. Gen. Conway remarked, "You fire with deliberation, Gen. Cadwalader." "I do," replied he, "when I aim at a traitor." The general then fired, and wounded his antagonist, as was then supposed, mortally. Under this belief, Gen. Conway, in a note to Gen. Washington (recorded by Marshall), acknowledged the injustice he had done him, and entreated his forgiveness; he however recovered, but sank ever after into merited neglect and insignificance. Gen. Cadwalader's first wife was Elizabeth, widow of Edward Lloyd, of Talbot county, Maryland, by whom he had: Anne, wife of Robert Kemble, whose only child, Mary, became the wife of Gen. William H. Sumner, of Massachusetts; Elizabeth, wife of Archibald McCall, of Philadelphia, and mother of Maj.-Gen. George A. McCall, of United States Volunteers, of Maria, wife of Gen. Samuel Ringgold, member of congress from Maryland, and the mother of Maj. Samuel Ringgold, of the United States Army, who brought the artillery arm to such a state of efficiency, and lost his life in the Mexican war, at the battle of Palo Alto, and of Rear-Admiral Cadwalader Ringgold, of the United States Navy. Gen. Cadwalader's second wife was Williamina Bond, of Philadelphia, who died in England in 1836, forty years after the death of her husband. Their children were: Thomas (7); John; and Frances, who married, in 1800, David Montague Erskine, son of Lord-Chancellor Erskine, then secretary of the English Legation at Washington, and afterwards minister to this country and to the courts of Wurtemburg and Bavaria. He succeeded his father, in 1823, as second Lord Erskine. Their eldest son, Thomas, was peer from 1855 to 1876, succeeded by the second son, John Cadwalader, the present peer, their third son, David Montague, was, for many years, colonial secretary at Natal, their fourth son, Edward Morris, was secretary of legation at St. Petersburg, and, successively, minister to Greece and Copenhagen. He died in April, 1883. Elizabeth, one of their daughters, márried Sir St. Vincent Keane Hawkins Whitshed, Bart., their daughter, Elizabeth Sophia, married Maj.-Gen. Arthur Cavendish Bentinck, heir-apparent to the Duke of Portland, of whom their son, William Bentinck, is now heir-presumptive. Another daughter of Lady Erskine, Jane Plummer, married James Henry Callender, of Stairforth Castle, Sterlingshire, whose children, at their parents' death, became wards of the Duke of Argyle, whose second son, Lord Archibald Campbell, married the youngest, Jane Sevilla Callender. Their son, Neil Diarmid, should the Marquis of Lorne, eldest son of the duke, and now governor-general of Canada, have no children, is likely to become Duke of Argyle. Singularly enough, then, this Philadelphia lady was the daughter-in-law of a peer, the wife of a peer, the mother of two peers, and the great-grandmother of heirs-presumptive to two of the oldest and most distinguished dukedoms of Great Britain—that of Argyle, in Scotland, and that of Portland, in England.

Thomas (7), son of John (4), was a student of the University of Pennsylvania, a member of the Philadelphia bar ; was appointed in the war of 1812 against England, successively, colonel and brigadier-general of militia, and was engaged in the defence of Baltimore. After the war, he was made major-general of United States Volunteers. He died in 1840, aged 61, having married, in 1804, Mary, daughter of Col. Clement Biddle, quartermaster-general of the Revolutionary Army, and a descendant of William Biddle, of England, who came over in 1678, in the ship Shield, from Hull. Their children were : John (8); George (9) ; Thomas; Henry ; and William.

John (8), son of Thomas (7), who died January 26th, 1879, was a graduate of the University of Pennsylvania, a member of the Philadelphia bar, and district judge of the United States. He married, first, Mary, daughter of the eminent jurist, Horace Binney, by whom he had Mary, first wife of William Henry Rawle ; and Elizabeth, wife of George Harrison Hare, United States Navy. His second wife was Henrietta Maria, daughter of Charles N. Bancker, of Philadelphia ; had children : Frances, died unmarried ; Sarah Bancker ; Charles E., a physician, and lieutenant-colonel of Pennsylvania Volunteers during the Rebellion ; Anne, married Rev. Mr. Roland; and John, a graduate of the University of Pennsylvania, and by profession a lawyer, married, in 1869, Helen Mary, daughter of J. Francis Fisher, of Philadelphia, whose wife was a daughter of Henry Middleton, member of congress from South Carolina and minister to Russia.

George (9), son of Thomas (7), who died February 3d, 1879,

was appointed brigadier-general of United States Volunteers, in the Mexican war. He was distinguished for his bravery at the battles of Contreras and El-Molino del Rey; was breveted major-general for gallantly at Chapultepec, and equally distinguished at the battle of Churubusco and the battle of the causeway leading into the city of Mexico. During the Civil war, he served as major-general of United States Volunteers. He married Frances, daughter of Dr. James Mease, and granddaughter of Maj. Pierce Butler, of South Carolina, one of the framers of the federal constitution and senator of the United States.

NOTE.—Thomas Lambert, of Hansworth, Yorkshire, England, a sensible and worthy man of large fortune, and a member of the society of Friends, emigrated to this country on account of his religion. He settled at Lamberton, so called from him, now a part of Trenton. He married, first, Ellen, daughter of Mahlon Stacy, of the same place, England, afterward of Trenton. His children were· Thomas; John; James; Samuel; Elizabeth, married Mr. Biles, had children, Samuel, Thomas, and Benjamin; Hannah, married Mr. Hodge, and lived in Philadelphia; Mary; Ruth, married Mr. Adams; and Pliny. He mentioned in his will, dated 1693, his wife Elizabeth, so that he had, at least, two wives.

Thomas (2), son of Thomas (1), styled yeoman and merchant, who died 1732, date of will, had four wives. By the first, he had one child, Elizabeth, wife of Daniel Biles, by whom she had: Thomas, who married, and had one child, Thomas, died unmarried; Margaret, wife of Daniel Biles; she had sons: Thomas, a captain in the army, and Robert. By his second wife, Anna Kimble, he had: Hannah, married Col. Lambert Cadwalader; Achsah, died unmarried, aged 73; and Margaret, died unmarried, in 1746. One of Mr. Lambert's wives was named Mary, another Margaret, and his surviving wife mentioned in his will, was Anne, by whom he had no children; one wife, Anne, was a daughter of Thomas Wood.

The Robert Chambers Family.

This early record of the Robert Chambers family is due to the researches of Mrs. Dr. Edwards Hall (Margaret M. Chambers), of New York.

We have traditional evidence that the Chambers family of Middlesex county, New Jersey, are directly descended from Robert Chambers, of Stirling, near Edinburgh, Scotland. He was a Presbyterian, and, with thousands of others, suffered persecution during the reign of Charles II. and James II., in 1683 and 1685.

John, Robert, and Marion Chambers embarked at Leith, August, 1685, on the Henry and Frances, of New Castle, and arrived at New Perth (now Perth Amboy) the following November, after a long and disastrous voyage of fifteen weeks.

John (1) owned land in Old Windsor township, near Allentown, in 1802. He had at least one son, John (2).

John (2), son of John (1), moved to Allentown in 1709, was an elder in the Presbyterian Church of that place, and was a delegate to the first Presbytery of New Brunswick, in 1738. It is believed he had children: James, died young, in 1741; Robert (3); John (4), an elder in the First Presbyterian Church, Trenton, in 1760; and Martha.

Robert (3), son of John (2), lived and died, in 1774, on his inherited estate, in Middlesex county. He was noted for his piety. He married Elizabeth, daughter of John Hammell, of Burlington, N. J., by whom he had children: John, died young; William, died a young man; David, was a captain in the Revolutionary war, lived near Hamilton Square, where he was buried, having married Rachel Stille; Robert (5); and Elizabeth, married Matthias Mount.

Captain Robert (5), son of Robert (3), born July 28th, 1758, although but 18 years old, was in the Revolutionary war; was with Washington in the battle of Trenton. "In the Historical Society of Pennsylvania, there is a $50 continental note, which he received as part pay for his services in the army." He died January 26th, 1813, aged 55, having married Francina, daughter of John Reeder, (see Reeder family, No. 4); she died July 18th, 1814. The remains of both rest under the northeast corner of the First Presbyterian Church, Trenton, as indicated by marble slab in the outside wall. Their children were: John, died in infancy; Hannah, born September 3d, 1784; Mary, born October 16th, 1786, died young; Robert (6), born July 2d, 1788; Abigail C., born October 7th, 1790; Reeder (7), born February 21st, 1792; Montgomery (8), born August 30th, 1796; Francina, born March 2d, 1799; David (9), born August 2d, 1801; Andrew Reeder (10), born December 27th, 1804.

Hannah, daughter of Capt. Robert (5), married, first, William Conover, of Monmouth; had one son, died in infancy. Second, Maj. Peter D. Cattell, by whom she left one son, Andrew C., a resident of Philadelphia, who married Eliza H., daughter of Charles Egner; their children are Henry S., Emma E., Edward E., Charles E., Andrew C., and Lillie.

Robert (6), son of Robert (5), a justice and a much-esteemed merchant of Trenton, was a director of the Trenton Banking Company and of the Mechanics' and Manufacturers' Bank. He was the founder of Chambersburg, N. J. He died 1865, aged 77, having married Catharine, daughter of Abner Houghton and Margaret Van Dyke.* Their children were: Abner H., died in child-

*Jans Vandyke (1), who, with his brothers, Nicholas and Hendrich-Thomas, emigrated to this country in 1652. They were the sons of Thomas Jans Vandyke, of Amsterdam. Jans had children: Thomas, Derrick, Charles, Peter, Achias, Hendrick, John (2), Antie, Angenetie and Marichie.

John (2), son of Jans, who died 1765 (date of will), aged 59, married Anna Vankirke. She died 1764, having had children: Tuentie, born April, 1707, wife of Johannes Emans; Catrina, born April, 1708, wife of Girardus Beekman; Jan. (John) (3), born November, 1709; Roeloff, born May, 1710; Mattys (Mathias) (4), born August, 1714; Abraham, born October, 1716; Simon, born October, 1718; Isaac, born June, 1721; Jacob, born November, 1723; and Anna, born June, 1728, wife of Albert Voorhees.

John (3), son of John (2), married, first, Margaretta Barriclo, by whom he had Anna; Charity; and John (5). By his second wife, called Garrite, in his will dated 1778, had Frederick; Abraham; Jacob; Roeloff; Ann; Jane; Tuntie; Elsie; Catrina; and Sarah.

John (5), son of John (3), married Rebecca, daughter of Roeloff Vandyke, son of John Vandyke, and had a daughter, Margaret, wife of Abner Houghton and mother of Catharine, wife of Judge Robert Chambers, of Trenton, and of Eliza, wife of Abram Beekman, of Griggstown.

Mattys (4), son of John (2), married January, 1740, and had children: John, born 1752; Mathew (6), born 1753; Anne, born 1755, married Capt. Aaron, son of Richard Longstreet, near Princeton, whose daughter, Eleanor, married Maj. Cornelius Cruzer; Margaret, born 1758, married Maj. John Gulick, of Kingston; Tuentye, born 1759, married John Bayles, of Kingston; Catrina, married Judge Frederick Cruzer; Sarah, married Col. William Scudder, of Princeton; and Ellen, married Judge Berrien.

Mathew (6), son of Mattys (4), married Lydia, daughter of Richard Longstreet, of

hood; Theodore Van Dyke, died 1867; Margaret Matilda, married Dr. Edwards Hall, a physician of New York city, a graduate of Hamilton College and of the Medical College of Albany, a brother of Hon. Willis Hall, a lawyer, and formerly attorney-general of New York state, both sons of Rev. Nathaniel Hall, of Middle Granville, N. Y.; they have two daughters, Charlotte Chambers and Sarah Frances; Abner Reeder (11); and Robert and Mary Frances, both died in childhood.

Abner R. (11), son of Robert (5), a trustee of the First Presbyterian Church of Trenton, and a director of the Trenton Banking Company, married Margaret Ann, daughter of John Waydell, of New York city. Their children are: Catharine H.; Robert; Margaret W.; Abner Reeder; Sarah Frances; Mary Elizabeth; and Josephine.

Reeder (7), son of Robert (5), married Jemima, daughter of Asher Howell, (see Howell family, No. 14.) Their children were: Asher, died young; John H., married Josephine, daughter of George Sayen, resides in Philadelphia; has daughters, Adele Josephine and Francis Georgiana; Phebe Frances, married Francis D. Way, of Philadelphia; and Mary Anna.

Abigail, daughter of Robert (5), married, first, Dr. John A. Hendry, a physician of New York, by whom she had: Charles F., married Miss Kelly, whose children are Mary, Elizabeth, Julia, Edwin, and Paul; Mary F., married Ashbel S. Thompson, a lawyer of New York city; William W., married Sarah Overman; Juliet A., married Dr. Isaac Munn; has children: Mary, wife of Charles O. McCord, Sarah C., wife of John M. Hewitt, and Juliet L., wife of Edwin Clark; John A., married Sarah Rulon, whose children are: Mary, William, Emma, Annie R., wife of William W. Cooper, Sarah, and Edwin; Elizabeth K., died young; Edwin A., married, first, Annie G. Dixon; second, Sarah R. Burke, of Easton, Pa., whose children are: Frances, died young, and John B., a lawyer of Philadelphia; Abbie A., died unmarried; and Hannah E., married Isaac Benners, of Philadelphia; her children are: Abbie E., died young, Henry C., Edwin H., and William W. Her second husband was David Carver. She died November 30th, 1882, aged 92.

Princeton, and by her had Mary, wife of Rev. James Carnahan, D. D., president of Princeton College, whose daughter, Hannah, became the wife of William K. McDonald, a lawyer of Newark, and Lydia, wife of Rev. Luther H. Vandoren; Elizabeth, born 1782, married Rev. William Neil, D. D., president of Dickinson College; Dr. John, born 1785; Isaac, born 1787; Lydia, born 1789, married John Nevius; Gertrude, born 1793, married Rev. Henry R. Rice; and William James, born 1795, married Margaret Nevius.

Dr. Montgomery (8), son of Captain Robert (5), a physician of Philadelphia, married Eliza, daughter of Dr. William Duffield, whose children were: William D., died unmarried; and Andrew Reeder, married Emma, daughter of Samuel Taitt, of Philadelphia.

Francina, daughter of Capt. Robert (5), married Samuel W. Hollingshead, of New York, whose children were: Amanda, married Joseph Wiggins; Sarah, married Amos Ayres; she left children: Emma, wife of George Moore, Andrew C., lives in Philadelphia, and Ella, wife of Howard W. Van Artsdalen; Henry, married in Missouri, now resides in Camden, N. J.; has one child; and Emma, married John Anistaki, a graduate of Yale College, a druggist of New York, afterward of Trenton, whose children are: Samuel, John S., and Frances, wife of William Schultz.

Judge David (9), son of Capt. Robert (5), was a merchant of St. Louis; was a member of the common council—an alderman; was elected judge of the city courts, and of the courts of general sessions. He removed to San Francisco, and became one of its prominent bankers. The close of his life was spent at Burlington, N. J., where he died, November, 1880, aged 80, much esteemed for his Christian character and unblemished integrity. He married Catharine, daughter of Gen. Price, of Ringoes, N. J., and had children: Robert; David; William; Mary; Virginia; all of whom died in childhood: Horace, married, and died in San Francisco, in 1866, aged 34, leaving one son; and Walter, educated at Burlington College and Harvard University, practiced law at the New York bar for several years, until he made his residence in Burlington.

Andrew R. (10), son of Capt. Robert (5), born December 27th, 1804, was appointed by Gov. Johnson as his aid-de-camp; also served on the staff of Gen. Bennett, with the rank of colonel. He was a successful and wealthy merchant of Philadelphia, noted for his benefactions and unobtrusive charities. He died December 3d, 1871, aged 66, having married Sarah Ann, only child of William Hyde. Their children are: Sarah Frances, died young; and Charlotte H., married, first, Warner Draper, of Boston, whose only child is Sarah C. She married, second, Clarence Cowton, of Philadelphia.

John (4), son of John (2), lived in Trenton as early as 1734; was an elder in the First Presbyterian Church there, in 1760. He died 1778, aged 66, having married Susannah, daughter of

Henry and Hannah Carter, of Trenton, previous to 1748. She died August, 1799, aged 71. They are both buried on the west side of the yard of the Presbyterian church. Their children were: John and Robert, died young; William, born May, 1749, fell a victim to small-pox, at Ticonderoga, in 1777; Henry (12), born October, 1753; and David R., born September, 1759, were in the Revolutionary war, and, with their cousins, David and Robert, were participators in the battle of Trenton. They crossed the Delaware with Washington, and being familiar with the country, were placed in the front rank, and led the advance of the left wing down the Scotch road to Trenton; and Susannah, born November, 1761, married Alexander Calhoun; resided in Trenton, and had children: Catharine, born 1784, wife of Daniel Baker, and Alexander, born 1778, died, aged 36.

Capt. Henry (12), son of John (4), at the close of the war bought property at Springfield, near Mount Holly, N. J.; still in the possession of his descendants. He died there, aged 69. He married Elizabeth Fox, and had children: Susannah, died in infancy; Achsah, married John Irick, had one child; William T., married, and had two daughters; John (13); and Mary, married Joseph Deacon, had one son, Henry.

John (13), son of Henry (12), a noble and upright man, died October, 1880, aged 82; is buried at Mount Holly. He married Eliza Haines, and had children: Henry; and Bessey, died young; Susan, married Samuel F. Peterson, and has children: John, died young, Eliza C., wife of Paul Lippencott, Mary, wife of James Willet, Achsah I., wife of William I. Tomlinson, Olivia Berrens, wife of Joseph L. Siner, Anne D., wife of Dr. Henry Shivers, Susan, died, aged 21, Laura F., wife of Benjamin A. Lippincott, Fannie, died in infancy, and Gertrude V.; Samuel H., married Mrs. Frances Kimble (Woodward); has one child, Charles; Annie D., married Ridgway S. Deacon; and George H., died, aged 34.

Martha, daughter of John (2), married James Hamilton, a Scotchman, living in Princeton, by whom she had sons: David; and James, who was an elder in the First Presbyterian Church of Princeton till his death, 1815. He married Sarah Anderson, by whom he had: Martha, married Rev. Enoch Burt, and had one daughter; Mary, married Rev. Jared D. Fyler, D. D., whose children are James H., Louisa, and Jared Dudley, a physician of St. Louis; Rhoda, married Mr. Harrison; Sarah, married Rev.

Charles Fitch; lives at New Albany, Ind.; has two sons and one daughter; Elizabeth, died unmarried; Rebecca, married Rev. Jonathan Huntington; David, died young; and James, professor in the University at Nashville, Tenn.

The John Chambers Family.

John Chambers (1) came from Antrim, North of Ireland, about the year 1730, and settled in Trenton, New Jersey, where he died, in 1747, aged 70, and is buried in the First Presbyterian churchyard. He built a mud house on the northeast corner of Second and Quarry streets, (now State and Willow.) He had sons, David (2); and Alexander (3); and five daughters. One daughter married Mr. Bell, then Mr. Jackson; one, Mr. Browning; one, Mr. Rosehook; another, Mr. Gaw.

David (2), son of John (1), resided in Philadelphia. One of his daughters married a Mr. Claypoole, a descendant of Oliver Cromwell, and left descendants: Abraham; David; and Elizabeth, who married, first, Mr. Copper, and afterward Mr. Matlack, and left a son, James Copper, who married Elizabeth, daughter of James Chambers, his second cousin.

Alexander (3), son of John (1), was born in Ireland in 1716, and died in Trenton September 16th, 1798. He continued at the corner of State and Willow, carrying on the trade of turning, spinning-wheel, and chair-making. He was one of the first trustees of the First Presbyterian Church of Trenton, which office he held for forty-two years, and treasurer of the board for thirty years. He was an active, enterprising citizen, and a liberal supporter of the church, to which he left, by bequest, £30. He married Rose Crage, who was born at Belentopen, in the parish of Clownish, within the mile of Monaghan, Ireland, in 1720, and died November 23d, 1780, and is buried in the yard of the First Presbyterian Church, Trenton. Their children were: John (4); David (5); James, married a Miss Baylis, and had a daughter, Elizabeth, who married James Copper; Alexander (6); Rose, married Mr. Wright; Margaret, married Mr. Snedeker; Elizabeth, died October 18th, 1770, aged 27; and Mary, died April 13th, 1757, in infancy.

John (4), son of Alexander (3), was born March 3d, 1741, and died in Trenton November 13th, 1813; his wife, Elizabeth Story, of Cranbury, born May 12th, 1749, and died June 3d, 1821. Their children were: Rose, born January 22d, 1776, married Septimus Evans, of Geneva, N. Y., where she resided, and died 1809, aged 33, leaving one child, Hetty; Hetty, born March 7th, 1780, died March 25th, 1809; John (7); and Alexander, born August 27th, 1784.

John (7), son of John (4), born October 18th, 1782, and died in Trenton November 10th, 1834; was a member of the board of trustees of the First Presbyterian Church of Trenton for eleven years. He married Elizabeth, daughter of John Scudder, (see Scudder family, No. 20,) by whom he had children: John Story (8); and James Copper, died in infancy.

John S. (8), son of John (7), was clerk of the board of trustees of the First Presbyterian Church for sixteen years and elder since 1866. He married Emma, daughter of Benjamin Fish, (see Fish Family, No. 7.) Their children are: John Story, graduated at the Rensselaer Polytechnic College, Troy, N. Y., a civil engineer; William Moore, died, aged 22, August 23d, 1871; Benjamin Fish, a graduate of Princeton College, is a lawyer of Trenton; and Thomas Stryker.

Col. David (5), son of Alexander (3), who died 1842, aged 94, was appointed colonel of the Third Hunterdon Regiment in 1776, and the next year to the colonelcy of the Second Regiment, which he commanded till near the close of the war, and was in active service. He married Ruth, daughter of Daniel Clark, (see Clark family, No. 3.) She died 1813, aged 58, having had children: Daniel, died in childhood; Alexander, died, aged 10; Phebe, died in infancy; Sarah, born August, 1778, married William Hyer; Rose, born 1780, married John Fisher, and had two daughters: Emeline, wife of George Baldwin, of New York, and Susan, wife of Beach Vanderpool, of Newark; they have five children: William, Beach, James, Eugene, and Wynant; Clark (9), born December, 1782; John, died in infancy; Elizabeth, born February, 1787, married Samuel Disbrow, of Cranbury, died 1835; had children: William, Angeline, Elizabeth, married Mr. Birchherd, Edward, and Horatio, married Miss Schenck; Margaret, born August, 1789, married John Van Dyke, and died 1815; had a daughter, Sarah, wife of John Beekman; David, married Samatta Slayback, and went to New Orleans; Gilbert, died in infancy; and Mary, born 1797, married John Lewis, of Cranbury, and had children: David C., married Rose Stonaker, Cicero, married, and resides in Oregon, Emeline, married Reuben Tuker.

Clark (9), son of Col. David (5), married Mary, daughter of John Guild, (see Guild family, No. 3,) and had issue by her: Ruth, married William McKean, whose children are: Mary, wife of Charles Whitehead, Sarah, wife of Charles B. Cogill, Jennie, wife of John Murphy, William, lives in New York city, Hetty, wife of Thomas Glasebrook, of Indianapolis, and Clara, wife of Edward A. Phillips; John, died unmarried; Henrietta, married Aaron H. Van Cleve, (see Van Cleve family, No. 26); Frances, married Capt. William Ashmore, whose children are: Henry, married Mary Rowley, William, married Alice Reese, Mary, wife of John I. Kinsey, of Easton, Pa., Jennie, and Fanny, wife of John J. Sager; Lydia, married Dr. Robert Stansbury; Mary Ann, married Alexander B. Green, (see Green family, No. 19); Annie, married Francis Lowthrop, whose children are: Mary, wife of Thomas Henderson, and Francis; Emeline, married Thomas Halloway, of Philadelphia; David, not married; Abigail and William, both died in childhood.

Sarah, daughter of Col. David (5), married William Hyer, son of Col. Jacob Hyer, who commanded a regiment at the battles of Trenton, Princeton, and Monmouth, in whose regiment her father, for a time, had command of a company. Mr. Hyer was a graduate of Princeton College; was admitted to the bar in 1789. He received his commission as adjutant of the Fourth Regiment of the Middlesex militia, 1794. He was elected clerk of the Supreme Court in 1807, which office he held for six years, when he was appointed clerk of the Court of Chancery, by Gov. Pennington. He died in Philadelphia, 1840, aged 74. Their children were: Alexander C., married Ann Torrence, of Boone county, Ky.; Rosetta, married George Malin, of Frankfort; Elizabeth, married Judge Peter Lott, son of Dr. Charles Lott. Judge Lott was a graduate of Princeton and a lawyer. He settled in Illinois, and during the Mexican war, commanded a company of volunteers in the regiment of Col. Bissell, of that state, and with his company and regiment, supported Bragg's battery, in the battle of Buena Vista, in which he was wounded.

Alexander (6), son of Alexander (3), was just old enough to enter the army under Washington, and was appointed one of the guides to the battle of Trenton. He was a prominent and enterprising merchant, and carried on an extensive business for many years. He was the first to establish Bloomsbury as a port for sloops, and built a wharf and storehouse there. At the death of his father, was elected in his place, to the trusteeship of the church, in which office he continued for twenty-five years, till his death, in 1824. He married, first, Miss Hunt; second, Miss Eyre, by whom he had: Richard, who married Miss Bispham, and had a daughter, who married, and resided in Virginia; had a large family; John (10); Eliza, married Andrew De Armond; Mary, married John Roberts; and James, died unmarried. By his third wife, Margaret Mott, he had children: William B. (11); Anna M., married James Cowden; Margaret, married Evan I. Way, of Philadelphia; Sarah, died unmarried; and Lydia, died in childhood.

John (10), son of Alexander (6), married Ellen Rogers, and had children: Richard, who left a son, Henry; Alexander, had sons, John and Frank, and a daughter, Mary; Elizabeth, married William Ayres, and had children: Ralston, John, Montgomery, Lewis, and Mary; and Mary, married William Johns, and had a son, George.

William B. (11), son of Alexander (6), married, first, Elizabeth George, and had a son, Amos George. By his second wife, Margaret A. Kuglar, had a son, William B., whose children are William W. and Mary.

Margaret, daughter of Alexander (3), born February 23d, 1746, and died May 9th, 1791, having married Garret Snedeker. Their children were: Alexander, born November 1st, 1775, married Lydia Perrine, and had two sons and seven daughters; Abraham, born April 16th, 1778, married Miss Gulick, had two sons and two daughters; Rose, born July 13th, 1780, died May 15th, 1830, married John Davison, and had eight sons and three daughters; and Isaac G., born October 2d, 1782, died February 22d, 1862, married Ann Salter, had children: Garret I., lives at South River, Margaret, wife of James Buckelew, of Jamesburg, and two others.

The Clark Family.

Charles Clark (1), one of the first settlers of Ewing township, came from Long Island in company with John Burroughs, about the year 1700. They were then unmarried. Mr. Clark bought and lived, till his death, on the night of the battle of Trenton, December 26th, 1776, on the place near the church, now owned and occupied by Edward S. MacIlvaine. He was in a room whose floor was covered with weary, worn, and sleeping soldiers. He was supposed to have been in the act of hanging his watch over the mantel, when he fell into the open fire and there burned to death. His condition was first discovered by his negro servant. Mr. Clark was a trustee of the First Presbyterian Church from 1757 to 1775, during all which time he was not absent from a meeting of the board. He left £20 to the church, for the support of the minister. He died, aged 88, having had by his wife, Abigail, who died November 12th, 1762, aged 77, children: Benjamin (2); Daniel (3); Abigail, married Daniel Howell, (see Howell family, No. 3.)

Benjamin (2), son of Charles (1), succeeded his father in the trusteeship in 1777, and was also a magistrate, held in high estimation. He died November 25th, 1785, aged 54, having married Elizabeth Mershon, and by her had children: John (4), born 1764; Benjamin (5); Abigail, married Theophilus Phillips, (see Phillips family, No. 10,) and at his death, John Brown, and died 1844, aged 89; buried in the Lawrenceville church-yard; Elizabeth, married Capt. Reeves; Sarah, married Daniel G. Howell, (see Howell family, No. 39); Anna, married Dr. Reeves, son of Capt. Reeves.

John (4), son of Benjamin (2), married Tabitha Liscomb. Their children were: John, married Mary M. Marshall; Maria, married James Lacony; Sarah, married John A. Insley.

Benjamin (5), son of Benjamin (2), married Mary, daughter of Peter Howell, (see Howell family, No. 41); had children: Elizabeth, married Joab Sexton; moved to Genesee, N. Y.; Sarah, married Absalom Krewson; Rebecca Ann; and Benjamin. Mr. Clark's widow moved to Genesee county, N. Y.

Daniel (3), son of Charles (1), who was also a trustee of the church from 1766 to 1788, married Elizabeth Lott, and had children: Daniel (6); Samuel (7); Phebe, married Amos Hutchinson; Mary; Abigail, married Solomon McNair; Elizabeth, married William Barber; and Ruth, born February 14th, 1755, married Col. David Chambers, (see Chambers family, No. 5.)

Daniel (6), son of Daniel (3), married Hannah, daughter of Jasper Smith, of Lawrence. Their children were: Charles, married Elizabeth Lyons, of Sunbury, Pa.; Mary, married Joshua Anderson; Elizabeth, married, in succession, Henry Runyon and Mr. Kingman; Jemima, married Thomas Combs, of Freehold; Enoch, married Mercy Green, of Easton, Pa.; William, married Sarah Graham, in Philadelphia; and Smith.

Samuel (7), son of Daniel (3), who died 1819, aged 47, married, first, Sarah Cox, who died 1802, aged 32, leaving children: Daniel, married Miss Knowles; William, not married; Samuel, went to Buenos Ayres, S. A.; John, died at Natchez, Miss.; second, Phebe, daughter of John Howell, (see Howell family, No. 38,) and their children were Sarah; Letitia; Elizabeth, married Thomas Clendenen, of Philadelphia.

The Coleman Family.

Timothy Coleman (1), by his second wife, Hannah Waters, had children: Timothy (2); John (3); and Sarah, married Elias Smith.

Timothy (2), married Sarah Lemon, and had by her: Julia Ann, married Elias Hankins; Jane, married Daniel Thorn; Susan, married Mr. Berkendale; Eliza, married William Smith; Thomas, married, and lives West; George and Charles, both married, and went West.

John (3), son of Timothy (1), died August 30th, 1866, aged 87; married Mary Baremore, who died January 23d, 1879, aged 95. Their children are: James B. (4); Nathaniel (5); Sarah, married Charles Waters; and Lewis (6).

James B. (4), son of John (3), married Theodocia Hutchinson, and had children: Mary, married Samuel Bennet; Harriet, died, aged 5; Elizabeth, married Randolph B. Totten; John H., married Margaret Bennet; Christiana; and Sarah Jane.

Nathaniel (5), son of John (3), married Jane, daughter of James Cummings Green, (see Green family, No. 50,) by whom he had: Phebe; and Sarah, second wife of Elijah Webster Lanning, (see Lanning family, No. 19.)

Lewis (6), son of John (3), married Hannah Baldwin, whose children are: Jane, wife of Welling Primmer; Moses; Mary Frances, wife of Joseph Sutphen; Nathaniel; Virginia, wife of Charles Case; Charles, died in youth; and Jedediah, married Lillie Case.

The Cook Family.

Anthony (1), the head of this family, married Keziah Roberts, by whom he had children: Jonathan (2); Anthony (3); William, not married; Wincy, not married; Polly, married Nathaniel Reed; Eliza, married David Olden; and Jane, married James Burroughs.

Jonathan (2), son of Anthony (1), married Mary, daughter of Richard Howell, and had by her, children: Anthony (4); Henry (5); Richard, married Elizabeth Reed; John (6); Keziah, married James Furman; and Elizabeth, married Samuel Green, (see Green family, No. 60.)

Anthony (4), son of Jonathan (2), by his marriage with Sarah, daughter of James Grant, had children: William G. (7); Elizabeth, married Emanuel Wright; Mary, married William Reed; Elias (8); James (9); Henry; Jonathan, married Julia Paxson, and had sons, Edward and Frederick; and John, married Elizabeth Dundas; has children: Monroe, Ellsworth Lincoln, Mary, and Sarah.

William G. (7), son of Anthony (4), who died June 19th, 1875, aged 69, married, first, Susan, daughter of Jacob Herbert; second, Elizabeth, daughter of William Grant, and widow of Lieut. Westcott, of the United States Navy, by whom he had children: Edward G., a graduate of Princeton College and a lawyer of Trenton; William G.; Henry H.; Hampton W.; and Walter I.; married, third, Mary E., daughter of Thomas S. Allison, ex-secretary of state of New Jersey and paymaster U. S. A.

Elias (8), son of Anthony (4), married Anna Thompson, and had children: Henry, married Carrie Lalor; Frank; Annie; Mary; and William.

James (9), son of Anthony (4), married Jane, daughter of Richard Hunt, (see Hunt family, No. 27,) by whom he had children: E. Rosseau, married Letitia Neeley, had one daughter, Minnie, died young; and Mary, married William H. Brace; had children, Lillie and Lulu.

Henry (5), son of Jonathan (2), who died 1835, aged 50; married Elizabeth Brown, who died 1853, aged 57, having had children: Theodore, married Elizabeth, daughter of William B. Grant; Eleanor; John; Henry; Charles; Howell; and Elizabeth, married Samuel Lamb.

John (6), son of Jonathan (2), who died 1853, aged 63, married Marcia Roscoe, who died 1829, aged 36, leaving children: Mary Ann, married Charles B. Howell; John, married Elizabeth, daughter of Enoch Burroughs; Richard (10); Marcia, wife of George H. Tindall; Wilson B., married Sarah Wearts; William R., died unmarried; and Sarah, died, aged 12.

Richard (10), son of John (6), married Ellen C. Conover, and had children: Mary, married William Worrell; William, died unmarried; Elizabeth; Susan, married John Johnson; Sally Ann, died young; and George.

Anthony (3), son of Anthony (1), married Sarah Kane, and had children: Charles (11); and Jane, married Henry Reed.

Charles (11), son of Anthony (3), married Sarah, daughter of Noah Lanning, and had children: Theodocia; Anthony, married Rebecca Primmer, and has children: Charles, Sarah, Milford, and Georgiana; Rachel, married Joseph Hart; Sarah Ann; Louisa, died young; and George S., married Cornelia, daughter of Charles Green, (see Green family, No. 39,) and has children: Alfred, died young, Charles, and Lillian.

The Cooley Family.

The family of Cooley is of English origin. The name is borne by many very respectable families, and by families, also, of illustrious rank. I may mention one as an illustration—that of the Duke of Wellington, whose family name is Cooley. Arthur Wellesley, Duke of Wellington, (say Clarke & Dunlap, in their History of the Duke, pages 25, 26, and 27,) was the son of Garret, created Viscount Wellesley, son of Richard Cooley, who was the first that received the name of Wellesley, or Wesley, as heir to his first cousin, Garret Wellesley, who left him all his large estates, on condition of his taking his arms and name, which he did. This Richard Cooley was the grandson or great-grandson of Sir Richard Cooley, spelled sometimes Cowley, and Colley, of Rutland county, the home, from time immemorial, of the Cooleys.

At what period Benjamin Cooley (1), the earliest known American ancestor of Dr. Eli F. Cooley, emigrated to this country, is not known. He was born 1620; was a resident of Springfield, Mass., which was settled in 1636, of which town he was one of the three selectmen, in 1646. He afterward moved across the river Connecticut to Longmeadow, of which he was one of the earliest settlers. He was one of the committee to lay out the town of Suffield, in 1670. He was a man of wealth, and left large landed estates in Springfield and Longmeadow, besides other property. He died 1684, six days before his wife, Sarah, by whom he had issue: Bethia, born January, 1644, married Henry Chapin; Obadiah (2), born 1647; Eliakim (3), born 1649; Daniel (4), born 1651; Sarah, born 1654; Benjamin, born 1656; Mary, born 1659; and Joseph, born 1662, married and died, leaving children. The Cooleys of East and West Springfield, Longmeadow, and Hartford, are of this family.

Obadiah (2), son of Benjamin (1), married Rebecca Williams, and had by her, children: Rebecca, born 1671; Mary, born 1675; Obadiah, born 1678; Anna, born 1681; Joseph (5), born 1683; and two others.

Joseph (5), son of Obadiah (2), married Margaret MacRanny, and by her had children: Aaron (6); Caleb, born 1722; and Margaret, born 1726.

Aaron (6), son of Joseph (5), who died 1793, aged 77, married Ruth Mears, and had children: Ruth, born 1757, married Oliver King, of Wilbraham; Margaret, born 1759, married William Hancock, of Enfield; Jerusha, born 1761, married Oliver Burt; Lucinda, died in infancy; Lucinda, born 1765, married Oliver Collens, of Springfield; Tirza, born 1767, married Peter Terry, of Enfield; Aaron (7), born 1770; Lois, born 1774; and Lewis, born 1776.

Aaron (7), son of Aaron (6), who died 1807, aged 37, married Sarah, daughter of Daniel Boardman, of Dalton, and by her had Aaron Boardman, a merchant of Philadelphia.

Eliakim (3), son of Benjamin (1), married Hannah, daughter of Thomas Tibbals, whose children were: Eliakim, married Griswold, daughter of Mathew Beckwith; Samuel; Mercy; and Hannah, wife of Hezekiah Parsons, son of Benjamin Parsons, of Springfield, Mass., formerly of Exeter, Devonshire, England.

Daniel (4), son of Benjamin (1), married Eliza, daughter of the first Simeon Wolcott, of Windsor, and had children: Benjamin; Daniel (8); Simeon (9); John; Thomas; William; and Elizabeth, married Mr. Field.

Daniel (8), son of Daniel (4), born 1683, married and had a son: Daniel (10).

Daniel (10), son of Daniel (8), born 1711, married Frances McKintree and had a son: William (11), born 1736.

Deacon William (11), son of Daniel (10), married Sarah Mather a descendant of the Rev. Cotton Mather, and had children: Sarah, born 1762; William, born 1763; Trifosa, born 1767; Dorothy, born 1768; Abigail, born 1770; Timothy Mather (12); Alexander; James (13), born 1780; and Abigail.

Rev. Dr. Timothy M. (12), son of William (11), an eminent divine, of East Granville, Mass., who died 1859, aged 88, married Content Chapman, who died 1860, aged 84. Their children were: Timothy C., died 1852; Isaac Augustine, lives in Pittsfield, Mass.; William B., of the same place; Eliza Content, wife of J. B. Spelman, a merchant of New York; Phineas R., died 1835; Harriet, lives in Granville; Susanna, died 1831; Samuel M., of Pittsfield; Jane Ruth, lives in East Granville; and Mary Ann, died 1838.

James (13), son of William (11), who died 1851, aged 72, was a lawyer of distinction, resident in East Granville, and a member of the state senate, married Almira, daughter of Captain Israel Parsons. Their children were: James P., died in childhood; Mathew Martin, died in infancy; Louisa Maria, died in childhood; Timothy Mather (14); and James Parsons.

Timothy M. (14), son of James (13), married Sarah I. Andrews, whose children were: Benjamin Franklin, rector of the church at Easthampton; Ellen Louisa, wife of C. S. Snow; Elizabeth M., died 1870; and Frederic Bradley, died in childhood.

Simeon (9), son of Daniel (4), with his family, was one of the forty families that settled Sunderland, Mass. (then Swampfield.) He died 1746, aged 60, having married Elizabeth, daughter of Samuel Gunn, of Sunderland, who died 1744, having had: Elizabeth, wife of Joshua Scott, died 1798, aged 87; Martha; Miriam; Simeon (15); Mary; Emma; Gideon; Lucy, died in infancy; Lucy, wife of Richard Montague; and Freedom.

Simeon (15), son of Simeon (9), who died 1805, aged 85, married Bethia Ashley, niece of the Rev. Joseph Ashley, minister of Sunderland, who died 1808, aged 75, having had children: Martin (16); Gideon; Mercy, married Col. Melser Hunt, and died 1850, aged 90; Rinnah (17); Ruth, wife of Spencer Russell, moved to Chicago; Sarah, wife of Stephen Clary; Thirza; and Israel, married Martha Morse and had children: Mary, Fanny, Martin, and George.

Martin (16), son of Simeon (15), married, first, Irena Montague, and had by her: Lucy and Rufus; second, the widow Rebecca Childs, by whom he had Irena and Lemuel.

Rinnah (17), son of Simeon (15), who died 1827, aged 69, married Lucy, daughter of Joseph Field, of Sunderland, (see Field family, No. 19.) Their children were: Eli Field (18); and Phila, married Amos Marsh and by him had children: Laura; Almeda, died 1832; Eli Cooley; Austin Lysander; Francis Emerson, died 1836; Lucy; William; and Edward Field.

Rev. Eli Field (18), son of Rinnah (17), and Hannah, daughter of Col. William Scudder, (see Scudder family, No. 110,) were married October 15th, 1807, by the Rev. Samuel Stanhope Smith, D. D. She died April 6th, 1817, aged 29, and is buried at Cherry Valley, N. Y., to whom the ladies of the Presbyterian church there erected a monument with the following inscription: "To the memory of one whom it were unpardonable to lay down in silence, and of whom it were difficult to speak with justice; for her true character will look like flattery, and the least abatement of it is an injury to her memory." Their children were: A daughter, died in infancy; William Scudder (19); Sarah Lucinda, third wife of Morgan Scudder, (see Scudder family, No. 22); Catharine; Hannah Maria, born in Cherry Valley, N. Y., died October 12th, 1843, and is buried in the Ewing church-yard; and Samuel Stanhope Smith (20). By his second wife, Catharine, daughter of Col. Thomas Henderson, M. D., of Freehold, who died 1854, is buried in Springfield, Ill., he had children: Rachel Henderson, wife of Dr. Thomas Spencer Hening, of Steubenville, Ohio, whose children are: James Courtney, married Mary Moore, of Stillwater, Minn., Mary G., Jennie, Anna, and three died young; and Mary Green, wife of Thomas H. Bergen, son of the Rev. John Bergen, D. D., of Springfield, Ill., where they reside. His third wife was Amy, daughter of Pierson Reading, (see Reading family, No. 19.)

William Scudder (19), son of Rev. Eli Field (18), born in Princeton, died February 7th, 1882, in the city of Philadelphia. He was for many years identified with the educational interests of that city, so widely and justly famed, not only for its public schools, but for its select and classical institutions of learning. He was a graduate of Princeton College and for a number of years was associated with the faculty of that institution. From there he went South and taught for several years in Virginia and North Carolina, then went to Philadelphia and established a select classical academy, and for thirty-five years remained at its head and successfully prepared hundreds of young men for entering college and business life. Professor Cooley was one of the oldest as well as ablest instructors in Philadelphia, and many of our prominent men in church and state now living, who came under his training and tuition in their early life, can bear testimony to the thoroughness and efficiency with which he conducted his system of teaching. He was well known in literary circles and was highly esteemed for his mental endowments and cultured attainments. His disposition was genial and social, and he possessed to a marked degree that faculty often found wanting in men of varied learning, of readily imparting his knowledge to those around him. His memory is enshrined in the hearts of those who knew him best as a thorough student, an honest man, and a Christian gentleman.

Catharine, daughter of Rev. Eli Field (18), married, first, Col. Joseph Purdy, a lawyer of Doylestown, Pa., and chief clerk of the United States Sub-Treasury till the law was repealed, and by him had: Anna, wife of Robert Allen, of Springfield, Ill., major of an Illinois regiment, in the Union army; and Catharine, died in infancy. She married, second, Rev. Garish Barrett, of Springfield, N. Y., and died May 16th, 1859. He died August 3d, 1857, aged 60. Both are buried in the Presbyterian church-yard of Springfield, Otsego county, N. Y. Their children are: William Cooley, a graduate of Princeton College and the Jefferson Medical College of Philadelphia, married Anna, daughter of John Crist; Charles Scudder, was a graduate of Princeton College, in which he gained the Metaphysical Fellowship, studied two winters in Edinburgh, Scotland, one in Berlin, and two years in the Theological Seminary at Princeton, is settled at Baltimore, Md.; and Sarah Lucinda, died in childhood.

Stanhope S. (20), son of Rev. Eli F. (18), became a merchant of Trenton; was deacon in the First Presbyterian Church there. He afterward removed to Ewing; was an elder in the church of that place till his death, September 30th, 1875. He married in 1841, Harriet, daughter of Isaac Welling, (see Welling family, No. 5.) Their children are: Emma, died August 31st, 1857, while a pupil at Dr. Charles C. Beatty's Seminary, Steubenville, Ohio; Virginia, died in childhood; Stanhope Field, died in infancy; Hannah Louisa; William Henry, married Emma, daughter of Forman Rose, (see Rose family, No. 4); has children: Edith R. and Walter F.; Alice Scudder, went, in 1877, as a missionary to Soo-Chow, China, and there married Rev. Alvin Parker, of Missouri; Isaac Welling, a graduate of the Polytechnic College at Philadelphia; Spencer Hening, married Martha, daughter of Willard Perry, resides at Chippewa Falls, Wis.; and Bessie W.

The Rev. Eli Field Cooley, D. D., son of Rinnah and his wife, Lucy Field, was born in Sunderland, Mass., October, 15th, 1781, pursued his preparatory classical studies at the Academy of Hartford, Conn., entered the College of New Jersey, was graduated by that institution in 1806, and soon after graduation, was elected a tutor in it, which office he declined. As the Presbyterian Church had no established Theological Seminary at that time, he pursued his theological studies under the Rev. Dr. Samuel Stanhope Smith, president of the college. He was licensed by the Presbytery of New Brunswick, October 3d, 1809, and received a call from the First Presbyterian Church of Cherry Valley, Otsego county, N. Y., and was there ordained and installed by the Oneida Presbytery,

Rev. Dr. James Carnahan, late president of Princeton College, then of Utica, preaching the ordination sermon. During the ten years of his pastorate, the additions to the church were large, especially the last year, when, as the result of a revival, about one hundred were added to it.

Although the relations between pastor and people had always been very pleasant, and the ever-prevailing affection had been greatly strengthened by the closing events of his pastorate, yet the severity of the climate proving too great for the delicate health of his second wife, he was constrained to separate from a congregation to whom he was bound by reciprocated attachments, which were not severed by the closing of his ministration, there, and to accept a call from the church of Middletown Point, now Matawan, N. J. Here he was installed June 2d, 1820, the Rev. Isaac V. Brown preaching the installation sermon. During his short pastorate there of three years, one period of serious attention to religion, largely increased the church membership. Though the congregation was very liberal for one so young and small, yet the salary which they could afford proved entirely inadequate to the necessities of a large and growing family. He was obliged again to retire reluctantly from his connection with his people, to whom he was bound by the harmony which had always existed, and by their multiplied marks of kindness and affection, which never ceased to be cherished in grateful remembrance.

He next accepted an invitation to become their pastor, tendered by the First Church of Trenton, now Ewing. He removed thither on the 10th of April, 1823, and was installed on June 4th of the same year, and continued to minister to them till July 19th, 1857, when he preached his farewell sermon, the presbytery dissolving the pastorate at his own request, his congregation generously continuing his salary six months longer.

Finding his salary, soon after he came into the congregation, still insufficient, though managed with the utmost economy, to defray the ordinary expenses of a large family and the proper education of his children, he felt reluctantly constrained, as many other clergymen have been, to resort to some other means of increasing his income ; this was to cultivate a farm which he purchased some three or four years after his settlement in Ewing, and successfully managed.

The long continuance of Dr. Cooley in his pastorate was not due to his having no calls to leave it. He had at least three from other congregations, with offers of a larger salary than he was receiving, and three to accept agencies in the service of the church, with a salary in one case four times the amount of his congregational one, which his friends pressed him with great urgency to accept. But Dr. Cooley was a man of kindly feelings and strong attachments. He preferred, therefore, remaining with the congregation to which he was ministering to transferring his services to another field, but the crowning motive that induced him to decline the agencies was, that he had consecrated himself to the gospel ministry. He therefore felt it a solemn duty incumbent on him to preach the gospel so long as his health permitted, and a congregation desired his ministrations.

No man took a more lively interest in all the Christian and benevolent operations of the day, or in any movement, the tendency of which was to advance the cause of religion or promote the general welfare of society. He was one of the first few who originated and met in Trenton to establish the New Jersey Historical Society; was one of the earliest and firmest supporters of African colonization. He and the Rev. Andrew Oliver, of Springfield, and James Fennimore Cooper, of Cooperstown, N. Y., were sent as delegates by the Otsego County Bible Society as delegates to the convention which met at New York, May 11th, 1816, and founded the American Bible Society, in whose behalf he ever after continued to interest and exert himself. Through his instrumentality the legislature was induced to make the first appropriation for the support of the blind and of the deaf and dumb. He was an early and strenuous advocate of the temperance reformation, and by adding to his precepts his example of entire abstinence from intoxicating drinks, his persevering labors were eminently successful, and the present temperate generation of this region have reason to bless his memory for the good he accomplished in this respect.

The Rev. Mr. De Veuve remarks, in his funeral discourse: "To delineate correctly the character of any one, is by no means an easy task. We are here to-day to contemplate the character of one who has not lived in vain; of one endowed with such a combination of qualities as rendered him a very useful man; of one whose character was adorned with such graces as shed a steady light throughout his long career, a light which did not pale as he drew near the end of his race, but which rather increased in brilliancy, burning steadily on to the mouth of the tomb, and there going out without a flicker. While Dr. Cooley's whole character was one that should belong to a Christian minister, some traits were, as usual, more fully developed than others. If he had one Christian excellence to a higher degree than another, it was *prudence*, both in speech and in action. He was a man that suffered himself to pronounce very few judgments upon the character or conduct of others, and even those few were marked by unusual charity and discrimination. Through a long life, he was often obliged to shape his course between jarring interests, and occupy positions peculiarly trying to this virtue, yet every trial only gave stronger evidence of his unusual prudence. Dr. Cooley was a very *persevering* man—a man not easily daunted by difficulties nor cast down by disappointments. The record of his early ministry, and the whole course of his private life reveal no ordinary development of this virtue. Combined with *perseverance* was *industry*. Few hours of his long life were wasted in pleasure, or even passed in beneficial recreation. In the work of the ministry and the varied concerns which occupied his mind, his labors were unremitting; his days were so crowded with business, that only by entering his study before dawn, and encroaching upon the hours of sleep necessary to sustain his intellectual toil, was he able to keep up the routine of study and writing.

"This reference to his multifarious duties leads to a notice of the matters about which he was so busily employed. In addition to his qualifications for the ministry and pastorate, Dr. Cooley was endowed by his Creator with a very decided talent for business. He possessed also an unusual skill for building. From this fact, he was chosen by the trustees of the College of New Jersey, in the year 1833, and in subsequent years, as one of a committee of trustees to plan and superintend the construction of the East and West Colleges, and other edifices connected with the institution. So well did he execute this work—so promptly and efficiently, as well as economically—that when the State of New Jersey determined on the erection of a lunatic asylum, he was chosen by the legislature a member of the building committee. Without doing injustice to truth, it may be claimed that the burden of the work devolved upon him. Of the faithful manner in which his trust was discharged, the noble structure, reared with so much economy and judgment, on the banks of the Delaware, will bear the strongest testimony. As long as it stands, it will irrepressibly witness his wisdom and his skill. At the time of his death, Dr. Cooley was engaged in preliminary arrangements in relation to the new theological seminary at Princeton, of which he was also a trustee. In these various labors, an opportunity was offered of bringing to a conspicuous light many other marked features of Dr. Cooley's character, especially his thorough *integrity.* Not only do I refer to the strict reckoning of all moneys passing through his hands, but more particularly to the watchfulness with which he saw to all matters, and the precision with which he insisted on a *quid pro quo* for every dollar expended. In the exercise of economy, he was admirable, and it would be no vain supposition to declare that the college treasury and the state treasury must have been saved many thousands of dollars by it, in the construction of these institutions. He was a man that carried the same nicety of precision into the care of moneys entrusted to him, that he did into his own private affairs—not that he was wanting in liberality; he was kind and generous to the full measure of his means. His life was not spent in accumulating; his earnings were judiciously employed upon his family, and in a systematic support of various schemes of benevolence, and he died little the richer for his industry and ability.

"Dr. Cooley's preaching was characterized by soundness and simplicity—he made no attempts at display, no show of learning, offered no conceit of philosophy, but the simple unadorned, and, what is more rare in our day, the unadulterated gospel of our Lord and Saviour, Jesus Christ. When delivering a written discourse, his manner was quiet, but when speaking without notes, there was a solemnity, an earnestness, an unction in it and his language which arrested fixed attention. Never have I listened to him with greater pleasure and profit than but three Sabbaths since (the last time he was permitted to enter God's earthly courts), when raising his imposing form to its full height, his voice swelled through the house in an earnest appeal to men to turn and live, pleading with them over the emblems of Christ's broken body and shed blood, to find peace in believing. During his long term of service in the ministry, he was blessed of God with many tokens of favor. At Cherry Valley, Middletown Point, and at Ewing, he was permitted to enjoy precious revivals, when large numbers were gathered into the church, so that he will not stand alone when his account is rendered to his Master, but, surrounded by a goodly number saved through his instrumentality, he can rejoicingly say, 'Here, Lord, am I, and the souls thou hast given me.' In the private relations of life, Dr. Cooley was noted for an even-tempered consistency—never extreme in his opinions, conservative without being narrow, moderate but firm, of decided views, but not obtrusive, and possessed of a degree of humility not often seen. Few men could have displayed the prudence which he has since his relinquishment of the pastorate. Retiring to his farm, in the midst of the congregation, he has been the unobtrusive observer of events, ever ready to assist his successor, and treating him with a fatherly regard; he has proved the wise counsellor, the faithful friend, the consistent Christian. The closing years of his life were singularly pleasant and peaceful. He has ripened for Heaven, and 'Has come to his grave, in a full age, like as a shock of corn cometh in his season.' It may be said of him, as was said of his life-long friend, Dr. Carnahan, for thirty-one years the esteemed president of the College of New Jersey, we have in him an example of a 'well-rounded, finished life;' nothing was left but to die and enter upon his reward."

He died April 22d, 1860, and is buried in the Ewing churchyard.

It is not inappropriate to add to this record of Dr. Cooley the mention, in brief, of his successors to the pastorate of the Ewing Church. His immediate successor was the Rev. Prentiss De Veuve, who was installed October 15th, 1857, and after seven years of acceptable labor among this people, he received a call from the Second Church of Germantown, Pa. The Rev. David J. Atwater, son of Dr. Lyman H. Atwater, was called November 25th, 1864, and remained till 1871. During his ministry, the old brick church was replaced by a new stone edifice, which was dedicated November 20th, 1867. The Rev. George L. Smith succeeded Mr. Atwater in 1871, and he resigned in 1879, to accept a call to the First Church of Cedarville, N. J. The present pastor of this old congregation is the Rev. Dr. Samuel T. Lowrie, son of Judge Walter H. Lowrie, of Pennsylvania. He was formerly connected with the Western Theological Seminary of Alleghany, Pa., was installed April 22d, 1879. His interest not only in the present, but in the past, of his people, has been a great incentive to the improving and beautifying of the old graveyard that surrounds the church, where many whose names are recorded in this book have been buried.

The Dean Family.

John Dean (1) came to Ewing township early in the eighteenth century, and purchased the place on the Delaware next above Gen. Thomas Cadwalader's, which still remains in the possession of his descendants. He died 1760, leaving children: Stephen (2); John; Jacob, who settled in Pennsylvania, and had a son, Jesse, whose daughter, Mary, became the wife of Stephen Dean (4); Martha, married Benjamin Green, (see Green family, No. 5,) and died 1768, aged 57; Elizabeth, married Mr. Lane; Hannah, married Mr. James; one of them moved to Virginia, the other to Pennsylvania; Mary, died 1736, aged 27.

Stephen (2), son of John (1), whose will, recorded in 1791, is probably the year of his death, married Anna, daughter of Joseph Reed. Their children were: John (3); Mary, married John Hart, (see Hart family, No. 11); Phebe, married Benjamin Hendrickson—was his third wife, (see Hendrickson family, No 4.)

John (3), son of Stephen (2), died September 1st, 1831, aged 76; married Mary, daughter of Richard Hart, (see Hart family, No. 4.) She died October 26th, 1826, having had children: Hulda, died 1848, aged 70; Sarah, died 1848, aged 72; and Stephen (4.)

Stephen (4), son of John (3), married Mary, daughter of Jesse Dean, of Pennsylvania. She died January 10th, 1829, aged 31, having had children: Elizabeth, wife of Samuel B. Cook, son of Daniel Cook, whose children are: Priscilla, wife of John Stephens, of Phillipsburg, Emily, wife of Grenville B. Little, of Freehold, Adeline, Lewis D., Mary K., Edward, and Milcelet; Lydia, wife of Joseph Campbell, of Pennsylvania; her children are: Thomas Ross, George Henry, and Stephen D.; and George, married Sarah Ann, daughter of Amos Reeder, (see Reeder family, No. 8); their children are: Albert Augustus, George Edgar, Eva, and Cora.

The Dickinson Family.

Samuel Dickinson (1), ancestor of that family in Trenton, was a resident of Maryland and Chief Justice of Kent county, Maryland. By his marriage with Mary, daughter of John Cadwalader, (see Cadwalader family, No. 1,) he had children : Henry ; John (2); and Philemon (3).

John Dickinson (2), son of Samuel (1), bred to the bar by a course of study both in Philadelphia and at the Temple, London, early and actively engaged in public life. We find him, as early as 1764, a member of the assembly of Pennsylvania, in the debates of which he exhibited that solidity of reasoning, and eloquence of manner for which he was afterwards so eminent. During its sessions, Dr. Franklin introduced a petition, drawn up by himself, begging the king to take the control of affairs, on account of the weakness of the proprietary government. This, as endangering their liberties, Mr. Dickinson, already distinguished for his learning, talents, and success, opposed, with all the force and weight of argument and eloquence that characterized his speeches, but in vain ; he found himself in a small minority, and the land of Penn became a royal province, and so continued until, by the strength of her own right and that of her sisters, she had thrown off the oppressive dominion to which she had consigned herself. The next year, 1765, Mr. Dickinson was sent as one of the four delegates of Pennsylvania, to the congress of delegates from all the provinces, held in New York, to devise measures in opposition to the stamp act. No man, perhaps, then nor afterwards, did more, by his speeches, and especially with his pen, to arouse and sustain the spirit of resistance of that day to the arbitrary and oppressive measures of England, than did Mr. Dickinson. The promptitude and unanimity that prevailed in the assembly of Pennsylvania, and the union of the colonies generally, in protesting against the wrong of taxation without representation, have been, with great justice, ascribed to the judicious and eloquent essays of Mr. Dickinson, sent forth to the world as "Letters from a Farmer in Pennsylvania to the Inhabitants of the British Colonies." These papers, in which the rights of the colonies were maintained with great clearness and vigor of reasoning, contributed greatly to arouse a spirit of opposition to the unwise and unreasonable pretensions of Great Britain. They were republished in every colony, and the people of Boston, in town meeting assembled, voted a letter of thanks to their "patriotic, enlightened, and noble-spirited author." His various tracts and essays, and the important papers and addresses, which came from his pen between the stamp act congress of 1765 and the close of the first continental congress of 1774, gave him a wide and just fame. These letters Dr. Franklin caused to be published in England, calling the attention of the people of Great Britain to them, and requesting any to answer them satisfactorily, if they could be so answered.

A company of the most distinguished gentlemen of Philadelphia, known as the "Schuylkill Colony," expressed the high estimation in which they held his writings and services in promoting the welfare of his country, by electing him a member of their society, for his "patriotic productions in behalf of the rights, and liberties, and privileges of the present, as well as of the rising and future generations in America, and for good service done by him to the British plantations in America (1768)."

A man of dauntless courage and inflexible determination, no personal consideration ever deterred him from accepting the post of danger conferred on him by his fellow-citizens. We find him often, therefore, presiding at those immense gatherings held in Philadelphia, to resist royal usurpations, a position which exposed its occupant to the no small peril of prison or the halter.

The assembly of Pennsylvania, influenced by instructions drafted by Mr. Dickinson, as chairman of a committee of fifty, composed of men most distinguished for wealth, morals, and intelligence, requesting them to appoint delegates to attend a congress of deputies from all the colonies, to effect one general plan for obtaining redress of grievances, unanimously approved of holding such a congress, to which they sent Mr. Dickinson as one of the seven to represent Pennsylvania. This congress, of which Peyton Randolph was president, met in 1774, at Philadelphia, and adopted a petition to the king, the "elegant composition" of Mr. Dickinson, and closed its short but important session of eight weeks after having called another, to meet the next year, in the sam place. At this, the congress of 1775, Mr. Dickinson, Dr. Franklin and five others were present as representatives of Pennsylvania. A declaration, of which Mr. Dickinson was the author, embracing the principles contained in the instructions of the Pennsylvania convention, and setting forth the causes and necessity of then taking up arms, and which was directed to be published by General Washington, on his arrival at the camp, in 1775, was adopted by it, and also a second petition to the king, the product of Mr. Dickinson's pen. It was those documents, principally, that the Earl of Chatham, on the floor of parliament, pronounced, "for solidity of reasoning, force of sagacity, and wisdom of conclusion, to be unsurpassed."

To the eventful congress of 1776, which sat, also, at Philadelphia, Mr. Dickinson, with Dr. Franklin, Robert Morris and four others, was again delegated. During its early sessions, Richard Henry Lee, of Virginia, introduced his celebrated resolution :

"*Resolved*, That these United Colonies are, and of right ought to be, free and independent states ; and that all political connection between them and the states of Great Britain is and ought to be totally dissolved."

This resolution, the delegates of Pennsylvania were instructed by the assembly not to vote for, and though these instructions were afterwards reversed, yet not so easily were the convictions of all the delegates. Many of the members of that congress, and some, too, of the warmest and most eminent patriots of the day, treasuring in their memories the lessons of the past, dreading the ruin, the desolation, and the immeasurable calamities that civil war ever draws in its train, fearing, too, that the very liberties which they were attempting to establish might, if rashly hazarded, be wrecked in the ruins of their country, hesitated to make the fearful adventure, regarding, too, as they did, immediate action as premature, believing that, as England had already receded from some of her most offensive and arrogant pretensions, that she would ultimately abandon them all, were reluctant to engage in acts of open hostility to the mother country, while a milder course seemed possible, and that thus the freedom and prosperity of their country might be preserved, without imperiling their all. One of those who thus hesitated was Robert Morris, afterwards financially the right arm of the confederacy. "And when we mention as one," says Sanderson, "that great and good man, John Dickinson, we give sufficient proof that the cause of these sentiments was no unmanly fear."

Although Mr. Dickinson was one of the most able of the opposers of the declaration, as being impolitic at that time, yet, after the vote in its favor was passed, no man was a more active and efficient promoter of the cause, or more fearless and animated in pressing it to a prosperous termination. "There was no actor in the Revolution," says Judge Conrad, "whose life and character were more direct and transparent, nor any man in our public council whose integrity, courage and devotion were more unquestionable and less questioned than those of John Dickinson." The rules for the guidance of his political life, which, after the passage of the resolutions, he affirmed on the floor of congress, are worthy of lasting remembrance and imitation. "Two rules," said he, "I have laid down for myself, in this contest, to which I have constantly adhered, and still design to adhere—first, on all occasions where I am called upon as a trustee for my countrymen, to deliberate on questions important to their happiness, disdaining all personal advantages to be derived from a suppression of my real sentiments, and defying all dangers to be risked by a declaration of them, openly to avow them; secondly, after thus discharging this duty, whenever the public resolutions are taken, to regard them, though opposite to my own opinions, as *sacred*, because they lead to public measures in which the common weal must be interested, and to join in supporting them as earnestly as if my voice had been given for them." These honorable sentiments, his whole career in public life fully illustrated. But Mr. Dickinson's exertions were not confined to civil duties exclusively; they were devoted to military matters as well, in which he engaged with great ardor. Early in 1775, Philadelphia began to set her house in order, and prepare for possible contingencies. She raised six battalions of associators, or volunteers, Pennsylvania troops in the service of the United Colonies, of the first of which, Mr. Dickinson was appointed colonel, and he, with Col. Cadwalader, was directed by the committee of safety, of which he and Dr. Franklin were members, to inspect the ordnance and military stores, and put them in order. He was also an active adviser in constructing the military defences of the city, and in 1776, he was ordered by congress to march with his battalion to New York, to aid in defence of the city, should it be attacked. So that, although he was opposed to the declaration, as being too early, yet he could boast of being the first member of congress to take up arms and march at the head of his forces to meet the enemy. In 1777, he was promoted to the rank of brigadier-general. In 1779, the assembly of delegates unanimously chose him to represent her in congress, and in 1781, elected him her president. In 1782, he was chosen as a member of council of Pennsylvania, and the same year, was elevated to the presidency of the provincial commonwealth, to which office he was unanimously re-elected in 1783, and for a third term in 1784, and was succeeded in the office by Dr. Franklin. When, during his administration, in an address to the Chief Justice and judges of the counties, he holds forth his views of his own and their responsibility in promoting the good condition and moral prosperity of the people over whom they are called to preside, we cannot withhold our admiration of his sentiments, and the earnestness with which he would impress on the judges the importance of their using their influence in enforcing on the people those measures and observances which tended to promote their happiness and general welfare. "Regarding," says he, "the offices we hold as merely bestowed for the purpose of enabling us to contribute to the happiness of the people, and persuaded that you view those held by you in the same light, we do not doubt but that you will cheerfully afford your aid in carrying into execution any measure that has a tendency to promote so desirable an end. You, gentlemen, well know how vain are laws without manners. These cannot be expected unless the strictest attention be paid to the instruction of youth, and the inculcation of a true love and fear of the Supreme Being. In republics, where the people themselves govern, virtue is essential to their prosperity. It is our wish that you would be pleased strongly to recommend in the several counties the establishment of schools, attention at places of public worship, provisions for ministers of the gospel, and observance of the Sabbath." He was chosen president of the convention held 1787, at Annapolis, to take into consideration matters relating to the trade of the United Colonies. He participated, also, as a delegate from Pennsylvania, in the deliberations of the convention held at Philadelphia in 1788, presided over by Washington, to frame the federal constitution, and with his usual ability, advocated with his pen its reception by all the states. During the later years of his life, he resided at Wilmington, Del., of which state he was chosen governor, and was, in 1792, a member of the convention which framed the constitution of that state. In 1769, the trustees of Princeton College expressed their estimate of his exalted literary abilities and his eminent legal knowledge, by conferring on him the then rare honor of doctor of laws.

Mr. Dickinson was ever the warm advocate and supporter of the cause of education and friend of literary institutions. Of this he gave evidence by founding and liberally endowing Dickinson College, at Carlisle, Pa., which perpetuates his name. He also presented to Princeton College £100, the interest of which was to be given as often as the trustees saw fit, to the student who should compose the best dissertation on one of the following subjects:

"A zeal for religion, clear of bigotry and enthusiasm."

"A liberality of sentiment, unstained by licentiousness"

"A purity of manners, free from censorial austerity."

"What are the most proper measures to be adopted by government for promoting and establishing habits of piety among a people."

"No one or more of the United States can ever derive so much happiness from a dissolution of the Union as from its continuance."

(This last was competed for in 1788. History of College of New Jersey, by Dr. M'Lean, vol. I., page 334.)

After his withdrawal, through the pressure of declining years, from the active scenes of public life, he spent his retirement in devotion to his books and favorite literary pursuits, and in the enjoyments of society, of which, through his varied knowledge and cultivated taste, his elegance of manners, and kindness of heart, he was at once both the delight and ornament. He closed his useful career February 14th, 1808, aged 76, having married, first, Mary, daughter of the second Isaac Norris, speaker of the house of assembly of Pennsylvania; second, Sarah, daughter of James Logan. Their children were: Sarah, died 1855, aged 84; three died young; Maria, married Albanus Logan, son of Dr. George Logan, of Philadelphia.

Philemon Dickinson (3), son of Judge Samuel (1), was born April, 1739, at Crosia, Talbot county, Md., and educated at Philadelphia. He afterwards made Trenton, N. J., his residence, and was placed in command of the military forces of that state. He was a man of a spirit as undaunted in the field as his brother was in the cabinet. Of his daring courage in the face of danger, he gave many signal proofs, during the war of the Revolution. He took part in the flank movement at Trenton, January 2d, 1777, followed by the victory at Princeton; and when, after that, the American army took up its winter quarters at Morristown, Gen. Dickinson was placed in command of the advanced post, on the west bank of the Millstone, while the British army lay at New Brunswick. It was here that an action took place, small in the numbers engaged, but important in its effects, and which fully illustrated his characteristic boldness and bravery. On the opposite bank was a mill filled with flour and grain for the American army. This was too tempting a prize for the British to resist. For the purpose of capturing it and plundering the surrounding region, they sent out a large foraging party, under cover of a battalion of four hundred regulars, supported by three field-pieces. Gen. Dickinson promptly determined to repel them. With a body of militia, not quite equal in number, he forded the river—the water was middle deep—and with the bayonet, charged them so vigorously and with such impetuosity, that they broke and fled, leaving behind them provisions, wagons, horses, arms—everything but themselves, and nine were so unfortunate as even to do that, and became prisoners. This successful result, accomplished by raw soldiers over regulars, and that, too, by the bayonet alone, the boasted weapon of the English, had a very inspiriting effect on the army, and seems to have afforded especial pleasure to the commander-in-chief, as may be seen by the following communication of Gen. Washington to congress:

HEADQUARTERS, Jan. 22d, 1777.

To the President of Congress:

SIR—I have the pleasure to inform you that Gen. Dickinson, with about four hundred militia, has defeated a foraging party of the enemy, of an equal number, and has taken forty wagons and upwards of a hundred horses, most of them of the English draft breed, and a number of sheep and cattle, which they have collected. Dickinson's behavior reflects the highest honor on him, for his troops were all raw. He led them through the river, middle deep, and gave the enemy so severe a charge that, although supported by three field-pieces, they gave way, and retreated with so much precipitancy that Gen. Dickinson had an opportunity of making only nine prisoners.

When, in the next campaign, Gen. Washington, after crossing the Delaware, had determined, contrary to the advice of his officers, except Wayne, Greene, La Fayette, and Cadwalader, to give battle to Gen. Clinton, retreating across the Jerseys, he assigned to Gen. Dickinson the duty, with others, of harassing him and delaying his march until he could come up with him. Gen. Clinton, with the gallant Morgan hanging on his right flank. Gen. Maxwell, commanding the Jersey continental troops, on his left, Gen. Scott in his rear, and Gen. Dickinson in his front, "who," says a historian, "destroyed the bridges and opposed his progress with remarkable energy," was so retarded by these incessant and spirited assaults, that he was able to advance no further than Monmouth Court House, before Gen. Washington had reached within striking distance. On the night before the battle, Gen. Dickinson, with the New Jersey militia, was stationed in the rear of the enemy, and in close proximity, to give notice of his earliest movement. When the corps of observation, composed of seven hundred men, under Col. Grayson, had come up with the enemy, they found him already engaged with Gen. Dickinson's force, who had attacked with his usual spirit, but who was obliged to retire before overpowering numbers. This was the opening skirmish of the day, and, had it been followed up by the advance of Lee, as ordered by Washington, instead of a retreat, the result would, in all probability, have been more disastrous, if not fatal to the British arms, instead of his mere escape and only a partial victory to the American cause.

Gen. Dickinson was greatly distinguished for his zeal and devotion in the cause of his country, for the eminent ability which he brought to her aid, and for the important services he rendered her, not only in his military capacity, but in his civil as well. In the early congress, he was a delegate from Delaware, and represented the State of New Jersey in the senate of the United States, in 1790, for four years. Though not a member of congress, he was one of the three commissioners—Robert Morris and Gen. Schuyler being the other two—appointed by congress to locate the federal capital near Trenton. At the close of the war, he retired to his estate on the bank of the Delaware, above the falls, near Trenton, where, in February, 1809, at the age of 70, he ended a life crowned with honor, a large part of which had been employed in defending and establishing the liberties of his country and promoting her welfare.

He married, first, Mary, and afterward Rebecca, daughters of Dr. Thomas Cadwalader, (see Cadwalader family, No. 2,) who died August 5th, 1791, having had children: Mary, who married George Fox, and had two children; and Samuel (4), born April 4th, 1770.

Samuel (4), son of Philemon (3), died November 4th, 1837, aged 67, having married Anne, daughter of Samuel Meredith, first treasurer of the United States; had children: Mary, married William C. McCall; had a son, William C.; John (5); Philemon (6); and Samuel, died July 18th, 1852, aged 46, who was educated at Mount Airy Military School, under Col. Raumfourt; was captain in the United States Army during the Mexican war, and died in Trenton, not long after his return to his family; he married Martha, daughter of William Gibson, a Scotch merchant of New York; had children: Anna, Henry and Charles, died in infancy, Mary, married John Graham, William, died young, and Wharton, married Emily Hughes, daughter of Lieut. Edward Albert Bosson.

John (5), son of Samuel (4), married, first, Elizabeth Barlow, and by her had Margaret McCall, who married Samuel Meredith, son of Thomas; and John, married Anne Herbert, and had children: Henry and Laura V. His second wife was Ury Drake, by whom he had: Lambert C., married Elmira, daughter of William Hankinson; Samuel, a druggist of Trenton, married Anna Skillman; Edith, married Samuel E. D. Hankinson; Anne, married George Shew.

Philemon (6), son of Samuel (4), was graduated by the College of New Jersey in 1822; was, for more than forty years, until his resignation, 1881, president of the Trenton Banking Company, and prominent in the various interests of the city. His children, by his wife, Margaret C., daughter of Charles Gobert and Charlotte T. Ogden, his wife, are: Philemon, died unmarried; Emily, married Richard F. Stevens, son of James A.; Samuel Meredith, a lawyer of Trenton, and purser in the United States Navy during the Civil war, married Garetta Moore, of Newtown, L. I.; Mary M.; George F., married Janie Parrott, niece of Robert Parrott, the distinguished inventor of the gun known by his name; and Charlotte, married Garret D. W. Vroom, a lawyer of Trenton and son of ex-Gov. Vroom.

The Ewing Family.

Findley Ewing (1), a Scotch Presbyterian, and his wife, Jane, left Scotland in the days of persecution, and settled in Londonderry; there, for his bravery at the battle of the Boyne, King William presented him with a sword. Their son, Thomas (2), born in Londonderry, Ireland, owing to troubles in that country, came to America, in 1718, and settled in Greenwich, Cumberland county, N. J., and there married Mary Paget, of English descent, and had ten children. The youngest, James (3), came first to Trenton as a representative of Cumberland county in the Legislature, in 1774, and made it his residence in 1779. He was for years auditor of public accounts, and commissioner of loans under the government. He was mayor of Trenton from 1797 to 1803. He was both trustee and elder of the First Presbyterian Church of Trenton. He died October 23d, 1823. His wife was Martha Boyd, by whom he had one son, Charles (4), born June 8th, 1780.

Charles (4), son of James (3), was a student at the Trenton Academy, and graduated at Princeton College with the highest honors of the class of 1798, was admitted to the bar in 1802, and was appointed Chief Justice of New Jersey in 1824, and was among the greatest ornaments of the New Jersey bar. Ewing township was given its name in honor of him. He married Eleanor Græme, eldest child of Rev. James F. Armstrong, who was, for thirty years, pastor of the First Presbyterian Church of Trenton, and for some time preached in the Ewing Church. Their children were: James; Francis A. (5); Emily Augusta, first wife of Henry W. Green; Susan Mary, second wife of Henry W. Green, (see Green family, No. 32); Charles; and Eleanor Græme, wife of Caleb S. Green, (see Green family, No. 33.)

Dr. Francis A. (5), son of Chief Justice Charles (4), was a graduate of Princeton College and of the medical department of the University of Pennsylvania, and practiced his profession in Trenton.

He was an elder in the First Presbyterian Church of Trenton. He married Adeline Nottingham, and had children: Louisa; Eleanor Græme; Frances A.; Charles; Bessie; Mary A.; Robert L.; and Emily Maud.

The Field Family.

Zechariah Field (1,) the paternal ancestor of the Rev. Eli Field Cooley, came, about 1630 or 1632, probably from Hadleigh, Suffolk county, England, first to Boston. As early as 1639, he removed, in company with the Rev. Mr. Hooker and others, to Hartford, in which, and its vicinity, he owned large tracts of land. He removed to Northampton in 1659. Two years afterwards, he was appointed, with five others, to lay out a tract of land on the west side of Connecticut river, for house-lots, in that part of Hadley which is now Hatfield. He received a grant of land in the new township, where he resided till his decease, in 1665, aged 65, leaving a wife, Mary, by whom he had children: Mary, married Joshua Carter, who removed to Deerfield, and, with all Capt. Lathrop's command, was killed in the unfortunate Indian battle of Bloody Brook; Zechariah (2); John (3); Samuel (4); and Joseph (5); all born between 1643 and 1658.

Zechariah (2), son of Zechariah (1), killed at Deerfield, married Sarah, daughter of John Webb, an early settler of Northampton; had children: Zechariah, born September 12th, 1669, died young; Ebenezer (6), born October 31st, 1671; and John, died young.*

Ebenezer (6), son of Zechariah (2), removed to Guilford, Conn., married Mary Dudley, and died 1713, aged 42, having had children: David (7); Mary; Samuel; Ebenezer; Joareb; Ann; and Zechariah.

David (7), son of Ebenezer (6), by his first wife, Mary Bishop, had Sarah; Benjamin; David; and Ichabod; by his second wife, Catharine Bishop: Anna; Samuel; Ebenezer; by his third wife, Abigail Stone; Timothy (8); Abigail; Catharine; and Mindwell.

Captain Timothy (8), son of David (7), was an officer of the Revolution, married Anna, daughter of David Dudley, and had eight children: Mina; Lois; Mina, second; Rev. Timothy; Mary; Rev. David Dudley (9); Abigail; Anna. He died 1770, aged 73.

---

* In 1704, a band of French and Indians attacked Deerfield, burned the town, massacred many of the inhabitants, and carried off the remnant, prisoners.

Rev. Dr. David Dudley (9), son of Timothy (8), was settled, first, in Haddam, Conn., where he remained many years, and afterwards in Stockbridge, Mass. He married Submit, daughter of Capt. Noah Dickinson, of Somers, Conn., a lady of remarkable brightness of mind and loveliness of character. She died 1861, aged 79, having had children: David Dudley, an eminent lawyer of New York, the author of the Civil and Criminal Code, extensively adopted in the United States; Emilia Ann, married to Rev. Josiah Brewer, missionary to the East; Timothy Beals, an officer in the United States Navy; Mathew Dickinson, a civil engineer; Jonathan Edwards, three times president of the Massachusetts senate; Stephen Johnson, who has been for twenty years one of the judges of the Supreme Court of the United States; Cyrus West, a merchant of New York, of world-wide fame as the originator of the ocean telegraph, and for his indomitable energy in carrying the work though to its accomplishment; Henry Martyn, a Presbyterian clergyman, the editor of the New York "Evangelist" and author of many books; and Mary E., who was married to Joseph F. Stone, a merchant of New York. Of these nine children, five are dead; only four, David Dudley, Stephen J., Cyrus W., and Henry M., are now living.

John (3), son of Zechariah (1), whose name appears among the volunteers that fought against the Indians at Turner's Falls, settled in Deerfield, but his family was broken up by the massacre, in 1704, perpetrated by the French and Indians, and he removed to Coventry. He married Mary, daughter of James Bennet, of Northampton, or of Alexander Edwards. She was taken prisoner and carried off to Canada by the Indians, but in a few years was ransomed and returned. They had children: John, taken captive, but ransomed and returned with his mother; Mary, born 1674, died young; Zechariah, born 1676; Benjamin, born 1679; Mary, born 1681, was captured and carried to Canada by the Indians, was adopted by them, became enamored of forest life, married an Indian chief, and though she afterward visited her relatives, no persuasions could induce her to leave her husband and remain with them; Bertha, born 1684, married John Allis; Sarah, born 1688, married Nathaniel Peck, was killed in the massacre; Ebenezer, born 1690, was slain by the Indians, in Deerfield; and Abilene.

Samuel (4), son of Zechariah, was also among the volunteers in the fight with the Indians at Turner's Falls, 1676. In revenge, as was supposed, he was shot down in his field by the savages, in 1697. He married, in 1676, Sarah, daughter of Thomas Gilbert, of Springfield; had children: Samuel, born 1678, who married Sarah Edwards, lived in Deerfield, and had two sons, Samuel and Col. David; Thomas (10), born 1680; Sarah, wife of Samuel Warner, of Springfield; Zechariah (11), born 1685; Ebenezer (12); Mary; Josiah, married, and had children, Josiah and Elizabeth; Joshua, born 1695, married Elizabeth Cooley, of Springfield, had children, Nathaniel, Ebenezer, and Elizabeth.

Thomas (10), son of Samuel (4), married Abigail, daughter of Hezekiah Dickinson; had children: Samuel, died young; Abigail, wife of Abiel Abboth, of Windsor, Conn.; Moses (13); Samuel, a physician of Saybrook, married Miss Lord; had children: Samuel, a physician, Henry, Fanny, and William, a physician; Sarah; and Simeon, a physician of Enfield, who married Margaret Raynold; their children are: Simeon, a physician, Margaret, Mary, Peter, and Edward, a physician.

Capt. Zechariah (11), son of Samuel (4), married Sarah, daughter of Philip Mattoon, of Northfield; had children: Seth; Catharine, wife of Mr. Willard; Gains; Dr. Ebenezer; Samuel; and Paul.

Ebenezer (12), son of Samuel (4), married Elizabeth, daughter of William Arms; had children: Ebenezer; Moses; Aaron; Elizabeth, married Ebenezer Wells; and Joanna, married Phineas Wright.

Capt. Moses (13), son of Thomas (10), married Rebecca Cooley, and had children: Rebecca, wife of Azariah Woolworth; Elijah, died young; Oliver (14); Moses, married Lydia Champion; Diadema, wife of Stephen Williams and Jacob Ribbe; Aaron, died in childhood; Aaron, a physician, married Maria Burt; Alexander, married, first, Flavia Colton; second, Jerusha Burt; Sarah; and Naomi, died in youth.

Oliver (14), son of Moses (13), married Anne Cooley, whose children are: Moses; Annie, wife of Justin Smith; Naomi, wife of Noah Ashley; Elijah, married Cynthia Terry; Mary, wife of Stephen Ashley; and Caleb C. (15).

Caleb C. (15), son of Oliver (14), married Sarah Colton, and had children: Oliver, married Lucinda Hatch, and their children are: Ella, Moses, Adelaide, and Sarah; Flavia, married George Gleason; and Moses (16).

Moses (16), son of Caleb C. (15), married, first, Abbie, daughter of Jonathan Pierson, of Newark, and had by her: Flavia; Frederic; Pauline; Mary Adelaide; and Flavia Adelaide. Second wife was Annie, daughter of Charles Pierson; children by her: Edward; William; and Annie.

Capt. Joseph (5), son of Zechariah (1), lived a considerable time in Northampton, then moved to Hartford, where he died, February 15th, 1735, aged 78. He married, first, in 1683, Joanna, daughter of John Wyatt, of Hartford; second, the widow Mary Belting. By his first wife, he had children: Mary, born 1684, married Ebenezer Boswell, of Hatfield; Joanna, died young; Joseph (17); Joanna, married Thomas French, of Deerfield; their children are: Mary, born 1719, Freedom, Abigail, Thomas, Freedom, Thomas, Abigail, and Joanna; Lydia, married John Bliss, of Long Meadow, and became the mother of Judge Bliss, of Wilbraham; Jonathan (18); Martha, born 1699; and Abigail, born 1702—no information of them; Israel; and Thankful; both died young.

Deacon Joseph (17), son of Capt. Joseph (5), moved to Sunderland, where he died February 4th, 1754. He married Mary Smith, of Hatfield, who survived him many years. Their children were; Elisha, married and removed to Bennington, then to Cornwall, Vt.; Mary, became the second wife of Daniel Clark, had one child, Irena; Abigail, died young; Abigail, wife of Samuel Field, of Northfield, and had children: Mary, Silas, Mary, Submit; Samuel, Asenath, and Abigail; Joseph (19); Thankful, wife of Benjamin Graves, of Sunderland; Martha, wife of Deacon Belden, of Amherst; Experience, married, first, Elijah Clark, of Northampton; had seven or eight children; second, Simeon Parsons; she died 1817, aged 85; Sarah, wife of Simeon Lyman, of Northfield, had ten children; Jonathan, married Elizabeth Cooley; and Israel, born March 27th, 1741.

Joseph (19), son of Joseph (17), succeeded his father in the office of deacon, in Sunderland, which he held many years. He died 1798, aged 75, having married Ruth Parker; their children were: Elijah (20), born 1754; Lucy, married Rinnah Cooley, (see Cooley family, No. 17); Rebecca; Thomas, died young; Mary, wife of Heman Farnum, lived several years in Sunderland, then in Bushland; Joseph, died in infancy; Martha; Ruth; Joseph (21); Submit; Thomas, born 1777, died at Oriskany Falls, aged 77.

Elijah (20), son of Joseph (19), married Tryphena, daughter of Capt. Abner Cooley. They lived some years in Sunderland, then removed to Hawley, where they died, leaving children : Wealthy, born 1785, wife of William Ferguson; Olive, wife of Edmund Langley; Theodore, married Deborah Taby; Rosamond, wife of Calvin Cooley; Tryphena, wife of Zephaniah Lathrop; Pindar, married a Congregational minister at Oriskany Falls.

Rev. Joseph (21), son of Joseph (19), born in the same house where his father, grandfather and great-grandfather died; was graduated at Dartmouth College, 1792; was minister, for a time, at Fairfield, N. Y., afterward at Charlemont, Mass.; represented his district in the legislature, for a time; died in 1839, having married Sabra, daughter of Rev. Mr. Emerson, of Conway; by her had children : Constant, graduated at Williams College; Caroline, married John Hooper, son of Hon. Robert, of Weston, Mass.; and Joseph, a physician, went to Texas and joined as surgeon-in-chief the unfortunate regiment of Col. Fannin, the remnant of whose regiment, after a battle, were, the next morning, shot by order of the commander, Dr. Field being the only one spared, that he might attend the wounded Mexican officers. He was carried to Mexico, but in about two months, he and a German, catching each a mule, at twilight, rode till their animals were exhausted, then walked for two days, when they reached friendly whites. He married Miss Jones, of Hudson, N. Y., sister of Dr. or Gen. Calvin Jones, of Memphis, Tenn., and settled in Galveston, Tex.

Submit, daughter of Joseph (19), became the wife of Gains Lyman, of Northampton, afterward a merchant of Hartford, Conn. Their children were: Winchester, born 1799; Christopher, married Cecelia Breckenridge; Orra Almira, married James Bolles; Julia Ella; Jane Rachel; Hannah Submit, married Chester Judson; Theodore, married Mary Nickols.

Jonathan (18), son of Capt. Joseph (5), moved to Sunderland in 1719, married, first, Harriet Billings, of Hatfield, by whom he had four daughters; second, Esther Smith, by whom he had: Seth (22); William; Jonathan; Moses; Esther; and Editha.

Seth (22), son of Jonathan (18), married Mary, daughter of Israel Hubbard, of Sunderland, and had by her: Roswell; Rufus; Martin, late Gen. Field, of Newfane, Vt.; Spencer; Orlanda; and Sally.

The Fish Family.

The family of Fish is of English origin, and more remotely, as the ancient mode of spelling the name, Fisch, indicates, of Saxon. The American progenitors of that name, who came from Kent county, England, must have arrived soon after the landing at Plymouth, as Nathaniel, John and Jonathan were residing at Lynn, Mass., before 1637, when they were removed to Sandwich, on Cape Cod. Of these, Jonathan Fish (1), at least, joined the settlement at Newtown, L. I., soon after its foundation, in 1652, and was evidently a person of note there, from the frequent mention of his name in an official capacity. He died in 1663, leaving a widow, Mary, and sons: John; Samuel; and Nathan (2). Of these, Samuel died about 1700, without issue, and John removed to New Jersey, probably to Elizabeth.

Nathan (2), son of Jonathan (1), remained at Newtown, and died at an advanced age, in 1734, having had fourteen children: Jonathan (3); Nathan; Mary; Samuel; John; Thomas; Susannah; Ambrose; and Benjamin (4)—twins; Sarah; Nathaniel; Hannah; Temperance; and Elnathan.

Jonathan (3), the eldest son of Nathan (2), was also a man of prominence in the town, to which he gave the lot on which the present Presbyterian Church stands. He died in 1793, aged 43, his wife, Mary, surviving, by whom he became the ancestor of Col. Nicholas Fish, distinguished in the Revolution for bravery and patriotism. Laying aside his law books, he commenced his career as major; was at the battle of Long Island, was wounded at Monmouth, participated in the capture of the British armies, both at Saratoga and Yorktown, and stood high in the confidence of Gen. Washington. After leaving the army, he was made adjutant-general of New York, and died 1833, having become, by his marriage with Elizabeth, daughter of Peter Stuyvesant, among others, the father of Hamilton Fish, at one time governor of the state, afterwards a representative of his state in the senate of the United States, and secretary of state of the United States.

Benjamin (4), seventh son of Nathan (2), was born May 12th, 1697; married January 11th, 1728, Sarah, daughter of Joseph Moore, of Newtown, (see Moore family, No. 4,) who was born September 29th, 1706, removed to what is now Ewing, about 1745, and died October 18th, 1773. Their children were: Elizabeth, married Amos Hart; Rebecca, married John Phillips, of Pennsylvania, (see Phillips family); Nathan; Joseph; Samuel; Benjamin (5); John; and Nathaniel. The posterity of Samuel and John is found in the counties of Salem and Gloucester, N. J., and that of Nathan in Butler and Union counties, Pa., of whom is the Rev. Reeder M. Fish, of Lewisburg.

Benjamin (5), son of Benjamin (4), was born on Long Island, August 10th, 1740; married Abigail, daughter of Joshua Howell, (see Howell family, No. 4,) and died suddenly, July 2d, 1808. Mrs. Fish was born March 15th, 1750, and died November 11th, 1822. Their children were: Israel, born July 14th, 1772, married October 25th, 1797, Mary, daughter of Richard Slack, of Hopewell, and, without issue, died July 10th, 1860; Peter, born March 7th, 1774, died in infancy; Asa, born January 5th, 1777, married, successively, Margaret, daughter of Garret and Lamartie Conover, who died August 16th, 1822, and Rachel, daughter of William Anthony, and, without issue by either, died February 28th, 1851, from the effects of a fall; Nathan (6); and Benjamin (7).

Nathan (6), son of Benjamin (5), was born December 10th, 1779, and died July 7th, 1865, having married, March 7th, 1805, Sarah, daughter of John Smith, of Lawrence. She died April, 1859, aged 75. Their children were: Mary, a mute; Elizabeth, died in infancy; Eliza, married Abram Skirm, whose children are: Asa F., married Margaret, daughter of William and Sarah Cook, Charles Henry, married Elizabeth, daughter of Job White, (see White family, No. 4), Emily Maria, Elizabeth, married Benjamin Vancleve, and Margaret, married James G. Vancleve.

Benjamin (7), son of Benjamin (5), was born in Ewing township, November 15th, 1785, and removed to Trenton in 1808, where he at first engaged in mercantile business, and later in the transportation of merchandise across the state. On the organization of the Camden and Amboy Railroad Company, in 1830, of which he was a projector and incorporator, he was elected a director, and continued to be such until the time of his death. For more than forty years he was a director of the Trenton Banking Company, and in 1834 he was a member of the legislature of the state. He was elected a trustee of the First Presbyterian church of Trenton on December 8th, 1825, and at the time of his death was the president of the board. He married Maria, daughter of William Sackett Moore, (see Moore family, No. 12,) on April 7th, 1812, and died suddenly in Trenton, on June 22d, 1880. Their children were: William Sackett, died in infancy; Jonathan Sackett, born May 19th, 1815, married Emeline, daughter of Dr. John Howell, (see Howell family, No. 44,) and died April 29th, 1872, whose children were: Emily Augusta, married F. Augustus Auten and Frances Maria, died young; Rebecca Ann, died in infancy; Clementina Elizabeth, died in infancy; Asa Israel, born February 17th, 1820, was graduated at Harvard College and also at the Law School; he became a member of the Philadelphia bar, and conducted with ability the editorial department of the "Law Journal," of that city; he was honored with the degree of LL. B. by the University of Pennsylvania, and with the degree of LL. D. by Kenyon College; he married Elizabeth H., daughter of Ralph Shreve, and died in Philadelphia on May 5th, 1879; his only child, Henry S., died in infancy; Benjamin Moore, born May 18th, 1822, and died unmarried, May 21st, 1874; Emma Maria, born December 27th, 1825, married John S. Chambers, (see Chambers family, No. 8); Augustine Hallett, born November 18th, 1828, was graduated at the College of New Jersey in 1847, and at the medical department of the University of Pennsylvania in 1851. He settled in Philadelphia, and was a practitioner of medicine in that city; he married Sarah P., daughter of Rev. Lewis Cheeseman, of Philadelphia, and died at Cooperstown, N. Y., August 3d, 1872, without issue; and Robert L. Stevens, died in infancy.

The Furman Family.

Richard Furman (1) was one of the early emigrants from Long Island to Lawrence, where he resided, and died 1752, date of will. He left a wife, Sarah, and children: Jonathan (2); Josiah (3); Frances; Elizabeth, married Mr. Kitchen; Mary, married Mr. Clark; and Sarah, married Mr. Clawson.

Jonathan (2), son of Richard (1), married, first, Frances, daughter of Robert Lanning, (see Lanning family, No. 1,) and had issue: Joshua (4); Daniel (5); Nathaniel (6); Robert (7); Richard, married Sarah Henderson; had children: David, Jonathan, and Sarah; Elizabeth, wife of Ralph Biles; Sarah, wife of Nathaniel Temple, (see Temple family, No. 7); Mary; and David, entered the army and never returned. He had a second wife, Mary.

Joshua (4), son of Jonathan (2), died February 20th, 1840, aged 86, having married, first, Sarah Jones, whose children were: Andrew (8); Israel (9); Fannie, wife of Henry Vanpelt; Mary, wife of George Lanning, (see Lanning family, No. 40); Jemima, wife of Amos Lanning, (see Lanning family, No. 29); his second wife was Sallie, daughter of Thomas Hendrickson, (see Hendrickson family, No. 16.)

Andrew (8), son of Joshua (4), died 1858, aged 83; married Jane Reed. She died 1854, aged 80, having had issue: Nathaniel, died in 1840; William Madison (10); Scudder; Andrew; Matilda; Mary; Elizabeth; Sarah, wife of John Titus.

William M. (10), son of Andrew (8), married Elizabeth Riley, widow of Ralph Furman, and had children: Daniel, married Louisa, daughter of Morgan Beakes; Rebecca, wife of William Mathews; Sarah, married John Blackwell; David; and George.

Israel (9), son of Joshua (4), married Sarah, daughter of Levi Ketcham, and had children: Joshua, married Susan, daughter of Ralph Hunt; Levi, married Mary, daughter of Asa Burroughs, of Hopewell; and Ralph, married Elizabeth Riley, whose children were: Elizabeth, wife of Mr. Hughs, Deborah, Hannah, and Harriet.

Daniel (5), son of Jonathan (2), married, first, Eunice, daughter of William Reed, (see Reed family, No. 1); had one son, Ezekiel (10); second, Elizabeth, daughter of Amos Hart, (see Hart family, No. 15.)

Ezekiel (11), son of Daniel (5), died 1857, aged 82; married Rebecca, daughter of Amos Hart, sister of his father's second wife. Their children were: Aaron (12); and Amos (13).

Aaron (12), son of Ezekiel (11), married Jemima, daughter of John Lanning, (see Lanning family, No. 13); had issue: Levi, married Anna Maria Howard; Henry, married Keturah Cheves; and Rebecca.

Amos (13), son of Ezekiel (11), married, first, Martha, daughter of John Lanning, (see Lanning family, No. 13); children are: Gilbert, married Amanda, daughter of Charles Reed, (see Reed family, No. 11); and Ann Eliza. He married, second, Clarissa Reed, widow of Samuel McMurray.

Nathaniel (6), son of Jonathan (2), died 1831, aged 89; was both an elder and trustee of the Ewing Church; married Elizabeth, daughter of William Welling, (see Welling family, No. 1.) She died 1815, aged 66, leaving children: Theophilus (13); Nathaniel, married, first, Sarah, daughter of Reuben Hunt, (see Hunt family, No. 33); second, Sarah, daughter of John Temple, (see Temple family, No. 11); he moved to Ohio, and there married, third, Miss Williamson; has a son, George, now living in Ohio; Lydia, wife of Newhall Nutt, has a son, William, who married Rhoda, daughter of George Garwood; Elizabeth, died 1825, aged 46; Rachel, died 1810, aged 29; Nancy, wife of Joseph Gray; Hannah, wife of Israel Green, (see Green family, No. 58); Mary, died 1825, aged 43; and Joseph; had by his first wife, Sarah, daughter of Titus Hart, (see Hart family, No. 16), a daughter, Louisa, who married John Hagerman, and moved to Ohio; by his second wife, Lydia, daughter of Joshua Reed, (see Reed family, No. 5,) he had: Ira; Randolph; and Cornelius.

Theophilus (14), son of Nathaniel (6), was an elder in the Pennington church. He married Mary, daughter of Elijah Lanning, (see Lanning family, No. 10); had children: Frances; John, married Miss Ketcham; Mary; Elijah, married Miss Bowes; and Nathaniel, married Ruth Higgins, who has a son, Higgins, married Caroline, daughter of William Hunt.

Robert (7), son of Jonathan (2), married Elizabeth, daughter of Daniel Lanning, (see Lanning family, No. 6.) They had children:

James (15); Frances, married Anthony Reed; and Elizabeth, not married.

James (15), son of Robert (7), married Kesiah, daughter of Jonathan Cook, (see Cook family, No. 2,) and had children: William, died in infancy; Jonathan C. (16); Enoch, died a young man; Mary, married Jesse Crosley; Samuel, died young; Kesiah; James (17); Sarah M.; and Henry C. (18).

Jonathan C. (16), son of James (15), married Elizabeth Jones, and had children: Enoch, died in infancy; Enoch, died when a young man; Jonathan, married; Margaret Ann, married Isaiah Cotral; and Charles, married Miss Obert.

James (17), son of James (15), married, first, Eliza Arey; second, Rebecca, her sister, by whom he has one son, William P.

Henry C. (18), son of James (15), married Sarah Matilda, daughter of Amos Lanning, (see Lanning family, No. 29,) and had children: Amanda, married Peter Williamson; Kesiah, married Isaac Dunn; Mary Elizabeth, married Charles Mitchell; and Rebecca, married John R. Elrath.

Josiah (3), son of Richard (1), whose will is dated 1788, had a wife, Mary, and children: Agur; Mary, married Mr. Smith; and Sarah, married John Johnson. Though no Josiah is mentioned in the will, (no uncommon occurrence, when children have already been provided for,) yet the following—Josiah (19)—was probably a son of his.

Josiah (19), son of Josiah (3), died 1803, having married Ruth Baraclift. Their children were: Richard Way (20); John (21); Josiah, not married; Barzilla, married Elizabeth Middleton, had a daughter, Hannah, wife of Robert Field, of Burlington county; Matilda, married Aaron Pitman; Achsah, married Mr. Satcher; Rebecca, married Mr. Calhoun, had Thomas, Josiah, and perhaps others; and Mercy, married Mr. Esdel.

Richard W. (20), son of Josiah (19), died 1813; had by his first wife, Hannah Middleton: George (22); and Josiah (23); by his second wife, Sarah Rickey: Thomas; John, not married; Rickey, went West; William; and Hannah.

George (22), son of Richard W. (20), died 1870, aged 85, having married Margaret Kelly; had children: Hannah, wife of Abel North, of Philadelphia; Sarah, wife of Mordecai Middleton; Elizabeth; Richard Way (24); David, married Mary Paxon, of Philadelphia; Phebe Ann; and Samuel, married Deborah Deverell; lives in Philadelphia.

Richard Way (24), son of George (22), married Ann Eliza Tilton, and had issue: Charles; Ellen; William S.; George M.; William; Hannah; Louisa; and David.

Josiah (23), son of Richard (20), married Sarah Williams, and had by her: Susan, married Lewis Breese; Mary, wife of Spencer Sutphin; Richard, married Miss Disborow; Theodocia, wife of Jacob Parent, of Allentown; Ruth, wife of Daniel Bowers; Thomas, married Susan, daughter of Samuel Ellis, of Burlington; and John.

John (21), son of Josiah (19), married, first, Miss Burroughs, by whom he had: Sarah, not married. By his second wife, Miss Steward, had: William, who married Elizabeth Wildman, of Pennsylvania; and Steward, married.

The Green Family.

William Green (1), ancestor of the families of that name in this region, dissatisfied with some new relation in his father's family, left his native land, England, at the early age of twenty, and landed at the port of Philadelphia. Soon after, desirous of returning, and finding no vessel about to sail from that port, he went to New York, but not meeting with an opportunity immediately, visited Long Island. He there became acquainted with the family of John Reeder, recently arrived from England, whose sister, or daughter, Joanna, in process of time, he married, and removed to Ewing township, about 1700. He purchased three hundred and forty-five acres of Col. Daniel Coxe, the deed bearing date 1712, and on it erected the first brick house in the township, which is still standing, having on the west end the date, 1717, and is owned and occupied by his descendant of the fifth generation, Henry Green. His qualities were such as to give him distinction, for he was appointed one of the first judges of Hunterdon county, and from the frequent mention of his name in public affairs and important business transactions, he was evidently a prominent and useful citizen. His children were: Richard (2); Joseph (3); William (4); Benjamin (5); John; Jeremiah, who removed to North Carolina; Isaac, married, and removed to Sussex county, N. J., where his descendants are to be found; Joanna; Sarah; Esther; and Mary. Of the daughters, there is no record. He died, as is indicated by his antique tombstone in the Ewing church-yard, in 1722.

Richard (2), son of William (1), who died 1741, married Mary, daughter of George Ely, of Trenton, and had children: Richard (6); George (7); Rebecca, wife of Samuel Moore, (see Moore family, No. 16); Christian, wife of Joseph Moore, (see Moore family, No. 17); and William, died 1754, probably unmarried, or without children, as he leaves his property to his brother Richard, £300 to his eldest sister's three sons, Richard, William, and

Elijah Moore; a legacy to his youngest sister's three sons, Ely, Moses, and Ephraim Moore; also to his mother, Mary; and his plantation to his brother George, when 19.

Richard (6), son of Richard (2), who died 1797, married Phebe, daughter of Nathaniel Moore, (see Moore family, No. 6,) whose children were: William R. (8); Nathaniel (9); Richard (10); Enoch (11); John (12); Samuel, not married; Benjamin (13); Joseph (14); George (15); Rebecca, wife of William B. Green (54); Sarah, wife of Samuel Moore, (see Moore family, No. 21); and Mary, married Daniel Stillwell, and went to Ohio.

William R. (8), son of Richard (6), who died 1818, married Elizabeth, daughter of James Burroughs, (see Burroughs family, No. 4.) She died 1842, aged 84, leaving children: Samuel (16); James B. (17); and Nancy, wife of Joseph Green (56.)

Samuel (16), son of William R. (8), died January 30th, 1812, aged 31, having married Sarah, daughter of Jedediah Scudder, (see Scudder family, No. 14.) Their children are: Jedediah, married Rachel Paxton, has one child, Mary; Ira, went to New Orleans, and was never heard from; Ephraim, married Mary Bassett, of Philadelphia, lives in Quincy, Ill., and has children, Frances, Henry, and Lewis.

James B. (17), son of William R. (8), was a trustee of Ewing Church and a man of influence; died October 23d, 1847, aged 63. He married Catharine, daughter of William Anthony, (see Anthony family, No. 2,) who died May 25th, 1866, aged 80. Their children were: Nancy, wife of John Scudder, (see Scudder family, No. 18); William A. (18); Martha, wife of John Vancleve, (see Vancleve family, No. 17); Alexander (19); Elizabeth, married, first, Theodore Johnson; second, Thomas Cain; lives in Philadelphia; her children are: Thomas, Jennie, Cassie, and James; James B. (20); Catharine, married Harvey Johnson, of Pennsylvania; and Edward, married Catharine, daughter of John Sager, of Trenton; live in Sydney, Ohio.

William A. (18), son of James B. (17), married Eliza, daughter of Ephraim Roberts, (see Roberts family, No. 3); lived at Schuylkill Haven, where he died 1853, leaving children: Alfred; Ephraim, married Miss Skirm; Mary, married Richard Jones; and Augusta, married Mr. Dye.

Alexander B. (19), son of James B. (17), was a merchant of Trenton, now a resident of Ewing; was a member of the state legislature; is an elder in the Ewing Church. He married, first,

Mary Ann, daughter of Clark Chambers, (see Chambers family, No. 9,) who died May 4th, 1848, aged 34, leaving children: Louisa, wife of Harvey Fisk, a wealthy banker of New York, of the firm of Fisk & Hatch, and son of Rev. Joel Fisk, a Congregational clergyman, who died 1856, aged 60, and who, with his wife, Clarinda Chapman, who died 1878, aged 78, is buried in the Ewing church-yard; Alexander, who, at the age of 23, promptly responded to the call of his country, and was one of those brave men of the Fourteenth New Jersey Volunteers, Lieut. Col. Caldwell Hall commanding, who laid down their lives in the desperate fight at Monocacy Bridge, against overwhelming numbers; and Mary. His second wife was Jane Rice, of Trenton. His third, Mary, daughter of Daniel Cook. His fourth, Clementine Davis, of Columbia, Pa.

James B. (20), son of James B. (17), a trustee of the Ewing Church, married, first, Deborah, daughter of Cornelius Moore, (see Moore family, No. 2.) She died August 14th, 1855, aged 34, leaving children: Theodore, who entered the Union Army, and, as lieutenant, but commanding Company I, of the Fourteenth Regiment of New Jersey Volunteers, fell, gallantly fighting, in the battle of Winchester, Va., September 19th, 1864, aged 20; and Albert, died in childhood. By his second wife, Maria, daughter of Benjamin Vancleve, (see Vancleve family, No. 16,) who died 1877, aged 59, has a son, John, married Marion, daughter of George Potts. His third wife was Eleanor, widow of Ephraim Woolsey, (see Woolsey family, No. 9.)

Nathaniel (9), son of Richard (6), who died September 25th, 1831, aged 75, married Sarah, daughter of Daniel Howell, (see Howell family, No. 37.) Their children were; Armitage (21); Mary, wife of Maj. John Howell, (see Howell family, No. 40); Ann, married Bradly Atwood, and moved to Memphis, Tenn.; and John, who, by falls, had broken his bones more than twenty times, but by his last fall, his spine was so injured that his body and limbs were entirely paralyzed and apparently dead, except the vital organs and the brain, yet he lived sixteen weeks after the injury—a remarkable case; he died January 14th, 1827.

Armitage (21), son of Nathaniel (9), was a merchant of Trenton; died July 19th, 1854, having married, first, Anna Maria, daughter of Daniel Williams, of Freehold, and had children: Augustus (22); Amanda, died in childhood; and Nathaniel (23). His second wife was Susan, daughter of John Moore, (see Moore family, No. 27.)

Augustus (22), son of Armitage (21), married Eliza Ann, daughter of John Green (51), and moved to Illinois. Their children are: Frederic A.; Francis O.; Elizabeth; Louisa; Robert; Nathaniel; Stephen; John G.; Isabella; and Augusta.

Nathaniel (23), son of Armitage (21), a lawyer of Pekin, Ill., married Charlotte Storms, and has children: Lily; Theodore; Frederic; Douglass; and Don Morse.

Richard (10), son of Richard (6), married, first, Martha, daughter of Christopher Howell, (see Howell family, No. 2,) by whom he had a daughter, Martha, wife of Charles Reeder, (see Reeder family, No. 5.) By his second wife he had: Ely; Mary; Elizabeth; and perhaps others. He lived in Pennsylvania.

Enoch (11), son of Richard (6), resided in Trenton; married Miss Davis, of Philadelphia, and had children: David, married Fanny Carman, and lived in Trenton; Susan, wife of Caleb Carman; Sarah, wife of Thomas Hamilton; and Maria, wife of Samuel Tucker.

John (12), son of Richard (6), one of the first settlers of Easton, Pa., died March 9th, 1854, aged 88, having married Rhoda, daughter of Daniel Howell, (see Howell family, No. 37,) who died September 19th, 1859, aged 73. Their children are: Enoch (24); Charles, married, first, Elizabeth Maxwell; second, Mrs. Latimer; Richard, married Sarah, daughter of Samuel Sherrod, of Washington, N. J.; William (25); Elizabeth, wife of David Deshler; and Lydia.

Enoch (24), son of John (12), married, first, Mary, daughter of George Beidelman, and had children: Ellen, wife of Whitfield S. Johnson, a lawyer of Sussex, and for several years secretary of state of New Jersey, whose children are: William M., a lawyer of Hackensack, Mary M., Emily E., Laura C., Elizabeth B., Margaret G., and Ellen Green; George B., married Ann Disbrow; resides in Jersey City; Mary, wife of George Woodruff, merchant, of New York; John; Joseph; Henry, a graduate of Lafayette College, a lawyer of Easton and judge of the Supreme Court, married Ann Hultsizer, of Easton; has children: Caroline, wife of Hiram Howland, of Indianapolis, Frances, wife of Henry E. Potter, of Orange, N. J., Frederic, and Ada; and Margaret, married Henry Johnson, a lawyer of Muncy, Pa. Married, second, Catharine Teneyck, of Princeton.

William (25), son of John (12), married, first, Elizabeth, daughter of Henry Beidelman; and, second, Jane Sherrard, and had children: Sarah, wife of Rev. John Kugler, of Warren, N. J.; Theodore, married Miss Kinsey; Frank; John; Louisa; Mary; and Howard.

Benjamin (13), son of Richard (6), removed to Easton, Pa.; died 1852, aged 82, having married there, Elizabeth, daughter of Robert Traill, a lawyer, and by her had children: John (26); Traill (27); Robert Traill, married Catharine Van Camp; Elizabeth, wife of John Stewart, of Greenwich, N. J.; and Maria, wife of Enoch Clark, of Monroe county, Pa.

John (26), son of Benjamin (13), a merchant, married Sarah, daughter of Nathaniel Hart, of Trenton (see Hart family), whose children are: Edward; Juliette; Kate; and Jane.

Dr. Traill (27), son of Benjamin (13), a physician, honored with the degree of LL. D., professor of chemistry in Lafayette College, and the liberal donor of funds to that college, to establish an observatory. He married Harriet, daughter of Loammi Moore, of Morristown, and has children: Ella; Frances; and Edgar Moore.

Joseph (14), son of Richard (6), married, first, Julia Hiling; had one daughter; married Mr. Hays. By his second wife, no children.

George (15), son of Richard (6), married Henrietta Hiling, the widow of Bertram Galbraith; had children: Charles, died, aged 26; George, married Miss Wharton, of Morrisville; has six children, and lives in Missouri; and Henrietta.

George (7), son of Richard (2), who died August, 1777, aged 39, married, May 4th, 1769, Anna, daughter of the Rev. Caleb Smith, (see Smith family, No. 4.) He settled in Lawrence, on the farm purchased of John Dagworthy. They had children: Caleb Smith (28); Charles Dickinson, born November 28th, 1771, was graduated at Princeton, studied divinity, died April 23d, 1857; James H., born January 7th, 1774; a merchant in western New York, died 1801; and Richard Montgomery (29). His widow married, September 20th, 1786, Capt. Benjamin Vancleve, (see Vancleve family, No. 5,) and died March 30th, 1789, aged 40.

Caleb Smith (28), son of George (7), who died August, 1850, aged 80, by his union with Elizabeth, daughter of Aaron Vancleve, (see Vancleve family, No. 10,) who died December 20th, 1836, aged 64, had children: Jane, wife of Rev. Thomas Kennedy, a Presbyterian clergyman, had one child, Mary, married Alfred D. Green; George S. (30); John C. (31); Henry Woodhull (32); James, died unmarried; Mary; Cornelia; Ellen, married Rev. Joseph W.

Blythe, who was for many years pastor of the Second Church, Cranbury, N. J., whose children are: Margaret, Ellen, Smith, William, and Lillie; and Caleb Smith (33).

George S. (30), son of Caleb Smith (28), an elder and trustee of the First Presbyterian Church of Trenton, and prominent in the business circles of that city, married, first, Sarah, daughter of Judge William Kennedy, of Warren county, who died 1843, aged 39, leaving children: William Henry (34): Sarah Elizabeth, married Rev. John T. Duffield, D. D., professor of mathematics in the College of New Jersey, whose children are: Rev. George Howard, graduate of Princeton College and Seminary, John Thomas, graduate of Princeton, Helen G., Henry, graduate of Princeton, Sarah, and Edward Dickinson; Anna Corilla, married, first, Rev. Edward D. Yeomans, was pastor of the Fourth Presbyterian Church of Trenton, and had children: George Green, a graduate of Princeton, Anna, and Elizabeth, her second husband is the Rev. Minot Morgan; Edward T., a graduate of Princeton College, in the class of 1854, a member of the bar of Trenton, married, first, Julia Thompson, has a son, Walter; second, Charlotte, daughter of Chief Justice Mercer Beasley, by whom has Annie and Charlotte. His second wife was Anna M., daughter of John Kennedy, brother of Judge William Kennedy, by whom he had: Virginia; Mary; and Emma, who married Frederick C. Lewis, has children, Edith and George Green.

Prof. William Henry (34), son of George S. (30), was born in Groveville, N. J., January 27th, 1825; graduated at Lafayette College, Pa., 1840; studied theology in the Princeton Seminary; was for three years assistant teacher of Hebrew there; was pastor of the Central Church, Philadelphia; thence he was called, in 1851, to be a professor in the Princeton Theological Seminary, where he now is. Among his publications are, a Hebrew Grammar and Chrestomathy, a Commentary on Job, a Vindication of the Pentateuch, from Colenso's Aspersions. He married, first, Mary Elizabeth, daughter of Stephen Colwell, of Philadelphia, who died March 29th, 1854, aged 26; second, Elizabeth Hayes. Their children are: Mary Elizabeth, wife of William Libbey; and Helen Hayes.

John Cleve (31), son of Caleb Smith (28), by his skill in business and success in the China trade, became an eminent and wealthy merchant of New York. He was a munificent patron of benevolent and educational institutions. He married Sarah, daughter of George Griswold, a merchant of New York city, and had three children, all of whom died in early youth.

Henry W. (32), son of Caleb Smith (28), graduated at Princeton College at the early age of 16, and was admitted to the bar in 1825. His great acumen, his eminent abilities, his thorough legal attainments, and his untiring industry and devotion to business, united to unswerving integrity, soon raised him to the highest rank in his profession. In 1846, his eminent fitness elevated him to the chair of Chief Justice, which he filled with great acceptance for fourteen years, when he was raised to the still higher position of Chancellor, in which office he remained till nervous prostration and failing health compelled his retirement, greatly to the regret of the whole bar. Besides his two high judicial positions, he occupied many others, to the great benefit of the community. He was, in 1844, a member of the constitutional convention, and commissioner of the sinking fund of the city of Trenton for many years. He was an elder of the First Presbyterian Church of Trenton, president of the board of trustees of the Princeton Theological Seminary, and a trustee, for more than a quarter of a century, of Princeton College, of which he was a liberal benefactor, having established in it a $10,000 fellowship of mental science. He aided many indigent students in gaining their education. His benefactions to the church, to benevolent institutions, and to the cause of education, though unknown at the time, were exceedingly generous, and when, on December 19th, 1876, he ceased from earth, he left behind a memory most fragrant, both as a man and a Christian. By his first marriage, with Emily Augusta, daughter of Chief Justice Charles Ewing, who died 1837, aged 29, he had a daughter, Emily, wife of William B. Blackwell, lawyer, of New York, who has a son, William B. By his second wife, Susan Mary, sister of his former wife, he had five children, died in infancy, and Charles Ewing, a graduate of Princeton College and a lawyer of Trenton, who married Mary Potter, has children: Helen G., Henry W., John C., and Susanna L.; he is now a trustee of Princeton College and of Princeton Theological Seminary.

Judge Caleb S. (33), son of Caleb Smith (28), was also a graduate of Princeton, adopted the profession of law; was made judge of the Court of Errors and Appeals, is a manager of the New Jersey Lunatic Asylum, director of the Trenton Banking Company, and president of the Trenton Savings Bank. He married Eleanor

Græme, daughter of Charles Ewing; has one son, Elmer Ewing, a graduate of Princeton, a lawyer of Trenton, who married Sue E., daughter of Capt. William E. Hunt, (see Hunt family, No. 15, has children, Elmer E. and William E.

Richard M. (29), son of George (7), who died November 2d, 1853, aged 78, was a man of strong mind and generous feelings. He was graduated by the College of New Jersey; was, in the early part of his life, a merchant in western New York, where he accumulated a handsome fortune, then settled in Lawrenceville. His children, by his wife, Mary, daughter of Dr. Thomas Henderson, of Freehold, who died January 13th, 1849, aged 70, were: Thomas Henderson (35); Charles Gustavus (36); Alfred Dickinson, first a merchant of Trenton, afterwards a lawyer of Burlington, Iowa, married Mary, daughter of Rev. Thomas Kennedy, and resided, for his health, in Italy, where his wife and two children are buried; he was consul at Naples, at his death, in 1867; Matilda; and Sidney Breeze (37).

Dr. Thomas H. (35), son of Richard M. (29), who died 1879, received his degree of A. M. from Princeton, and of M. D. from the University of Pennsylvania; practiced his profession, lastly, in Brooklyn. He married Mary, daughter of Jacob Gulick, of Kingston, and had by her: Charles, a druggist of Brooklyn, married Maria, daughter of Dr. Alfred Dayton, of Matawan; Lydia S., married Alfred Sampson, of New York; at their early death, left a daughter, Mattie S.; Richard Montgomery, married a daughter of John Ward, of Brooklyn; and Kate Nelson, married George McFarlane.

Charles G. (36), son of Richard M. (29), educated at Princeton, a merchant of Trenton, and married Sarah Ann, daughter of John S. Maxwell, by whom he had children: Maxwell, a lawyer, settled in Burlington, Iowa, married Elmira Schenck, of that place; Matilda, died young; and Louisa, married James Peasley, cashier of the Bank in Burlington, Iowa.

Matilda, daughter of Richard M. (29), married Samuel M. Hamill, D. D., son of Robert Hamill, of Norristown, Pa., who was graduated by Jefferson College, Pa., received his theological education at Princeton, was president of the New Jersey Historical Society, a director of the New Jersey State Lunatic Asylum, a member of the board of trustees of the Princeton Theological Seminary, and Principal of the High School established at Lawrenceville, N. J., more than sixty years ago, over which he has presided most of that time, and which has, under his able management, continued to extend, far and wide, its beneficent influence. Their children are: Mary, wife of Edward P. Wood, a Presbyterian clergyman, and son of James Wood, D. D., professor of theology at New Albany, and president of Hanover College; Robert, died young; Isabella; Maxwell; Richard; last three died in childhood; Charles, died, aged 18, while a student in Princeton College; Hugh H., a graduate of Princeton, a lawyer of Trenton, who married Elizabeth, daughter of Barker Gummere; Maud; and Samuel M., a graduate of Princeton.

Sidney B. (37), son of Richard M. (29), occupied the homestead in Lawrenceville; married, first, Ellen, daughter of Dr. Horatio Sansbury, of Princeton. She died 1866, aged 40, leaving children: Horatio S., died, aged 18; Mary M., died in youth; Catharine H., died young; and Alfred Dickinson. His second wife was Maria Grey, of Princeton, who died 1877, leaving children, Charles and Nellie.

Joseph (3), son of William (1), was an elder of the Ewing Church; died March 12th, 1784, aged 85, having married Elizabeth Mershon, who died March 12th, 1775, aged 61. Their children were: Jemima, born August 2d, 1742, married James Hunt; Sarah, born August 19th, 1744, wife of Thomas Smith; Ann, born March 20th, 1748; and Joseph (38).

Joseph (38), son of Joseph (3), who died February 23d, 1826, aged 75, married Hannah, daughter of Richard Lanning, (see Lanning family, No. 4.) She died February 2d, 1828, aged 65, having had children: Charles (39); Elizabeth, born March 5th, 1784, married Enos Hart; Ann, born December 6th, 1785, married Abijah Lanning; Isaac, died in childhood; Rachel, born March 6th, 1789, married Asher Hill, and died 1825; Rhoda, died in infancy; Jemima, born January 12th, 1793; Sarah, born March 14th, 1795, married John Hendrickson, (see Hendrickson family, No. 9); Burgis Allison, born November 14th, 1796, married, and lived in Illinois; Enoch Wilson, born March 14th, 1799, married Susan Cook; Margaret, born January 3d, 1801, second wife of Asher Hill; Lydia, born February 3d, 1803, married Samuel B. Green (60); and Mary, died in childhood.

Charles (39), son of Joseph (38), who died 1859, aged 77, married Eliza, daughter of Josiah Hazard, widow of Charles Hendrickson. Their children are: Joseph, died in childhood; John; Cornelia, married George Cook; Elizabeth, married George Fowler; Amanda; Sarah; and Charles.

William (4), son of William (1), who died 1786, aged 84, was one of the corporators of Trenton First Church (now Ewing) from 1756 to 1764. He married Lydia, daughter of Enoch Armitage, by whom he had Enoch (40); William (41); Joanna, wife of Christopher Howell, (see Howell family, No. 2); and Mary, wife of Daniel Howell, (see Howell family, No. 37.)

Rev. Enoch (40), son of William (4), was graduated by Princeton College, and after a course of theology, was licensed to preach, and became pastor of the Presbyterian Church of Deerfield, N. J., 1766. He served for a short time as chaplain in the Revolutionary army, and there contracted the camp fever, of which he died, December 2d, 1776, aged 42; is buried in the aisle of the church. He married Mary, eldest daughter of Rev. Charles Beatty, (see Beatty family, No. 2,) who retained, in vigorous exercise, her mental powers, which were of a high order, till her death, May 2d, 1842, in the 96th year of her age. She is buried in the grounds of the Presbyterian Church, corner of Fourth and Pine streets, Philadelphia. Their children were: William Enoch (42); Ann, married Benjamin Guild, (see Guild family, No. 4); and Charles Beatty (43.)

William E. (42), son of Enoch (40), a man of high moral character, was suddenly cut off by injuries received from being dragged around the field by his horse, his foot being entangled in the halter, July 31st, 1813, aged 41. He married Charity, daughter of John Guild, (see Guild family, No. 3,) by whom he had: Enoch, died unmarried; Mary Ann; Charles Beatty, a graduate of Princeton, was admitted to the New Jersey bar, but practiced his profession in Livingston, Miss., where he died, unmarried, September 17th, 1834, aged 30, a young man of much promise; Elizabeth G.; Philip Physic, a merchant, died October 29th, 1860, unmarried; and William E. His widow married Pierson Reading, (see Reading family, No. 19.)

Elizabeth G., daughter of William (42), married James W. Moore, D. D., and settled at Little Rock, Ark., and had children: William E., a graduate of Princeton, became a merchant; married Sallie A. Washington, of Somerville, Tenn,; was a captain in the Confederate army, and fell at the battle of Chickamauga, September 20th, 1863; Mary W., married William B. Nash, of Virginia; Charles Beatty, a graduate of Princeton College, a lawyer of Little Rock, served in the Southern army as a staff officer, with the rank of major, he married Louisa B., daughter of Rev.

Joshua F. Green; James W., a physician, surgeon in the Confederate army, married Maggie, daughter of Rev. Dr. Lapsley, of Nashville, Tenn.; Alexander, died young; Henry W., a graduate of the University of Virginia, a lawyer; Philip G., died young; and Elizabeth L.

Charles B. (43), son of Rev. Enoch (40), became a member of the New Jersey bar, 1802; removed to Natchez, Miss., where he soon became distinguished, and gained a lucrative practice. He was many times returned to the house of representatives, of which he was once speaker; was also a member of the Senate. In the military service, he was elevated to the rank of general, and was known, the latter part of his life, as Gen. Green. He married Mrs. Helen Andrews, daughter of Col. Girault, of Mississippi, and by her had seven sons and six daughters—only three attained maturity: William, married, and resided in New Orleans; had children: Charles, William, Stewart, and Helen; Cordelia, married Mr. Rowan; and Helen, married Mr. Ross, of Port Gibson.

William (41), son of William (4), who died October 30th, 1815, aged 72, married Phebe, daughter of Samuel Moore, (see Moore family, No. 16,) who died February 16th, 1837, aged 84, having had children: Enoch, a physician, went South, and died young, at Savannah, Ga.; Elijah, not married, died 1850, aged 68; Samuel (44); Lydia, married Israel Carle; Rebecca, maried John Welling, (see Welling family, No. 3); Sarah, died May 28th, 1828, aged 44; and Mary, wife of John Jones, (see Jones family, No. 4.)

Samuel (44), son of William (41), died April 1st, 1859, aged 68, having married Mary, daughter of Henry Perrine, of Monmouth, who died November 25th, 1847, aged 52. Their children were: Emily, wife of Henry Bilyeu; William A. (45); Phebe, wife of Francis Sneed; Henry (46); Lydia; Sarah, wife of David Jeffries; Hannah, wife of Henry Lanning; Lewis, went to Australia, and there married; and John, married Elizabeth, daughter of William Scudder, (see Scudder family, No. 23); has children, Margaret and Sarah.

William A. (45), son of Samuel (44), married Catharine, daughter of Joseph Moore, (see Moore family, No. 35,) whose children are: Maxwell, married Harriet Vancleve; Mary, wife of Col. Ridgeway; and Joseph, married Helen Forker.

Henry P. (46), son of Samuel (44), married Virginia, daughter of Amos Reeder, (see Reeder family, No. 8.) Their children are:

William, married Augustine, daughter of William Scudder, (see Scudder family, No. 23); Frederic, married Mary Lee; Anna, died in youth; Florence, died in childhood; Henry; and Reeder.

Benjamin (5), son of William (1), who was one of the first common councilmen of Trenton after it was made a borough, married Martha, daughter of Stephen Dean, (see Dean family, No. 2.) She died May 30th, 1768, aged 57, having had children: Joseph (47); Elizabeth, died in childhood; Benjamin (48); Martha, died aged 21; Hannah; Deborah, wife of Timothy Howell, (see Howell family, No. 8); Hezekiah, died unmarried; Charity, married Philip Hendrickson, (see Hendrickson family, No. 5); and William, died 1736.

Joseph (47) son of Benjamin (5), who died 1806, aged 69, married Elizabeth, daughter of Rev. Mr. Gillis, a Presbyterian clergyman. She died March 13th, 1826, aged 80. Their children were: Richard (49); James Cummings (50); John (51); Archibald, died 1783, aged 16; Joseph, died 1845, aged 58, not married; Jane, died in infancy; Martha, died 1796, aged 19; Phebe, wife of Timothy Burroughs, (see Burroughs family, No. 11,) moved to Illinois, and died 1867, aged 67; Jane, married Ezekiel Quick, of Amwell; and Sarah, married Edward Hepburn, and died 1855, aged 68.

Richard (49), son of Joseph (47), married Jane, daughter of Jacob Quick, of Amwell, who died 1852, aged 81. They had one child, Martha, who married Samuel T. Atchley, whose children are: Richard G., Jane, Charles, Sarah, and David.

James Cummings (50), son of Joseph (47), died January 3d, 1852, aged 78, having married Kesiah Baldwin, who died October 3d, 1848, aged 68, by whom he had children: Maria, married Andrew Reed, (see Reed family, No. 12); Archibald, for several years an elder of the Ewing Church, died 1863, unmarried; David (52); Jane, wife of Nathaniel Coleman, (see Coleman family, No. 5); Sarah, wife of Charles E. Scott; Eliza, died 1858; Andrew (53); Martha, wife of George Smith; and Daniel, married Elizabeth, daughter of Job Mershon, and has children: Archibald, Louisa, and Edward.

David (52), son of James Cummings (50), married Rhoda Vankirk, and had children: Elizabeth, married William Burd; James; and Jane, married Armitage Green.

Andrew (53), son of James Cummings (50), married Susan, daughter of Job Mershon; had children: Emma; Sarah; Mary Elizabeth; Fanny; Corydon; and George.

John (51), son of Joseph (47), married Elizabeth, widow of Enoch Vankirk, daughter of Stephen Blackwell, of Hopewell, and had children: Stephen B., died in Illinois; not married; Eliza Ann, wife of Augustus Green (22); David, died in infancy; Louisa Jane, wife of Timothy Howell, (see Howell family, No. 26); and Rachel.

Sarah, daughter of Joseph (47), married Edward Hepburn, and died 1855, aged 68, having had children: John; Sarah; Mary, wife of George Reed, (see Reed family, No. 6); Jane, married, successively, Stephen Moore and Henry Wood; William, married Matilda, daughter of John Stout; Elizabeth, wife of Daniel Stout; Edward, married Elizabeth, daughter of William Hendrickson, (see Hendrickson family, No. 10); and Harriet, wife of William Titus.

Benjamin (48), son of Benjamin (5), whose will is dated 1797, married Rebecca, sister of Joshua Jones, by whom he had William B. (54); Benjamin (55); Noah, married Barbara Allen, of Easton, where he resided, they had a son, Benjamin, who married Ann Ashmore, and moved to Illinois; Joseph (56); Ralph (57); Israel (58); and Elijah (59.)

William B. (54), son of Benjamin (48), who died January 13th, 1837, aged 75, by his marriage with Rebecca, daughter of Richard Green (6), who died May 4th, 1817, aged 52, had children: Samuel B. (60); Enoch, married, and moved to Illinois; Abijah, married, and went to Kentucky, where he died, leaving one daughter; William, married, in Philadelphia; Rebecca, wife of William Hendrickson, (see Hendrickson family, No. 10); Ely, married his cousin, Deborah, daughter of Joseph Green (56); and Mary, married, in succession, Montgomery Phillips and Peter Vanzandt.

Samuel B. (60), son of William B. (54), married, first, Elizabeth, daughter of Jonathan Cook, (see Cook family, No. 2,) and had children: Mary, first wife of William Reed, (see Reed family, No. 13); and Jonathan, married Elizabeth, daughter of Elias Hart, (see Hart family, No. 18,) has one daughter, Lydia, wife of William Morris; his second wife was Lydia, daughter of Joseph Green (38), whose children are: Armitage, married Jane, daughter of David Green (52,) have one daughter, Ella, wife of Samuel Atchley; and Mary Elizabeth.

Benjamin (55), son of Benjamin (48), died April 10th, 1826, having married, first, Hannah, daughter of Joseph Tindall, (see Tindall family, No. 2,) and had a son, George, who married, successively, Miss Temple, Rachel Phillips, and widow Urie Cole, and died 1855, aged 62. His second wife was Elizabeth, sister of his former wife, and widow of Jacob Hendrickson, by whom he had: Noah (61); Benjamin (62); Thomas (63); Hannah, wife of John Hull; and Mercy.

Noah (61), son of Benjamin (55), resided in Princeton; married Mary Loughbury, and had children: James, married; Samuel, married Miss Evert; Mary E., wife of William Hutchinson; and Anna.

Benjamin (62), son of Benjamin (55), resided in Lawrence; married Sarah Loughbury, and had children: Sarah, married Mr. Denston, and lives in Brooklyn; Benjamin; John; Addison; and William.

Thomas (63), son of Benjamin (55), married, and died 1844, having had children: Aaron, married, and lives ih Princeton; Benjamin, married Margaret Plew, of Illinois, and lives in Texas; Charles, married Anna Robins; lives in Kingston; Mary I., wife of Mr. Wells, of Long Branch; Rachel; Henry; and Elizabeth.

Joseph (56), son of Benjamin (48), married, first, Nancy, daughter of William R. Green (8), by whom he had: Rebecca, wife of John B. Moore; Elizabeth Ann; and Maria. His second wife was Martha, daughter of Timothy Howell, (see Howell family, No. 8), by whom he had: Sarah; and Deborah, wife of Ely Green.

Ralph (57), son of Benjamin (48), who died 1828, aged 86, by his wife, Sarah, daughter of John Welling, (see Welling family, No. 2,) had children; Mary, wife of Lemuel Franklin; Lydia, wife of Robert Aitkin; Wesley H.; Matilda; Ralph H.; Theodocia; and Hannah Louisa.

Israel (58), son of Benjamin (48), died 1819, aged 39, having married Hannah, daughter of Nathaniel Furman, (see Furman family, No. 6,) whose children are: Susan; Eliza, married John Gallager; Nathaniel F., married Eliza Bradis; and Eleanor, died 1824, aged 17.

Elijah B. (59), son of Benjamin (48), died 1828, aged 46, having had children, by his wife, Mary, daughter of William Anthony, (see Anthony family, No. 2): Anthony, married Elizabeth McKinney; Catharine, wife of William Lyons; Emeline, wife, first, of Charles Keylman; second, of Judge Bentley, of Williamsport; and John Biles, a merchant of Philadelphia, married Mary Bradley, and has children, Mary and Elizabeth.

The Guild Family.

The Rev. John Guild (2), for nearly fifty years pastor of the Church of Hopewell or Pennington, was the son of John (1) and Esther Guild, of Wrentham, Mass., was graduated at Harvard University, Cambridge, was licensed to preach 1737, and was ordained and appointed, in 1741, over the Church of Hopewell, and one-fourth of his time over the Church of Maidenhead, and also, after the death of Mr. Cowell, supplied the vacant pulpit of the Trenton Church. Mr. Guild's pastorate extended through an eventful period in the history of the church, during which he conducted himself with exemplary wisdom, and also through the troubles of the Revolution. Though a clergyman, and therefore a non-combatant, yet he was too well known as a firm and earnest patriot, to escape the alarms and depredations occasioned by prowling bands of British soldiery. At one time he was obliged to fly for refuge, with his children, to Pennsylvania, the enemy, in the meantime, ravaging the country, entering his house, destroying his papers, tearing his books, converting his church to barracks, hacking and cutting the pews, and breaking to pieces the marble-topped communion table, and committing other acts of wanton destruction, to the terror of the inhabitants.

The Rev. John Guild's funeral sermon was preached by the Rev. Samuel Stanhope Smith, president of the College of New Jersey, and his epitaph, still to be seen on his monument, in Pennington church-yard, was composed by the Rev. Dr. John Woodhull, of Freehold.

In memory of the
Rev. John Guild,
Pastor of this congregation 47 years,
who departed this life
July 10th, 1787,
aged 75 years.

In yonder sacred desk
I spent my painful breath
In warning sinners of eternal death.
Now dust and ashes, I
From this cold marble cry:
Sinners, be warned and to the Saviour fly.

By his marriage with Charity, daughter of Ralph Hunt, of Stony Brook, and sister of Azariah Hunt, a man prominent in public business, who died 1776, aged 44, had issue: John (3); Charity, wife of George Muirheid, (see Muirheid family, No. 4); Phebe, married Titus Hart, (see Hart family, No. 16); Mercy, married Jesse Christopher, whose children are: Charles, married Rebecca Lippincott, John, not married, Charity, married John Davison; and Catharine, married Ephraim Scudder, (see Scudder family, No. 25); Mary, the wife of John Howell, (see Howell family, No. 38); Esther, the wife of John Welling, (see Welling family, No. 2); Margaret, wife of John Price Hunt, (see Hunt family, No. 12); Benjamin (4); and Ralph, married Sarah Emley; no children.

John (3), son of Rev. John (2), who died 1825, aged 75, resided in Ewing, and married Abigail, daughter of Daniel Howell, (see Howell family, No. 3)—she died 1818, aged 62—and by her had: Charity, born September 24th, 1781, married, first, William E. Green, (see Green family, No. 42); and, second, Pierson Reading, (see Reading family, No. 19); Mary, born November 17th, 1784, married Clark Chambers, (see Chambers family, No. 9); Elizabeth Howell, born April 28th, 1791, became the wife of John C. Moore, (see Moore family, No. 24); Ann Green, born November 25th, 1793, married Thomas Millett, whose children are: John, Antoinette, William, and Thomas, a lawyer; John, born 1797, not married.

Benjamin (4) son of John (2), was a merchant at Pittstown, and afterwards at New Brunswick, where he died, 1815, aged 41, having married Ann, daughter of Rev. Enoch Green, (see Green family, No. 40,) a woman of great worth, who, after the death of her husband, removed to Philadelphia, where she lived till her death, 1846, aged 73. She is buried in the cemetery of Princeton. Their children: John, a shipping merchant of Philadelphia, died 1826, aged 32, in Vera Cruz, Mexico, while on a visit there; Maria, is buried in Princeton; Christiana B., buried in Princeton; Elizabeth; Ralph (5); Charles B. Green, was graduated by Princeton College, and died there, while pursuing his theological studies; and Ann Matilda, married Galbraith Stewart, of West Philadelphia; she died 1849.

Ralph (5), son of Benjamin (4), was connected with Stevenson & Co., shipping merchants, of Philadelphia; and while on his return from a trading expedition to the interior of Mexico, was taken prisoner by a horde of pirates, who were lying in wait for them, and held in captivity two months, when a United States vessel came to their relief, broke up their fortified nest, after having killed sixteen of them, and released their captives. Mr. Guild afterwards became a merchant of St. Girardeau, Mo., was receiver of the land office, and was also a major in the state militia; and was at one time on an expedition against the Indians, acting as aid to the major-general. He married Ellen M., daughter of Elijah P. Hunt, (see Hunt family, No. 20,) of Easton, and afterwards took up his residence in retirement, at Princeton.

The John and Joseph Hart Family.

John Hart (1) and Joseph Hart (2) came to Hopewell township near the beginning of the eighteenth century, as the name of John is signed to an agreement dated August 26th, 1703. They are believed to be brothers from the fact that they came together, purchased farms adjoining each other, and, above all, from the striking resemblance that their descendants bear to each other, even to the fourth and fifth generations, for they are remarkable for their light eyes and hair and a peculiarly fair complexion, which caused them to be designated as the "White Harts," to distinguish them from the descendants of Maj. Ralph Hart and Capt. Edward Hart, called, from their black hair and eyes and dark skin, the "Black Harts."

John (1), whose will is dated 1753, had a wife, Sarah, and children: John (3); Richard (4); Mary, wife of Benjamin Moore, (see Moore family, No. 8); Elizabeth; and Joanna, who probably died unmarried, as her property was administered upon in 1783, by Israel Moore.

John (3), son of John (1), the date of whose will is 1774, married Hannah, daughter of Theophilus Phillips, (see Phillips family, No. 2); had children: Elijah (5); Maj. John, died unmarried 1812; left £10 to the Pennington Church, and his property to his brother's (Elijah's) children; Philip (6); Abner (7); Fanny, married Joab Mershon; Rebecca, married John Marshal; Abigail, became the second wife of Joab Mershon.

Elijah (5), son of John (3), married Rebecca Mershon, and by her had Richard; Nathaniel, died 1820, probably not married; a daughter, married Mr. Phillips, and had a daughter, Frances; Catharine, married Mr. Hunt, and had sons: Charles, Theodore, and Elijah, and perhaps others.

Philip (6), son of John (3), died 1831, aged 76; married Hannah Palmer. She died 1829, aged 74. Their children were: Joseph, who married Catharine Houghton, had a son, Edmond, who lives in California; Edmond, died 1818, aged 26; John (8); Abner (9); Palmer; Israel; Susan; Clara, wife of Louis Dunn, of Trenton; Elizabeth, wife of Elijah Atchley.

John (8), son of Philip (6), married Ure Golden, and had children: Hannah, died, aged 18; Catharine, married Howell Dalzall; Sarah, married Byard Updike; John, married Rosa Updike; William; Theodosia; Harriet; Washington; and Joshua, killed on the railroad.

Abner (9), son of Philip (6), married Abigail, daughter of Richard Hunt; had children: Noah, married Elizabeth Phillips; Cornelia, died, aged 15; Wilson, married Hannah Banbridge; and Eleanor.

Abner (7), són of John (3), born 1762, married Jane, daughter of Creinyonce Vancleve, (see Vancleve family, No. 4,) and had by her: John Vancleve (10); Joab, born 1788, married Jane Pettit; Aaron, married Miss Leonard; Fanny, married John Blackwell; Catharine, married Aaron Titus.

John Vancleve (10), son of Abner (7), became a merchant, resident in Philadelphia, married Keziah, daughter of Theophilus Moore, (see Moore family, No. 23,) whose children were: Theodore, graduated at Princeton College, but died young; Alexander, also a graduate of Princeton, and a physician of Philadelphia, married Mary, daughter of Dr. Israel Clarke, of or near Lawrenceville; John, killed while young; Frederic, married, has two sons in Callfornia; Cornelia, married Judge Oswald Thompson, of Philadelphia; has children: Cornelia, married Mr. Kelley, a lawyer of Philadelphia, Helen, wife of Rev. Dr. James Knox, of New York, and Julia; Theophilus P. M., married Jane, daughter of John Ellis, of New York; has children: Henry Ellis, Oswald Thompson, Lizzie, and Adele.

Richard (4), son of John (1), died 1773, having married Margaret Snowden, who survived her husband till 1817, aged 92, leaving children: John R. (11); Margaret, wife of Jacob Ashton; Mary, wife of John Dean, (see Dean family, No. 3); Sarah, wife of Timothy Hart, (16); Joseph, inherited the homestead on Rogers road; married Sarah, daughter of Andrew Huff; Asher (12); Hannah; Phebe; and Elizabeth, wife of Daniel Carpenter.

John R. (11), son of Richard (4), died 1845, aged 92; was buried in Pennington; his wife was Mary, daughter of Stephen Dean, of Ewing, (see Dean family, No. 2); she died 1807, leaving children: Naomi, married John Baldwin; Annie, married Jonathan Grey; Phebe, not married; Richard (13); Dean, married Mary, daughter of John Farley, of Titusville; has children, George, Alfred, Mary E., and Emeline.

Richard (13), son of John (11), married Elizabeth, daughter of Amos Lanning, (see Lanning family, No. 25,) by whom he had children: Jerusha, married Moses Burroughs, (see Burroughs family, No. 18); John R., married Eliza, daughter of Philip Burroughs, (see Burroughs family, No. 8); lives at Lambertville; Amos Lanning, married Elizabeth, daughter of Isaac Smith; has children: Isaac S., Mary Ann, Sarah Elizabeth, Richard H., and Susan E.

Asher (12), son of Richard (4), died 1846, aged 86, and was buried with his first wife and daughter, Mary, in the Lawrenceville cemetery. He married, first, Abigail, daughter of Samuel Hunt. She died 1820, aged 58, leaving children: Samuel Stockton, married Jemima, daughter of Daniel Lanning; Rebecca, died 1846, aged 56; Abigail Hunt, wife of Smith Williams; Margaret; and Mary, died 1828, aged 56. His second wife was Sarah, daughter of John Temple, (see Temple family, No. 6); she died 1840, aged 80; is buried in the Ewing church-yard.

Joseph (2), brother of John (1), the other ancestor of the "White Harts," whose will bears date 1776, married, and had children: Joseph (14); Amos (15); Abigail, married Joshua Reed, (see Reed family, No. 3); Mary, married Jeremiah Woolsey, (see Woolsey family, No. 4); Naomi, married John Howell, (see Howell family, No. 7); and Lois.

Joseph (14), son of Joseph (2), died 1794; married Frances, daughter of Theophilus Phillips, (see Phillips family, No. 2.) Their children were: Timothy (16); Theophilus, died young; Aaron (17); Joseph; Amos, married Mary, a daughter of Capt. Timothy Titus, (see Titus family, No. 36,) and removed to the lake country of New York, where their descendants are to be found; Israel (18); Susan, married John Phillips; and Jane.

Timothy (16), son of Joseph (14), married Sarah Hart, and had by her: Theophilus, an elder of the Ewing Church, died unmarried, 1854, aged 64; Israel, settled in New York state; Lott; Phebe, married Obadiah Akers, and removed to New York; Hannah, married Mr. Vliet; Jane, married Ralph Herron; Hulda; and Joseph, married Theodosia Stout; removed to New York state; had children: George, died 1855, aged 36, Eveline, died

1858, Catharine, died in infancy, Jesse, died 1843, William A., married Mary S. Heacock, Kate E., and Aaron.

Aaron (17), son of Joseph (14), died 1853, aged 85; married Rebecca, only child of Amos Moore, (see Moore family, No. 19.) She died 1826, aged 54, leaving children: Amos, who died 1826, aged 33; Ann, married James Burroughs, (see Burroughs family, No. 23); Smith (20); Aaron (21); and George (22).

Smith (20), son of Aaron (17), married Ann, daughter of Richard Scudder, (see Scudder family, No. 24.) Their children are: Joseph Scudder, married Elizabeth, daughter of John Neely, of Bucks county, Pa.; Rebecca, married John R. Hendrickson, son of Timothy; Dr. Israel, a graduate of Lafayette College, a physician of the University of Pennsylvania, married Marie Josephine, daughter of Peter Tellier, of Easton, Pa.; Sarah, married Joseph Frisbie, merchant, of Pennington; Alfred, married Catharine Tellier, sister of the former; Margaret; and Frances, died in infancy.

Aaron (21), son of Aaron (17), married Rebecca, daughter of Noah Stout. Their children are: Mary Ann; Noah; Amos, married Elizabeth Wilson; Elizabeth, died in youth; Sarah, married John Schenck; Frances, died young; Charles, married Margaret Swan; Augustus, married Ada, daughter of Burroughs Matthews.

George (22), son of Aaron (17), was president of Quaker City Insurance Company; died 1871; resided in Philadelphia. He married, first, Elizabeth Graham; second, her sister, Mary; had Aaron, who married Alice Bowker, of Clarksville; and Joseph, married, and resides in St. Louis.

Israel (18), son of Joseph (14), lived in Pennington till his death, 1828, aged 56. He married Mary, daughter of John Davison. She survived her husband till 1856, aged 75. Their children were: John D., married Elizabeth Welling, widow of Dr. Springer, and died 1838, aged 32, having had one son, Israel; died in infancy; Rebecca Ann, married Simeon Phillips, of Woodbridge, children: William and Mary; Mary; and Frances, died, aged 19.

Amos (15), son of Joseph, married Miss Burrowes, and had by her, children: Mary, second wife of Ralph Lanning, (see Lanning family, No. 3); Elizabeth, wife of Daniel Furman, (see Furman family, No. 5); Rebecca, wife of Ezekiel Furman, (see Furman family, No. 10); Foster Burrowes (23); Asher (24). His second wife was Elizabeth, daughter of Benjamin Fish, (see Fish family, No. 4,) whose son, Asa, probably it was, who married a Miss

Nourse (?), and had children: Asher, Reuben, Anna, and a daughter, married Theophilus Phillips. His third wife was Margaret Marlin.

Foster Burrowes (23), son of Amos (15), died 1830, aged 64; lived in New Hope, Pa. He married, and had children: Foster B., died young—killed by a fall from a tree; William, married Mary, daughter of Samuel Stockton, of Trenton; he was a volunteer in the Union ranks; was taken prisoner, and was supposed to have died in Libby prison; Susan, married Robert Mellen, a lawyer of New Hope, Pa.; Phebe, died 1803; Eliza Ann, died 1807; Sarah Ann, died, 1810.

Asher (24), son of Amos (15), married Mary, daughter of William Moore, (see Moore family, No. 31.) Both he and his father-in-law moved to Coshocton, Ohio. He had children: Eliza, married Benjamin Webb; Lois, married Nathaniel Webb—both sons of Dr. Webb, who after the decease of Mr. Hart, married his widow.

The Ralph and Edward Hart Family.

Major Ralph Hart (1) was one of the earliest settlers of Hopewell, and is believed to have come from Stonington, Conn., preceding his brother, Capt. Edward (2), a few years. He purchased and occupied a farm adjoining the Lawrence line, on the road leading from Ewingville to Lawrenceville. He married a Furman, it is supposed, and left, at his death, 1749, a widow, Sarah. His children were: Benjamin (3); Samuel (4)—who shared equally the homestead; Ralph (5); Josiah (6); Mary, married John Carpenter, of Jamaica, Long Island, whose children are; Hezekiah, John, married Ann, daughter of Creinyonce Vancleve, (see Vancleve family, No. 4), Mary, wife of John Hunt, of Pennington, Sarah, wife of Augustin Moore, Hannah, wife of Maj. Stephen Burrowes, and Catharine, wife of Israel Moore, (see Moore family, No. 11); Mercy, married Joseph Tindall; Martha, married Robert Lanning; Elizabeth, married Joseph Jones; and Abigail, married Stephen Lanning, (see Lanning family, No. 2.)

Benjamin (3), son of Ralph (1), died 1806. By his marriage with Hannah Cook, of Trenton, had children: Parmela, died December 4th, 1827, aged 75; married Nathan Harker (Harcourt), and had a son, John, who died 1827, aged 39, having married Deborah Hart; Martha, married a Hart or Salathiel Peirson; Jemima, married Jehiel Pierson; Stephen; William, married Hannah, daughter of Daniel Lanning, (see Lanning family, No. 6); died 1826, aged 88; his children were: William, Israel, married Mary, daughter of John Lanning, Jemima, married Joseph Pierson, and Elizabeth; John; Absalom, married, and had children: Daniel, Absalom, and Mary, wife of Frank Plumley; Elijah (7); Benjamin; Elisha; Mercy; Hannah; Abigail, died 1846, aged 84; Mary; Sarah; Nathaniel; and Ralph, who died March 8th, 1830, aged 73, having had by his wife, Hannah Carter, who died March 14th, 1835, aged 83, children: William, John, Phebe, Sarah, Susan, Elizabeth, and Martha.

Elijah (7), son of Benjamin (3), married Elizabeth, daughter of

John Lanning, of Lawrence, whose children were: Nathaniel; John; Edward; Elijah; Benjamin; Martha, wife of Elias Golden; Charity, wife of John Hoagland; and Parmela, wife of John Golden.

Samuel (4), son of Ralph (1), had children by his wife, Sarah Webster, of Long Island; Ralph (8); Elias, married Abigail Price, of Lawrence; had children: Ruth, wife of Isaac Howell, and Elias, went South; Samuel, married Martha Smith; died 1779, leaving children: Elias, George, Philemon, and Mary; Elizabeth, wife of John McCollomb; Mary, married John Welling, (see Welling family, No. 2), and died, aged 99; Hannah, died 1793; Sarah, married Jeconiah Smith.

Ralph (8), son of Samuel (4), as a member of a company of volunteers, participated in the battle of Monmouth; died October 14th, 1829, aged 80. He married Sarah, daughter of Richard Lanning, (see Lanning family, No. 4); had children: Nathaniel; Daniel (9); Elizabeth, died 1840, aged 38; Matilda; Eleanor; John, died young; Levi (10); Zenas, with his father, moved, in 1815, to Elizabeth, Miami county, Ohio, having married Elizabeth, daughter of Joseph Green; have children: James, Levi, William, Joseph Green, Mary, and Elizabeth; Charles (11); Andrew, joined the army in the war of 1812; was captured with Gen. Hull; having been exchanged, he rejoined it, and was never more heard of; and Wilson C., moved to Troy, Ohio, and married Mary Lowry.

Daniel (9), son of Ralph (8), died February 26th, 1854, aged 82, having married Elcy, daughter of James Grant; she died August 18th, 1828, aged 60; had children: Enoch, married Sarah Moon, and died, March, 1835, aged 37; Pierson, married Margaret Smith, and died January, 1853, aged 45.

Levi (10), son of Ralph (8), married Nancy Fulmore, and in 1811, removed to Troy, Ohio, and had children: John Maxwell, married, and lived in Troy; Ralph S., a lawyer and a judge, residing in Dayton, Ohio; James H., also a member of the bar; in the late war was colonel of the Seventy-first Ohio Volunteers, and commissioned brigadier-general by brevet; Isaac W., lives in Attica, Iowa; and Sarah Ann, wife of John F. Clark, a Methodist clergyman; has one daughter.

Charles (11), son of Ralph (8), moved to Miami county, Ohio; died 1862, aged 79; by his wife, Nancy, had children: Eleanor; William, died 1870; Levi, died 1865; Caroline, died 1833, aged 17; James H; Wilson C., died at Murfreesboro, Tenn., while in the United States service, 1863; Henry M., resides in Brownsville, Neb.; and Martha Ann.

Ralph (5), son of Ralph (1), who died 1872, married, first, Jemima, daughter of George Woolsey, (see Woolsey family, No. 3,) by whom he had a son, Noah (12); second, Miss Updike; third, Penelope (Merrill), mentioned in his will. By which wife the following children were born, is not known: Jerusha, wife of Moses Hart; Hannah, wife of Lott Phillips; Elizabeth, wife of Francis Blackwell; and Mary, wife of George Smith, (see Smith family, No. 9.)

Dr. Noah (12), son of Ralph (5), was a physician, who studied his profession, first, in Philadelphia, and afterward continued his studies in London and Edinburgh; resided in New York; was considered one of the most eminent physicians of the day. He married a daughter of the Rev. Charles McKnight, a member of the New Brunswick Presbytery. He died early, leaving a daughter. His widow married Mr. Sinnickson, of lower New Jersey.

Josiah (6), son of Ralph (1), who died March 22d, 1799, married Mary, daughter of John Titus, (see Titus family, No. 4.) Their children were: Elijah (13); Rebecca, born July 19, 1741, married Thomas Wilson; Andrew (14); Nathaniel (15); Sarah, born March 6th, 1748, married Andrew Smith, (see Smith family, No. 9); Elizabeth, married Jacob Ege; Titus (16); Mary, married Ishi Vancleve, (see Vancleve family, No. 9.)

Elijah (13), son of Josiah (6), married Kesiah, daughter of Edward Hunt, whose children are: Enoch (17); Philip, married Nancy Hoff; Hannah, married Edmund Phillips; Phebe, married Asher Atchley; and Betsy, married Peter Phillips.

Enoch (17), son of Elijah (13), a deacon in Ewing Church, married Mary, daughter of Daniel Howell, (see Howell family, No. 6); had children: Elias (18); Daniel, married Mary, daughter of Edmond Roberts, they had one child, Deborah, wife of Henry Whitenack; Elijah, married Keturah, daughter of Jonathan Smith, (see Smith family, No. 8,) and their only daughter is Mary, wife of Baker Hill.

Elias (18), son of Enoch (17), married Sarah, daughter of Joseph Titus, whose children are: Enoch, married Cornelia Cain, their children are: Sarah, Mary E., and Anna; Elizabeth, wife of Jonathan Green; Joseph, married Sarah, daughter of Simeon Phillips; have children, Simeon and Laura.

Andrew (14), son of Josiah (6), who died 1817, married Elizabeth, daughter of Adam Ege, and had by her: Asa, married Rebecca, daughter of Benjamin Temple, (see Temple family, No. 12); Amos, married Hannah, daughter of Capt. Timothy Titus, (see Titus family, No. 36); Abner (19); Adam, married Charity Baldwin, and had Samuel and Joseph; Hannah, married Job Robbins; Mary, wife of Theophilus Stout; Sarah, wife of John Phillips; and Rebecca.

Abner (19), son of Andrew (14), married Mary Updike, and had children: Andrew, married Esther Golden; William, married Caroline Baker; John, married Penelope Blackwell; Wilson, married Miss Chamberlain; and Maria.

Nathaniel (15), son of Josiah (6), was chosen one of the first seven trustees of the Presbyterian Church of Hopewell, in 1786. He married Abigail, daughter of Joseph Scudder, (see Scudder family, No. 11,) and had by her: Elizabeth, born May 5th, 1778, married Levi, son of John Knowles, whose children are: Nathaniel, married Ann M. Lambert, Ralph, married Mary Hoff, Mary, Abigail, married Henry Platt, Eliza, married Lewis Shallcross, two Sarahs, and Levi, married Elizabeth A. Croskey, and his children are: James R., Julia, Mary, Gen. Oliver, Fannie, William B., and Lizzie; Josiah, born October 21st, 1782, who was also a trustee of Hopewell Church, died May, 1864, having married, first, Elizabeth, daughter of Israel Moore, (see Moore family, No. 11); she died August 16th, 1850, aged 67; his second wife was the widow Jane Boss (Poor), of Philadelphia; Mary, born December 15th, 1784, married Ephraim Roberts, (see Roberts family, No. 3,) and Joseph Scudder (20).

Joseph Scudder (20), son of Nathaniel (15), born September 14th, 1788, married Abigail, daughter of Sackett Moore, (see Moore family, No. 10.) They had children: Nathaniel, married Jane Atchley, whose children are: Mary, wife of Smith Scudder; Lizzie, wife of Mr. Buckman, Scudder, married Willhannah Scudder, and Emma, wife of Aaron Cook; Sackett Moore, married Mary Blackwell; have children: Lizzie, wife of Harrison Muirheid, and George.

Titus (16), son of Josiah (6), a deacon in the Pennington Church, died 1797, aged 40. He married, first, Rebecca, daughter of Joseph Scudder, (see Scudder family, No. 11,) and had: Samuel, not married; Mary, became the wife, first, of Noah Stout; second, of Benjamin Hendrickson, (see Hendrickson family, No. 7); Noah, not married; Abigail, married Thomas Blackwell;

Sarah, married Joseph Furman; Rebecca, born January 2d, 1791, married John Stout, whose children are: Maria, Titus, married Mary Ann Krewson, Henry, Jonathan, Rebecca, wife of Elias Welling, Elizabeth, wife of Henry Krewson, Sarah, and John. His second wife was Phebe, daughter of Rev. John Guild, (see Guild family, No. 2.) She died 1834, aged 76, leaving children: Esther, born May 8th, 1795, married Peter Blackwell, and had children: Elizabeth, wife of Enoch Titus, Susan, wife of George Titus, brother of Enoch, Mary, married Moore Hart, Noah, and Samuel, not married; Chatty, became the second wife of Reuben Titus, (see Titus family, No. 28,) having by him one son, John Guild, who married Emma, daughter of Wesley Burroughs, (see Burroughs family, No. 24.)

Edward Hart (2), brother of Ralph (1), was of English origin, and came, at an early part of the century, and shortly after his brother, to Hopewell, from Stonington, Conn., as Mrs. Axford, his great-granddaughter, states that she has often heard her grandfather, John, the Signer, say, calling himself, at the same time, a Yankee. Before the establishment of a Presbyterian Church at Pennington, within three miles of which Mr. Hart settled, he carried his son, John, to the Presbyterian Church of Maidenhead, where, December 31st, 1713, he was baptized, as church records show, by the Rev. Jedediah Andrews, pastor of the Presbyterian Church on Washington Square, Philadelphia. He was a zealous supporter of the church, in which he was a ruling elder, and a commissioner to the Presbytery of Philadelphia, to place into the hands of Rev. John Guild the call of the Pennington congregation. He was a man of influence, and active in conducting not only the civil concerns of the township, but its military matters as well. "Edward Hart," says Sanderson, the able biographer of the Signers of Independence, "was one of those brave and loyal colonists who generously lent their aid to the military operations of England. He exerted himself so far as to raise a corps of volunteers, the 'Jersey Blues,' then for the first time so called. With this corps he marched into Canada, and arrived before Quebec in time to participate in the victory of Wolfe."*

---

*This latter part of Sanderson's, though it has often been quoted, is undoubtedly incorrect. The battle of Quebec took place June 13th, 1759. Mr. H. had ceased from the living before August, 1752, as a deed of conveyance, signed by his sons, John and Daniel, proves. On two other occasions, 1715 and 1746–7, England summoned her colonies to aid against their enemy, the French. It was doubtless on one of these that Mr. Hart raised his corps.

Captain Edward (2), by his wife, Martha, had children: Edward (21); Daniel (22); John (23); Martha, not traced; Sarah, became the wife, successively, of Timothy Temple, (see Temple family, No. 4,) and Stephen Burrowes, by the latter of whom she was the mother of Maj. Stephen Burrowes, and of Sarah, wife of Andrew Reeder, of Lawrence.

Edward (21), son of Edward (2), was an active and useful citizen. His name frequently occurs in connection with the official business of the town. He married, and had at least one child. Moses, who married Jerusha, daughter of Ralph Hart (5), who died 1835, aged 91, twenty-three years after her husband, who died 1812, aged 71. Their children were: Nathaniel W., married Jane, daughter of Joseph Reed, who had one child, Sarah, wife of John Green, of Easton, Pa., (see Green family, No. 26); Jemima, died 1821, aged 57; Catharine, died unmarried, 1840, aged 71; Moses, not married; and Amos, married Hannah Waters.

Daniel (22), son of Edward (2), married, and was killed while young, by a negro, leaving a son, Levi (24), who married Mary, daughter of Elnathan Hunt, and removed, in 1820, to the lake country of New York. Their children were: Daniel, died young; John H. (25); Charity, wife of Nathaniel Bryant, who moved to New York state; Sarah, wife of John Stout, of Rocky Hill; and another daughter.

John H. (25), son of Levi (24), married Elizabeth, daughter of Capt. Timothy Titus, of Pennington, (see Titus family, No. 36,) and removed, about 1820, to Seneca county, N. Y., where he died, at the age of 80, having had children: Titus, married, and lives at Trumansville, Tompkins county, N. Y.; Daniel, married, and lives at Romulus, N. Y.; Enoch, married, and resides in Varick, Tompkins county, N. Y.; Eliza; Amanda; and Mary, wife of John R. Smith.

John Hart (23), Signer, son of Edward (2), was born, according to the statement of Mrs. Axford, his granddaughter, in Stonington, Conn., from where he came, in early childhood, to Pennington, and was baptized at the Presbyterian Church of Lawrence, by the Rev. Jedediah Andrews, pastor of the Presbyterian Church on Washington Square, Philadelphia. As his father was a man of property and influence, we may presume that his son received, if not a classical, at least as good an education as was at that time attainable. In his New Jersey home, advanced to manhood, he employed his time in the pursuits of agriculture and in discharging the duties of such minor offices as his fellow citizens chose to confer upon him. Though surrounded by all the appliances of ease and affluence, devoted to the charms of domestic society, in which his kindly nature eminently fitted him to indulge, yet he was not an inattentive and unconcerned observer of his country's danger, from the unjust encroachments of British power upon her liberties. Though office had no charms for his unambitious nature, yet he yielded a prompt response to the call of duty and threatening danger. His entrance into more eminent public life was signalized by his having been chosen, in 1761, to represent his district in the colonial legislature, to which he continued to be annually elected until 1772. During this period, some of the most important resistant and revolutionary movements took place, of all of which, John Hart was one of the most active and resolute promoters. At its sessions, he protested, and recorded his vote against the stamp act, against taxation without representation, against interfering with the liberty of the press and trial by jury, and especially, by his vote, did he refuse to grant further supplies to maintain the king's troops, quartered in the province, which refusal of the legislature caused its dissolution by the angry royal governor, Franklin. Such, in 1774, was the alarming condition of affairs, that a convention was deemed necessary, to take measures for the defence of the colony. To this body, known as the provincial congress, Mr. Hart was annually elected a delegate from Hunterdon county, till its dissolution, in 1776, and from his position as chairman of most important committees, he was evidently a leading member. He also shared, throughout its existence, the onerous and important duties of the committee of safety, appointed by the provincial congress. Before the dissolution of this congress, a constitution and state government were formed, which continues to this day. At the first meeting, in August, at Princeton, under the new government, of the legislature, to which Mr. Hart had been returned from Hunterdon county, he was, without a dissenting voice, chosen speaker of the house. Owing to the persistent encroachments of royal power upon the rights of the colonies, the time had come, in the opinion of many, for more active measures. Accordingly, a congress of colonial representatives was convened, in 1774, at Philadelphia. To this august body, Mr. Hart was elected as a fit representative of the firmness and moderation of the people. Thus, within a period of a few months, did he fill three positions of the first importance—that of member to the provincial congress, of speaker of the assembly, and of delegate to the continental congress. This congress proposed to accomplish its ends by pacific measures, but these failing, a similar congress was called, to meet at the same city the next year, 1775. Of this illustrious congress, Mr. Hart was appointed a member by the general assembly of New Jersey. He attended its sittings till its adjournment, in August. The members of the first and second continental congresses and many of the third, though boldly opposing the exactions and encroachments of Great Britain, were by no means unanimous in their desire of cutting loose, *at once*, from their allegiance, and of adopting the resolution offered in congress by Richard Henry Lee, of Virginia, "that all political connection between the colonies and Great Britain be dissolved," as their hope of reconciliation with the parent country was not yet extinct. When, therefore, four of the five delegates chosen by the first legislature under the new government, to represent them in the congress of 1776, declined to accept, from unwillingness to take the step contemplated by Lee's resolution, which they regarded as at least premature, five others, of bolder spirit, were elected, viz., Richard Stockton, Dr. John Witherspoon, president of Princeton College, Judge Francis Hopkinson, Abraham Clark, and John Hart, who, though not equal, in professional ability, to the first three, yet was adjudged by the people their worthy associate, and fully their peer in soundness of judgment, in boldness and firmness of purpose, and in pure and enlightened patriotism. These men voted for Lee's famous resolution, but the glory in which the name of John Hart and his compeers is embalmed, culminated when, on the 4th of July, 1776, fully alive to the peril which threatened their property, their lives, and their families, undismayed, they affixed their names to that immortal document which announced to the world the freedom of their country and her entrance into the family of nations.

On these men, and such as these, it was that the great William Pitt, Earl of Chatham, in his place on the floor of parliament, pronounced his celebrated eulogium : "I must declare and avow that, in the master states of the world, I know not the people, nor the senate, who, under such a complication of difficult circumstances, can stand in preference to the delegates of America, assembled in general congress at Philadelphia. For genuine sagacity, for singular moderation, for solid wisdom, manly spirit, manly sentiments, and simplicity of language, for everything respectable and honorable, they stand unrivaled." We have said that Mr. Hart was elected speaker of the first assembly in the spring of 1776. When, in the same year, the army of Washington, yielding to the overwhelming superiority of the British force, was obliged to leave New Jersey and cross the Delaware, the legislature also became a fugitive, and, after fleeing from place to place, was obliged to disperse, but when, after recrossing the Delaware, Washington, by the re-inspiriting battles of Trenton and Princeton, had relieved the state of the enemy, the legislature, at the summons of Mr. Hart, convened at Trenton, in January, 1777, and again unanimously elected him its speaker, an honor that he continued to hold till his failing health compelled his resignation. The prominence of Mr. Hart's position, and his well-known fidelity to the cause of liberty, brought down upon him the intense hatred and vengeance of the British, who, after ravaging his estates, destroying his extensive mills and other improvements, reduced him to a condition of hopeless poverty. But not in the loss of property alone did he suffer ; his children were driven, in exile, into the neighboring provinces, and he, though hunted down with relentless diligence, was prevented from following them, by his sense of duty to his country, and by his devoted affection for a sick and beloved wife, whose dying couch he could visit only by stealth, and at the midnight hour, being compelled, in the meantime, in order to evade the vigilance of his pursuers, to seek the obscurity of caves and outhouses, and to share with its occupant, on one occasion, the kennel of a dog. Such were the trials and deprivations which this persecuted but unshaken patriot was forced to endure, while discharging what he regarded his sacred obligations to his country. Yet he was not permitted to live to see the triumph of the cause and the principles which had absorbed the devotion of his public life. At about the age of 72, honored and beloved by all that knew him, he closed the evening of an active life, rendered illustrious by his piety, integrity, patriotism, and practical wisdom.

Mr. Hart, though a Presbyterian, having been baptized into the communion of this church, and reared in its faith, and worshiped in its sanctuary, yet could embrace within the folds of his truly Christian and catholic spirit, other communions as well. He gave to the Baptist Society of Hopewell the ground on which their church edifice is built, and he no doubt attended service within its walls, in the declining years of his life, as it was near his residence; and had not war made such havoc of his property, we should doubtless be able to record many kindred acts of beneficence, illustrating the kindly promptings of his liberal soul. Of Mr. Hart, no reliable portrait exists, so far as is known, but he is represented by his cotemporaries as having had black hair and eyes, a dark complexion, and a very fine personal presence; as a man of a gentle expression of countenance, of simple, though pleasing manners, of unblemished purity; as one to be relied on in every exigency, and of uncompromising integrity in the management of public and private trusts—so that, not without reason did his friends and acquaintances confer upon him the epithet of "Honest John Hart."

Mr. Hart was buried in the family and neighborhood burying-ground of John Price Hunt.

The State of New Jersey, with a tardy but honorable sense of justice, determined, by act approved April 5th, 1865, to erect over his grave a monument to his memory. This, with appropriate ceremonies and an oration by Gov. Joel Parker, was dedicated July 4th, 1865. The monument, set up in the burying-ground of the old Hopewell Church, to which his remains had been transferred, is a plain, four-sided pyramidal shaft of Quincy granite, bearing on its faces the following inscriptions, viz.:

[Front]—

JOHN HART,
A Signer of the Declaration of Independence
from New Jersey,
July 4th, 1776. Died 1780.

[Right side]—

Erected by the State of New Jersey,
by act approved April 5th, 1865.
Joel Parker, Governor;
Edward W. Scudder, President of Senate;
Joseph T. Crowell, Speaker of the House;
Jacob Weart,
Charles A. Skillman,
Zephaniah Stout,
Commissioners.

[Left side]—

First Speaker of Assembly,
August 27th, 1776;
Member of the Committee of Safety,
1775–1776.

[Rear]—

Honor the Patriot's grave.

Mr. Hart is claimed by the Baptists as a member of their communion, and is so represented to be in a printed volume of theirs; undoubtedly incorrect. Besides evidence given in the memoir, a receipt of his, as late as 1769, for the payment of his dues to the Presbyterian Church of Pennington, is found recorded in its books.

He died 1780, aged about 72, having married Deborah, youngest daughter of Richard Scudder, of Ewing, (see Scudder family, No. 8,) who died October 26th, 1776, aged 55. Their children were: Sarah; Jesse (26), born September 19th, 1742; Martha, born April 10th, 1744; Nathaniel (27), born October 29th, 1747; John (28), born October 29th, 1748; Susannah, born August 2d, 1750; Mary, born April 7th, 1752, died, aged 30; Abigail, born February 10th, 1754; Edward (29), born December 20th, 1755; Scudder, born December 30th, 1757, died young; a daughter, born March 16th, 1761; Daniel (30), born August 13th, 1762; Deborah, born August 21st, 1765.

Jesse (26), son of John (23), married Martha Mattison, of New Jersey, and removed to Washington, Pa.; had children: John, who married, and had children: Deborah, wife of John Armstrong, of Beaver county, Pa., and Martha, wife of John Cowan; Mattison, married Mrs. Thompson, had two daughters, and lived in Allegheny City; Scudder, a prominent business man of Pittsburg, a pioneer in the navigation of the Ohio, and a skillful meteorologist, having furnished weather calculations, of great accuracy, for many years, for the daily press; with unimpaired faculties, he closed a Christian life, in 1867, aged 92, having married Anna Anderson, of Beaver county, Pa., and Willamina Eichbaum, of Pittsburg; no children; Deborah, wife of Maj. Robert Darragh, of Beaver county, died 1866, aged 90, a woman of ardent piety and of singular excellence; Maj. Darragh survived her six years, dying in his 91st year, highly esteemed for his intelligence, integrity, and moral worth; their children were: John S., married Sarah Allison, sister of Hon. John A. Allison, register of the United States treasury, Martha A., wife of Hiram Stowe, of Ohio, Cinthia B., wife of Dr. Milo Adams, Jesse, died young, was captain in the One Hundred and Fortieth Regiment of Pennsylvania Volunteers; married Marianna, daughter of Lewis Reno, James, Hart, Mattison, married Josephine Cooper, and Scudder, married Catharine, daughter of Hon. D. Weyand; Anna, wife of Dr. John Dickey, who died at Fort Meigs, 1813, while connected with the United States Army; had sons, John and Newton; and Aaron, largely engaged with his brother in the transportation business, married Miss White, and had children: Jesse, married, Emily, wife of Nicholas Beckwith, John, married at Madison, Ind., George, married, no children, Monroe, married, and had children, and Sophia, wife of Joseph Langhorne, and lived at Maysville, Ky.

Nathaniel (27), son of John (23), married Betsy Stout, of Hunterdon, N. J., and moved, in 1795, to Mason county, Ky., where he died, at the age of 83, having had children: Sarah, married Henry Voorhies, of Hunterdon, N. J., and died, aged 68; Mabel; Zephaniah, married Mary Arms, of Kentucky, lived in Warren county, Ohio, and there died, aged 89; Betsy, died, aged 78; Mary, wife of Stephen Bayless, of Mason county, Ky.; Charlotte, wife of Elijah Houghton, of same place, died, aged 33; John (31); Zebulon Stout, married Nancy Thomas, of Kentucky, died, aged, 78, leaving children: Alanson, Joseph, and Jeremiah; and Nathaniel, married Unity Jane Marshall; lived in Boone county, Mo.; had sons, Joseph and Alfred.

Judge John (31), son of Nathaniel (27), lived in Lebanon, Ohio; married, first, Mary Corwine, by whom he had children: Zephaniah; William C.; and Francis. His second wife was Hannah Pumeo, by whom he had Jeremiah P.

John (28), son of John (23), about the year 1770, emigrated to Point Coupee, La. During the troubles that occurred there some years after, he, with many others (English and Americans), became the victim of the oppressive measures pursued by the Spanish authorities there. He was seized, confined eight months in prison, and lost, by confiscation, his large body of slaves and the handsome property which he had accumulated. On his release, he went to Cuba, met with great success as a merchant, at first, but with reverses afterward. He finally returned to Hopewell, and by his energy, succeeded again in gathering a comfortable estate. But now the enmity entertained by the British against the father was transferred to the son. His buildings were burned, his property destroyed; and to escape further persecution, by removal, he sold the remnant of his once large possessions, took his pay in continental currency, which, by its rapid depreciation, left him, in the decline of life, poverty stricken and disheartened. By his marriage with Catharine, daughter of George Knowles, of Tacony, Pa., he had children: Mary, wife of Jacob Vandergrift;

Susannah, wife of Joseph Hall, of Philadelphia; Elizabeth, wife of James Bowyer; Sarah, wife of William Reed, of Philadelphia; moved to Ohio; and John (32).

John (32), son of John (28), married Mary, daughter of John Shreves, an Englishman, of Philadelphia; had by her: Thomas, married Anna Robinson, of Philadelphia county, resided near Pittsburg; Mary, wife of George W. Smith, of Philadelphia; Catharine, married Henry Bartram; Elizabeth, wife of James Loughead, of Philadelphia; Frances, wife of Richard Rankin, of Staunton, Va.; Deborah, wife of David Davis, of Philadelphia; Rebecca, wife of Dallas Kneass, of Philadelphia; Susannah, married, in succession, Joseph, son of Dr. Huyck, of Philadelphia, and Richard Roberts, of New Jersey; John, married Mrs. Sarah Paulin (Kerr); and Abigail, wife of Dr. James Shaw, of North Carolina, a surgeon of the United States Army, resident in Philadelphia.

Edward (29), son of John (23), married Nancy Stout, of Hopewell, and removed, previous to the year 1794, to Beverly, Randolph county, now West Virginia. His children by her were: John, married Deborah, daughter of Moses Stout, of Hopewell; Edward, married Catharine Phillips, of Randolph county, West Virginia; Elijah, married Margaret, daughter of Daniel Hart (No. 30); Joseph, a justice of the county, married, successively, Miss Kittle and Miss Pickens, by whom he had children: David, Bosworth, Joseph, and Alexander, all of whom rendered efficient service in the late war, on the side of the Union. When the Rebels retreated from Beverly to Rich Mountain, before Gen. McClellan's advancing forces, Mr. Elmer Hart, to whose house David had fled, furnished him with a horse, and with instructions to pilot the army of Rosecrans, by a private path, around the Rebel batteries, at the base of the mountain, to the top, where he participated in the fight and victory, the result of which secured West Virginia to the Union. For this service, he was promoted to a captaincy, and was afterwards made quartermaster, and died in the service, at Nashville, Tenn. His father, Joseph, as justice, administered the oath to the entire force captured. I may here remark that the children and grandchildren of both Edward (29) and Daniel (30) Hart, in their energetic action on the side of the Union, during the late unhappy war, seem to have inherited not only the name, but the virtues and patriotism as well, of their distinguished ancestor.

Daniel (30), son of John (23), married Margaret Bund, of New Jersey, in 1788, and with his family, removed to Beverly, Randolph county, Va., in 1794, whither his brother Edward had preceded him. He was a gentleman of high character, and commanding influence in the community, having filled the magistracy and other public offices for many years. As a mark of estimation, he was, in 1819, by a handsome majority, elected to represent the county in the general assembly of his adopted state. He died 1848, aged 86, his wife surviving him two years, aged 84, by whom he had children: Sarah, remained in New Jersey with her grandmother, and married Jonathan Tappan, of New Jersey; Margaret, married Elijah, son of Edward Hart (29), and after his death, Eli Butcher; James M., married Nellie Chenowith, of Virginia; John S., his twin brother, married Jemima Slagle; Elmer, born 1795, married Parmela Carper; has children: Ira, lives at Clarksburg, Caroline, and another daughter; Parmelia, married Thomas Powers; Hugh, married Elizabeth See; Jerusha, married Daniel Capita; and Elizabeth, married George Buckey.

Sarah, daughter of John Hart (23), married Jacob Wykoff, of Hopewell, whose children were: Mary, born 1762; John, born 1763, father of Samuel S. Wykoff, an eminent merchant of New York; Isaac, born 1766, married Eleanor Merril; Sarah, married Mr. Lane, father of Jacob W., ruling elder in the Presbyterian Church of Princeton, N. J.; and Anna, wife of John Kinney.

Abigail, daughter of John Hart (23), who died about 1832, married Moses Stout, of Hopewell. Their children are: Deborah married John, son of Edward Hart (29); Rachel, married Abraham Quick; Theodella, married John Schenck, of Amwell, N. J.; Sarah, married Sidney Prall, of Amwell; Asher, died unmarried; Edward, married Miss Briece; Scudder, left home at an early age, and was never heard from; Simpson, married Abigail Bryant.

Deborah, daughter of John Hart (23), died May 18th, 1848, having married Joseph, son of Nicholas Ott, of Amwell. Their children were: Abigail, wife of Samuel Larrue, who had children: Joseph, Phemus, John H., David O., Samuel, Isaac, and Hamilton; David S., married Hannah Young, of Ringoes; and Permelia, married Peter S. Low; children: Richard, Sarah, and John.

Susannah, daughter of John Hart (23), and her husband, Maj. John Polhemus, son of Hendrick, of Somerset county, N. J., an officer of the Revolutionary army, were both buried in Ronaldson's cemetery, Philadelphia, she having attained the age of 82, in 1832. They had children: Ellen; Deborah, married John McCarr; Sallie; Hannah, wife of Rev. Mr. Miller, had children, Sarah and Susan; Polly, married Mr. West; Ann; Margaret, a twin sister, wife of John Kneass; John, a lieutenant in the Continental Army, was with Gen. St. Clair in 1791, died unmarried; Montgomery, married Ann Vanzandt, of New Jersey, whose children are: Janet, John, Charles, and Susan, wife of Jesse Godley, a prominent merchant of Philadelphia her children are: Montgomery, lives in San Francisco, Franklin, died unmarried, Henry, married, Sophia, married Mr. Weygandt, William, married Mary Sitgreave, Charles, and Caroline.

Ellen, daughter of Susannah Polhemus, by her marriage with Capt. John Axford, had children: John; Samuel; Charles; Thomas; Abram; Montgomery; Abby; Susan, married Mr. Albertson; Sallie; Rebecca; Martha; Ellen, wife of William Axford; and two died in infancy.

Sallie, daughter of Susannah Polhemus, married Capt. Peter Kurtz, who, with his father-in-law, Maj. Polhemus, was taken prisoner soon after the battle of Monmouth, and confined for a long time in that grave of our brave soldiers, the old sugar-house of New York. They had children: Harriet; Richard, married Mary Jackson; George, married Louisa Vultee; Henry; Mary, married Truitt; and Ellen, married Henry P. Bockus.

Ann, daughter of Susannah Polhemus, became, first, the wife John Fimeton, of Philadelphia, whose children are: Thomas McKean, who married, successively, Mary and Sallie Day, no children; Ann and John, died young. Her second husband was Capt. John Pascal, of Philadelphia, by whom she had Aurora, wife of Dr. George W. Chambers, of Philadelphia; Mary, married Frederic Charleton, of England; Julia, wife of Col. Charles B. Reess; Charles Lacroix, married Marie Stewart, daughter of Capt. Malcolm Campbell, of Argyleshire, Scotland, and had Kate C. and James C.; George W., died young; Sallie Ann, wife of Jacob Holahan; Susan, died young; and Adaline, wife of Charles W. Lilliendahl, of New York.

Sarah, daughter of Hannah Miller and granddaughter of Susannah Polhemus, by her marriage with Christian Kneass, a merchant of Philadelphia, became the mother of Caroline, wife of James Magee, a merchant of Philadelphia, whose children are: James Horace and daughters; Napoleon, married Caroline Vultee; Frederic; Horace; Sarah, wife of Samuel Sparhawk; Virginia; Cora; and Horn R., who married Sarah, daughter of Judge Williamson, of Delaware.

The family of Polhemus originated in the Netherlands, where it attained considerable celebrity, one of its members, Eleazar Polhemus, a learned jurist, having been burgomaster of Antwerp as early as 1310. From this region came Johannes Theodorus Polhemus, a minister of the Reformed Church of Holland, and the progenitor of the entire American family.

He was first settled in Itamarca, Brazil. Thence he came, in 1654, to New Amsterdam, when, having immediately received a call to Flatbush, he took up his residence there till 1665, when his services were given to the Brooklyn congregation till his decease, June, 1676, where he was greatly esteemed as a "worthy pastor, and a pious, godly, and edifying preacher." His widow, whose maiden name was Catherine Van Werven, survived him several years.

His children were: Theodorus; Daniel; Elizabeth, married Denys Tennisz; Adriana, married John R. Senbering; Anna, married Cornelius B. Van Wyck; and Margaret, married William G. Cornell.

Daniel P., son of Johannes, was captain of the King's County Troop, supervisor of Flatbush, and county judge. He married Neeltie, daughter of Cornelius Vanderveer, and died 1730, having sons: Cornelius, settled at Hempstead, L. I.; Daniel, in New York; Hendrick, in Somerset county, N. J.; and Jacob, at Haverstraw, N. Y.

Hendrick Polhemus, son of Daniel, married, and had three sons, one of whom was Capt. Cornelius, grandfather of Jane, wife of Henry S. Randall, of Cortlandville, N. Y.; another, Maj. John, who married Susannah, daughter of John Hart, signer of the Declaration, of whom, an active and gallant officer of the Revolution, the following brief notice is subjoined, together with a short extract from his journal, as not being wholly uninteresting:

At the outbreak of the Revolution, when affairs, even to the most sanguine, wore a gloomy aspect, Maj. Polhemus, then young, in the vigor of life, in good circumstances, deeply impressed with the importance of the crisis and the necessity of prompt action on the part of every true patriot, was among the foremost at the summons of his country, to step forward and lay his services and his property at her feet. He was appointed by congress, fourth captain in the First New Jersey Regiment, commanded by Col. Lord Stirling.

The company of eighty-six men which he recruited were without arms and equipments. These, as the public purse was empty, he was desired by his colonel to furnish, with a promise of re-imbursement. This he did, mortgaging his property to raise the money.

His first active service was in the army which invaded Canada, being present in the battle of Three Rivers and several skirmishes.

"On my return," remarks the major, in his journal, "Jersey was so overrun with the British that I could not go to my home. My wife had left all, and fled for safety to the mountains, where I found her.

"In a day or two, I joined the army at Newtown, Pa. Soon after, December 26th, 1776, we moved from Newtown, crossed the Delaware to Trenton, took about one thousand Hessians, recrossed the Delaware, and confined our prisoners in Newtown jail and yard. There being a severe snow storm, the officers were quartered in the same house with Gen. Patterson and myself.

"On the 3d of January, 1777, we attacked the British at Princeton, routed and drove them to New Brunswick. I was left with a rear guard to secure the stores, take care of the wounded, and bury the dead.

"I then obtained leave to visit my home and mill at Rocky Hill. Our army passed on the left side of the Millstone river, where our mill stood, the British on the other side. One morning, being not more than three miles distant, they sent a body of men, belonging to the Fifty-fifth Regiment, to burn the mill and cut down the bridge; but, as they hove in sight, a company of militia with a field-piece, opened on them with such effect that they retreated in great haste, luckily for us too, for we had there four hundred bushels of wheat and a great quantity of flour. The mill belonged to John Hart, my father-in-law, and myself; he was then a member of congress and a signer of the Declaration of Independence. On going to the mill we found a number that Morgan's rifles had killed, whom we buried; the sick and wounded we paroled. The next day I joined the army on Street's mountain, where we remained watching the enemy that lay at New Brunswick, till they left. We then traversed the State of

New Jersey, keeping near the mountains, crossed the Delaware, and on reaching the Brandywine, in Delaware, September 11th, 1777, we had a severe engagement with the British, which lasted till dark, losing on our side more than five hundred men and a field-piece of wrought-iron, commanded by Captain Jones. Our colonel had his horse killed, and the General Marquis De La Fayette while standing near me was wounded in the leg by a musket ball. Slapping his hand on the spot where the ball entered, he exclaimed 'Bon! bon! for America.' Quartered in the same house I asked him what he meant by 'Bone for America,' he replied, 'Good! good! it is a holy cause.'

"On the 4th of October we attacked the British at Germantown, and drove in their pickets, excepting General Stephen, who had gained the rear of their army to come up and enclose them, but he did not come till too late.

"The British left their tents and part of their guns after cutting off the limbers, and fled, some to the mills, others to Chew's stone house, having some field-pieces with them. We were ordered to storm it, which we did, losing all the captains of our battalion in killed and wounded, except myself. Major Witherspoon was killed at my side, and Colonel Nash wounded. Lieutenant Hurley was taken and hung on a tree without benefit of the clergy (because he had formerly belonged to the king's dragoons). General Stephen not appearing, the enemy wheeled about, came down from the hills, and in their turn drove us. Had Stephen come up as he should have done, we could have taken the whole army, for he had a large body of five hundred men.

"After marching and countermarching for some time we took up our winter quarters at Valley Forge, built log huts, dug wells, and made a bridge over the Schuylkill. I hoped now to obtain leave to visit my family, but Lord Stirling refused me on the ground that every field officer of the regiment had gone home—he then appointed me major." The major was next, in June, 1778, in the battle of Monmouth, and as he remarks, "in the hottest of the battle on that intensely hot day." Not long after he was taken prisoner with his son-in-law, Captain Peter Kurtz, thrown into a dungeon of the Provost prison, New York, where he was kept during that winter of unusual severity. "There, with nothing to lie on but the cold floor, through want of covering, and food, which was poor and scanty, I suffered terribly."

He was afterwards transferred to the old sugar-house, where so many of our poor soldiers died of cold, pestilence, and starvation, and finally at the intercession of Dr. Bainbridge, father of the commodore, and of other friends, he was released on parole.

Near the close of the war Major Polhemus retired prostrated in health on account of his many years of severe and active service and his long imprisonments, poor from the wasting of his property by necessary neglect during his absence, but rich in the honor of having gallantly aided in the achievement of his country's independence.

The Hendrickson Family.

John Hendrickson (1), as indicated by his name, was born of ancestors who had their origin in the land of De Ruyter von Tromp and Erasmus. His two sons, William (2); and John (3) became inhabitants of Ewing in the infancy of the settlement.

William (2), son of John (1), purchased a farm, but finding the title defective, and having been required, as a condition of retaining it, to pay for it a second time, he preferred to resign it, and removed to Sussex county. He had by his wife Joanna, sister of Jacob Reeder: Amaziah born May 1st, 1737; John, born February, 1739; Benjamin (4), born August 21st, 1743; Jacob, born November 10th, 1748; Anna, born May 29th, 1741; and Philip (5), born 1745.

Benjamin (4), son of William (2), after the death of his father returned, at the age of seventeen, to Ewing, and purchased a plantation occupied by his grandson, William H. (10), on which he resided till his death, January 24th, 1832, aged 89. He married, first, Mercy, daughter of Ralph Jones; by her had children: Israel (6); Benjamin (7); Elijah (8); and Jacob, who married Elizabeth, daughter of Joseph Tindall, (see Tindall family, No. 2,) and died November 21st, 1797, aged 29, leaving an only child, Letitia. His second wife was Joanna, daughter of Timothy Temple, (see Temple family, No. 7.) His third wife was Phebe, daughter of Stephen Dean, (see Dean family, No. 2,) who survived him till June 26th, 1842, aged 89.

Israel (6), son of Benjamin (4), was elected a trustee of the church in 1811, an office which he continued to fill until his death, May 3d, 1835, aged 70. He married Rachel Anderson, of Pennsylvania, who died February 14th, 1858, aged 89. Their children were: Phebe, married Benjamin Hill; Charles, died young; John (9); Mercy, married Charles Hill; Elizabeth, married Jedediah Hill; Maria, married David Hill; William (10); Joanna, married, first, Enoch Vankirk; had children: Benjamin, and Rachel, married David Howell, her second husband was John Hazard ; had children : Ellen, and Amanda, wife of William Rose ; Israel (11); and Martha, married Randal Hunt.

John 19), son of Israel (6), died September 30th, 1864, aged 72, was also a trustee of the Ewing Church. He married Sarah, daughter of Joseph Green, (see Green family, No. 38,) who died December 20th, 1869, aged 74, having had children : William, married Phebe Anderson ; Ebenezer Rose, married Alice Leigh ; Lydia ; Enoch, married, first, Anne E. Waters, second, Hannah D. Roads ; Rachel, married Levi Farr, of New York city ; Hannah ; Mary, married John Symms.

William (10), son of Israel (6), died July, 1881, aged 81, married Rebecca, daughter of William B. Green, (see Green family, No. 54,) and by her had : Elizabeth, married Edward Hepburn ; Rachel, married George Fox Crozier ; Charles, died, aged 20 ; Richard, married Elizabeth Leigh, and removed to Illinois ; Montgomery, married Virginia, daughter of Lott Howell ; Marcia, died, aged 19 ; Israel, married Annie Rulon ; William G., married Licia Rotes ; Louisa ; Virginia ; David ; and George, died in infancy ; and Wesley, married Rebecca Leigh.

Israel (11), son of Israel (6), died September 27th, 1880, aged 78 ; married Eleanor, daughter of Anthony Smith, of Lawrence, whose children were : Anna Maria, married Stephen Blackwell ; John, married Emeline, daughter of Stephen Brearley, (see Brearley family, No. 14) ; Elizabeth, married Wykoff Hendrickson ; Rachel, married Joseph Conard ; Frances, married Crook Conard ; Louisa, married William Henry Howell ; Reeves, married Mary Creamer ; and Jefferson, married Miss Compton.

Benjamin (7), son of Benjamin (4), died January 28th, 1829, aged 62. He married, first, Sarah, daughter of Nathaniel Temple, (see Temple family, No. 7,) who died July 6th, 1809, aged 36, having had one son, Charles, who married Eliza, sister of John Hazard, and died September 12th, 1827, aged 33. His second wife was Mary, daughter of Titus Hart, (see Hart family, No. 16,) widow of Noah Stout. His children by her were : Sarah, married Joseph B. Anderson, (see Anderson family, No. 6,) and died 1836 ; Matilda, became the third wife of Joseph B. Anderson ; Cornelia, married Aaron Burroughs, (see Burroughs family, No. 26); Elizabeth, married Jonathan Forman Rose, (see Rose family, No. 4); Marcia, married Thomas F. Howell ; Charity, married Samuel Howell—both sons of Samuel Howell, (see Howell family, No. 25);

Julia Anna, married Bradley Atwood Howell, son of Maj. John Howell, (see Howell family, No. 40); Benjamin, married, first, Virginia, daughter of Aaron Moore, (see Moore family, No. 13); second, Anna Mary, daughter of James Brooks.

Elijah (8), son of Benjamin (4), who served as trustee from 1807—thirty-five years—and who died July 7th, 1863, aged 85, married Elizabeth, daughter of Ralph Lanning, (see Lanning family, No. 8.) She died 1840, aged 75, having had a daughter, Rebecca, who married Elias Welling, (see Welling family, No. 6); and Reuben (12).

Reuben (12), son of Elijah (8), who died 1859, aged 66, married Isabella, daughter of Noah Lanning, (see Lanning family, No. 27,) whose children are: Jacob (13); and Elijah, married Rebecca Maples.

Jacob (13), son of Reuben (12), married Mary Hough, of Pennsylvania, whose children are: Marcia, married William H. Fay, of Philadelphia; Benjamin, married Mary, daughter of Dr. John W. Scudder, (see Scudder family, No. 128); and Frank.

Philip (5), son of William (2), resided in Lawrence till his death, December 2d, 1817, aged 72. He left children by his wife: Charity, daughter of Benjamin Green, (see Green family, No. 5), who died March 19th, 1819, aged 67: Martha, wife of James White, (see White family, No. 3); Mary, wife of William Baker; Richard, died unmarried, October 17th, 1865, aged 92; Joanna, wife of Joseph Brearley, (see Brearley family, No. 20); William (14); and Rebecca married Roswell Howe, a teacher, resident in Lawrenceville.

William (14), son of Philip (5), died in 1831, aged 42, married Anna, daughter of Edmund Burke; she died in 1860, aged 65, having had children: Philip (15); James Monroe, married Louisa Vanvleit; Charity Matilda, the second wife of Rev. Jesse Davis, settled at Hightstown.

Philip (15), son of William (14), married Christiana, daughter of Charles Reeder, (see Reeder family, No. 5,) of Lawrence, whose children are: Charles; Emma; Mary married Rev. James Worden; Matilda, married Alexander G. Vancleve; Lewis; and William.

John (3), son of John (1), one of the earliest settlers, also purchased a farm, on which he continued to live. At the time of the first charter of the Presbyterian Church, he, with two others, John Chambers and Joseph Green, was elected an elder. By his wife, Sarah Pearce, he had children : William, died, aged 12 ; Timothy, appointed to the eldership in 1771, married Elizabeth Kellum ; Richard, not married ; Martha, wife of John Rose ; Rhoda, wife of John Burroughs, (see Burroughs family, No. 6); Sarah, wife of Hezekiah Young; Phebe, not married; and Thomas (16).

Thomas (16), son of John (3), by the election in 1796, made trustee of the church, died 1822, aged 83, having married Ruth, daughter of Richard Burt, who died 1817, aged 79. Their children were : Hannah, married John Reeder, of Pennsylvania ; John, died, aged 20 ; Keziah, married Philip Burroughs, (see Burroughs family, No. 8,) who died 1833, aged 68; Timothy (17) ; Richard ; Sarah, the second wife of Joshua Furman, (see Furman family, No. 4,) and died 1864, aged 94—no children ; Phebe, married Joseph Tindall ; Moses, died unmarried, 1831, aged 56 ; Huldah, died September 21st, 1870, aged 92 ; Mary, died in childhood ; Jemima, married Joseph Burroughs, (see Burroughs family, No. 12).

Timothy (17), son of Thomas (16), died February 7th, 1848, aged 76. His wife, Eunice, daughter of Elijah Lanning, (see Lanning family, No. 10,) died August 15th, 1839. Their children are : Elijah L. (18); James ; and John R., a trustee of the Ewing Church, married Rebecca, daughter of Smith Hart, of Pennington, (see Hart family, No. 10,) by whom he had one son, Charles, died in early childhood.

Elijah L. (18), son of Timothy (17), represented his district in the legislature, in 1853 ; has been a trustee of the Ewing Church since 1858. He married Louisa C., daughter of Richard Hunt, (see Hunt family, No. 27,) whose children are : Cornelia, married Edward M. Burroughs ; Frances ; and Anna L., married George L. Howell.

The Hill Family.

Isaac (1), married, and had children: Richard (2); Smith, died January 9th, 1822, aged 71, and is buried in the Ewing church-yard; Mary, married William Howell; and probably others. A Samuel Hill, who died 1785, aged 69, is buried in the Ewing church-yard, of which church he was an elder.

Richard (2), son of Isaac (1), removed from Flemington to Ewing township in 1804, purchased a farm on the Delaware, on which he erected a handsome house, which he occupied till his death, and was succeeded in it by his son Wallace. He died 1826, aged 67, having married Elizabeth, daughter of Jasper Smith, who died January 28th, 1837, aged 60. Their children were: Jonathan, went to New Orleans, and was never heard from; Jasper Smith, a merchant of Trenton, died February 3d, 1847, unmarried; Enoch, married Delia Ann, daughter of Dr. Stillwell, of New York, is a merchant in Mount Pleasant, Iowa; Samuel, died July 14th, 1825, aged 27; Sally Ann, second wife of Morgan Scudder, (see Scudder family, No. 22); Daniel, married, and lives on the Susquehanna; Elias, married Elizabeth Anderson; James, married Mary Ashmore, lived and died in Iowa, leaving one daughter, Elizabeth; Theodore Wallace, married Caroline, daughter of Col. Elias Gilkyson, of Bucks county, Pa.

The Houston Family.

It may be said of the Hon. William Churchill Houston, that the memory of a man should be perpetuated who was the pupil of Dr. Samuel Finley and of Dr. John Witherspoon, presidents of the College of New Jersey, and the fellow tutor of the Rev. Samuel Stanhope Smith, who was afterward president of the college, and was the associate of Hamilton, Jefferson, Madison, Monroe, Chase and Ellsworth, in the congress of the confederation, to say nothing of his own merits as a man of genius and of virtue, and as one equally distinguished on the rolls of science and in the halls of legislation.

Mr. Houston, who in his early years adopted the State of New Jersey as his future residence, was a native of Sumter county, S. C., son of a planter of property and distinction, and a member of the society of Friends. Young Houston early exhibited a strong proclivity for learning, and earnestly besought his father to furnish him the means of obtaining a liberal education. To these solicitations the father turned a deaf ear, in deference to the society, who did not at that time favor such a course. But yielding at last to the anxiety and earnestness of his son, he offered to furnish him with a horse, equipments, clothes, and £50 in money, to do with as he pleased. This would release himself from responsibility and from giving offence to the society.

The son gladly accepted the offer, left the paternal roof and turned his face northward. Harvard, Yale, William and Mary, and Nassau Hall, were the only collegiate institutions, at that day, in the colonies. His choice fell on Princeton, then, as ever since, held in high estimation at the South. He was admitted to its Freshman class, and at the same time took charge of the classical school connected with the college.

This he taught while keeping up with his classes in college, and was graduated in 1768 with distinguished honor, receiving from the college authorities a silver medal, (then not so common as since,) still in the possession of his grandson, William C. Houston, of Philadelphia. Immediately after his graduation he was appointed tutor, and two years later, when a professorship of mathematics and natural philosophy was established, he was unanimously elected to this office, the duties of which for more than twelve years he discharged with fidelity and signal ability, to the entire satisfaction of the board of trustees, until his resignation in 1783. He was also treasurer of the college. During the temporary suspension of the college exercises in 1776 on the approach of the enemy, he offered his services in a military capacity, which were accepted, and he was appointed captain in the Second Battalion of Somerset county militia, but resigned the same year. He was also sent to the assembly from that county in 1777, but resumed the duties of his chair as soon as the safety of the college permitted. Amid the demands of his professorship he found leisure to pursue a regular course of legal study, and was admitted to the bar in 1781, and on his resignation in 1783 removed to Trenton.

Though the resolution which he adopted at the outset of his professional career, never under any circumstances to undertake a cause of the justice of which he was not fully satisfied, might seem calculated to restrict the limits of his business, yet such were his high abilities and profoundness of his knowledge that he soon attracted to himself a large and lucrative practice.

To Mr. Houston was assigned during his official life the filling of many important and responsible trusts and positions. He was made surrogate of Hunterdon county, New Jersey, was receiver of continental taxes from 1782 to 1785, was appointed clerk of the Supreme Court from 1781 to 1788, was for a time secretary of the congress of the confederation, and on the 25th of May, 1779, was elected a member of that body, to which he was re-elected four times. In its deliberations and measures he took an active and prominent part. It was while a member that Mr. Houston evinced his discriminating judgment of character and his devotion to the commander-in-chief of our army, by giving expression to his views in a letter written to Governor William Livingston:

"My object in sending these documents, is to communicate the noble and dignified sentiments of the commander-in-chief, and to give some idea of the difficulties he has to encounter. If ever a man deserved gratitude and confidence, he does, and the more especially as his modesty will never allow him to be sated with the former, nor his goodness of heart to abuse the latter. * * * * * The virtues of this amiable man as a citizen are no less conspicuous than his spirit and perseverance as a soldier."

This was at a time when officers of the highest rank, such as General Conway and General Charles Lee, were endeavoring to supplant him in the estimation of congress, and to shake their confidence in his conduct of the war. An act of Mr. Houston's about this time, which forcibly illustrates his patriotism, his sympathy and his generosity, ought not be allowed to sink into oblivion.

In 1779, the troops of the state in the continental army continued to be in a most destitute condition, especially with regard to pay and clothing, and a touching appeal was made by the officers, at the same time setting forth their grievances. During the recess of the legislature, the necessities of the troops became so urgent that three individuals—Gov. Livingston, Robert Morris, and William Churchill Houston—interposed for their relief, and requested the treasurer of the state to furnish the commissioners of clothing any sum not exceeding £7000, to supply clothing, for which they would be responsible, if the legislature would make no appropriation. (Mitford.)

Mr. Houston had the high honor of being one of the five commissioners, of whom the Hon. David Brearley, Chief Justice of the state, was another, appointed by congress to settle the dispute between Pennsylvania and Connecticut, in relation to the Wyoming lands. They met in Trenton between November 12th and December 30th, 1782. Jonathan Dickinson Sergeant was one of the agents of Pennsylvania, in whose favor the decision was made, known as the "Trenton Decree." One of the last public honors conferred on Mr. Houston was that of sending him as a delegate to represent New Jersey in the important convention of commissioners from different states, which met at Annapolis September 11th, 1786, and which closed its labors by suggesting the convention which formed the constitution of the United States, and which accordingly met at Philadelphia on November 3d of the same year. To this able and distinguished body, also, over which Washington presided, Mr. Houston was appointed a delegate, but failing health prevented his attending its sessions.

Mr. Houston, in 1788, already in an advanced stage of consumption, determined to seek the balmy air of the South, but had proceeded no further on his way thither than Frankford, Pa., when he was arrested by the hand of death. He was carried to Philadelphia and buried in the yard of the Third Presbyterian Church, at the corner of Fourth and Pine streets.

Thus died, in the very vigor of manhood, though ripe in honors, a man of ability, eminent, of honor unimpeachable, and of integrity unsullied.

He is represented as having been, in person, tall, dignified, and graceful, with a countenance of extreme intelligence, though grave and uniformly serious. His eloquence, not brilliant, derived its force from his profound knowledge, and from his truth and earnestness, which rarely failed to produce conviction.

William C. Houston (1) married Jane, daughter of the Rev. Caleb Smith, (see Smith family, No. 4,) of St. George's Manor, L. I., pastor of the Presbyterian Church of Orange, and his wife, Martha, daughter of Rev. Jonathan Dickinson, president of Princeton College. She died in 1796, aged 41, and is buried in the Lawrenceville cemetery, having had children: William Churchill (2), a skillful and opulent merchant of Philadelphia, married Susannah Somers, of Philadelphia, and had by her, one daughter; Louisa Ann, wife of Dr. John Vancleve, of Princeton, (see Vancleve family, No. 21); Elizabeth, wife of Horace G. Phillips, (see Phillips family, No. 32,) removed to Dayton, Ohio; George S. (3); Mary, wife of the Rev. Isaac V. Brown, D. D., of Lawrenceville, of whose church he was pastor, and where he established, and conducted for many years, a very successful classical academy; she died in 1834, aged 49, having had children: Rezeau, a graduate of Princeton College, was tutor in the same, and died while passing through his theological course in 1833, aged 25; George Houston, graduated by the College of New Jersey, a member of the bar, of the state senate, and of congress, and was appointed judge of the Supreme Court, which office he was holding at his death, in 1865; he married a daughter of Sheriff Gaston, of Somerville, and left several children; William C. H., also a graduate of Princeton, a lawyer and the editor of a paper, died young, unmarried. Residing in Mr. Houston's family was his sister, Elizabeth, who became the wife of Capt. Jonathan Phillips, of Lawrenceville, (see Phillips family, No. 29.)

George S. (3), son of William (1), married Mary Forman, and by her had issue: George, died in 1833, aged 8, is buried in the Lawrenceville graveyard; William C. (4); and Eliza, wife of David

K. Este,* son of Charles, who, for a time, resided in Paris, France, but ultimately lived in Philadelphia, whose children are : Charles, Lucy P., Lillian, Florence May, and Elizabeth Worthington.

William Churchill (4), son of George (3), a successful and wealthy merchant and a prominent and influential citizen of Philadelphia, united in marriage to Mary B., daughter of Joseph Solms, had by her : Mary B., wife of Francis H. Williams, son of Joseph ; William C., married Helena, daughter of William Hunter, Jr., of Philadelphia ; Elizabeth Dickinson, wife of Charles C. Dunn, Jr., son of Charles, of Philadelphia ; Ida ; Sidney ; Maud ; and Frederic.

---

*Capt. Moses Este, of Morristown, served in the U. S. Army of the Revolution, was severely wounded in the battle of Monmouth, and found among the dead and dying by Col. Hamilton, who had him cared for. He recovered, was made a collector of revenue, and died, aged 85. His wife was Anne, daughter of David Kirkpatrick, who, with his father, Alexander, emigrated from Watties Neoch, Dumfriesshire, Scotland, first to Belfast, thence, in 1736, to this country, settling at Mine Creek, Somerset county, N. J. She was sister of Andrew Kirkpatrick, for many years Chief Justice of New Jersey, and aunt of the Rev. Dr. Jacob Kirkpatrick. The family was a distinguished one in Scotland. Captain and Mrs. Este's children were: Hannah, who married Mr. Nottingham, of England, her daughter, Adelaide, married Dr. Francis Ewing, son of Chief Justice Charles Ewing, of Trenton ; David K., a graduate of Princeton, a distinguished jurist established at Cincinnati, was made president judge of Hamilton county, and afterwards judge of the Supreme Court of Ohio ; he married, first, in 1819, Lucy Ann, daughter of William Henry Harrison, president of the United States, one of his four daughters reached maturity, and married Joseph Regnolds, of Baltimore, his second wife was Louisa, daughter of Judge William Miller ; Charles, married Mary Johnson, whose son, David K., married Eliza, daughter of George S. Houston (3).

The Howell Family.

It is believed on good family tradition that the first American ancestor of the Howell family came from Kent county, England. Daniel Howell (1) came to Ewing, New Jersey, from Long Island; he purchased and lived on the land which has continued in the family, last inherited by a great-great-granddaughter, married to Alfred Muirheid.

The deeds for his land were one from Samuel Coxe and John Hutchinson, dated 1702, and one from William Worrell, dated 1705.

Daniel (1), died April 25th, 1732, aged 52, having married Mary, sister of Ebenezer Prout's wife; she died September 26th, 1760, aged 76, and had children: David (2); Phebe, born September 28th, 1707, married John Scudder, (see Scudder family, No. 10); Elizabeth, born January 9th, 1709, married William Pearson; John, died January 13th, 1732, aged 20; Hannah, born February 24th, 1714; Daniel (3), born February 24th, 1716; Mary, born February 6th, 1718; Abigail, died January 31st, 1746, aged 26; Joshua (4), born October 11th, 1722; Prudence, died January 13th, 1734, aged 10; Hezekiah (5), born August 7th, 1727.

David (2), son of Daniel (1), died October 24th, 1775, aged 70, having married Mary Baker, she died January 15th, 1786, aged 79, had children: Daniel (6); John (7); Timothy (8); David (9); Joseph (10); Amos; also a daughter that married a Mr. Hartley, and had at least two children, Lydia and Amos, mentioned in her will.

Daniel (6), son of David (2), died February 27th, 1812, aged 73, married Deborah, daughter of Stephen Rose, (see Rose family, No. 1,) who died November 4th, 1825, aged 84. Their children were: Elizabeth, wife of James Anderson, of Newtown, Pa., removed to Ohio, and died 1817, aged 53, having had children: Ephraim, married Sarah Moon, and Charles, married Ruth Bunting; Mary, wife of Enoch Hart, (see Hart family, No. 17,) Ebenezer (11); Patience, died January 8th, 1819, aged 41, having married Ralph Phillips, had children : Simeon, married Lucretia Williamson, Ann Eliza, wife of Azariah Phillips, Sarah, wife of Jacob Williamson, Howell, married Jane Hunt, and William; Deborah, became the second wife of James Anderson; Daniel (12); Henry Baker, died July 2d, 1854, aged 71, having married Hannah Corlies, of Trenton, and had children : Elizabeth, Joseph, Henry, James, Hannah Ann, and Lydia, married Joseph Sawyer; Jonathan, died 1869, aged 83, married Virginia Hankinson, have children: Charles B., married Sarah Olcott, of Pennsylvania, and Deborah, married Edgar M. Moon, of Maryland; Ephraim, died 1813, aged 43, married Elizabeth Robinson; Phebe, died April 26th, 1861. aged 82; and Eunice, died July 18th, 1862, aged 88.

Ebenezer (11), son of Daniel (6), died October 28th, 1813, aged 45, married Hannah, daughter of Alexander Biles, of Lawrence, and had children: Elizabeth, married Andrew Brown; Rachel, married Charles Bailey; Stephen, married; Ebenezer, married Hannah Rosecrantz; Phebe, married Charles Hart; William, married Sarah Ann Carman; Martha, married Wilson Servis.

Daniel (12), son of Daniel (6), married, first his brother Ebenezer's widow, by whom he had Ephraim, married Elizabeth Belford, and Nancy, wife of Simeon Reeder. He married a second time in the West, and had children: Daniel; Samuel; Eunice; and Mary.

John (7), son of David (2), was an elder in the Ewing Church in 1771, died 1779, aged 52, having married Naomi, daughter of Joseph Hart, (see Hart family, No. 2,) who died 1803, aged 67, having had children: Ezekiel (13); Asher (14); Susanna, died April 13th, 1836; Noah (15); John (16); Huldah, born 1768, married Daniel Anderson, had one child, Huldah Ann; Ezek (17); Mary, born 1773, married John Burroughs, (see Burroughs family, No. 20); Joseph (18); Abner (19).

Ezekiel (13), son of John (7), died 1831, aged 76, having married Charity, daughter of Richard Lott, (see Lott family, No. 2,) who died 1847, aged 90. Their children were: Richard Lott (20); Vincent, who died 1834, aged 48, having married Jane Margeram, had children: Matthias, married Phebe, daughter of Abner Hunt, Eliza, who was blind, Letitia, married Aaron Doble, and Vincent, died young; Letitia, married Benjamin Howell (23); Mary, married John Clawson, had children: Hetty Ann, married John W. Neal, Emeline, married Voorhees Hunt, Huldah married

William Mooney, and George married Emeline Fowler; Huldah, married Jason Roe, had children: Lott Howell, who married, first, Garetta Quick, had Sarah and Hulda, second, Sarah Quick, sister of the former; Mary Ann, wife of James Miller, she has children: James, Jason, Alexander, Charles, and Christine, married Charles Van Deventer; and Charles, married Mary Vansant, have children: Alethia Ann, married Ira Bennet, Sarah, married Aden Carver, Mary, married Mr. Carver, Esek, married Jane Scudder.

Richard Lott (20), son of Ezekiel (13), married Susanna Baker, whose children are: Ezekiel, married Maria Dansbury; Mary Matilda, married, first, Heber Belden, has a son Heber, married Margaret, daughter of Dr. Vandevere, of North Branch; second, Asher Schenck, by whom she had a son George; Frances Elizabeth, married, first, Richard Lilly, had a daughter Emma; second, Peter Stout; Ellen, married Amos Gilkyson; Asher; and Theodore, married Elizabeth Hughes, whose children are: Elijah, Mary, wife of Dr. Herman Shafer, Julia, wife of William West, George L., married Anna L. Hendrickson, and Maggie, wife of Lambert L. Howell.

Asher (14), son of John (7), died 1807, aged 50, married Phebe, daughter of Joseph Howell (10), whose children were: Letitia, wife of David Howell; and Jemima, wife of Reeder Chambers, (see Chambers family, No. 7.)

Noah (15), son of John (7), died 1801, aged 38, having married Hannah Lawrence. Their children were: Jesse (21); Elizabeth; Sarah, married Benjamin Muirheid, (see Muirheid family, No. 7); and Mary, married Job White, (see White family, No. 4.)

Jesse (21), son of Noah (15), married Deborah, daughter of George Muirheid, (see Muirheid family, No. 4.) Their children are: Elizabeth, wife of Dr. Crane; Sarah, wife of James Pollock; Ellen, wife of William Maxwell; Jesse, married Eliza Smith, children, Judson and Eliza; George, married.

John (16), son of John (7), married Mary Keyser, and had children: George; John; Joseph; Asher; Hulda; Jane; and Naomi.

Ezeck (17), son of John (7), married Magdalena Keyser, and had children: George; Joseph; Lorenzo; Mary; Amanda; Susan; and Ann.

Joseph (18), son of John (7), died April 17th, 1853, aged 77, having married Mary, daughter of Jesse Hough, and had children: Ezeck; Elvira; John, died, aged 22; Mary, married Isaac I. Robbins, and died 1845; Adaline, died 1828, aged 14; Joseph (22); Amanda, wife of Imlah Moore, (see Moore family, No. 36); Lydia Ann, wife of Charles Moore, his brother; and Adaline.

Joseph (22), son of Ezeck (17), died 1858, having married Elizabeth Livensetter, of Pennsylvania; left children: John L., married Sarah, daughter of Rev. Dr. Hall, of Trenton; Charles; Fanny; and Elizabeth.

Abner (19), son of John (7), married Anna, daughter of Edmund Burroughs, (see Burroughs family, No. 21,) whose children were: Liscomb, who married Ursula Mount, and had children: John, Anna, Lizzie, Virginia, and Mary; Asher, married Ruth, daughter of Enos Titus, (see Titus family, No. 23); children: John, Charles, Ann, and Almena; John, died young; Abner; and Susan, died in infancy.

Timothy (8), son of David (2), died 1804, aged 61; married Deborah, daughter of Benjamin Green, (see Green family, No. 5); she died 1832, aged 82. Their children were: Benjamin (23); David (24); Israel, married Hetty Vannoy; Samuel (25); Mary, died unmarried, 1816, aged 38; Martha, became the second wife of Joseph Green, (see Green family, No. 56); Phebe, married Abner Hunt, of Hopewell; and Sarah, died, aged 10.

Benjamin (23), son of Timothy (8), died 1822, aged 49, having married Letitia, daughter of Ezekiel Howell (13), who died 1879, aged 93, by whom he had: Lambert, married the widow Matilda West, and died 1841, aged 24; Charity, wife of Gershom C. Sergeant; they have children: Mary Jane, wife of Dr. C. W. Larison, Lambert, a lawyer of Lambertville, married Sarah Scarborough, Joseph, Letitia, and Garetta, wife of George Vancinderin; Letitia, married John C. Titus, son of Nathaniel; Timothy (26); and David, married Rachel, daughter of Enoch Vankirk; have children: Benjamin, Russel, Larison, Inez, and Howard.

Timothy (26), son of Benjamin (23), died 1864, aged 49, having married L. Jane, daughter of John Green, (see Green family, No. 51,) whose children are: John G., a lawyer of Trenton, married Hannah A., daughter of Amos Reeder, (see Reeder family, No. 18); Lambert L., a graduate of Princeton, a lawyer of Trenton, married Maggie, daughter of Theodore Howell; and Caroline.

David (24), son of Timothy (8), died 1837, having married Letitia, daughter of Asher Howell (14), by whom he had: Ann

Amanda, died, aged 8; and Phebe, married George Gatchell, of Philadelphia. His second wife was Sarah Lupp.

Samuel (25), son of Timothy (8), died 1868, aged 76, having married Sarah Ford, who died 1873, aged 83. Their children were: Thomas (27); and Samuel (28).

Thomas (27), son of Samuel (25), married Marcia, daughter of Benjamin Hendrickson, (see Hendrickson family, No. 7.) Their children are: David, married in Kansas City; Mary, wife of Alexander Hunt; William, died young; Julia, wife of Samuel Hutchinson; Alonzo, married Lizzie, daughter of Benjamin White; and Sarah, married Joseph Golden.

Samuel (28), son of Samuel (25), married Charity, daughter of Benjamin Hendrickson, (see Hendrickson family, No. 7.) Their children are: Benjamin; Sarah, married Benjamin Reiff; Deborah, married Mr. Bedle; Lizzie, married Frank Rogers; Samuel, married Cora Lampson; and Chattie.

David (9), son of David (2), died 1785, aged 54; married Keturah, daughter of John Scudder, (see Scudder family, No. 10.) Their children were: Absalom, married Miss Vansant, resided in Pennsylvania; Prudence, married; Patience, married Mr. Thompson; Charity, married Mr. Reed; and Israel, who died 1787, aged 29, married Susannah Fleming, and had children: Mary, second wife of Jacob Vancleve, (see Vancleve family, No. 25), David, Anna, and Parmela, last three died young. His widow married John Reeder, (see Reeder family, No. 6,) and died 1836, aged 75.

Joseph (10), son of David (2), was born 1729, removed to Pennsylvania, where he resided till his death about 1800. He married the widow Jemima Barber, daughter of John Burroughs, (see Burroughs family, No. 3,) who died 1824, aged 99. Their children were: Samuel (29); David (30); Timothy (31); Phebe, married Asher Howell (14); Jemima, married Mr. Coursen; Elizabeth, married William Burroughs; Polly; Martha, married Joshua Vanhorn; and Susan, married Edmund Burroughs, (see Burroughs family, No. 21.)

Samuel (29), son of Joseph (10), was an elder in the Ewing Church till his death, 1834, aged 80. He married Sarah, daughter of William Cornell; she died suddenly on her way to Philadelphia in 1823, aged 58, leaving children: William (32); and Mary, married Charles Taylor, of Taylorsville, Bucks county, Pa., whose children are: Burroughs, Sarah, Charles, Elizabeth and Howell.

Esquire William (32), son of Samuel (29), who was a magistrate, died 1842, aged 56, having married Abigail, daughter of John Howell (38); she died 1854, aged 69. Their children were: Charles, died 1832, aged 22; Samuel (33); John, a graduate of Princeton College and Seminary, married Jane Cox, of Western Virginia, where he was settled till his death, leaving children: John, William and Maria; Addison Alexander (34); Horatio Stockton (35); William (36); Sarah Maria, married Rev. William H. McCarer, a Presbyterian clergyman, settled at Evansville, Ind.

Samuel (33), son of William (32), married, first, Harriet Cook, of Philadelphia, by whom he had Horatio, married Maggie Conway; Joshua, married Anna E. Wilkins; William A.; Sarah M.; and Mary C.; his second wife was Mary, half sister of the former.

Dr. Addison Alexander (34), son of William (32), a physician, married Isabella, daughter of Richard Beatty, (see Beatty family, No. 7,) of Allentown, N. J., where he practices. Their children are: Isabella B., wife of Edward J. Wright, a merchant of New York; John B., a graduate of Princeton College and Seminary, and is a missionary in Brazil, South America; Catharine Louisa, married Wilson Reynolds, of Connecticut, and moved to Iowa; and Susan, married Charles Reeves.

Horatio Stockton (35), son of William (32), was a graduate of Princeton College and Seminary. He married Isabella Graham, of New York city, and was settled at Delaware Water Gap. He was chaplain during the war, and killed in the hospital by a stray ball, during the battle of Gettysburg. He left children: Mary P., wife of Frederic B. Carter; Horatio Stockton, married Catharine D. Leonard; and James Wilson.

William (36), son of William (32), a merchant of Philadelphia, where he married Hester Roberts, of Montgomery county, Pa. Their children are: Mary A., married Isaac B. Bunting; John R., married Flora M. Shannon; Clara; William, married Sarah Jane McHenry; Lydia R.; and Warren R.

David (30), son of Joseph (10), lived in Taylorsville, Pa., married Susan Scott, and by her had: Elizabeth, not married; Samuel, married Joanna Johnson, and had children: Susan, Phebe, Letitia, and Theodore; Charles, married Mary, daughter of Samuel Taylor, had one son, David; Moore Scott, married the widow of his brother Charles, and had children: Susanna, Elizabeth, and Lydia; Joseph, married.

Timothy (31), son of Joseph (10), married Mary or Rebecca

Ketcham, of Pennington, N. J.; had children: Levi, married, first, Sarah, daughter of John Reeder, (see Reeder family, No. 6); second, Rebecca Marjoram, by whom he had children: John; David; Sarah; Mary; and Martha.

Daniel (3), son of Daniel (1), died 1763, aged 46, having married Abigail, daughter of Charles Clark, (see Clark family, No. 1.) She died 1785, aged 69. Their children were: Daniel (37); Charles, died young; Prudence, died in infancy; Phebe, married Job Phillips, (see Phillips family, No. 7); Eunice, married John Phillips, went West, had a daughter, Sarah; John; Hezekiah, died 1754, aged 23; Abigail, married John Guild, (see Guild family, No. 3.)

Daniel (37), son of Daniel (3), married Mary, daughter of William Green, (see Green family, No. 4.) Their children were: Rhoda, born 1766, married John Green, of Easton, Pa.; Sarah, married Nathaniel Green, brother of John, (see Green family, No. 12); Elizabeth, died in youth; Daniel G. (39); at his death, 1779, aged 36, he left £20 to the Presbyterian Church.

Daniel (39), son of Daniel (37), died 1852, aged 75; married Sarah, daughter of Benjamin Clark, (see Clark family, No. 2,) and had children: Elizabeth, married John G. Muirheid, (see Muirheid family, No. 6); John, married, had a daughter, Sarah, wife of Henry Sanford; Charles, married Esther Hyatt, had children: Thomas, Charles, Alfred, Daniel, William, Elizabeth, Margaret, Sarah, Caroline, Ella, Mary; William, married Ellen Sutphen, had children: Robert, Peter, and John G.; Robert, married Harriet Judson, had a daughter, Harriet; Joseph; and Mary, died in infancy.

John (38), son of Daniel (3), died 1823, aged 74; was an elder in the Ewing Church. He married Mary, daughter of Rev. John Guild, (see Guild family, No. 2.) Their children were: Phebe, married Samuel Clark, (see Clark family, No. 6); Charles, died in childhood; Letitia, died 1839, aged 56; Abigail, married William Howell (32); and John (40).

Maj. John (40), son of John (38), was an elder in the Ewing Church till his death, 1855, aged 56. He married Mary, daughter of Nathaniel Green, (see Green family, No. 9,) by whom he had children: Edward, died in childhood; Bradley Atwood, married, first, Julia, daughter of Benjamin Hendrickson, (see Hendrickson family, No. 7); second, Arabella Morgan, have one son, Charles; Theodore Sitgreaves, married Phebe, daughter of John

Jones, (see Jones family, No. 4,) had children, Mary and Alfred; Sarah Ann, wife of Alfred Muirheid, (see Muirheid family, No. 8.)

Joshua (4), son of Daniel (1), married Rebecca Reed, and had children: Abigail, wife of Benjamin Fish, (see Fish family, No. 5); Phebe, married John Fleming, of Pennsylvania; Mary, wife of Peten Elvish, of Hesse Cassel; Peter (42); Amos (42); Levi, married Nancy, daughter of Daniel Clark; and Lott (43).

Peter (41), son of Joshua (4), died 1812, aged 64; married Sarah Preston, who died 1816, aged 66. Their children were: John (44); Charles, married Rachel Erwin, had one son, John, died, aged 21; Phebe, married Abner Scudder, (see Scudder family, No. 15); Mary, married Benjamin Clark, (see Clark family, No. 5); and Rebecca married Peter Hahn, of Philadelphia, has one daughter, Caroline, married Dr. George B. Wood.

Dr. John (44), son of Peter (41), an eminent physician of Trenton, died 1860, aged 81, having married Lydia, daughter of Benjamin Taylor, of Philadelphia, had children: Peter, also a physician, married Adelaide, daughter of James Pratt, of Bridesburg, their children are, Anna, wife of James Whittaker, and Edmund, married ——— ; Benjamin, married Miss Pearce, whose children are William, Benjamin, Hammot, Henry, and Emeline; Charles, married Miss Cunningham, have children: Emma, married, Mr. Bedell, and John, married Miss Wallace, of Virginia; James, died 1866, aged 56; Theodore; and Emeline, married Jonathan Fish.

Amos (42), son of Joshua (4), married Martha Jones, and had children: Elizabeth, married, first, Mr. Miller, and, second, Mr. Prentiss, both of Philadelphia; Maria, married Dr. Coldwell, of Philadelphia; and Rebecca, married Samuel Wooley.

Lott (43), son of Joshua (4), died 1841, aged 73, married Lydia Hartupee, who died 1855, aged 84. Their children were: William, married Jane Cammeron, and has children: Eliza Jane, Louisa, and Mary; Rebecca, married Joseph McGill, her children are: John, Lydia, Lott, Joseph, William, and Benjamin, last four live in California; Daniel, married Mary Chambers, had children: Emma, Eliza, Sarah, Philie, and Alfred; Charles, married Nancy Worrill; Lott, died 1860, aged 51, having married Fanny Walker, whose children are William Henry, Virginia, and Alfred; Sarah, married Jonathan Howell, of Hopewell; Jane, married Joseph Walker, whose children are Charles and Adeline; and Elizabeth, married John Fowler, their children are Daniel and Wilson.

Hezekiah (5), son of Daniel (1), was an elder in Ewing Church, died 1800, aged 73; married Hannah Ellett; had children: Ellett (45); Aaron, died 1800, not married; Marcia, married Mr. Douglass, captain of a packet ship; after his death, she married Mr. Durant, of Santa Cruz, after, resident of Norfolk, Va., by whom she had Marcia, Hannah, and Matilda.

Ellett (45), son of Hezekiah (5), was a lieutenant of the First Hunterdon Regiment, and assistant quartermaster. He died 1821, aged 64, having married Catharine Flick, of Philadelphia. She died 1808, aged 49, leaving children: Philip (46); Douglass, who was killed at the age of 21, by being thrown from a horse; Ann, married Matthew Galbraith, of Philadelphia, had one son, James, killed while young; Eliza, married Abraham Tenbrook, of Philadelphia, whose children are: William, married Margaret Lee, of Philadelphia, Philip, married Catharine Stewart, and Elizabeth; Marcia, died 1820, aged 33; Mary, died 1819, aged 26; Harriet; Hannah, married John R. Vogdes, an eminent professor in the University of Pennsylvania, and lawyer of Philadelphia, whose children are: James and Julia; Catharine, married Theodore Titus, (see Titus family, No. 19.)

Philip (46), son of Ellett (45), was killed by being thrown from a carriage, in 1833, aged 55; married Mary Erwin, of Pennsylvania. Their children are: Mary Ann; Catharine, married David H. White, of Philadelphia; Eleonora, wife of James Hoy, of Trenton; Julia, wife of Joseph Exton; Louisa; Philipina, married Commodore Armstrong, of the United States Navy, grandson of Rev. James Armstrong, he died in Pensacola, 1854, aged 29; Sarah, married James Southard, son of Isaac, for a time treasurer of New Jersey; and three sons, died in infancy.

The Christopher Howell Family.

Christopher Howell (1), whose death is recorded April 25th, 1779, at the age of 90, is in no way related, so far as can be ascertained, to Daniel Howell, the ancestor of most of the Howells of this region. He and his wife, Johanna, came, at an early period, from Long Island, and settled on a farm in Ewing township. She died October 31st, 1789, aged 91, having had children: Christopher (2); Obadiah, was, from 1762, for nine years, a trustee of the First Church of Trenton (now Ewing), he married, at the age of 60, Polly Cherry; Stephen, married, and had several children; Josiah (3); Isaac (4); Rhoda, married, successively, Mr. Rue and Mr. Scott; and Abigail, married Mr. Dumont, and lived in Warren county.

Christopher (2), son of Christopher (1), who died 1802, date of will, married Joanna, daughter of William Green, (see Green family, No. 4.) She died 1802, leaving children: William, married Mary, daughter of Isaac Hill, of Flemington, and died April 10th, 1801, aged 43; Martha, married Richard Green, (see Green family, No. 10); and Mary, died unmarried.

Josiah (3), son of Christopher (1), died 1801, date of will. By his wife, Margaret, had children: Edward, married, and lived near Harbortown, and had children: Peter, Hannah, and others; Andrew, lived in Somerville, and was a judge many years, in Somerset county; Burt; and a daughter, married Mr. Wright, and had children: Mary, Sarah, Margaret, and Benjamin.

Isaac (4), son of Christopher (1), who died April 28th, 1814, aged 79, married Hannah Carter, who died August 11th, 1804, aged 68. Their children were: Robinson (5); Henry (6); Israel (7); Ezekiel (8); Spencer (9); Isaac, married Elizabeth, daughter of John Phillips, who died February 2d, 1879, aged 83; Christopher (10); Obadiah (11); Susan, married Joseph Redman, and had children: Woolston and Charles; Hannah, married Joseph Welling, (see Welling family, No. 3.)

Robinson (5), son of Isaac (4), married Mary Miller, of Sussex county, and had children: Nancy; Mary; Kenora; Cornelia; Phebe; Hannah; Isaac; William; and Robertson.

Henry (6), son of Isaac (4), died February 16th, 1826, aged 63, having married Rebecca Jones, and had children: Isaac, married Elizabeth Hart; Henry, married Elizabeth Ann Laterette; James, married; Christopher, died 1829, aged 40; Elijah, not married; Joseph, not married; Ralph, went West; Mary, married Nathaniel Lanning, (see Lanning family, No. 18); Rhoda, wife of Ralph Lanning; Obadiah, not married; Abigail, died 1831, aged 34; and Hannah, married William Marcellus, and had children: Rebecca, wife of Simon Mathews, Elizabeth, wife of Joseph B. Crosdale, Mary, wife of Joseph M. Bennet, Hannah, wife of Daniel McNeal, Anna, wife of John B. Goheen, and Sarah, wife of John Dobbins, of Philadelphia.

Israel (7), son of Isaac (4), died September 15th, 1835, aged 48, having married Agnes Hickey. She died September 17th, 1852, aged 70. Their children are: Israel, married Sarah Carter; Samuel; Liscomb; Charlotte, wife of W. P. Wright; Lydia, wife of Enoch Jones; Charles; Elizabeth; Susan; and Naomi.

Ezekiel (8), son of Isaac (4), married Charity, daughter of Joseph Brittain. She died March 5th, 1847, aged 90. Their children were: Susan; Hannah; Isaac; Charles; Sarah; William; and Joseph.

Spencer (9), son of Isaac (4), married Mary Abel, of Easton, Pa., and had children: Spencer; Ezekiel; Fanny; and Rebecca.

Christopher (10), son of Isaac (4), married Mary, daughter of John McCollen, and had children: John; Henry; Prudence, wife of William Updike; Susan, wife of Samuel Biles; Sally, wife of Ralph Carlisle.

Obadiah (11), son of Isaac (4), died November 30th, 1844, aged 78, having married Sarah, daughter of William Biles. She died June 25th, 1833, aged 62. Their children were: Cornelia; Ezekiel, not married; Elizabeth, not married; William C. (12); Charles, married Mary Ann, daughter of John Cook, and had a daughter, Sarah, wife of William White; George S., married Letitia, daughter of William Yard, whose children are: George, Sarah E., and Frances; Sally Ann, married Richard Lilly; and Obadiah, married Louisa, daughter of James Tantum, and has children: Emma, wife of Leonard Kittenger, and Charles.

William (12), son of Obadiah (11), married, first, Hannah, daughter of John Borden, by whom he had Evalina, wife of

Thomas Gandy. By his second wife, Eve, daughter of Samuel Lawrence, he had: John; and William, cashier in the Bank of Freehold. By his third wife, Eliza, daughter of Richard Howell, who died at the age of 93, he had: Mary L.; and Joseph W.

Cornelia Howell, daughter of Obadiah (11), married John Hazard, a teacher, and had children: Howell, a Presbyterian clergyman, a graduate of Princeton Theological Seminary, married Ellen, daughter of William Stout; Mary, first wife of George Hunt, a resident of Philadelphia; Elizabeth, married Charles B. Smith; Jane, married Derrick H. Clifford; Sarah, married John Primmer; and Cornelia, married Mr. Hart.

The Hunt Family.

In the company of Englishmen that came to Long Island in 1652, to plant the town since known as Newtown, was Ralph Hunt (1). He was one of the seven patentees to whom, in behalf of themselves and associates, a grant was made by Gov.-Gen. Richard Nicholl, of the land on which Newtown was afterward built. He was, for many years, one of its first magistrates, and actively and prominently engaged in its business interests, as the records abundantly prove. He died 1677, leaving children: Ralph, removed to Jamaica; Edward (2); John, was, for several years, a magistrate; Samuel (3); Mary; and Ann, wife of Theophilus Phillips, (see Phillips family, No. 1.)

Edward (2), son of Ralph (1), became a man of estate, and died in Newtown, 1716, having married Sarah, daughter of Richard and Joanna Betts, who came from England to Ipswich, Mass., in 1648, thence to Newtown, L. I. Their children were: Edward (4); Richard, settled in Hunterdon county, N. J.; Ralph, there is good reason for believing that this is the Ralph who, in his will, made 1732, styles himself of Maidenhead, bequeathing one hundred and fifty acres in Hopewell to Edward, his brother, probably; Thomas; Jonathan (5); Sarah, married Silas Titus, (see Titus family, No. 3); Martha; Elizabeth; Hannah; and Abigail.

Edward (4), son of Edward (2), born February, 1684, came to Hunterdon county, N. J. He married Elizabeth, daughter of Jonathan and Hannah Laurenson. They had at least one son, John (6).

John (6), son of Edward (4), died 1769. By his wife, Margaret, had issue: Noah (7); Wilson (8); John (9); Jonathan, went South; Enoch, a colonel in the British army, his property administered upon in 1762, by Noah; Gershom, removed to North Carolina, in which state, and in Kentucky and Mississippi, his descendants are to be found; Daniel; Johanna; and Charity.

Noah (7), son of John (6), received the homestead, died October 5th, 1805, aged 81. By his wife, Sarah, he had children: Stephen, a trustee of the Pennington Church, who married Ruth Hunt, and had two sons, Noah H. and Asa R., both died young; and Achsah, married Josiah Vankirk, their daughter, Sarah, died in 1880, in her 93d year, by her marriage with Peter Z. Schenck, became the mother of John V., married Sarah A. Beaumont, Jane E., wife, first, of George W. Coryell, second, of Charles Steadman, Louisa, wife of Dr. Henry P. Welling, (see Welling family, No. 7,) Mary, wife of Dr. George White, (see White family, No. 6,) and of Rev. Noah Hunt, a graduate of Princeton College and Gambier Theological Seminary, was settled, first, at Chicago, afterward rector of Emmanuel Church, Baltimore, and now fills the rectorship of St. Ann Church, Brooklyn, in 1858, was editor of the "Western Churchman," Chicago, and in 1867, of the "Protestant Churchman," New York, he married Anna Pierce, daughter of Nathaniel G. Pendleton, of Cincinnati.

Wilson (8), son of John (6), who died 1782, aged 67, married Susannah, daughter of Mr. Price, of Wales. She died 1783, aged 68, leaving had children: Elijah, married, and died in 1760, aged 31, having a daughter, Hannah, died young, and Rachel, married Mr. Lightfoot; James (10); Abraham (11); Nathaniel, died 1825, aged 81, having married Miss Peets, of New York, and had children: Theodocia, Sallie, Wilson, Johns, of New York, and Fitz-Randolph; John, married, and had a daughter; Susanna, wife of Maj. Peter Gorden, U. S. A., of Trenton, who died 1823, aged 71; Margaret, married Mr. Johnes, of Lawrence; Charity, wife of Dr. De Camp, of Stoutsburg, surgeon in U. S. A., who died 1776, aged 23; John Price (12); Enoch, not married; Abigail, wife of Col. Stout; Joanna, died unmarried; and Naomi, married Peter Lott, to whose children, Peter and Naomi, mentioned in his will, he leaves property, he also mentions a granddaughter, Ruth Phillips, who may have been the child of another daughter married to a Phillips.

James (10), son of Wilson (8), died at the age of 93, having married Jemima, daughter of Joseph Green, (see Green family, No. 3,) by whom he had children: Joseph, married, and had children: Nancy, Peter, and Dora, he removed to the lake country of New York; Elijah, died unmarried; Peter (13); James, died unmarried; Wilson (14); Jonathan, took the homestead, married Mrs. Parks; Elizabeth, wife of Thomas Cox, of Monmouth; Susan, married John T. Blackwell; Rhoda, wife of David Mount; Jemima, wife of Jonathan Blackwell; and Nancy.

Adj.-Gen. Peter (13), son of James (10), was a trustee of the First Presbyterian Church of Trenton. He was a wealthy merchant, and had a spacious store at Lamberton, where was also his mansion; he died at Charleston, S. C., 1810, aged 42, where he was buried with military honors. By his marriage with Maria, daughter of Moore Furman, of Trenton, he had issue: Sarah Ann; Maria; Susannah Matilda; Furman; Peter—all of whom died unmarried; and William (15).

Capt. William Edgar (15), son of Peter (13), a captain in the United State Navy, was supposed to have perished at sea, while in command of the Levant, as nothing was ever heard of the ill-fated vessel, her captain, or crew. He married, first, Susan, daughter of Dr. James Clark, of Trenton, by whom he had children: Moore Furman; Annie and Sue, died young; James Clarke, captain in United States Regular Cavalry; Virginia H., wife of Lieut. Peter Hargous; William and Aubelsue, died young; and Annie Bellville, wife of Edward S. McIlvaine, (see McIlvaine family, No. 8.) By his second wife, Annie, sister of his former, he had: Sue, wife of Elmer E. Green; and Matilda, wife of Cleveland Hillson.

Wilson (14), son of James (10), married, and had children: William; George, resides in Monmouth county; Sarah; Thomas, of Brooklyn; and Wilson G., of New York.

Abraham (11), son of Wilson (8), became an eminent merchant of Trenton, and by his energy and great business talent, accumulated a large fortune. He was, for fifty-seven years, a trustee of the First Presbyterian Church of Trenton, to which he left, at his death, October 27th, 1821, aged 81, $100, and the same to the Episcopal Church. He was, for several years, postmaster of Trenton, and appointed by Benjamin Franklin, postmaster of the United States. He married, first, Theodocia Pearson, who died March 4th, 1784, aged 39, having had children: Pearson (16); Wilson, died, not married; Abram, died 1799, not married; Robert, was graduated at Princeton, admitted to the bar in 1799, removed to the South, and died, unmarried; Philemon, died young; Theodore (17); John Wesley (18); Theodocia; Charles; and Henrietta; last three died unmarried. His second wife was Mary Dagworthy, who died April 4th, 1814, aged 66.

Pearson (16), son of Abraham (11), who died November 4th, 1828, aged 63, married Rachel, sister of Charles and Joseph Higbee, of Trenton. She died April 7th, 1836, aged 71, having had children: Abraham, died young; Robert, a physician, established in Covington, Ky.; Theodocia Philadelphia, died 1844; Sallie, died 1818; and Westley P., who married Elizabeth, daughter of John Gulick, of Kingston, N. J., and their children were: Wilson, died 1856, William Edgar, died at St. Paul, Minn., and Louisa W.

Theodore (17), son of Abraham (11), captain in the United States Navy, married Anna Lucas, of St. Louis, by whom he has: Charles; Theodocia, married Henry Patterson, of Elizabeth, resides at St. Louis; Julia, wife of Maj. Turner, U. S. A., of St. Louis; and others.

John (18), son of Abraham (11), removed to Lexington, Ky., where he married Catharine Gross, and had children: Mary, wife of John H. Hanna; Theodocia, married George F. Strother, member of congress, of St. Louis; Robert Pearson, married Sallie Ward, widow of Col. Bigelow Lawrence, of Boston; Eleanor H., wife of Richard Curd; Henrietta, married Col. Calvin Morgan, of Huntsville, Ala., and became the mother of the noted General John Morgan, of the Confederate Army; Thomas; Catharine; Francis, married Julia, daughter of Dr. Elisha Warfield; Ann; and Charlton, married Rebecca Warfield, whose children are Elisha W. and Mary Thomas.

John Price (12), son of Wilson (8), married Margaret, daughter of Rev. John Guild, (see Guild family, No. 2.) Their children were: Azariah (19); Wilson Price, was the hero of Irving's "Astoria." John Jacob Astor, of New York, fitted out two expeditions for the mouth of the Columbia river, Oregon—one by sea, the other by land. The conduct of the land expedition was entrusted to Mr. Wilson P. Hunt, who is represented by Irving to have been a man "scrupulously upright and faithful in his dealings, amiable in his disposition, and of most pleasing manners." His enterprising spirit had early led him to engage in commerce at St. Louis, then a frontier town, where, by the knowledge which he gained of Indian tribes and traders, from his intercourse with them, he became especially fitted for his position. The skill with which he conducted the expedition over the new, perilous, and hitherto almost untrodden route of between two and three thousand miles, fully justified the high opinion that was entertained of his abilities. He was a partner in the company, and ultimately became the head of the establishment, at Astoria. He married Anna Lucas, widow of Theodore Hunt (No. 17), no children: Elijah (20); John Guild (21); Charity, wife of Joseph Wilson, of Asbury; Susan, wife of James Stevenson; Hetty, died 1862; and Mary Price, wife of John Bruere, of Allentown.

Azariah (19), son of John Price (12), married Widow Salter (Borden), whose children are: Borden; Philip L.; John, of Cape Girardeau; Robert, resided at St. Louis; Margaret, married William Pearson, of the United States Navy; and Mary, married Henry Pearson.

Elijah (20), son of John Price (12), settled in Easton, Pa., and married Susan, daughter of Capt. John Barnet, of that place, by whom he had children: Ellen, wife of Ralph Guild; and John, married Maria White, of Easton.

John Guild (21), son of John Price (12), married Rebecca, daughter of Samuel Titus, and had by her: Samuel, died in Cuba; Wilson, married Hannah Blackwell; Robert, married, first, Miss McPherson, second, Sarah Lemon; John Stevenson, married, first, Caroline Atchley, second, Henrietta, daughter of John Jones, (see Jones family, No. 4); their children are Joshua and Guild.

John (9), son of John (6), married, and had children: John, who married Mary Carpenter, and died 1789, had a daughter, Eliza, wife of John Welch, of Boston; Wilson; Margaret, wife of James Wilson, of Amwell; and Rebecca, wife of Gershom Lambert.

Jonathan (5), son of Edward (2), came to this township not long after 1700. He married Phebe, daughter of Content Titus, (see Titus family, No. 2.) Their children were: Edward (22); Jonathan (23); Richard (24); Phebe; Elizabeth; and Hannah, who became the second wife of Andrew Muirheid, (see Muirheid family, No. 2.)

Edward (22), son of Jonathan (5), married Hannah Drake, and had children: Oliver (25); Benjamin, born March 1st, 1758, married Sarah, daughter of Samuel Furman, and had one child, Margaret, wife of Elias Scudder Hunt; Varnel (26); Willah, born March 25th, 1763, married Thomas Skillman, of Cranbury; Charlotte, married her cousin, Israel Hunt; Sarah; Richard (27); Jonathan, born 1770; Mary, born 1772; Joab, born 1775; Hannah, born 1777; and Henry, born 1780.

Oliver (25), son of Edward (22), born August 16th, 1754; lived on his estate, near Princeton, known as Cherry Hill. He married Elizabeth, daughter of Samuel Furman, and had children: Sarah, married Richard Bond, of Trenton; Elizabeth, wife of Rev. David

Bartine, of the Methodist Church; Samuel Furman, graduated at Princeton with honors, was a lawyer of Cincinnati, where he died; and John (28).

Dr. John (28), son of Oliver (25), graduated at Princeton and at the New York Medical College. He settled in the Miami valley, Ohio, where he practiced his profession over forty years. He married there, Amanda Baird, and had children: Elizabeth; Oliver; Anna, died young; John R.; Samuel F.; James; Alethia, wife of Isaac Wetherby; Edith, died young; and Anna.

Varnel (26), son of Edward (22), married Achsah Pierson, and had by her: Pierson; Siliman; Eliza; Jonathan, died in Mississippi; Theodore, not married; Hannah; Jane; Benjamin, died in Mississippi, not married; Caroline, married Mr. Smith; and Charlotte, married Mr. Smith.

Richard (27), son of Edward (22), born May 4th, 1768, and died 1833; married, first, Ruth Smith. She died November 24th, 1824, having had children: Cornelia, died 1841; Abijah; Elias Scudder, who married, first, Margaret, daughter of Benjamin Hunt, and had children, Richard and Abijah, died young, his second wife was Hannah Bateman; Randolph S.; Mary V.; Joab, studied medicine, and practiced his profession in Mississippi, where he died, not married; Jane, wife of James Cook, (see Cook family, No. 9); and Charles. His second wife was Sarah, daughter of Jedediah Scudder, (see Scudder family, No. 14,) and widow of Samuel Green. She died September 11th, 1872, aged 89, leaving a daughter, Louisa C., wife of Elijah L. Hendrickson, (see Hendrickson family, No. 18.)

Jonathan (23), son of Jonathan (5), married Abigail North, and had children: Daniel; Israel (29); Jonathan (30); Jesse (31); Richard (32); Jeremiah, died unmarried; Reuben (33); Rebecca, married Benjamin Lawrence; Mary C.; Abigail; and Abijah, lived in Mississippi, and died there, unmarried—he fell in a duel with Poindexter.

Israel (29), son of Jonathan (23), married Charlotte, daughter of Edward Hunt. Their children were: Mary, wife of Rev. John Boggs, of the Baptist Church, whose children are Elizabeth and Mary Jane; Charles, died young; Hannah, married John Vanderveer; John, married Lucy Servis, and had children: David, Wesley, and Dr. John; and Wesley, married Louisa, daughter of Joab Titus, of Hopewell.

Jonathan (30), son of Jonathan (23), married, first, Miss Stout, and had children: David, married Miss Calvitt, of Mississippi, in which state he owned and lived on a large plantation. He was an earnest friend of education, and became one of the founders of Oakland College of that state, of which he was ever after the generous supporter; he was also the liberal contributor of $50,000 to the Colonization Society; Andrew, a successful physician, resident at New York, where he married; and Henry, located near Ringoes, and married Ida Z. Schenck, their children were: Jonathan and Anna Mary, wife of Dr. Jacob Ludlow, of Easton, Pa. His second wife was Mary Salter.

Jesse (31), son of Jonathan (23), married Elizabeth, daughter of John Hunt. He removed to Cincinnati, where he became wealthy. Their children were: George N., not married; Louisa, died young; Jane Frances, married Hon. Nathaniel G. Pendleton, formerly member of congress, and father of Hon. George H. Pendleton, United States senator from Ohio, and of Anna P., wife of Rev. Noah Hunt Schenck, D. D.

Richard (32), son of Jonathan (23), married Miss Stevens, whose children are: Benjamin, went south and was drowned; Margaret, married Mr. Hamilton; and Maria, married.

Reuben (33), son of Jonathan (23), who died 1832, aged 58, married Valeria Mershon, she died 1834, aged 60, having had children: Jeremiah, settled in Ohio; Lewis, settled and died in Missouri; Harvey, went west and there died; Dr. Charles, located in Illinois; James, a lawyer, settled in Ohio; Cicero (34); Augustus (35); Catharine, married Ralph Mershon, whose children are: Eleanor, Harrison and Lewis; Juliet; Eleanor, married Dr. John Thomas, has a daughter Eusebia; Sarah, married Nathaniel Furman, principal of the High School at Newtown, Pa.

Dr. Cicero (34), son of Reuben (33), a physician at Ringoes, married Annie, daughter of Robert Iredell, of Hatborough, Pa. Their children are: Robert I., married Catharine Skillman; Frances M., wife of A. J. McCrea; Mary, wife of Andrew Blackwell; Louisa, wife of Jacob J. Fisher.

Augustus (35), son of Reuben (33), married Wilhemina Williamson, and resides in Philadelphia. Their children are: David W.; Cicero; Annie I.; Sallie W.; Mary K.; Emma; and Howard A.

Richard (24), son of Jonathan (5), died January 1st, 1821, aged 83, having married Jemima Blackwell, she died January 9th, 1814, aged 64, both buried in Pennington. Their children were: Phebe, wife of Henry Vandyke, of Princeton; Elizabeth; Kesiah; Harriet; Catharine, married Mr. Grover; Jemima, wife of Abram Vanpelt; Jonathan, who died December 10th, 1848, aged 67; married Rebecca Blue, who died April 15th, 1852, aged 71, buried in Pennington, they had children: Richard, went west, Maria, Ezekiel, Eliza, Martha Ann, and Blackwell.

Samuel (3), son of Ralph (1), came from Long Island to Maidenhead, N. J. His will is dated January 15th, 1717. His children were: Samuel (36), who inherited the homestead; Ralph; and John owned land on Stony Brook, in Maidenhead and Hopewell; Elizabeth; Anna; Mary; Thomas; Jesse; and Edward.

Samuel (36), son of Samuel (3), will dated March 13th, 1752, by his wife, Abigail, had children: Samuel (37), inherited the homestead; Richard (38), inherited the Coxe tract of 460 acres; John, who died unmarried; and Thomas (39), inherited the Bainbridge tract of 650 acres; Ralph (40); Sarah, married Mr. Price; Martha, married Sampson Dildine, and had children: Uriah, died unmarried, aged 90, Abby, wife of Enos Goble, died aged 96, Samuel, died unmarried, aged 92, Richard, married Anna Opdike, Abraham, John, Ralph, Thomas, married Dorothy Divers, and Sarah; and Abigail, married John Oxford, an Englishman, their children were: Samuel, married Margaret McDonald, John, married Eleanor Polhemus, Joanna, Nancy, wife of John Kenney, president of the Belvidere Bank, Abigail, wife of William Parks, Abraham, married Polly McMurtry, Jonathan, married Ellen Kenney, Sarah, wife of Thomas Bowlsby, and Martha, wife of Robert Oxford.

Samuel (37), son of Samuel (36), will dated 1783, by his wife, Sarah, had children: Samuel, who inherited the homestead farm; he was taken prisoner by the Tripolitans, money was sent out to redeem him, but he never returned. His sisters: Abigail; Rebecca; Sarah; Anna; and Elizabeth, inherited the farm. One of them married a Hunt; Elizabeth, married Philip Van Cleve, whose descendants are now living on a part of the old place.

Richard (38), son of Samuel (36), of Sussex county, N. J., whose will was dated 1814, had children: Richard; David, a physician, married Sally Roy; Samuel; Joseph; Thomas, married Catharine Dodder; John; William, of Morris county, N. J., married Miss Cooper; Ralph, went west; Sarah, wife of George Armstrong; Elizabeth, wife of John Hankinson; Patty, wife of John ——, a member of congress; and David, practiced medicine in Newton, N. J., died, leaving two children.

Thomas (39), son of Samuel (36), was a prisoner three years during the French and Indian war. In 1770, he married Tabitha Cook, whose children were : Abraham, married, first, Miss Allen ; second, Eunice Wells ; third, Elizabeth Everett ; Thomas, married Miss Turner ; Samuel, married Miss Greer ; Sarah, wife of Joseph Allen ; Daniel, married Mary Kercuff ; Rebecca, wife of William Allen.

Ralph (40), son of Samuel (36), married May 7th, 1768, Elizabeth, daughter of Joseph Phillips, of Maidenhead, (see Phillips family, No. 8). Their children were : John (41) ; Joseph, born December, 1769, married Ann Hibler, died 1829, no children ; Samuel (42) ; Theophilus (43) ; Ralph (44) ; Richard, died unmarried ; Thomas (45) ; Sarah, died March 12th, 1859, aged 81, having married Samuel Wells, had a daughter, Eunice, wife of Ralph Dildine ; Abigail, wife of Joseph Hill ; Martha, died unmarried, 1827, aged 40 ; Mary, wife of Absalom Price, died June 4th, 1850, aged 67 ; and Elizabeth, wife of Charles Roy, whose children were : Theophilus, Robert, Sarah, Martha, and William.

John (41), son of Ralph (40), who died 1846, aged 77, married Anna, daughter of Samuel Hill, she died January 31st, 1854, aged 80. Their children are : Sarah ; and Joshua, died in infancy ; Samuel, born June 5th, 1814, married Mary P. Hill ; and Mary, born August 22d, 1818, wife of Daniel Budd.

Samuel (42), son of Ralph (40), married Sarah Coats, and had children : Abraham, married, and lives in Michigan ; John, married, and lives in Tennessee ; Ralph, married, and lives in Michigan ; and Mary Ann, married, and resides in Michigan.

Theophilus (43), son of Ralph (40), died October 15th, 1846, having married Margaret Armstrong, and had children : Elizabeth, wife of Hampton Andress ; Sarah Ann, wife of Benjamin A. Potter ; Dorinda, wife of George Turner ; Theophilus, married Miss Hunt ; and Margaret, wife of Peter C. Osborn.

Ralph (44), son of Ralph (40), died 1858, aged 73, having married Hannah Budd, and had children : Theodore, married Celeste Struble ; Joseph B., married Phebe Roof ; Julia E. ; Adeline D., wife of J. Miller Hager ; Abby M., wife of Charles Hardin.

Thomas (45), son of Ralph (40), died January 21st, 1864, having married Eliza Wigton, and had children : Martha, wife of Jacob Wigton ; Mary Louisa, married Mr. Mains ; William, married Miss Hibler ; Savilla, wife of James Decker.

The Jones Family.

John Jones (1) was a native of Wales, settled in Pennsylvania, and by his wife Katharine, a native of Holland, had sons: Joshua (2), and two others. Their mother gave each a sixteen-dollar gold piece, one of which is still in the possession of one of her great-great-great grandsons.

Joshua (2), son of John (1), came from Pennsylvania, in the year 1758, purchased a farm in Ewing, on which he resided, and married Prudence, daughter of John Scudder, (see Scudder family, No. 10,) he died 1811, aged 85, she two years afterwards, aged 82, having had children: Benjamin (3); Mary, died 1821, aged 54; and Phebe, married Isaac Wynkoop, and had children: Mary, wife of Isaac Lanning, Joshua, married Catharine Anderson, and Isaac, married, first, Rachel, daughter of Jesse Hunt, and second, Maria, daughter of Abner Scudder, (see Scudder family, No. 15.)

Benjamin (3), son of Joshua (2), who died 1820, aged 60, married Catharine, daughter of Joshua Anderson, of Pennsylvania, she died 1833, aged 69, having had children: Joshua, married Rebecca, daughter of James Cole, no children; John (4); Daniel A., married Sophia Manly, and died in Kentucky; Elias S., married Margaret Mackey; Charles, married Margaret Cook; Isaac Brearley, married successively Isabella Morrison, and Hannah, daughter of Lott Phillips; Joseph; Elizabeth, married, first, Allen Holcomb, second, William Wilson; Prudence, married Cornelius Anderson; and Mary, married John M. Schamp.

John (4), son of Benjamin (3), who died September 23d, 1868, aged 82, married Mary, daughter of William Green, (see Green family, No. 41,) she died March 2d, 1858, aged 70, having had children: Enoch G. (5); Amos Scudder, not married; Lydia, died 1858, aged 47; Joshua, married Elizabeth Corlies, of Trenton; Alfred, married Caroline Mathews; William (6); Samuel A., married Susan Barnes, of Philadelphia; Henrietta, married John S. Hunt; and Phebe, married Theodore S. Howell.

Enoch G. (5), son of John (4), married Margaretta, daughter of James Hay, and had children: Richard, married Mary, daughter of William A. Green, (see Green family, No. 18); Lamar, married Mary Williamson; and Cornelia, wife of Alfred Reeder.

William (6), son of John (4), married Elizabeth, daughter of John Wesley Burroughs, (see Burroughs family, No. 24,) whose children are: Sarah; Mary Ellen; Lydia; and John, died in infancy.

The Lanning Family.

There is a tradition in this family that three brothers, of the name of Lanning, came originally from Wales, and settled on Long Island. They removed, soon afterward, to New Jersey. One bought land in the northern part, another in the southern section of the colony, and Robert, from whom the Lannings of this part of the colony descend, settled in Maidenhead, now Lawrenceville. His name is found among the grantees of the land on which to build a church in that village, in 1698–1699.

Robert (1) is thought to have married Miss Hart. Their children were: Stephen (2); Ralph (3); Richard (4); John (5); Daniel (6); Robert (7); Frances, who was baptized at Maidenhead, July 13th, 1715, and married Jonathan Furman, (see Furman family, No. 2); Martha, married, first, Mr. Phelps, who lived in Warren county, N. J., and second, Mr. Allen, no children by either husband; Mercy, married Elijah Jones.

Stephen (2), son of Robert (1), died in 1780. By his wife, Abigail, daughter of Ralph Hart, (see Hart family, No. 1,) had children: Ralph (8); Robert (9); Elijah (10); Stephen (11); Sarah, who married Joseph Scudder, of Lawrenceville; Abigail, married Israel Jones, and had children: Elizabeth, the second wife of Joshua Reed, (see Reed family, No. 5), Ralph, who never married, Joel, who married Theodosia, daughter of Ralph Lanning, Stephen, who married Sarah, another daughter of Ralph Lanning, and Hulda, who died unmarried; Mary, married Mr. Cook, and they had children: Rebecca, Elias, and Hannah; Elizabeth, married Henry Pierson; Mercy, died unmarried, in 1784, aged about 80.

Ralph (8), son of Stephen (2), married Elizabeth Jones, sister of Israel Jones. She died March 17th, 1808, aged 68. They had children: Samuel, died unmarried, in 1814, aged 46; Joseph (12); Mary, married Joshua Reed, (see Reed family, No. 5); Elizabeth, married Elijah Hendrickson, (see Hendrickson family, No. 8); Abigail, died unmarried, in 1838, aged 78; Sarah, married George

Beaver, and lived in the upper part of Hunterdon county; Joshua, married, and had children, Lydia and Abner.

Robert (9), son of Stephen (2), married Jemima, daughter of John Smith, of Lawrenceville. Their children were: John (13); Nancy, died unmarried, in 1847, aged 84; Stephen, died young; Joshua (14).

Joseph (12), son of Ralph (8), married Mary Jones, who died May 10th, 1819, aged 44. He died April 24th, 1823, aged 54. Their children were: George, died 1830, unmarried; Samuel, married Frances Britton, and died October 26th, 1841, aged 34, and she died June 20th, 1858, in her 51st year; Mary, married Gilbert Roe, of Trenton, whose children were: George, Joseph, and Sarah.

John (13), son of Robert (9), died May 28th, 1852, aged 86. He married Elizabeth, daughter of Samuel Hart. She died January 21st, 1852, aged 81. Their children were: Samuel Hart (15); Jemima, who married Aaron Furman; Martha, who married Amos Furman, brother of Aaron, (see Furman family, Nos. 12 and 13); Ann, died unmarried, October, 1837, aged 37; Cornelia, died unmarried, October, 1854, aged 45.

Samuel Hart (15), son of John (13), died September 23d, 1851, aged 58; married Eleanor, daughter of Henry Cook. They had children: Eliza Ann, married William Ashmore; Henry (16).

Henry (16), son of Samuel Hart (15), married, first, Hannah, daughter of Samuel M. Green, (see Green family, No. 44.) She died October 14th, 1851, aged 23. Their only child was Hannah, wife of William Henry Reed. He married, second, the widow Matilda Ashmore (Hillman).

Joshua (14), son of Robert (9), married, first, Catharine Vankirk, and had children: Charles, who married Hannah, daughter of Matthias Perrine, of Cross Roads; John, married Sarah, daughter of Asher Temple, (see Temple family, No. 8.) who had a son, Benjamin; Stephen, married a daughter of Henry Killer; Jemima, married George Hunt, son of Theophilus Hunt; Elizabeth, married Nathaniel Tomlinson, (see Tomlinson family, No. 5); Mary Ann, married Samuel Craft, son of George Craft. He married, second, Leah Hoagland; no issue. He died August, 1863, aged 93.

Elijah (10), son of Stephen (2), married Sarah Mershon. He died October, 1793, aged 40, and she died December 11th, 1831, aged 79. They are both buried in the Ewing graveyard. They had children: Mary, who married Theophilus Furman, (see Furman family, No. 14,) and died in 1845; Eunice, married Timothy Hendrickson, (see Hendrickson family, No. 17,) and died August 15th, 1839, aged 60; Elijah (17); Nathaniel (18); Jemima, died, unmarried, in 1845, aged 55; Abigail, never married, and died March 10th, 1845, aged 64; Angeline, married John Paxson, and had children: Sarah, married Horace English, and lives in Philadelphia, Julia, married Jonathan Cook, son of Anthony Cook, Rachel, married Jedediah Green, and lives in Philadelphia, and Hannah, wife of George T. Price, of Cecilton, Md.

Elijah (17), son of Elijah (10), married Mary, daughter of John Burroughs, (see Burroughs family, No. 6,) and died in 1845. Their children were: Randolph; Edward; Sarah; Angeline, wife of Amos Phillips; Mary Frances, who married Edward Phillips, son of John Phillips; Charles Henry.

Nathaniel (18), son of Elijah (10), was, for many years, an elder in the Ewing Church. He married Mary, daughter of Henry Howell, and died January 25th, 1845, aged 69. His wife died May 25th, 1840, aged 52. Their children were: Elijah Webster (19): Elizabeth; Rebecca, married James L. Woodward; Nathaniel, married Harriet Gustin; James, a merchant in Philadelphia, married Rebecca Boyd; John, married Fanny Beach; Sarah, died young, in 1856.

Elijah Webster (19), son of Nathaniel (18), is an elder of the Ewing Church. By his first wife, Cornelia, daughter of William Mershon, who died 1854, aged 29, he had two children: William M., married Jennie Hemenway, and Wallace, married Bell Cadwallader; and second, by Sarah, daughter of Nathaniel Coleman, (see Coleman family, No. 5,) had children: Alfred M., married Ella G. Cox; Cornelia Jane; Herbert; Harry Webster.

Stephen (11), son of Stephen (2), who died 1798, married Elsie Reed, and had children: Samuel (20); Nathaniel (21); Daniel (22); John (23); Stephen (24); Naomi, died, unmarried;- Mary, died, unmarried.

Samuel (20), son of Stephen (11), married, and had children: Susan, who married Mr. Morris; Mary Ann, married in Philadelphia; Amy, wife of Mr. Lee, and lives in Ohio; Phebe, married, and lives in Pennsylvania; Elizabeth, married Mr. McKinney; Hetty, married, and lives in Ohio; Martha, married Mr. Jones, of Philadelphia; Rebecca, married in Ohio, as did Mahala; Nicholas, married, and settled in Ohio.

Nathaniel (21), son of Stephen (11), married Miss Lee, and had children: John, married in Warren county, N. J.; Amos, married Hulda Thorn, of Bordentown; Nathaniel, married; Samuel, married, and lives in Luzerne county, Pa.; Thisbe; Penina.

Daniel (22), son of Stephen (11), was a man of distinction, and was the proprietor of a large iron furnace at Oxford, Warren county, N. J., where he died, in the winter of 1862, aged 89. His children were: Charles; Stephen; Daniel; John; Eliza; Fanny; Polly; Mary; Mahala.

John (23), son of Stephen (11), married Rachel, daughter of Patrick Young, and had children: Jesse, who married Lucretia Wetherill, near Princeton; William, married Mary, daughter of Matthew Wetherill; Isaiah, married Lydia Carter, of Burlington; Elizabeth; Naomi; Susan.

Stephen (24), son of Stephen (11), died 1826; married Mary, daughter of Isaac Smith. Their children were: Horace, who married Jane, daughter of William Beatty, of Ewing; Enoch, who married Harriet Beatty; Smith, married Elizabeth Knox; Samuel, married Mary Beatty, sister of Jane and Harriet Beatty, aforementioned; Joseph, married in Philadelphia; Susan, married William Wells.

Ralph (3), son of Robert (1), was a second lieutenant in Captain Hunt's Company, First Regiment, Hunterdon Militia, in the Revolutionary War. He married, first, Elizabeth, sister of Jasper Smith, of Lawrenceville, and second, Mary, daughter of Amos Hart, (see Hart family, No. 15.) He died in 1798. His children were: Amos (25); Ralph; Daniel; Jasper (26); Noah (27).

Amos (25), son of Ralph (3), married Lois Reed, sister of Hezekiah Reed. Their children were: Amos (29); Ralph (30); William, who married Anna Appelgate, and moved to western New York; Sarah, married Asa Reed, (see Reed family, No. 10); Hezekiah, married Susan Boswell; Elizabeth, married Richard Hart, (see Hart family, No. 11); Jasper, married, first, Mary Vankirk, and second, her sister, Phebe Vankirk. They lived, also, in western New York.

Jasper (26), son of Ralph (3), married Keziah Reed, who died in 1812. They had one child, Abijah (28).

Noah (27), son of Ralph (3), married Theodosia Smith. Their children were: Isabella, who married Reuben Hendrickson, (see Hendrickson family, No. 12); Sarah, married Charles Cook, (see Cook family, No. 11.)

Abijah (28), son of Jasper (26), married Ann, daughter of Joseph Green, (see Green family, No. 38,) and had one child, Jasper, who married Rebecca Garwood, and had children: Maria, and Keziah, wife of Abner Jones.

Amos (29), son of Amos (25), married, first, Jemima, daughter of Joshua Furman, (see Furman family, No. 4,) in 1815, and had children: Jasper, who married Miss Budd, and lived in Wisconsin; Amanda, married Mahlon Fulton, of Phlladelphia; Eliza, married Smith Mitchner, of Philadelphia; Mary Ann, married Andrew Stanley, of Salem; Sarah Matilda, married Henry Furman, son of Joseph Furman. He married, second, Catherine, daughter of John Anthony, of Dutch Neck. Their children were: Amos, married Ann Mary Neil, of Trenton; Charles Wesley, married Sarah M. Wykoff, of Flemington; Theodore, married Mary Jane White; William, married Sarah McChesney, of Trenton; Henry B., married Mary, daughter of Edward Gardner, of Elizabcth; Emma, married Cruzer Snedeker; Martha; Caroline; Frederic.

Ralph (30), son of Amos (25), was, for many years, an elder in the Ewing Church, and died May 4th, 1843, aged 57. His wife died November 8th, 1842. She was Mary, daughter of Isaac Wynkoop, by whom he had issue: Isaac, a lawyer of Trenton, who married Ruth Van Schaick; Phebe, married Charles Torbert, of Bucks county, Pa.; Theodore, married Eliza Van Schaick; Rebecca, married Simon Prall, of Pennsylvania; Amos, married Elizabeth Wilkins; David, married Caroline, daughter of James Brearley, of Lawrenceville, (see Brearley family, No. 11); Elizabeth, married Simon Van Arsdalen, of Pennsylvania; Gerardus, married Amanda Norton; William, married Catharine, daughter of Joseph Rue Burroughs, of Hopewell, (see Burroughs family, No. 29); Ralph Augustus.

Richard (4), son of Robert (1), was a teacher, and married Sybil Rose, sister of the first Stephen Rose, and they had children: David (31); Phebe, who became blind, and died unmarried, July 21st, 1832, aged 83; Zenos, married Rachel Garretson; Hannah, married Joseph Green, (see Green family, No. 38); Rachel, married Joseph Knowles; Sarah, married Ralph Hart, (see Hart family, No. 8); Rhoda, married Mr. O'Neil, of Washington, D. C., by whom she had a daughter, Margaret, whose first husband was Lieut. Timberlake, of U. S. Navy. After his death she married General John Henry Eaton, U. S. Senator from Tennessee, afterward secretary of war during the administration of President Jackson. By both of these husbands she had children. Her third husband was an Italian named Antonio Buchignani, a teacher of music. One of her daughters married into the distinguished Virginia family of Randolph, and another Miss Virginia Timberlake, a young lady of great personal beauty, became the wife of the Duke de Sampago, of Paris, and the mother-in-law of one of the Rothschilds. Mrs. Eaton, for in after years she took the name of her second husband, died in 1879, aged 83.

David (31), son of Richard (4), died June 4th, 1824, aged 86. He was one of the guides to General Washington's army on the morning of the battle of Trenton. For anecdote of David Lanning, see Barber and Howe Historical Collections of New Jersey. He married Mary, daughter of Philip Palmer, who died September 21st, 1852, aged 88. Their children were: Ralph (32); William (33); Elizabeth; Susan, married Nathaniel Snook, died 1832, aged 30.

Ralph (33), son of David (31), married Phebe Ashton, and their children were: Amanda, married Joseph Stout; Margaret, married William Burroughs, son of Joseph Burroughs, no issue; Letitia, married William Doran; Sarah, married Peter Hoagland.

William (34), son of David (31), married Nancy, daughter of Emanuel Pidcock, and their children were named: Mary; Susan, who married William Savage, of Philadelphia; Charles, married Louisa Savage, of Philadelphia, whose children are named: William, Adelaide and Frances.

John (5), son of Robert (1), lived on his farm near Lawrenceville, still occupied by his grandson, Absalom Price Lanning (35). He died 1816, aged about 80, having married Martha, daughter of Edward Hunt, of Lawrence. They had children: Edward (34); Elizabeth, married Elijah Hart, (see Hart family, No. 7); Mary, married John Lawrence, of Princeton, a teacher, and in 1862, was in her 95th year; Sarah, died unmarried; Martha, in 1862, was in her 93d year; Abigail, married Thomas Hooper, of Dutch Neck; Charity, married Moses Allen, of Warren county, N. J.; Susan, married John Frenor, of Dutch Neck.

Edward (34), son of John (5), died in 1859, aged 85. He married, first, Ann, daughter of Benjamin Bryant, of Hopewell, she died in 1857, aged 52. Their children were: John; Benjamin; Margaret; Ann—all four died in childhood; Elizabeth, married Cornelius Vandyke; Sarah, married Horace Varian;

Martha Ann, married Jacob Golder; Absalom Price (35). He married, second, Rachel Hankins, who survived him—no children.

Absalom Price (35), son of Edward (34), married Henrietta Drake, and their children were named: John E., a graduate of Princeton, prosecutor of the pleas of Monmouth county, married Mary, daughter of William Scudder, (see Scudder, family, No. 121); Mercer, married Emma Garten; and Thomas.

Daniel (6), son of Robert (1), was baptized at Lawrenceville, in 1713, and his will is recorded in 1771. He married a sister of Jonathan Furman. He was a surveyor and lived near Ewingville. Their children were: Jemima, married Jasper Smith, of Lawrenceville, and died, aged 96; Hannah, who died about 1830, aged 88, married William Hart, son of Benjamin Hart, (see Hart family, No. 3); Elizabeth, who married Robert Furman, (see Furman family, No. 7,) died at 90 years of age; Prudence, married Samuel Cook, father of Justice Daniel Cook, of Lawrenceville, their only child was over 90 years of age at her death; John, a physician, died unmarried, aged 80, at Reading, Pa., where he practiced; Robert (36); Daniel (37); James (38); Enoch, died Young; Israel, died young. The children of Jasper and Jemima Smith were: Daniel, a graduate of Princeton College, a lawyer by profession, and resided in Sunbury, Pa; Asher, who lived at the homestead; Hannah, who married Daniel Clark, (see Clark family, No. 6); Sarah, married Elias Scudder, (see Scudder family, No. 16); Elizabeth, married Richard Hill; Jasper, died 1832, young; Prudence, married, first, William Mershon, of Lawrenceville, by whom she had children: Samuel and Mary, and second, Joseph Patterson, who died 1838, aged 58, by whom she had Mary, wife of Dr. Allison Perrine, of Monmouth county, she died in 1867, aged 90.

Robert (36), son of Daniel (6), lived and died in Sussex county, N. J., having married Sarah, daughter of John Coryell, and sister of Judge George Coryell, of New Hope, Pa. They had children: John (39); Daniel; Mary, married Israel Hart; Nancy; Frances; Prudence, married Mr. Van Syckle, of Sussex county; Sarah, married William, son of Judge Montgomery Reading, of Sussex county.

Daniel (37), son of Daniel (6), lived in Owego, New York, where he married Miss Warring. He afterwards removed to Canada, where he died, leaving children: Amos; Daniel; John; Robert, Hulda; Sarah; Mary.

James (38), son of Daniel (6), married Nancy Edge, of Philadelphia, and died in 1842, aged 89. Their children were: George (40); William, who married Harriet Smith, of Trenton; Elizabeth, married Joel Gordon, of Philadelphia; Rhoda, married Henry Ashmore; Nancy; Hannah.

John (39), son of Robert (36), lived in Owego, New York. Was an extensive merchant, owning several stores. He died by a fall through a trap door. His wife was a daughter of Judge Hallenbach, of Pennsylvania. They had children; Augustus, who married Amanda, daughter of Dr. Crystal, and he is a merchant residing in Wilkesbarre, Pa.; Matthias, married Ann Overton, of Owego, and lives on Wyalusing creek; John, married Juliet, daughter of Asa Trumar, of Owego, where he lives; Mary Ann, married John Rosette, a merchant, whose children are: Mary Ann, wife of Dr. John Ludlow, son of Rev. Dr. John Ludlow, provost of the University of Pennsylvania, Elizabeth, wife of John Brodhead, Ellen, wife of Anthony Drexel, the distinguished banker of Philadelphia, and Sarah; Sarah, another daughter of John (39), married Dr. Ezekiel Phelps, of Owego; Emily, married John Taylor, a lawyer of Owego.

George (40), son of James (38), lived in Morrisville, Pa. He married Mary, daughter of Joshua Furman, of Ewing, (see Furman family, No. 4,) and their children were: Enoch, married Mary, daughter of William Gillingham, of Morrisville, and lives in Philadelphia; Andrew; Joshua Furman, married Phebe, daughter of Dr. John Howell, of Philadelphia, in which city he is a merchant; William B., married Rachel, daughter of Abner Margeram, of Morrisville, Pa.; Sarah Ann, married Matson Preston, of Morrisville; Rebecca, married William Kitson; Mary, married Thomas Bailey, of Morrisville, and lives in Atlanta, Georgia.

Robert (7), son of Robert (1), married Judith Baker, living near New Brunswick, he died in 1808. Their children were: John; Daniel; Enoch; Robert; William; Deborah; Martha; Judith, who married a Mr. Abbott; Hester; Achsah; Susannah.

The Lott Family.

Much obscurity rests on the family of Lott, difficult, in the absence of family records, to remove. The family was originally from Holland. Their name appears early among the settlers of Flatbush and Newtown, L. I., and we find them intermarried with the most prominent Dutch families of those towns. From that region came Peter Lott and took up his residence in Trenton, while his brother Hendrick (1) purchased a large body of land some six miles further up the river, a part of which he afterwards sold to Joshua Jones and Amos Scudder. Who constituted his family it seems impossible now to determine with certainty. We know through the will of his brother Peter, in which he expresses his desire to be buried with his parents on Long Island, that he had a son Peter; this is he, probably, who lies in the Ewing Church ground, whose tombstone says Peter Lott, late of Long Island, died April 14th, 1753, aged 30. Elizabeth, who married Daniel Clark, about 1760, and Jane, who married Timothy Smith, were probably daughters of his. Individuals of this name seem to have married into nearly all the prominent families of Ewing and Pennington. We conjecture also that the following recorded name was a son of his :

Richard Lott (2), who died 1784, married Letitia Phillips ; issue, Theophilus, died young in 1786, leaving his property to his brothers, Richard and Peter and to his sisters Hannah, Jane, and others ; Ezekiel, married Anna Burrowes ; Richard (3); Peter, married Miss Burrowes, and went west ; Charity, married Ezekiel Howell, (see Howell family, No. 13); Mary, married Jonathan Muirheid, (see Muirheid family, No. 3); Abia, married Vincent Wetherill ; Hannah, married John Wetherill, of Cranbury, and had one child, Abia, married Isaac Scudder, (see Scudder family, No. 126,) of Cranbury ; Jane, died unmarried ; Fama, married Mr. Carlisle ; Catharine, married Thomas McDowell.

Richard (3), son of Richard (2), who died about 1847, aged 75, was twice married, first, to Fanny Burrowes, and by her had Lambert, not married; Theophilus, married Mary Lawyer, whose children are: Richard, married Mary Simpson, Francina, died, aged 20, John, died in youth, and Mary Ann; Abigail, married Ezekiel Rose, of Salem county; John, not married; Ebenezer, married Mary King, lived in Salem; Eliza, married Moses King, of Salem. By his second wife, Miss Applegate, he had one son, Richard, not married.

A Peter Lott died 1720, leaving five children, one of whom was Peter. The name was not unfrequent in the neighboring towns.

The McIlvaine Family.

The family of McIlvaine, in Scotland, is of great antiquity. The first of this family of whom we find record was Allane McIlvaine, who had a charter of the lands of Grumet and Attiquia from James V., October 16th, 1529. His son, Gilbert McIlvaine, had a charter of confirmation of the lands of Grumet from Queen Mary, dated May 4th, 1546. After several generations, William (2), son of Joseph (1), came to America, in what year is not known, having married Anne, daughter of Caleb Emerson and Mary North, a descendant of Right Hon. Dudley North. Caleb Emerson is descended, as is attested by a carefully preserved genealogy, from Sir Theophilus Emerson, a valiant knight, who came over with William the Conqueror, he being in the sixth generation from the German Robert Count Hobspruck. The children of this marriage were: William (3); Joseph (4); and Mary, who died November, 1818, aged 66, having married Governor Joseph Bloomfield, son of Dr. Moses Bloomfield, of Middlesex county, a member of the bar, a captain in a New Jersey regiment, ordered to Canada in 1775, was attorney-general of state, a trustee of Princeton College, elected governor in 1785, and for several successive terms, appointed brigadier-general in the war of 1812, and represented the state in congress from 1816 to 1821. He died October 3d, 1823, aged 70, and though a Presbyterian, is buried in the old church-yard of St. Mary's Episcopal Church, Burlington, N. J.

Dr. William (3), son of William (2), having received his medical education at Edinburgh University, became a physician, settled first in Bristol, afterward in Burlington. He married, first, Margaret, daughter of William Rodman, of Pennsylvania, she died February 22d, 1781, aged 29. Their children were: Hannah, died in infancy; Rachel; married Dr. Ruan; Mary Ann, married Gen. Jonathan Rhea; and Elizabeth, died in childhood, is buried with her mother in the Episcopal church-yard at Bristol. His second wife was Rebecca, daughter of William Coxe, of Burlington, she died September 13th, 1783, aged 23, leaving a daughter, Rebecca, wife of Joshua M. Wallace, of Philadelphia. His third wife was Mary, daughter of Edward Shippen, chief justice of Pennsylvania, and Margaret Francis, his wife, who was the daughter of Tench Francis, recorder of Philadelphia and attorney-general of Pennsylvania, son of John Dean, of Inismore, son of Rev. John F. Dean, of Leighton. He had, by her, children: William, died August, 1854, aged 68, not married; Edward Shippen (5); Margaret Shippen, died 1864, aged 76, not married; Joseph Bloomfield (6); and Maria, died 1869, aged 98, not married.

Edward S. (5), son of William (3), in 1813 settled in Ewing township, on a farm near the church, still owned and occupied by his grandson, Edward S. McIlvaine. He was a man of strong character and much influence, had one child, William Rodman (7), by his wife, Esther, daughter of William and Esther Rodman, of Bucks county, Pa., a lady of singular refinement and highly cultured mind, which she improved by travel abroad. The following lines addressed to her grandchildren were written by this most estimable Christian lady, prompted by the destruction of one of two venerable white oaks, that stood in the grave-yard of the Ewing Church, and which was destroyed by a tornado, June 3d, 1852:

Thou venerable oak, the churchyard tree,
With deep regret thy broken form we see.
Two hundred years or more the storms thou braved,
Unharmed, while round thy head the tempest raved.
A faithful guard through all that time thou kept,
Above the throng that 'neath thy shadow slept.
The wild tornado's breath hath o'er thee past,
And prostrate on the earth thou liest at last.
In time remote two white oaks had their birth,
Destined for many an age to grace the earth.
And here they stood when our forefathers came,
To build an altar to their Maker's name.
Men from afar—perchance beyond the deep,
This place they chose, their Sabbath rest to keep.
They built an altar of materials rude,
Unhewed the stone, and roughly dressed the wood.
'Twas blessed of Him whose promised dwelling place,
Is where His people meet to seek His grace.

Once in three weeks the stated pastor came,
With gracious message in his Master's name.
Reciprocated all the greetings kind,
Rejoiced in health and peace his flock to find.
The morning service o'er, beneath your shade,
They ate their bread and kind inquiries made—
How fared it with the brother pioneers,
What were their prospects, what their hopes and fears?

What news from home—afar beyond the sea?
Fight Hampden, Cromwell, still for liberty,
Or to his kingdom is King Charles restored?
Has promised but again to break his word?
Has Scotland sheathed the sword, or does she still
For conscience' sake oppose her sovereign's will?
Worship the faithful still in caves and dens,
In forest deep, or wild secluded glens?
For Wales who strikes to put oppression down.
Who nobly dares to wear a martyr's crown.
One to the other thus the tidings bore,
Of clime and kindred they would see no more.
That duty done, once more to praise and pray,
The church they entered- thus they spent the day.
They sought religion first, man's greatest good.
The path the fathers trod the sons pursued.
Their children to the Lord in covenant given,
They placed their feet in paths that led to Heaven.
By precept and example trained the youth
In all the ways of honesty and truth.
None caused their parents or their country shame,
Of them no record shows a felon's name.
When war's dark storm across the country came,
Bravely they faced it in their Maker's name.
With patriot zeal their country's battle fought,
Gained for posterity the boon they sought.
That duty done they left the camp and plain,
And homeward turned to till their fields again.
Time levels all, the old church passed away—
It served a holy purpose in its day.
And faithful men a new foundation laid,
Offerings of patient toil and substance made.
Well wrought, the building rose by careful hands,
Memorial of their zeal the church now stands.
And to this people, long the Lord hath given,
Grace, food, and peace, the richest gifts of Heaven.
Old Trees! when ye were young and small your shade,
There at your feet a stranger form they laid,
Now many others rest beside his bed.
For many a mossy stone the names disclose,
Of Hart, Reed, Scudder, Howell, Clark and Rose.
Hunt, Burroughs, Reeder, Hendrickson and Green,
Fish, Welling, Temple, Lanning, Moore and Dean,
Cook, Chambers, Carle and Muirheid, Furman, Lott,
And hundreds without stone to mark the spot.
These slow processions in their sad array,
From age to age have traced their mournful way.

From this enclosure, consecrated ground,
None shall awake until the last trump sound.
One name on earth and one alone is given,
Whereby this numerous host can enter Heaven.

William R. (7), son of Edward (5), who died January 13th, 1875, aged 55, was, for many years, a judge of the court of common pleas and a trustee of the Ewing Church. He married, in 1842, Christiana, only daughter of Jasper Scudder, (see Scudder family, No. 17.) Their children are: Edward Shippen (8); Jasper Scudder, graduated at Princeton College with the first honor of the class of 1862, at the age of 18, and graduated at the Theological Seminary, and went as a missionary to China, in 1868. He soon made himself proficient in the language of the country, and became one of the best Chinese scholars of the American board. So great was his zeal in his Christian work, that he would go where others deemed it unsafe, and in order to win the hearts of the people, he adopted the Chinese dress and partook of their food with them, which is considered by all missionaries a great sacrifice of comfort and health. He gave $5000 toward the purchase of land for a Presbyterian church in Tsi-nan-fu, Shantung, China, to which place he was the first to carry the news of the Gospel. It was there, on February 2d, 1881, aged 37, that he died, and is buried. Even the Chinese were impressed by his godly life, as they wrote upon his coffin, "Holy Teacher gone to God;" Maria, died, aged 18; and Francis, died in infancy.

Edward Shippen (8), son of William (7), is an elder and trustee in the Ewing Church; married Annie Belleville, daughter of Capt. William E. Hunt, (see Hunt family, No. 15.) Their children are: Margaret Shippen; Anna Belleville; and Maria.

Joseph B. (6), son of William (3), married Mariana, daughter of Commodore Alexander Murray, United States Navy, and by her had children: William; Alexander Murray (9); Mary; and Margaret S., married Rev. Mr. Dickinson.

Alexander Murray (9), son of Joseph B. (6), resides in Philadelphia. He married Mary, daughter of Dr. Joseph Olden, of Ewing, by whom he has children: Elizabeth Olden; Julia Murray; Bloomfield; William; Alexander; Rodman; Edward S.; and Mary.

Joseph (4), son of William (2), was colonel in the Revolutionary service; died just after the conclusion of the war, February 17th, 1787, aged 38, and is buried in the ground of the Episcopal Church, Bristol, leaving an only son, Joseph (10).

Joseph (10), son of Joseph (4), transferred his residence to Burlington; was a lawyer, and arose to high distinction in his profession, and for a time represented the state in the United States senate. He married Maria, daughter of Bowes Reed, of Philadelphia, by whom he had children: Bowes Reed (11); Bloomfield, was graduated at Princeton, married Miss Banker, and died 1826; Charles Pettit (12); Joseph, also a graduate of

Princeton, member of the bar, and recorder of the city, a district of which he represented in the legislature, died unmarried, 1826; Henry, a member of the legal profession, which he practiced in Philadelphia, he married, first, Matilda, daughter of Michael Nesbit, of Philadelphia, and second, her sister, Louisa, no children; William, died young; Emerson; Edward, married Miss Watson; Mary, married Rear-Admiral Frederic Engle, of the United States Navy, they have several children; Ellen, married Dr. Berkley, of Virginia, and at his death, married Mr. Harris, of Philadelphia.

Bowes Reed (11), son of Joseph (10), died 1866. He graduated at Princeton in 1812. The war breaking out shortly after, he entered the army, and was appointed aid-de-camp, with the rank of major, and served with credit during the war. At its close, he spent three years at Cadiz, Spain, engaged in mercantile pursuits. On his return, he engaged in the same employment at Lexington, Ky., and finally at New York, where, having accumulated an ample fortune, he died; 1866, aged 72, a model of purity, integrity, and Christian consistency. While at Lexington, he married Catharine S. Dusmesnil, by whom he has children: Reed; Charles; Henry; Edward; and daughters.

Rev. Dr. Charles Pettit (12), son of Joseph (10), was graduated by Princeton College and Theological Seminary. He was appointed chaplain and professor of ethics and revealed religion, at West Point, and of sacred antiquities in the University of New York; was made bishop of the Episcopal Church of Ohio; was president of Kenyon College and Theological Seminary. He was honored with the degree of D. D. in this country, with D. C. L. by Oxford, England, in 1853, and with LL. D. by Cambridge, in 1858. He ended his valuable life at Florence, Italy, whither he had gone for health, March, 1873, aged 75. He was the author of numerous works, none of which had a popularity equal to his "Evidences of Christianity." He was a man of broad and liberal views, and was not to be prevented from identifying himself with his clerical brethren of other denominations. A man of rare dignity and eloquence, both in the pulpit and on the platform, and equally distinguished for his eminent piety, his profound learning, and his exalted abilities. He married Emily, daughter of William and Rachel Coxe, of Burlington, by whom he had several children.

The Moore Family.

The English familes of Moore, says Riker, are believed to find their common head in Sir Thomas De Moore, who came over from Normandy with William the Conqueror, in 1066, his name being on the list taken at the port of embarkation (St. Valery); and also in the list of survivors of the battle of Hastings.

Rev. John Moore (1), was of English birth, though when and whence he emigrated, is unknown. As an independent minister he came from New England to Newtown, Long Island, soon after its settlement in 1652, and became their first minister, and continued to preach to them very acceptably till his death in 1657. He left children: John; Gershom, married the widow of Jonathan Fish, some of both of whose sons are believed to have removed to New Jersey; Joseph, lived at Southampton, and there died in 1726; Samuel (2); and Elizabeth, married Content Titus, (see Titus family, No. 2.)

Captain Samuel (2), son of Rev. John (1), became a grantee of land at Newtown, L. I., in 1662, and subsequently a large purchaser, and having filled many public offices, and served in the magistracy for a series of years, died in 1717, and his wife, Mary Reed, died in 1738, aged 87. Their children were: Samuel (3); Joseph (4); Benjamin (5); Nathaniel (6); Mary, married Nathaniel Woodward; Margaret, married Mr. Pretton; Elizabeth, married Mr. Hicks; and Sarah, married Daniel Coe.

Samuel (3), son of Samuel (2), married Charity, daughter of William Hallett, and had a son John; and daughter, Elizabeth, wife of Benjamin Moore (No. 18).

Joseph (4), son of Samuel (2), who lived at Newtown, L. I., and died there in 1760, aged 71, married successively Elizabeth and Sarah, daughters of Joseph Sackett. Of the seven children by his first wife, Sarah, married Benjamin Fish (see Fish family, No. 4), and removed to Trenton; of the eight children by his second wife, Sackett (7), and Benjamin (8), were twins, both moved to New Jersey, one to Hopewell, the other to Trenton.

Sackett (7), son of Joseph (4), died August 18th, 1753, aged 37, and is buried in the Ewing Church ground. He married his cousin, Abigail, daughter of Nathaniel Moore (No. 6), and had children: Nathaniel, born September 30th, 1741, married Mary Mershon; Captain Joseph, born August 14th, 1744, died unmarried; Joanna, born July, 1747, married Andrew Smith; Jesse (9); and Sackett (10).

Jesse (9), son of Sackett (7), was a trustee in the Pennington Church, died July 8th, 1839, aged 89, having married, first, Susanna Lawrence, who died March 10th, 1814, aged 63. His second wife was Hannah, daughter of Daniel Woodward, no children.

Sackett (10), son of Sackett (7), born January 7th, 1754, and died July 29th, 1820, having married Elizabeth Clifford, she died 1830, aged 62. They had a daughter, Abigail, wife of Joseph Scudder Hart, (see Hart family, No. 20.)

Benjamin (8), son of Joseph (4), died in 1792, aged 74, having married Mary, daughter of John Hart, (see Hart family, No. 1.) She died 1789, aged 73, having had children: Israel (11); William Sackett (12); Sarah, wife of Joseph Moore, of Newtown, L. I., whose children are: Mary, and Catharine, wife of Benjamin Titus.

Israel (11), son of Benjamin (8), died March 5th, 1829, aged 78, having married Catharine Carpenter. She died February 22d, 1835, aged 82. Their children were: Aaron (13); Sarah, born August 11th, 1777, died 1829; Mary, born April 12th, 1781, died 1801; Elizabeth, born January 29th, 1785, first wife of Josiah Hart.

Aaron (13), son of Israel (11), born October 23d, 1775, died December 17th, 1849, having married Sarah, daughter of Jeremiah Burroughs, (see Burroughs family, No. 9,) by whom he had children: Catharine Eliza, died young, 1832; Sarah, died in infancy; Mary Ann; and Virginia, married Benjamin Hendrickson.

William Sackett (12), son of Benjamin (8), died February 3d, 1825, aged 67, having married Elizabeth, daughter of Benjamin Moore (No. 18), of Hopewell. She died November 14th, 1828, aged 60. Their children were: Maria, married Benjamin Fish, of Trenton, (see Fish family, No. 7); Ann, became the second wife of Captain Lewis Parker, of Trenton, died August 3d, 1871; Benjamin (14); Eliza, died May 30th, 1880, aged 83; William, lived in Danville, Ill., married the widow, Mary Scott, and died April 16th, 1877 ; and Charles, died in infancy.

Benjamin (14), son of William Sackett (12), by his wife, Rebecca, daughter of Abner Scudder (see Scudder family, No. 15), had children : Abner Scudder, married Susan Dole, of Lynn, and died 1871, left children, Mary, Auther and Gertrude ; Caroline, married Frederic Dressler, of Philadelphia, whose children are : Charles and Emma ; William C., died 1872, not married ; Elizabeth, died, not married ; Israel, married Hester Ann Knox, of Philadelphia, and has children : Alexander, William, Mary and Lizzie ; Sarah, married Charles S. Moulder, of Philadelphia, whose children are : Charles, Benjamin, Sarah and Augustine ; Benjamin, lives in Boston, married Clorinda Wales ; and Georgiana, married John Townsend, of New York, has children : Kate and Maria.

Benjamin (5), son of Samuel (2), who by his marriage with Anna, daughter, of Joseph Sackett, was the grandfather of that truly pious, profoundly learned, and greatly venerated prelate, Benjamin Moore, president of Columbia College, of New York city, and bishop of the Episcopal Church of New York state, and grandfather of Dr. William Moore, of New York city, a man distinguished in the medical profession, who by his marriage with Jane, daughter of Nathaniel Fish, brother of Benjamin, who settled in Ewing, was the father of Nathaniel Fish Moore, also an eminent president of Columbia College, of which he was a graduate and professor of Latin and Greek ; he died aged 90.

Nathaniel (6), son of Samuel (2), came to this township from Long Island, in 1708, bought 500 acres of land about two miles from Pennington, on which he lived till his death, September 6th, 1759, aged 72. He married Joanna, daughter of the Rev. John Prudden, a Presbyterian clergyman of Newark, N. J., by whom he had children : John, (15); Samuel (16); Joseph (17); Benjamin (18); Phebe, married Richard Green, (see Green family, No. 6); Abigail, married, first, Sackett Moore (No. 7); second, Jonathan Smith, (see Smith family, No. 3); and Sarah, married Benjamin Temple, (see Temple family, No. 3).

Captain John (15), son of Nathaniel (6), who died September 3d, 1768, married, first, a daughter of Theophilus Phillips, (see Phillips family, No. 4,) of Lawrence, and had issue : Amos (19); John (20); Samuel (21) ; Nathaniel (22); Theophilus (23); Elizabeth, died December 7th, 1818, aged 67 ; Kesiah, married Mr.

Titus; Sarah, wife of John Smith, (see Smith family, No. 7); William; Joseph, married Miss Palmer. His second wife was Love, daughter of Ebenezer Prout, who died January 9th, 1776, aged 59.

Amos (19), son of Capt. John (15), who died April 29th, 1814, married, first, Ann a,daughter of Jonathan Smith, (see Smith family, No. 3); she died August 27th, 1777, aged 31, having had one daughter, Rebecca, wife of Aaron Hart, (see Hart family, No. 17.) His second wife was Dorothy Hutchinson, who died March, 1834, aged 86.

John (20), son of Capt. John (15), by his wife, Sarah, daughter of Henry Carpenter, of Ewing, had children: John C. (24); Elizabeth, wife of Rev. Asa Dunham; Sarah, wife of George Hunt, moved West; and Charles, married and went West.

John C. (24), son of John (20), married Elizabeth, daughter of John Guild (see Guild family, No. 3,) whose children are: John G. (25); Elizabeth, married Rev. Jacob Duy, a Lutheran clergyman of Germantown, and has children: Olivia, wife of Dr. Smiley, of New York, Raymond, died young, Cornelia, wife of Mr. Abby, Henrietta, wife of Paul Davis, of Philadelphia, Sallie, Helen, and Philip Melancthon; Cornelia, married the Rev. Daniel Miller, their children are: Elizabeth, Mary, wife of John Vancleve, Sophia, Susan, John, Margaret, and Catharine; Sarah, married Mr. Ward, of Hollidaysburg, had children: Elizabeth and Sarah; Charles, married Kate Heinichen; Abigail; Augustus; and Edwin; the three latter died young.

John G. (25), son of John (24), married, first, Elizabeth Lippincott, of Philadelphia, have children: Sarah; Edward; Raymond; Olivia; Charles; Emma; John; and Mary; married, second, widow Martha Hutchinson.

Samuel (21), son of Capt. John (15), married Sarah, daughter of Richard Green, of Ewing, (see Green family, No. 6); in 1782 made his home in Easton till his death in 1798. She died 1829, leaving children; Phebe, born July 17th, 1782, married, first, William Kelly, and lived in Batavia, Ohio; her second husband was Israel Gregg; she died at Hamilton, having had children by both husbands; Rebecca, born September 9th, 1783, wife of Samuel Kelly, lived in Cincinnati, Ohio, died 1871; Mary, born November 18th, 1784, married Dr. Edward Porter, of Frenchtown, and died 1838, leaving children: Edmond, Leonidas, and Thomas; Elizabeth, born July 17th, 1786, married William B.

Mott, had children: Sarah Ann, Edward T., Jane M., Marcia M., Elizabeth, and Mary; Nancy, born July 19th, 1787, married Thomas Kelly, brother of the two former, and died in Mellville, Ohio, in 1818; Martha, born October 3d, 1789, died unmarried 1858; Samuel (26); Sarah Green, born, June 22d, 1797, married Joseph Rapp; and Abigail, born November 19th, 1798, married Dr. John Hoff, of Easton, Pa., children: John P. and Elizabeth.

Samuel (26), son of Samuel (21), married November 7th, 1832, Elizabeth Wamsley, of Mansfield, and had issue: Samuel S., married Abigail Smith, of Elizabeth, N. J.; Martha, married Rev. Edward Townsend, of Maryland, a Methodist clergyman; Sarah G., died in infancy; Mary E., married William H. Cornell, of Ithaca, N. Y., lives in Titusville, Pa.; James W., married Rachel Flannery, of Pottsville, Pa., is a physician and professor of physics in Lafayette College; and Anna, married T. W. Doty, a lawyer of Mifflin, Pa.

Nathaniel (22), son of Captain John (15), married, Eleanor Van Brunt, resided in Trenton, had children: John (27); Cornelius (28).

John (27), son of Nathaniel (22), lived in Philadelphia, died February 12th, 1834, aged 69, having married Hannah, daughter of Joseph Price, of Harbortown; she died in 1835. Their children were: John, died young; Samuel; Hannah, married John B. Ellison, had children: Elizabeth, wife of Samuel Richards, William, married Ellen V. Walker, Rodman B., married Hannah Miller, and Meta, married Dr. George Ellis; Sarah, married, first, William G. Orr, had one son, John, who married, first, Orra Lee; second, Miss Preston, her second husband was Rev. Jared Dewing, one son, Thomas; Maria, was the second wife of George Link, of Philadelphia, whose children are: Susan, wife of Thomas Folwell, and Maria, died young, Eliza, married, first, Anthony Finley, of Philadelphia, second, Xenophon J. Maynard, of Trenton; Susan, married Armitage Green, (see Green family, No. 21.)

Cornelius (28), son of Nathaniel (22), who died 1819, aged 58, married Sarah, daughter of James Hill, of Trenton. She died aged 90, having had children: James, died young in Cuba; David (29); Charles; and William Hill (30).

David P. (29), son of Cornelius (28), resided in Philadelphia, he married, first, Mary Collens, whose children are: Cornelius; Sarah; Virginia; John M., married Miss Mason; Albert; Raymond; and Hannah. His second wife, was widow Azuba Withrop.

William Hill (30), son of Cornelius (28), was a resident of Philadelphia, married Hannah, daughter of Captain Davis, of Lancaster county, Pa., by whom he had issue: William Hill, married Susan, daughter of William Camm, of Philadelphia; Thomas B.; Emma, died in youth; and Hannah.

Theophilus (23), son of Capt. John (15), married Rhoda, daughter of John Phillips, of Pennington, and by her had children: Mary, married Samuel Holcomb, of New Brunswick, and her children are: Rhoda, wife of Peter Poole, Theophilus, married Elizabeth, wife of Rev. Stephen Meeker, of Williamsburg, Jane, died unmarried, Susan, wife of Mr. Molleson, a lawyer of New Brunswick, and Cornelia, wife of Dr. Augustus Taylor; Keziah, married John V. Hart, (see Hart family, No. 10); Letitia, married Jacob Holcomb, son of Jacob Holcomb, of New Brunswick, and by him had children: Maria, wife of Dr. Landis, Keziah, wife of Mr. Rekirt.

Samuel (16), son of Nathaniel (6), who died April 7th, 1803, aged 83, married Rebecca, daughter of Richard Green, (see Green family, No. 2.) She died September 28th, 1813, aged 87, having had children: William (31); Richard; Elijah; Samuel, died July 30th, 1816, aged 58; Rebecca, died February 24th, 1806, aged 46; Phebe, married William Green, (see Green family, No. 41); Mary, married Jonathan Smith; Hannah, married Titus Quick, of Amwell; Abigail, died March 22d, 1823, aged 66, leaving $4000 to the Pennington Academy; Joanna, died 1831, at an advanced age.

William (31), son of Samuel (16), married Elizabeth, daughter of John Davinson, of Pennington, and had children: Mary, married Asher Hart, (see Hart family, No. 24); Charles (32); Nathaniel, married in Ohio; John, married in Ohio; Elijah, not married; Sarah, died unmarried; Rebecca, married Cornelius Vankirk, of Pennington.

Charles (32), son of William (31), married Sarah, daughter of Daniel Woodward, whose children were: Eliza Ann, wife of John B. Taylor, of Taylorsville, Pa., have one daughter, Hannah Maria; Sarah, married Mr. Green, in Ohio; and Phebe.

Joseph (17), son of Nathaniel (6), resided near Pennington, died April 7th, 1804, aged 70. He married, first, Christian, daughter of Richard Green, by her had children: Ely, (33); Moses (34); Ephraim, a physician, not married; Elizabeth, married Col. John Van Cleve, (see Van Cleve family, No. 7.) His second wife was Mary, daughter of Reuben Armitage.

Ely (33), son of Joseph (17), was an officer in the First Hunterdon Regiment, 1776. He lived on his father's place, near Pennington, and died October 1st, 1812, aged 67, having married Elizabeth, daughter of Cornelius Hoff. She died 1839, aged 86. Their children were : Joseph (35); Sarah, third wife of Benjamin S. Hill ; Fanny, married Ira Jewell ; Elizabeth, married John Maxwell, of Savannah, Ga.

Joseph (35), son of Ely (33), who died May 9th, 1852, aged 72, married, first, Sarah B., daughter of Thomas Phillips, (see Phillips family, No. 11), and had children by her : Imlah (36); Charles (37); Ely (38); Thomas, married widow Ann Moore (Hill); Catharine, married William A. Green, (see Green family, No. 45); Elizabeth, became the second wife of Rev. Joseph W. Blythe. His second wife was Leah Wilson, who died 1841, aged 60.

Imlah (36), son of Joseph (35), married, first, Amanda, daughter of Joseph Howell, (see Howell family, No. 18,) and had children : Joseph H., married Mary Carr ; and Mary. His second wife was Rebecca, daughter of Benjamin Brearley, (see Brearley family, No. 21.)

Charles (37), son of Joseph (35), who died 1870, married Lydia Ann, daughter of Joseph Howell, (see Howell family, No. 18,) whose children are : Eckford ; and Charles.

Ely (38), son of Joseph (35), resided near Pennington, married Ann, daughter of Stout Hill ; had children : Elizabeth ; Jesse ; Mary Jane ; Joseph ; and Frank.

Capt. Moses (34), son of Capt. Joseph (17), was one of the patriots of the Revolution who promptly responded to the call of their country in her extremity. He commanded a company of "Jersey Blues," and was present at the battles of Trenton, Princeton, and Monmouth. He resided at Newton, Sussex county, N. J., till near the close of his life, about 1810, aged 60, having married, first, Elizabeth, daughter of Creinyonce Van Cleve, (see Van Cleve family, No. 4,) by whom he had a son, Col. Van Cleve, at one time sheriff of Sussex county, who married the widow of William Sausman. His second wife was a daughter of Abraham Coryell, of New Hope, Pa., by whom he had a son, Coryell, married. His third wife was Mary, sister of the former, by whom he had : Ely (39); and Sarah, married William Rittenhouse, moved to Wisconsin.

Hon. Ely (39) son of Capt. Moses (34), at an early period of his life transferred his sphere of action to New York city, and, through the force of talent, soon became a man of note. In 1834, he was elected from the city to a seat in congress, a position which he continued to fill for two terms with great credit, both as a speaker and a man of business, having been made chairman of several important committees. During this period, he edited the "National Trades Union," in New York. On his return, he was made president of the board of trade. He was also appointed surveyor of the port of New York, an office which he held till he was selected by President Polk, in 1845, to be marshal of the South District of New York. In 1838 and 1839, he was political editor of the "New York Evening Post," and in 1851, he owned and edited the "Warren Journal," at Belvidere. In 1853, he received the agency for the Miami and other tribes of Indians in Kansas, and in 1855, was appointed register of the United States land office, in Lecompton, where, having been highly honored by his adopted city, and having had confided to his charge many important trusts, by successive administrations, he died, at the age of 62, in January, 1860, and was buried on his farm, two miles from the city, with distinguished honors. He had children by his first wife, Emma, daughter of Gilbert Contant, of New York: Contant, died young; Emma, wife of John Coughtry, lives in Trenton; Mary, wife of G. U. Reynolds, is living in New Brunswick; Helen, wife of George C. Baker, of Washington, D. C.; Hampden, married, first, Sarah Sharp, second, Fanny Travers; and Ely, married Rose McKinney, resides in Lawrence, Kansas. Both sons belong to the editorial corps. His second wife was Mrs. Clara Baker.

The following is an extract of a speech of his, made in New York, in 1834, at a meeting held to urge contributions for the completion of Washington's monument:

"In no one instance, perhaps, was Washington's influence with the army so strikingly exemplified as in his attack on the enemy at Trenton. O'er and o'er have I listened with intense anxiety, in the day of my boyhood, whilst my now departed sire, who fought and bled on that proud field, recited with thrilling interest, all that related to the enterprise. 'It was on a December's night,' would he say, 'when our little heart-broken army halted on the banks of the Delaware. That night was dark, cheerless, tempestuous, and bore a strong resemblance to our country's fortune! It seemed as if heaven and earth had conspired for our destruction. The clouds lowered—darkness and the storm came on apace. The snow and hail descended, beating with unmitigated violence upon the supperless, half-clad, shivering soldiers; and in the roarings of the flood and the wailings of the storm was heard by fancy's ear the knell of our hopes and the dirge of liberty! The impetuous river was filled with floating ice. An attempt to cross it, at that time, and under such circumstances, seemed a desperate enterprise, yet it was undertaken, and, thanks be to God and Washington, was accomplished.

"'From where we landed on the Jersey shore, to Trenton, was about nine miles, and, on the whole line of march, there was scarcely a word uttered, save by the officers, when giving some order. We were well-nigh exhausted,' said he, 'many of us frost-bitten, and the majority of us so badly shod that the blood gushed from our frozen and lacerated feet at every tread, yet we upbraided not, complained not, but marched steadily and firmly, though mournfully, onward, resolved to persevere to the uttermost, not for our country—our country, alas! we had given up for lost—not for ourselves—life, for us, no longer wore a charm—but because such was the will of our beloved chief—'twas for Washington alone, we were willing to make the sacrifice. When we arrived within sight of the enemy's encampments, we were ordered to form a line, when Washington reviewed us. Pale and emaciated, dispirited and exhausted, we presented a most unwarlike and melancholy aspect. The paternal eye of our chief was quick to discover the extent of our sufferings, and acknowledge them with his tears, but, suddenly checking his emotions, he reminded us that our country and all that we held dear was staked upon the issue of the coming battle. As he spoke, we gathered ourselves up and rallied our energies; every man grasped his arms more firmly, and the clenched hand, and the compressed lip, and steadfast look, and the knit brow, told the soul's resolve.

"'Washington observed us well; then did he exhort us, with all the fervor of his soul, "On yonder field to conquer, or die the death of the brave." At that instant, the glorious sun, as if in prophetic token of our success, burst forth in all his splendor, bathing in liquid light the blue hills of Jersey. The faces which, but a few moments before, were blanched with despair, now glowed with martial fire and animation, Our chief, with exultation, hailed the scene; then casting his doubts to the winds, and calling on the "God of battles" and his faithful soldiers, led on the charge. The conflict was fierce and bloody. For more than twenty minutes, not a gun was fired; the sabre and the bayonet did the work of destruction; 'twas a hurricane of fire, and steel, and death. There did we stand,' would he say, 'there did we stand, "foot to foot and hilt to hilt," with the serried foe! and where we stood, we died or conquered.'

"The result of that action, gentlemen, is known to you all, as are also its bearings upon the fortunes of America. Had defeat attended our arms at that trying crisis, our cause was lost, forever lost, and freedom had found a grave on the plains of Trenton! But the wisdom and prudence of Washington secured us the victory, and, consequently, our liberty.

"How great our obligation, then, and how much it behooves us, at this time, to show our gratitude by erecting to his memory a monument that shall tell to after ages, not only that Washington was great, but that *we were grateful.* Let it no longer be delayed. To pause, is to invite defeat; to persevere, is to insure success."

Benjamin (18), son of Nathaniel (6), who died November 9th, 1813, aged 81, and is buried in the Ewing church-yard, lived on the homestead, near Pennington, and married his cousin, Elizabeth, daughter of Samuel Moore (No. 3), of Newtown. She died January 8th, 1803, aged 73, having had children: Augustine, married Sarah, daughter of John Carpenter, Sr., and died without children; Elizabeth, married William Sackett Moore (No. 12); and Sarah, married Daniel Woodward, and died 1842, aged 86, having had children: Hannah, second wife of Jesse Moore (No. 9), Sarah, wife of Charles Moore (No. 32), Mary, wife of Mr. Anderson, and Benjamin.

The Nathan Moore Family.

This family is not connected, unless distantly, with the other families of Moore, of this township. Nathan (1), by his wife, Naomi, had children: Cornelius (2); and Absalom (3).

Cornelius (2), son of Nathan (1), who died November 19th, 1853, aged 56, married Rachel Swan. She died July 23d, 1850, aged 53. Their children were: Nathan (4); Catharine, married John H. Latourette, of Trenton, whose children are: Clinton, Ella, and John, he resided in Fulton county, Ohio; Deborah, first wife of James B. Green, (see Green family, No. 20); Dewitt Clinton (5); Absalom B. (6); and Randolph H. (7).

Nathan (4), son of Cornelius (2), a merchant of Philadelphia, married Elvira E. Allen, of Bass River, Burlington county, where he resided. Their children were: William A.; Samuel A. B.; Rachel R.; Edward F.; Lyman B.; James G.; Dewitt C.; and Elvira V.

Dewitt C. (5), son of Cornelius (2), was a distinguished lecturer, especially in the temperance cause, of which he was an ardent advocate. He married Phebe A. Troutman, of Philadelphia, where he resided. Their children are: Frederick K.; Kate S.; and Mary V.

Absalom B. (6), son of Cornelius (2), married Elizabeth Thorn, of Trenton, lives in Lasalle, Ill., and had children: Randolph; Emma; and Sarah.

Randolph H. (7), son of Cornelius (2), married Sarah Brandt, of Trenton, and had children: Edward; Florence; and Albert.

Absalom (3), son of Nathan (1), who died December 31st, 1856, aged 58, married Eliza Ann Pierson, who died February 2d, 1861, aged 54, and had children: Sarah, married Amos Akers, and died 1861, aged 35; Cornelius, died September 2d, 1863, aged 34, having married Mary Moore, has a son, Charles; and Naomi, married Henry Thompson.

The Muirheid Family.

John Muirheid (1) was one of that valuable class of men which Scotland has sent us, having been born in Glasgow. After his arrival, his residence was, for a time, on Long Island, where he married, November 22d, 1706, Rebecca Bailey; removed to Hopewell, N. J., in the early part of the last century, and became a man of mark. He was both an elder and a trustee of the Presbyterian Church of Pennington, and was, in 1713–1714, appointed to be the first high sheriff of Burlington county, then including Hunterdon county. He died January, 1725; his widow, December 25th, 1759. Both are buried in the Ewing church-ground. They had children: Jane, born August 29th, 1710, and became the wife of Edward Burrowes, son of Thomas, and had children: John, Anthony, Zebulon, Edward, Hannah, wife of John Moore, Catharine, wife of Jesse Atchley, ancestor of all the Atchleys of this region, Rebecca, wife of Francis Reed, and Jane; George, born March 1st, 1711; John, born February 5th, 1713; William, born February 14th, 1715; Andrew (2), born February 11th, 1717; Rebecca, born December 25th, 1719; Ruth, born May 4th, 1723; and Elizabeth, born 1725.

Andrew (2), son of John (1), in 1745 bought a farm near Harbortown, on which he lived, and which is still the family homestead, and died 1794, aged 77, having married Elizabeth, daughter of Jonathan Waters. She died 1771, aged 49. Their children: John, born October 18th, 1750, died unmarried 1830; Deborah, born March 20th, 1753, died unmarried, 1784; Jonathan (3), born May 7th, 1755; William, born October 18th, 1757, died 1776; Rebecca, born February 8th, 1759, died unmarried, 1793; George (4), born June 25th, 1760; and Andrew, born December 7th, 1764, died 1830, at his residence in Amwell, having married, in succession, without children, Hannah, daughter of John Stevenson, and Anna, sister of Edward Hunt. Andrew Muirheid (2) had a second wife, Anne, who died September 10th, 1776, aged 45.

Jonathan (3), son of Andrew (2), was an officer in the Third Regiment of Hunterdon county, in 1777. He died 1837, aged 83, having married Mary, daughter of Richard Lott, (see Lott family, No. 2.) She died 1817, aged 57; had children: Andrew, not married; Elizabeth, wife of William Beakes, whose children are: Julia Ann, who became the second wife of Isaac Scudder, of Cranbury, (see Scudder family, No. 126,) Mary, wife of Aaron Stout, Jane, wife of Mr. Beatty, Rebecca, wife of Mr. Vancleve, Abigail, George, Samuel, and William; Mary, married James Disborough; William (5); Ann, married George Schenck; and Phebe, married, first, Andrew McDowell, second, George McDowell.

William (5), son of Jonathan (3), married Amy Housell, of Easton, Pa. Their children were: Mary, married Benjamin Ehrie; Sarah, married Benjamin Clark; and Jonathan, married, first, Miss Williamson, had a son, William, a lawyer of Jersey City, and by his second wife, had John and Benjamin C.

George (4), son of Andrew (2), was a trustee of the Presbyterian Church of Pennington. He married, June 9th, 1788, Charity, daughter of the Rev. John Guild, (see Guild family, No. 2.) Their children were: Deborah, married Jesse Howell, (see Howell family, No. 21); John Guild (6); Benjamin (7); William, not married; George, married Sarah, daughter of Amos Wilson, has one son, Abner Wilson; and Elizabeth, wife of George Woolsey, (see Woolsey family, No. 8.)

John Guild (6), son of George (4), was both an elder and trustee of the Pennington Church. By his wife, Elizabeth, daughter of Daniel Howell, (see Howell family, No. 39); had children: Mary, died in childhood; Charity, married John, son of the Rev. Benjamin Ogden, of Michigan; Charles H., married Elizabeth, daughter of Michael Nesbit, of Philadelphia, of which city he was a well-known and prominent business man; Sarah; Elizabeth, married Samuel Titus; Alfred (8); Henry P., a volunteer in the late war, and first lieutenant in Rush's Lancers; John Guild, married Prescilla, daughter of Joseph Bunn, of Pennington; and William Harrison, married Elizabeth, daughter of Moore Hart.

Alfred (8), son of John Guild (6), died May 25th, 1875, aged 44, having married Sarah Ann, daughter of Maj. John Howell, (see Howell family, No. 40.) Their children are: John Guild; Sarah, died in infancy; George; Anna; Henry; and Lillie.

Benjamin (7), son of George (4), by his marriage with Sarah, daughter of Noah Howell, (see Howell family, No. 15); had children: Maria, wife of John S. Van Cleve; John (9); William B.; and Susan.

John (9), son of Benjamin (7), sheriff of Mercer county in 1858, married Mary, daughter of Roswell Howe, and had children: Ella, wife of Aaron Van Cleve; and Charles.

The Phillips Family.

The Rev. George Phillips, of Boxford, England, with his wife, Elizabeth, and children, Samuel, Elizabeth, and Abigail, came over with Governor Winthrop, in 1630, and settled in Watertown, Mass. By a second wife he had Zerubabel; Jonathan; Theophilus; Annabel; Ephraim; Obadiah; and Abigail. His son, Rev. Samuel, settled at Rowley, Mass. One of the Rev. Samuel's sons was the Rev. George Phillips, graduated at Harvard, came to Jamaica, L. I., where he preached till 1697, when he removed to Setauket, L. I., and there remained till his death in 1739, and is buried in the Presbyterian church-grounds of that place.

The three brothers, Theophilus (1), Joseph, and Daniel, whose names appear among the grantees of the new charter of Newtown, granted in 1686, by Governor Dongan, of New York, are supposed by Riker, who carefully investigated the matter, to be the grandsons of the first Rev. George, either by the Rev. Samuel, or a brother of his.

The name of Theophilus (1), first appears in 1676, in the business transactions of Newtown, in which he was an active participant and a highly useful man. He was thrice married, first, to Ann, daughter of Ralph Hunt, (see Hunt family, No. 1,) by whom he had three sons: Theophilus (2), born May 15th, 1673; William, born June 28th, 1676, settled in New York; and Philip (3), born December 27th, 1678, who with his brother, Theophilus (2), removed to Maidenhead at least as early as March, 1698, as their names are among the grantees of a tract of land for a church. His third wife was Elizabeth, by whom he had children: Hannah; Elizabeth; and Mary.

Theophilus (2), son of Theophilus (1), by his wife, Elizabeth, had children: Theophilus (4); John (5); William (6); Joseph, had a wife, Mary, a daughter, Mary, and other children; Philip; Frances, wife of Joseph Hart, (see Hart family, No. 14); Hannah, wife of John Hart, (see Hart family, No. 3); Mary, wife of Benjamin Hunt, of Lawrence ; Job (7); and perhaps a daughter, who married her cousin, Abner, son of Philip (No. 3.)

Theophilus (4), son of Theophilus (2), whose will is dated 1762, by his wife, Abigail, had children: John ; William ; Frances, married Mr. Bainbridge ; Richard ; Joseph (8) ; and a daughter married Captain John Moore, (see Moore family, No. 15.)

Joseph (8), son of Theophilus (4), married, and had children : Mary, married ; Elizabeth, wife of Ralph Hunt, (see Hunt family, No. 40); Hezekiah, died unmarried, at an advanced age, near Newton, N. J. ; Joseph (9); and Theophilus (10).

Joseph (9), son of Joseph (8), married in 1785, Martha Schooley. Their children are: James, married Miss Wallace ; Benjamin, married ; Theophilus, unmarried ; Martha, married Mr. Haggerty ; Sarah, married Mr. Kennedy.

Theophilus (10), son of Joseph (8), married Abigail, daughter of Benjamin Clark, (see Clark family, No. 2,) and had by her children : Elizabeth, married William Smith ; Mary, married Henry Krewson ; Sarah, married Jacob Van Cleve, (see Van Cleve family, No. 25,) and Susan, married Justice Enoch Johnson, and had daughters: Sarah, wife of Alexander Schenck, and Fanny, wife of William Gulick.

John (5), son of Theophilus (2), married and had children : Thomas (11); Joseph, no children ; John (12); Theophilus (13); and William I. (14).

Thomas (11), son of John (5), married Catharine, daughter of William Phillips (3), resided in Hopewell. Their children were : William (15); John (16); Elijah, married ; Ephraim (17); Enoch (18); and Sarah, wife of Joseph Moore, (see Moore family, No. 35.)

William (15), son of Thomas (11), married Martha, daughter of Col. John Van Cleve, (see Van Cleve family, No. 7.) Their children are : John V., married Mary Biles, reside at St. Louis ; Thomas, died young ; Joseph M., married Mary Etta Sutphen ; Sarah, wife of William L. Titus ; Charles T., married Margaret Ann Biggs, resides in the District of Columbia ; Jane M., wife of Andrew I. Lanning ; Catharine, wife of W. L. Titus ; William R., married Mattie B. Holcomb ; Elizabeth ; and Millie.

John (16), son of Thomas (11), married, first, Elizabeth Sexton ; second, Ruth, her sister, by whom he had children ; Elizabeth, married, first, Mr. Humphrey ; second, William G. Marshall ; Ruth, married ; Catharine, married William G. Marshall ; John S., married Miss Hoff ; and William, died young.

Ephraim (17), son of Thomas (11), married and went West, had children : John ; Isaac ; Ephraim ; Charles ; Thomas ; Sarah ; and Catharine.

Enoch (18), son of Thomas (11), married Sarah Blackwell, and had children : David, married, first, Abbie Perrine ; second, Mary Blackwell ; and Martha.

John (12), who died 1831, aged 73, married Huldah, daughter of Benjamin Mershon, who died 1842, aged 78, having had children : Benjamin, married Elizabeth, daughter of Thomas Stevens ; James, a graduate of Princeton, married Catharine, daughter of Thomas Stevens ; Randall, a physician, died 1827, aged 25 ; and Abigail, wife of Amos Scudder.

Theophilus (13), son of John (5), who died 1840, aged 81, married Margaret, daughter of Joseph Disbrow. She died 1864, aged 96, having had children : Henry, D. (19); and John (20.)

Henry D. (19), son of Theophilus (13), died 1873, aged 80, having married Jane C. Fiester, who died 1855, aged 50. Their children are : John F., married Hannah, daughter of Richard Warne, of Warren county ; Reseau, married Joanna F., daughter of John Barcalew ; Henry, married Mary Vandervere, of Amsterdam, N. Y. ; Theodore, married Emma Breed, of Pittsburg, Pa. ; Juliet, wife of Andrew Titus, (see Titus family, No. 32); and Margaret, wife of Van Camp Bush, of Philadelphia.

John (20), son of Theophilus (13), an eminent physician, settled in Bristol, Pa., who died 1861, aged 71, having married Deborah, daughter of Dr. Gregg. She died 1869, aged 71. Their children were : Caroline, wife of Allen E. Bassett, a merchant ; Margaret Ann, wife of Symmington Phillips, son of the Rev. Dr. William Phillips, of New York ; Ann Eliza, married, first, Dr. William R. Phillips, son of Lewis Phillips (No. 22) ; second, Albert Phillips, son of the Rev. Dr. William Phillips ; and Mary, wife of Rev. Henry Bartow, rector of the Episcopal Church at Bristol, Pa.

William I. (14), son of John (5), married Frances, daughter of Col. Joseph Phillips (No. 33); had one daughter, Abby, married Isaac Savage.

William (6), son of Theophilus (2), was a man of large property, resided in Lawrence, and died 1806, aged 84, the date of his will. By his wife, Abigail, he had children : Ralph (21); Frances, a lady of great beauty, married Jonathan Deare, of New Brunswick, a lawyer, a representative from Middlesex county to the Provincial Congress in 1775 ; Sarah, wife of Henry Phillips, of

Pennington, whose children are: William, Ralph, John, and Henry; Kesiah, wife of Nathaniel Hunt, of Cranbury; Deborah, wife of David Johnes; and Elizabeth, wife of Evan Runyan.

Ralph (21), son of William (6), occupied the farm of 200 acres, left him by his father, he also owned a large body of land in Ohio, where, while on a visit, he died August 2d, 1827, in his 73d year, having married Ruth Stout, of Penn's Neck. She died 1827, aged 69, having had children: William R., who died 1821, aged 21, while a student in Princeton College; Juliet, wife of Manuel Eyre, of Philadelphia, died 1803, aged 17, is buried in the Lawrenceville church-yard; Lewis W. R. (22); Susan; Jonathan; Susan; Gideon; and Charles H.; last five died young.

Lewis W. R. (22), son of Ralph (21), was graduated at Princeton, resided in Lawrence, died 1855, aged 64, having married, first, Maria, daughter of Dr. John Smith, of Philadelphia, by whom he had children: William and Harrison, died in infancy; William R., a graduate of Princeton College, and of the Medical University of Pennsylvania, married Ann Eliza, daughter of Dr. John Phillips (No. 20), of Bristol, Pa., where he settled and died 1847, aged 24; and Lewis, married Carrie Evans. His second wife was Eliza Craig, widow of Rev. Aaron B. Jerome, by whom he had Juliet, wife of Rev. John M. Richmond, settled at Ypsilanti, Mich.; and Margaret, wife of Rev. Henry Myers, settled at Millville, N. J.

Job (7), son of Theophilus (2), lived near Titusville, married, first, Phebe, daughter of Daniel Howell, (see Howell family, No. 3), and by her had children: Richard; Abigail, married Mr. Vankirk; John, married, and had a numerous family; these three removed to Uniontown, Fayette Co., Pa.; Daniel (23); Joseph (24); and Hannah, wife of Rev. William Wetherill, a Methodist clergyman, of Bucks county, Pa. His second wife was Rachel Kerr, of Freehold, whose children were: Samuel, married Elizabeth Dippolt, of Trenton, where he resided till his death; Aaron, married Mary Brown, of Trenton; Phebe, wife of the Rev. Sylvester Hutchinson, a noted Methodist minister, near Hightstown; and Elizabeth, married George Farley, of Titusville, who removed to Cherry Valley, N. Y., where she died.

Daniel (23), son of Job (7), resided in Trenton, and married Ann, daughter of Archibald William Yard, (see Yard family, No. 7.) Their children were: Archibald William (25); Elias, died December 1st, 1868, aged 73; Juliet; and George, married Elizabeth Smick.

Archibald William (25), son of Daniel (23), died January 5th, 1877, aged 84, having married Margaret Anderson, who died September 16th, 1867, aged 66. Their children are: Daniel; Annie; and Robert, died young; Annie, wife of Thomas Barnes; America; Jane; Daniel, died, married Mrs. Olivia Conner; Charles C., married Rebecca P. Hopkins; Edward A., married Clara McKean; and William.

Captain Joseph (24), son of Job (7), succeeded to the homestead, near Titusville, and married Sarah, daughter of Judge Thomas Reading, (see Reading family, No. 7,) by whom he had children: Joseph Reading (26); John Howell (27); Mary, wife of John W. Phillips, of Pennington; and Phebe, married the Rev. Joseph Barlow, a Presbyterian clergyman of Franklin, Pa., and by him had children: Sarah, wife of William Dowd, Hattie, wife of J. H. Lippincott, professor in Dickinson College, Carlisle, Pa.; Rosalie, wife of J. Darwin Cooke, a lawyer, of Kansas City, John Reading, residing at St. Louis; Ellen; and Carrie.

Joseph R. (26), son of Capt. Joseph (24), married Elizabeth, daughter of John M. Vankirk, and removed first to Ohio, afterward to Kansas City, where he died leaving children: Edward, a prominent citizen, filling many posts of honor and trust; Frances, married Mr. Vantile; Mary, married; Martha, wife of Dr. Overstreet, a physician of Sedalia; and Sarah, married, and lived in Missouri.

Dr. John H. (27), son of Capt. Joseph (24), a physician, practicing at Pennington, afterward at Beverly, married Elizabeth A., daughter of James Carson, of Bucks county, Pa., whose children were; Josephine, died young; and Emily, the wife of Professor J. Fletcher Street.

Philip (3), son of Theophilus (1), came to Maidenhead at the close of the 17th century. He was probably the Philip who was commissioned in 1722 captain in a regiment of Hunterdon county, of which Judge Trent was colonel, and afterward in 1727 major of a regiment of foot of Hunterdon county, of which Governor Reading was colonel. He was evidently a man of influence. He died about 1740, the date of his will, in which he mentions his wife, Elizabeth, and children: Philip; Abner; Samuel (28); John; Esther; and Ruth.

Samuel (28), son of Philip (3), died 1770, the date of his will. By his wife, Ruth, he had children: Jonathan (29); Elias (30); John (31); Samuel; and Asher.

Capt. Jonathan (29), son of Samuel (28), entered the United States Army in 1775, a second lieutenant of Capt. Joseph Brearley's Company, Second New Jersey Battalion; promoted captain in Second Battalion in 1777, and captain in Second Regiment of the Continental Army in 1780. He served during the whole war, and was an original member of the Cincinnati Society. He died 1801, aged 57, having married, first, Mary, daughter of Joseph Phillips, son of Theophilus Phillips (No. 2.) She died 1785, having had children: Horace (32); and Samuel, died young. His second wife was Elizabeth, sister of the Hon. William Churchill Houston, (see Houston family, No. 1,) by whom he had: Churchill W., married Maria, daughter of Benjamin Baker, of Lawrence, he moved to the West, and there died.

Horace (32), son of Capt. Jonathan (29), moved to Dayton, Ohio, about 1804, where he became a large land-holder and an opulent merchant. He married Elizabeth, daughter of the Hon. William C. Houston, (see Houston family, No. 1,) by whom he had: Elizabeth, married John G. Worthington, and resides at Georgetown, D. C.; Dickinson, married Miss Green, of Dayton, Ohio, had three daughters and a son; and Mary Anna, married Robert Thurston, a lawyer and member of congress, and at his death, John G. Laine, a lawyer.

Maj. Elias (30), son of Maj. Samuel (28), was commissioned adjutant First Regiment of Hunterdon Militia, 1776, and was in active service during the war, as most of the New Jersey militia were, and was distinguished for his gallantry in partisan warfare. He died 1797, aged 42, and his wife, Elizabeth, daughter of Col. Joseph Phillips (No. 33), in 1819, aged 61, having had children: Ruth, died 1835, aged 31; and Sarah, married Mr. Vanhart, and died 1831, aged 39.

Maj. John (31), son of Samuel (28), who died May, 1831, aged 74, married Mary, daughter of Col. Joseph Phillips (No. 33), whose children are: Asher, major and paymaster in the war of 1812, married Sarah, daughter of Oliver Ormsby, merchant, of Pittsburg; Elias, a graduate of West Point and captain in United States service, married Mary Ormsby, sister of the former; Augustus, a graduate of West Point and captain in the United States Army, married, first, Miss Barron, of Providence, R. I., second, Miss Dewy, and had a daughter by each; William, went West, where he died, unmarried; and Mary.

Col. Joseph (33), may have been the grandson of the first

Philip (No. 3), but more probably of the first Theophilus, as a relationship is claimed by the older members of his family, more nearly with the latter. He was probably the son of Joseph, the names of whose children cannot now be ascertained. He resided in Lawrenceville, in the house afterward occupied by his son, Dr. Joseph, and still held by his grandson, James. He was a man of high distinction. In the Revolutionary war, was appointed major of the New Jersey Battalion, the first military organization of the state; was in the battle of Long Island; was promoted lieutenant-colonel, afterward colonel, of the First Regiment of Hunterdon county, 1777, which regiment was in almost constant service during the war. He died about 1788, aged about 70, having married Rebecca Griffin, by whom he had children: Abigail, wife of Capt. Edward Yard, (see Yard family, No. 8); Mary, wife of Maj. John Phillips (No. 31); Frances, wife of William Phillips (No. 14); Elizabeth, wife of Maj. Elias Phillips (No. 30); William, settled in Frankfort, Ky., where he left descendants; and Dr. Joseph, who was a surgeon in the United States Army, served with Gens. St. Clair, Wayne, and Wilkinson, was on the staff of the two latter, retired on the reduction of the army, and settled in Lawrenceville, where he married Mary C., daughter of John Moore, and died 1842, aged 76, she died in 1847, aged 83, having had children: James, Juliet, married Elisha Gorden, and Joseph, married Lydia Guskey.

The Joseph Phillips Family.

Joseph (1), the ancestor of one branch of the Phillips family, emigrated from Wales to Long Island, thence to Maidenhead.

He had brothers, Theophilus, Philip, and perhaps others. He was twice married, one wife being a Miss Lott, and had children by each wife. A son, William (2), born January 7th, 1702.

William (2), son of Joseph (1), was a deacon of the church of Maidenhead. He died January 3d, 1776, leaving a wife, Mary, and sons, William (3), Simeon (4), and others, and a daughter, Polly, who married John Carpenter, who had a son, John, who died 1828.

William (3), son of William (2), born May 21st, 1736, and died December 8th, 1778; married Ruth, daughter of Ephraim Titus, (see Titus family, No. 6,) and Mary, his wife, daughter of Enoch Armitage, a ruling elder and prominent supporter of the Presbyterian Church of Pennington. She died 1818, aged 80, having had children; Mary, born, December 4th, 1757, died aged 20; Catharine, born March 9th, 1761, died, aged 37, having married Thomas Phillips (No. 11); Sarah, born April 16th, 1763, married Mr. Davis, and had children: John, George, Ephraim, Charles, Joseph, and Eliza; Martha, born July 3d, 1767, died, aged 30; Ephraim (5); and Elizabeth, married Mr. Price.

Ephraim (5), son of William (3), born June 14th, 1770, and died March 5th, 1834, having married Sarah Smith, who died 1824, leaving children: George (6); and Mary, married Mr. Fiester.

George (6), son of Ephraim (5), born September 11th, 1803, and died in 1869; married Abigail, daughter of Levi Ketcham, of Pennington, and had children: Sarah Elizabeth; William Wilson Latta (7); Ephraim (8); George Eugene; and Frances E.

Dr. William W. L. (7), son of George (6), a graduate of Princeton, a physician, practicing in Trenton, entered the Union service in 1861 as surgeon of First New Jersey Cavalry, and in 1862 became surgeon-in-chief of Second Division of cavalry corps of the Army of the Potomac. He married, first, Margaret, daughter of Dr. John McKelway, of Trenton, by whom he had one daughter, Isabella, married Joseph Thompson, of Mays Landing. He married, second, Meta, daughter of Alexander McAlpine, by whom he has: William W. L.; Helen; and McAlpine.

Ephraim (8), son of George (6), married Mary McClure, whose children are: George E.; William E.; Mary A. B.; J. Walter; Robert H. C.; and Emma B.

Simeon (4), son of William (2), married Rebecca, daughter of John Titus, (see Titus family, No. 10.)

The Thomas Phillips Family.

Thomas Phillips (1), the ancestor of the Phillips of Ewing, was among the first settlers of Pennsylvania. He had children: John (2); Thomas; Baker; Aaron; Rebecca, wife of Mr. Hedley; Mary, wife of Mr. Stackhouse; Letitia, wife of Mr. Gauslen; and perhaps others; all of whom, except John, lived in Bucks county, Pa.

John (2), son of Thomas (1), owned the large grain mills at Ingham's Springs, Pa. He settled in Ewing, and married Rebecca, daughter of Joseph Fish. Their children were: Letitia, married William Young; Aaron (3); Sarah, married Thomas Phillips; Joseph, married Anna Hoff; Elizabeth, married Scudder Hoff; Levinia, married Isaac Primmer; John (4); and Abbie, married John Hockenbury.

Aaron (3), son of John (2), died March 2d, 1872, aged 84, having married Anna, daughter of Richard Smith. She died September 12th, 1871, aged 85. Their children are: John Smith (5); Joseph (6); Horace (7); Aaron, married Catharine, daughter of James Burroughs, whose children are Elmer and Charity; Maria, married Charles Clark; Cornelia, married Jonathan Beakes; and Israel, married Elizabeth La Rue, and has children: William, Harriet, Bert, Livingston, Frederick, and Lillie.

John S. (5), son of Aaron (3), married Joanna Temple, and has children: Wesley; Liscomb; Ann Elizabeth; Rebecca Ann; and Sarah Virginia.

Joseph (6), son of Aaron (3), married Mary Ann, daughter of William Young, and has children: Silvester; David; Louisa; Margaret; and Harriet.

Horace (7), son of Aaron, married Emily Shipes, whose children are: Horace; David; Annie; and Caroline.

John (4), son of John (2), married Mary, daughter of Anderson Smith; had children: Edward, married Mary Frances, daughter of Elijah Lanning, whose children are: Frank, James, and Mary; Scudder, married Sarah La Rue, and their children are:

Isabella, Henry G., Annie E., and Samuel; Amos, married Angeline, daughter of Elijah Lanning, whose children are: Sarah, and Mary; Anna, wife of Luther Vanpelt; and Virginia, married Mr. Voorhees.

The Potts Family.

Thomas (1), who resided at White Hill, was probably the son of Thomas that came over in the ship Shield, a Friend. He married Sarah Beakes, and had by her issue: Stacy (2); and Ruth, wife of Samuel Johnson, son of William Johnson, who came from Ireland, and bought in Flemington in 1731, 210 acres; he was a teacher and mathematician, and conducted a boarding school at Charleston, S. C., where he died. She with her five children returned to Trenton. Her second son, Thomas P., became successively teacher and merchant, and finally settled in Princeton, where he married Mary, daughter of Robert Stockton; he became one of the most brilliant and eminent members of the New Jersey bar, and died at New Hope, Pa., at the house of his son-in-law, Dr. Richard Corson; he was the father of Dr. William Johnson, of White House, Hunterdon county, who died 1867, aged 88.

Stacy (2), son of Thomas (1), after the close of the war removed from Trenton to Harrisburg, Pa.; he returned to Trenton, engaged in mercantile pursuits, was an active member of the society of Friends, was elected many years mayor of the city, and died 1816, aged 85, having married, first, Esther, daughter of John Pancoast, son of William Pancoast, of Bucks county, Pa., and had children: Mary; Sarah; Elizabeth, died young; Thomas (3); and William (4). His second wife was Margaret Yardley, of Bucks county, Pa., whose children were: Stacy (5); Joseph (6); Anna; Rebecca; and Thomas, died young.

Thomas (3), son of Stacy (2), by his wife, Rebecca, had children: Nathaniel; Thomas; Joseph; William; Rebecca, wife of Thomas Coxe; Ann, wife of William Folwell; and Mary, wife of John Coxe.

William (4), son of Stacy (2), married Mary, daughter of Theophilus Gardner, an eminent merchant of Philadelphia, of Scotch Presbyterian descent, and by her had children: Theophilus Gardner, a Presbyterian clergyman, settled in North Carolina, died unmarried; Stacy Gardner (7); Maria, wife of Samuel Loyd, of Philadelphia; Joseph C. (8); and William Stevens, born October 13th, 1802, at Fishing creek, Northumberland county, Pa.; he graduated at the Princeton Theological Seminary, became soon after pastor of the earliest Presbyterian church of St. Louis in 1828. In 1835, he was elected the first president of Marion College, which office he filled five years, when he resumed his pastorate at St. Louis, and there died 1852, having married Ann, daughter of Samuel Benton.

Stacy (7), son of William (4), who died April 9th, 1865, aged 66, was editor for many years of one of Trenton's papers, the "Emporium," was a lawyer, and was elevated to the bench of the Supreme Court. He was an elder in the First Presbyterian Church of Trenton, and was at times when appointed to its sessions a valuable member of the general assembly. He married, first, Ellen Eliza, daughter of Nathaniel Burrowes,* and sister of Rev. George Burrowes, D. D., and had by her, issue: Mary, wife of Andrew R. Titus (see Titus family, No. 32); Ellen, married, first, Mr. Vandergrift, of Trenton; second, Rev. F. R. Harbaugh, pastor of a church in Philadelphia; Gardner L., died aged 21; Stacy G.; Anna, wife of Dr. Helm, of Sing Sing; and two died in infancy. His second wife was Cornelia, daughter of the Rev. Dr. How, of New Brunswick, by whom he had two children died in infancy. His third wife, was Hannah Moore.

Joseph C. (8), son of William (4), a member of the Trenton bar. By his marriage with Elizabeth Sherman, of New Haven, had children: William Sherman, married in St. Paul; Anna Maria, wife of Joseph Loyd; Margaret, married Dorsey Gardner; Benjamin, married Martha Flagg; Olivia, died young; Elizabeth, wife of Joseph Coats; Joseph C.; and Ella, wife of Edward Coats. By his second wife, Maria Falon, he has one son, Stacy.

Stacy (5), son of Stacy (2), married Mary Somers. Their children are: Charles, city engineer, married Miss Boardley, and they

*Nathaniel Burrowes, who in 1790, married Elizabeth, daughter of David Stout, was the son of Foster Burrowes and Phebe Moore his wife, who was the son of Thomas Burrowes, who was the son of Thomas Burrowes first of Hopewell, who was the son of Edward Burrowes, of Jamaica, Long Island. Nathaniel Burrowes married as his second wife, Maria Coleman, of Lawrence, by whom, besides several other children, he had George, a graduate of Princeton College and Theological Seminary, was a tutor in the former, professor of languages in Lafayette College, Pa., and professor of Oriental and biblical literature in the Theological Seminary of California. He married, first, Helen, daughter of Charles Parker, of Trenton; second, Matilda Shotwell, an English lady, no children.

have children: Mary, Emma, Charles and Boardley; Mary Ann, wife of George Steerver, of Philadelphia; Rachel, married Dr. George Duhring, of Philadelphia; Maria, wife of William Evans, of Philadelphia; Emma; Esther; Sarah, wife of Robert Thompson; and Albert, married Emma Snider.

Joseph (6), son of Stacy (2), by his wife, Sarah Hyllyer, had children: Stacy; John, married Mary Ann Roscoe; Julia; Euphemia; Emily, wife of Samuel Kerr; Margaret, wife of Isaac Woodruff; Joseph E., a practitioner of law at Mays Landing, married Lucy Mull, of Bucks county, Pa.

Anna Potts, daughter of Stacy (2), lived in Trenton, became the wife of William Potts, son of Richard Potts and Rebecca Arney, his wife. Their children were: George S., married Mary Birdsel; Elizabeth, died young; Rebecca; James, died in youth; Margaretta; William Henry, married Hannah Stevens, had children: Herbert, Anna, Henrietta, Isabella and Henry; Thomas and Richard both died young.

Rebecca Potts, daughter of Stacy (2), married George Sherman, who came to Trenton in 1797, and purchased the "New Jersey State Gazette," which he edited with great ability and published till his death. Their children: George P., married Sarah Ann Bellerjeau; Anna P.; Margaretta, died 1831; Sarah T.; James T., who continued in the editorship of the same paper with success after his father's death, he married the widow Caroline H. Higbee, daughter of George Howell, of Philadelphia; Rebecca, died in infancy, and Olivia, married Ezra B. Fuller.

The Reading Family.

John Reading (1), with his wife, Elizabeth, and his two children, John (2) and Elsie, in the year 1686–1687, or, as Gordon states, before 1685, emigrated from England, and probably from London, or its vicinity, as he selected as his place of settlement, the second tenth, or that of the London Company, now Gloucester. When the town and township were laid off, Mr. Reading became the owner of some fifty lots, (building lots, probably,) besides many acres in the town and a body of land of 1200 or more acres in the township. Along his line lies the land of Daniel Reading, supposed to be his brother, containing 600 acres. A large portion of this land, Mr. Reading is thought to have sold before he made his large purchases near Amwell, and which were bequeathed mostly to his son, John (2). Mr. Reading represented Gloucester county in council in 1687, and 1688 was appointed recorder of deeds and surveys, and is named as clerk and recorder of Gloucester county from 1695 to 1701, (Leaming & Spicer's Laws of New Jersey.) Desirous of procuring a better education for his children than New Jersey at that early period afforded, they were sent, in charge of his wife, to England, where they remained for nine years, till their education was finished. Soon after her return, he removed to Howell's Ferry, or Mount Amwell, in what year is not known, though in 1707 we still find him representing Gloucester in council. He was also employed as an agent, with two others, to go to Caponokous and Nimhammoc, chiefs residing above the Falls, to pay the balance due on former purchases, and to make additional ones. This they did to the satisfaction of both parties. He was a surveyor, a man of large property and high standing, and after an active and useful public life, died in 1713 or 1714, and is buried in the grounds of the Buckingham meeting-house, Bucks county, Pa.

Gov. John (2) and his father, John (1), have frequently been confounded with each other. They have been taken to be one person. The acts of the councillor of Gloucester have been assigned to the governor, and the acts of the governor to the councillor. The Rev. George Mott, in his valuable "History of the Flemington Church," errs slightly, in stating that the commissioner to run the state line between New York and New Jersey was John Reading, Sr. James Logan, in a letter to Col. Coxe, says, "The commissioners for running the line June 27th, 1719, are Joseph Kirkbride and John Reading, Jr.," adding, in parentheses, ("Ye old man is deceased.") Mr. Reading's large purchases, amounting to several thousand acres, and his inherited property, rendered him one of the largest landed proprietors of that region. He was a surveyor, as was his father—in the early days of the colonies, a distinguished and profitable profession. He was a man of great influence and largely concerned in the active management of public affairs, and one whose piety prompted to deeds of judicious beneficence. Smith mentions, page 402, that a change took place in the body of councillors—four were suspended, five others were appointed, one of whom was John Reading. This, then—the close of 1713, after the death of his father, and to supply his place—was the commencement of his councillorship, an office which he held till his death, 1767. In 1746, Mr. Reading, as oldest councillor, succeeded, in the management of government affairs, President Hamilton, successor of Lewis Morris, first governor of New Jersey after its separation from New York. Again, by the death of Gov. Belcher, the administration of affairs devolved on John Reading, as president of council, the duties of which office he assumed with great reluctance. His name is first on the list of trustees of the College of New Jersey. He died November 7th, 1767, aged 81, and is buried in the grounds of the Presbyterian Church of Amwell. Over his grave has been erected, within a few years, a monument of Quincy granite, by two of his descendants, John G. Reading, of Philadelphia, and Franklin Reading, of Williamsport, Pa. He left £10 for the purchase of a chalice for the church at Amwell. He married, in 1720, Mary, daughter of Joris (Yoris) or George Ryerson, of Pequenac, Passaic county, and his wife, Ann Schoute. She died April 17th, 1774, aged 78, having had children: John (3), born 1722; George (4), born 1725; Daniel (5), born 1727; Joseph (6), born 1728; Richard, born 1732, married Catharine, by whom he had several children, in 1767, he offered for sale his lot lying a mile along the Delaware, of 456 acres, on which is a mill, a store, a stone house, with four rooms on a floor, and 600 acres elsewhere, he was appointed a justice of the county, after residing a short time in Trenton, he removed to Long Island, and died about 1781, his family is no further traced; Thomas (7), born 1734; Ann, married Rev. Charles Beatty, (see Beatty family, No. 2); Mary, married Rev. William Mills, of Jamaica, L. I.; Elizabeth, married John Hackett, of Hackettstown; and Samuel, born 1741, died 1749.

John (3), son of John (2), who died 1766, married Isabella, daughter of William Montgomery, of Ayr, Scotland; had children: John (8); Charles, married Abigail, daughter of Thomas Hunt, of Amwell, had a son, Henry; Rebecca; Montgomery, was a judge, removed to Sussex county; Alexander, married Sarah, daughter of Daniel Reading (5); Theodocia; and Mary.

John (8), son of John (3), who died November, 1820, aged 69, married Elizabeth, daughter of Joseph Hankinson, who died 1817. Their children were: Mary, died 1825, aged 53; William, killed by a fall from a horse, aged 19; John, died 1821, aged 46, not married; Ann; and Joseph (9). He leaves to his oldest male descendant a silver tankard, which his grandfather, Governor John, had given him, having on it the family coat-of-arms, and it was by him to be transmitted in the same way—now in the possession of Judge James N. Reading.

Joseph (9), son of John (8), who died 1853, aged 75, married Eleanor, daughter of Dr. John Grandon, of Hamburgh, Hunterdon county, and had issue by her: James Newell (10); Mary Ann, wife of William Hedges, of Somerville, who had a daughter, Elizabeth, wife of Rev. John Schofield; John Grandon (11); Philip G. (12); William (13); and Joseph H., married Sarah, daughter of Samuel Evans, of Trenton, have a daughter, Mary, wife of Robert C. Belville.

Judge James N. (10), son of Joseph (9), a graduate of Princeton, went to Missouri as president of a lead-mining company; after two years he removed to Morris, Ill., where he practiced law and is state judge. He married in 1836, Sarah C., daughter of Isaac Southard, New Jersey state treasurer, whose children are: Mary S., wife of Edward Sanford, of Saybrook, Conn., a lawyer of Morris, Ill.; Eleanor G., married Hamilton Longworth, died young; Julia N., wife of Lyman B. Ray, of Vermont; Henry S., a merchant of Morris, married Cornelia, daughter of Levi Hill; and Joseph, died in infancy.

John G. (11), son of Joseph (9), a successful merchant, now

resident in Philadelphia, married Sarah F., daughter of Henry H. Woodhull, son of Rev. Dr. William Woodhull. They have one daughter: Mary Anna, wife of Joseph Gazzam, of Pittsburg.

Philip G. (12), son of Joseph (9), married Evelina E., daughter of Samuel Evans, and has children: Joseph, who with his wife, Mary M., daughter of Alexander Slack, went seven years ago as a missionary to Africa; Charles N., married Ella F., daughter of Peter S. Hunt; and James, married Lilly May, daughter of John W. Fox.

William (13), son of Joseph (9), married Sarah M., daughter of Hugh Capner, and have children: Hugh C., married Louisa Blanchard, of Baltimore; and Joseph, married Elizabeth A. Marshall, of Virginia.

George (4), son of John (2), was a member of assembly for Hunterdon county, 1761, died 1792, aged 67, married, and had children: John Mullen; George; Elizabeth; Charles, married and had children: Thomas, and Henry; and Samuel, married a daughter of Samuel Governeur, of Newark; he was appointed captain, and promoted to the rank of major of the First Regiment of New Jersey in the Continental Army, was in the expedition to Canada, and was taken prisoner at the battle of Three Rivers.

Daniel (5), son of John (2), who died 1768, aged 41, married Euphemia, daughter of Col. John Reid, of Monmouth, and by her had children: John Reid (14); Daniel, married Jane Kenedy, had one son, Daniel, who by his will established a school at Flemington; Ellen, wife of James Montgomery, son of James Montgomery, of Eglinton, whose children are: Esther Ward, and William Reading, who attained the rank of brigadier-general in the regular army in the Mexican war, and was distinguished for gallantry in the battles of Palo Alto, Resaca de la Palma, and Molino del Rey, in Mexico, and was commander of the First New Jersey Volunteers at the battle of Bull Run; Ann, married Thomas Wood, and by him became the mother of the eminent lawyer, George Wood, of the New Jersey and afterward of the New York bar; Sarah, wife of Alexander Reading; Euphemia married Thomas Grey, of Flemington, N. J.; and Theodocia, married Rev. Thomas Grant, a Presbyterian clergyman of Flemington.

John Reid (14), son of Daniel (5), married Mary Ann Kennedy, by whom he had children: Robert (15); Daniel; Maria, wife of Henry Disbrow, whose children are: Daniel R., Robert, Edward

Wood, and Isaac; Theodocia, wife, first, of Nicholas Depue, by whom she had a son, Robert, who married Matilda Disborough, her second husband was Isaac Farlee, by whom she had children: Anna, wife of Augustus G. Richey, a lawyer of Trenton, Eliza, wife of Peter Coxe, George W., married Elizabeth, daugher of Mayor Opdyke, of New York; and John Reading, married Hannah, daughter of Isaac Scudder, (see Scudder family, No. 26.)

Judge Robert (15), son of John (14), who died 1850, aged 65, married Maria, daughter of Col. James Henry, and sister of Rev. Dr. Symms C. Henry. Their children were: Franklin, married Mary, daughter of Charles Hepburn, of Williamsport; Symmes; Harrison, married widow Harriet Bradshaw, (Morrison) of Wisconsin; R. Charleton, married Elizabeth Sproll; Eliza, wife of Edward Remington; Mary, wife of John Grandon, of Cincinnati; Elmira, wife of Alexander Gulick, of Kingston, N. J.; and Jane.

Joseph (6), son of John (2), was made captain of a company of militia by Governor Belcher, and was, in 1776, appointed judge of the Court of Common Pleas. His will is dated 1806. He married Amy Pierson, and by her had children: William (16); John, first lieutenant in Fourth Company Third Battalion of New Jersey, was at the battle of Quebec, he married Mary Harrison, of Princeton, had one daughter, married Henry Provost; Joseph (17); Samuel 18); Pierson (19); Amy, wife of Cornelius Harrison, no children: Sarah, wife of Finchen Helens; Elizabeth, wife of Samuel Boyle, whose children are: Theodocia, Anastasia, Amy, and Mary; Nancy, not married; Theodocia, not married; Rebecca, married John Anderson, and moved to Ohio, had sons, Robert and Joshua; and Mary, not married.

William (16), son of Joseph (6), married Nancy Emly, whose children were: Elisha (20); Joseph, married Nancy Doyl, no children; Asher (21); William (22); and George, married.

Elisha (20), son of William (16), married Anna, daughter of Joseph Reading (17). Their children are: William; Anastasia; Joseph; Lucy E; George Jackson.

Asher (21); son of William (16); married Margaret Wolverton, and had children: Nancy; John; Kensell; Sarah; Samuel; Mary; and Margaret.

William (22), son of William (16), married Elizabeth Sergeant, had children: Charles; Joseph; Sarah; Amelia; Emma; Taresia; and Asher.

Joseph (17), son of Joseph (6), married Lucy Emly, and had children: Amy, married George Opdycke; Anna, wife of Elisha Reading (20); John, married Martha Sergeant; Hannah, wife of Edmund Rittenhouse; Maria, wife of Joseph West; Theodocia, wife of Larison Stryker; and Lucy E., married William Kugler.

Samuel (18), son of Joseph (6), married, first, Ellen, daughter of Joshua Anderson, (see Anderson family, No. 1,) by whom he had children: William (23); Pierson (24); Joshua; Anderson; Eliza, married, first, Mr. Lambert, had a son, Joseph; her second husband was Cornelius Wilson, by whom she had children: Ellen and Cornelius; Ellen, married Joseph Reading; and Lucy. By his second wife, Susan, daughter of Isaac Rittenhouse, of Kingwood, he had Louis; and Theodocia, wife of Mr. Collens.

William (23), son of Samuel (18), married Deborah Coryell, of Kingwood, and had children: Samuel R.; Augustus; Sarah; Emma; and Joanna.

Pierson (24), son of Samuel (18), married Mary Gaw, and had children: Anderson; Ellen; Louis, married, first, Isabella Foster; second, Mrs. Shaw, daughter of Rev. D. W. Bartine; Victoria, married John Temple, of Louisiana; Pierson; Olivia, married William McCready; Charles, married Kate Mathews; and Mary, married Edward Solliday.

Pierson (19), son of Joseph (6), who died August 26th, 1847, aged 67, married, first, Mary, daughter of Samuel Opdycke, and Susanna Robeson, by whom he had children: Susan, married Robeson Rockhill, and had one child, John, a merchant of Philadelphia, who married Caroline (Burton), widow of John Guild Reading; Amy, became the third wife of Rev. Eli F. Cooley, (see Cooley family, No. 18); Joseph, died aged 16; Mary, wife of George Mason, whose children are: John, and Susan. His second wife was Charity Guild, widow of William E. Green, (see Green family, No. 42), by whom he had Pierson (25); John Guild died 1850, a merchant of Philadelphia, married Caroline Burton of that city, had one child, Robert, died young; and Alfred, married Miss Conner.

Major Pierson (25), son of Pierson (19), impressed with the spirit of adventure at an early age, was one of the first emigrants to California, then an almost unexplored region, and before the discovery of gold there. He became a large purchaser of lands which were afterwards confirmed to him by the United States. He was there when Commodore Stockton, indignant at the aggressions of the Mexicans and their insolence toward Americans, landed his crew, converting his sailors into artillery, and his marines into infantry, and with the aid of a few settlers extemporized an army. Major Reading, in command of a division of this little army, participated in that series of victories which won to our arms the country. Commodore Stockton with his characteristic energy, had chastised the natives, defeated them at all points, and had taken possession of the country, established a government and appointed Colonel John C. Fremont to govern it, before the news of the declaration of war by the United States had reached there. Major Reading was the Whig candidate for governor, but being defeated by a small majority, he would never afterwards, though often solicited, enter the arena of politics; he chose rather to look after the concerns of his large landed estate. His children were Jeannette, wife of Col. Robert Simson, a lawyer of San Francisco; Anna; Alice; Robert; Richard; and Nina, having married Fanny, daughter of Dr. Washington, of Washington, D. C.

Thomas (7), son of John (2), who died 1814, aged 80, was captain of the Sixth Company of the Third New Jersey Battalion, and took an active part in the operations before Quebec, in 1776, was appointed judge, was a trustee in the old Amwell church, a founder of the Flemington Presbyterian Church, and one of its first elders and trustees. He married Rebecca Ellis, and by her had children: Joseph, married Miss Waldron, had a son killed in battle; George, married Tace Reed; Francis (26); Ellis, married and had children: Thomas, Edgar, a physician, and others; Deborah, wife of Dr. Bertron, whose son, Samuel R., is a graduate of Princeton, and a Presbyterian clergyman resident at Port Gibson, Miss.; Sarah, married Capt. Joseph Phillips, of Pennington, (see Phillips family. No. 24); Harriet, married Jeremiah King; and Polly, not married.

Francis (26), son of Thomas (7), married a daughter of William Pond, and had children: William; Amanda; Henry; Austin; Gideon; John; and Miller, a physician.

Else Reading, daughter of John (1), became the wife of Daniel Howell, who resided in the upper part of the state, near Amwell, who died about 1730, date of his will, his executors being his brother-in-law, John Reading (2), and Mr. Rittenhouse. Their children were: Daniel; John; Elizabeth; Mary; Benjamin; and Joseph.

Daniel Howell, son of Daniel Howell and Else Reading, married Julianna Holcomb, and had children : Reading ; John, died unmarried ; and a daughter.

Reading Howell, son of Daniel Howell, was quartermaster of Second Regiment of Hunterdon county in the Revolution. He married Catharine, daughter of Edward Yerkers, and by her had issue : Clarissa, J., not married ; Henrietta M., married John J. Wheeler, of Philadelphia, whose children are : Catharine H., wife of Robert Clarkson, Edward H., of Pottsville, Anna M., married Edward Hammekin, of New York, and John H., of Philadelphia ; Harriet Ann, wife of Joseph Montgomery, of Philadelphia ; Courtland, married ; John Fisher, died unmarried ; Edward Y., a physician, died unmarried ; Rebecca ; and Catharine Augusta, wife of Gen. Thomas Flournoy, of Augusta, Ga.

The Reed Family.

William Reed (1), from whom most of that name in Ewing and Lawrence derive their origin, followed about 1700 the current from Long Island. He purchased of John Brearley, a farm in the western part of the township of Lawrence, near the boundary of Ewing, on which he settled and lived till his death, May 16th, 1762, aged 73, leaving children: Amos; William (2); Joshua (3); Joseph (4); and Eunice, married Daniel Furman, (see Furman family, No. 5.)

William (2), son of William (1), married, and had a son, Daniel, who married Sallie Pierson, whose children were: Nancy, wife of Abner Cook, died 1865, aged 86; and Naomi, not married.

Joshua (3), son of William (1), married Abigail, daughter of Joseph Hart, (see Hart family, No. 2,) and had children: Daniel Furman; Lois, married her cousin, Israel Reed (8); and Joshua (5).

Joshua (5), son of Joshua (3), died September 11th, 1831, aged 64. By his first wife, Mary, daughter of Ralph Lanning, (see Lanning family, No. 8,) had children: Abner, who died February 24th, 1847, aged 50, his wife was Isabella, daughter of Ralph Lanning, no children; Ralph, died young; Lydia, married Joseph Furman. His second wife was Elizabeth Jones, who died 1849, aged 72, by whom he had Levi; and George (6).

George (6), son of Joshua (5), married Mary, daughter of Edward Hepburn, and died September 7th, 1849, aged 41. Their children are: Alfred, born 1839, was a student of Rutgers College and the Law School of Poughkeepsie, N. Y. He practiced law first in New York, then in Trenton. He was elected mayor of Trenton in 1867. Was appointed judge of the court of common pleas in 1869, and has for several years been justice of the Supreme Court; he married Rosalba E. Souder; Amanda, wife of Edward T. Persons, of Illinois; and Dr. Edward H.

Joseph (4), son of William (1), married Else Lanning, and had children: John (7); Israel (8); Azariah (9); Elizabeth, married

Jacob Blackwell, and removed to another state; and Anna, married Stephen Dean, (see Dean family, No. 2.)

John (7), son of Joseph (4), married Catharine Hutchinson. Their children were: Elizabeth, married Abel Appleton, and went West; Theodocia, married James Grant; Sarah, married Benjamin Laird; Anna, married Thomas Quigley; Aaron, married Catharine Furman, of Monmouth; Joseph, married in Philadelphia; Pierson, married Eleanor Abbott; Abijah, married Jerusha Quick, went West; and John, married Rachel Lake.

Israel (8), son of Joseph (4), who died February 8th, 1825, aged 80, married Lois, daughter of Joshua Reed (3), had by her, children: Susan, died September 11th, 1851, aged 78; Asa (10); Eunice, died March 7th, 1857, aged 78; Bathsheba; and Abigail, married Thomas Quigley.

Asa (10), son of Israel (8), who was in the eldership of the Ewing Church until his death, January, 1847, aged 67, married Sarah, daughter of Amos Lanning. Their children were: Amos, died young; Charles (11); Andrew (12); Phebe, married William Barlow; Lois, became the second wife of Jesse Smith; and William (13).

Charles (11), son of Asa (10), died September 21st, 1875, aged 69, having married Elizabeth, daughter of Noah Tindall, (see Tindall family, No. 4,) whose children are: Phebe, married Charles Smith, son of Abijah Smith; Amanda, married Gilbert Furman; William Henry, married, first, Fanny, daughter of Andrew Green, second, Hannah, daughter of Henry Lanning; Mary Frances, married John Morris; and Israel, married, first, Mary Tindall; second, Mary Girton.

Andrew (12), son of Asa (10), died April 17th, 1868, aged 65, having married Maria, daughter of James C. Green, (see Green family, No. 50.) Their children are: Sarah, wife of Cornelius Coryell; Kesiah, wife of Jacob Maple; Amos, married Mary Taylor; James, married Emma Knowles; Susan Elizabeth, married Stephen Reed; and Edward, responded to the call of his country in August, 1862, was in the service two years, when he was killed in the battle of Cold Spring, Va.

William (13), son of Asa (10), married, first, Mary, daughter of Samuel B. Green, who died June 29th, 1849, aged 37, leaving a daughter, Sarah Elizabeth, married John Riley. His second wife is Gertrude Conover, (widow Updike), whose children are: George E., married Anna Coleman; Charles A., married Rebecca Coleman; and Edward, married Minnie Reed.

Azariah (9), son of Joseph (4), who died March 5th, 1833, married Elizabeth, daughter of Abraham Temple, (see Temple family, No. 2.) She died February 13th, 1841, aged 86, leaving children: Daniel (14); Azubah, married Noah Cook, and had children: Daniel, Clarissa, wife, first, of Samuel McMurray, second, of Amos Furman, Rosetta, Abigail, Azariah, married a widow Stilman; and John, married Elizabeth, daughter of Samuel Hart; Phebe, married Phineas Tomlinson, (see Tomlinson family, No. 4,) and died 1859; Deborah; David (15); John, died in youth; Joseph, married Jemima, daughter of Elijah Cook, no children; Rachel, married Abijah Smith; Abigail, married Isaac Mershon, and their children are: Martha, married William Wilson, Sarah, Mary, William, and Isaac—the last four died young; and Israel, who married in succession, Eliza, daughter of James Lilly, Martha Riley, and Elizabeth Ann Mount; by the first wife he had a son, Joseph, who died aged 20.

Daniel (14), son of Azariah (9), was lieutenant in Captain David Pierson's Company, Eighteenth Regiment of Hunterdon, in 1777. He married Sarah, daughter of Nathaniel Hunt, and had children: Azariah, married Mary, daughter of Henry Reed; John, died young; Elizabeth, married Abraham Voorhees, of Hightstown; Benjamin (16); William, married Elizabeth, daughter of Samuel Perrine, of Freehold; Joseph, died young; Sarah, married John Wilson, of Hightstown; Abner, married Lydia, daughter of John Hutchinson, of the same place, had by her: Joseph, and two daughters.

Benjamin (16), son of Daniel (14), who died 1865, was a man of handsome property, owning a large and valuable farm in the vicinity of Hightstown, of which place he was a resident; he was also president of the bank of that place. He married Lydia, daughter of John Story, of Cranbury, and had issue by her: Armstead, married Miss Anderson; Story, married Miss Hutchinson; Amanda, married Edward Applegate, member of the New Jersey assembly.

David (15), son of Azariah (9), married Melce, daughter of Jonathan Pierson, by whom he had: Adeline, married John Cunningham, of Monmouth; Sarah, wife of Joseph Curtiss; Phebe, wife of Elisha Reed, of Sandtown; Elizabeth; Enoch, married Maria Hagerman; Abraham T., married Esther Insley, of Trenton; Jonathan, married Rachel Anderson; Rebecca, married William Ford; and Azuba, married Enoch Ford.

The Reeder Family.

John Reeder (1), the earliest American ancestor of the families of that name residing in Ewing township and vicinity, was of English origin, having emigrated from that country before the year 1656, to Newtown, L. I. His name is found in that year, on the list of the residents of that town who purchased the title to their lands of the Indians, having failed to obtain it by patent from the Dutch governor, Stuyvesant. His son, John (2), came to Ewing in the early part of the eighteenth century, and married Hannah, daughter of Jeremiah Burroughs, also one of the first settlers of the township, and by her had a son, Isaac (3), whose name is signed to an agreement August 26th, 1703, and also Joseph Reeder's.

Isaac (3), son of John (2), purchased of Zebulon Heston the farm on which he afterward lived, and which still remains in the possession of one of his lineal descendants, Amos (14). He died 1763, aged 85. By his first wife, Elizabeth, widow of John Yard, he had a daughter, Sarah, who never married. By his second wife, Joanna Hunt, he had John (4), and Abia, died, aged 18.

John (4), son of Isaac (3), died 1788, aged 64, having married, January 18th, 1753, Hannah Mershon. She died 1781, aged 49, having had children: Isaac, born 1754, and died, aged 30, having married Rachel, daughter of Daniel Scudder, (see Scudder family, No. 12,) by whom he had no children; Charles (5); Andrew, married Sarah, daughter of Stephen Burrowes, died, aged 49; John (6); Francina, born 1758, married Capt. Robert Chambers, (see Chambers family, No. 5); Abigail, born 1760, died unmarried; Letitia, born 1761, married, first, Henry Krewsen, second, Joseph Hunt, whose children are: Peter, Mary, and Letitia; Absalom (7); Hannah, born 1764, wife of Amos Hartley, of Amwell, whose children are: Mary, Garret Schenck, John, and Amos; Abner, born 1766, married Hannah Wilkinson, of Pennsylvania; Benjamin, born 1768, died, aged 15; Amos (8); Rebecca, died, aged 12; Mercy, born 1774, wife of William Praul, of Amwell, had

William R., died young; and Elizabeth, wife of Solomon Landis, had one daughter.

Charles (5), son of John (4), who died 1861, aged 78, is buried in Lawrenceville. He married Martha, daughter of Richard Green, (see Green family, No. 10,) and had children: Sarah, wife of Timothy Baker, of Lawrence; Mary, married Louis Hutchinson; Christiana, wife of Philip Hendrickson; Charles; Louis; Abner; Isaac, died young; and Elizabeth.

John (6), son of John (4), died 1830, having married Susannah Fleming, the widow of Isaac Howell, by whom he had Isaac, who married Catharine Williams, and had children: Mary Ann, wife of Samuel Backus, and Catharine, wife of William H. Clark; Letitia, married Andrew Slack; and Sarah, married Levi Howell.

Absalom (7), son of John (4), married, October 16th, 1788, Christiana Smith, of Easton, Pa., where he resided. He died 1847, aged 84. Their children were: Andrew Horatio (9), born July 12th, 1807; Edward Augustus (10), born November 29th, 1812; and Abner Lucius, born July 29th, 1818, and died June 23d, 1833.

Andrew H. (9), son of Absalom (7), was appointed governor of Kansas territory by President Pierce, on June 29th, 1854, and was removed for his refusal to use his position to aid in making Kansas a slave state. He was elected the first delegate to congress from the territory, and first United States senator after its admission into the Union. He was appointed brigadier-general in the regular army, by President Lincoln, at the outbreak of the Rebellion. He died at Easton, July 5th, 1864, having there married September 13th, 1831, Frederica A., daughter of Col. Christian J. Hutter, by whom he had children: Harriet L., died in infancy; Emily C., died in infancy; Ida T., wife of William W. Marsh, of Schooley's Mountain, N. J., whose children are: Cora L., Jennie A., Ray, and Ethel; George Marchand (11); Emma Hutter, married J. Charles Ferriday, of Natchez, Miss., and died May 12th, 1865, her children are: Amelia, died in infancy, and Andrew Reeder; Howard James (12); Frank (13); and Andrew Jackson, died in infancy.

George M. (11), son of Andrew H. (9), was captain in the First Regiment of Kansas Volunteers; is now editor and publisher of the Easton "Daily Express." He married Mary Niles, and has children: Harold H.; and Donald M.

Howard James (12), son of Andrew H. (9), and his brother,

Frank, left Princeton College in their senior year, to enter the volunteer army. He was first lieutenant of First U. S. Infantry and captain of the One Hundred and Fifty-third Pennsylvania Volunteers. He is, by profession, a lawyer, and is ex-judge of the Court of Common Pleas of Northampton county, Pa. He married Helen Burke, of Easton, and has had children: Andrew, died in infancy; Leila B.; and John K.

Gen. Frank (13), son of Andrew H. (9), was colonel in the Nineteenth Pennsylvania Cavalry, collector of internal revenue under President Grant, and brigadier-general of National Guards of Pennsylvania. He is a graduate of the Albany Law School, and practices his profession in Easton, Pa. He married Grace E. Thompson, of Boston, Mass., and has children: Andrew Horatio; Grosvenor Lowrey; and Frank.

Edward (9), son of Absalom (7), married, January 9th, 1839, Harriet Stem, of Easton, Pa., and had children; Sarah B.; Ella E.; and Lucretia M.

Amos (8), son of John (4), died 1855, aged 85. By his first wife, Mary, daughter of Joseph Stillwell, of Monmouth, had children: Christiana, died 1816, aged 20; Joseph Stillwell, died unmarried, aged 26; Mary, married Jasper Smith Scudder, (see Scudder family, No. 17); Andrew, a merchant of Trenton, married Sallie Ann, daughter of Isaac Kremsen, by whom he had Emma and Stillwell, died young; and Hannah, married Abner Scudder. By his second wife, Rachel, daughter of Thomas Folwell, widow of Alexander Hemphill, of Pennsylvania, who died 1854, in her 72d year, had children: Amos (14); Caroline, wife of Nathan Folwell, a physician practicing in Ithaca, N. Y.; Matilda, wife of Henry Lefferts; William; Sarah, wife of George Dean; Virginia, wife of Henry P. Green, (see Green family, No. 46); and Amanda, wife of Oliver Bond, of Trenton.

Amos (14), son of Amos (8), married, first, Catharine Anderson; had one son, Alfred, who married, first, Maggie S. Covert, and, second, Cornelia, daughter of Enoch Jones, (see Jones family, No. 5.) His second wife is Mary, daughter of Holmes Large, by whom he has children: Stillwell: and Hannah, wife of John G. Howell.

NOTE.—Henry Krewsen (1) married Letitia, daughter of John Reeder (4). She died 1796, aged 36. Their children were: Henry (2); Absalom, married Sally, daughter of Benjamin Clark, (see Clark family, No. 5); and Isaac, married Louisa West, whose children were: Henry, Elizabeth, and Sally Ann, married Andrew Reeder, son of Amos (8).

Henry Krewsen (2), son of Henry (1), died 1857, aged 69, married Mary, daughter of Theophilus Phillips, of Lawrence, (see Phillips family, No. 10.) She died 1857, aged 71, having had: Letitia, wife of Samuel Roberts; Andrew; Horace, married, at Pittsburg, a young lady from England, he died in early manhood; William, died in youth; Mary Ann, married Titus Stout, son of John; and Henry, married Elizabeth, daughter of John Stout.

14

The Jacob Reeder Family.

Jacob Reeder was also one of the first settlers of Ewing township, and for a time an active participator in its concerns. He purchased a farm, on which he settled, but finding his title to it not good, and being required to pay for it a second time or resign it, he chose the latter alternative, and removed from the township. He married, about 1717, Anna, daughter of Robert Blackwell. We presume it is he who, by his will, dated 1760, at Amwell, leaves property to his wife, Elizabeth; to his granddaughters, Elizabeth and Anna, daughters of his daughter, Phebe; to his brother Benjamin; and to his nephew, William, son of his brother Joseph.

Whether Jacob Reeder was the brother of John (1), we are unprepared to decide, but presume that he was.

The Roberts Family.

Thomas Roberts (1), before the year 1727, resigned his home on Long Island for one in Hopewell. By his wife, Jane, who died 1804, he had children: Philip, died 1811; Edmund (2); and Sarah, married Mr. Pierson.

Edmund (2), son of Thomas (1), who died 1839, aged 82, held the office of elder, trustee and deacon in the Pennington Church. He married, first, Mercy Moore, died 1814; second, Elizabeth Hamilton, died 1817; third, Elizabeth Stillwell, died 1824; his children were: Samuel, died in youth; Ephraim (3); Elizabeth, wife of Benjamin Van Cleve, (see Van Cleve family, No. 16); and Philip, not married.

Ephraim (3), son of Edmund (2), died 1836, having married Mary, daughter of Nathaniel Hart, (see Hart family, No. 15); he died 1849, aged 65, had children: Samuel, married, first, Letitia, daughter of Henry Krewson, had two children, died in childhood; second, Sarah, daughter of Benjamin Van Cleve, (see Van Cleve family, No. 16,) widow of Benjamin Smith; Eliza, wife of William Green, (see Green family, No. 18); Edmund, married Frances Glenn; and Nathaniel, married Augusta Stillwell, of Amwell.

The Rose Family.

Stephen Rose (1), at an early period after the settlement of Ewing, came from Long Island with his sisters, Elizabeth, who died 1806, aged 90, unmarried, and Sybil, who became the wife of Richard Lanning, (see Lanning family, No. 4.) He was an elder in the church, and died August 16th, 1775, aged 65, having married Elizabeth, daughter of Ebenezer Prout.* She died January 30th. 1779, leaving children: Elizabeth, died unmarried, 1811, aged 63; Phebe, died January 9th, 1772, aged 33, married Amos Scudder, (see Scudder family, No. 13); Deborah, married Daniel Howell, (see Howell family, No. 6); Ebenezer (2); and Patience, died March 13th, 1785, aged 39, married Henry Baker, of Hopewell, who died January 3d, 1827.

Ebenezer (2), son of Stephen (1), succeeded his father in the eldership of the church, died April 20th, 1831, aged 87, having married Eunice, daughter of Stephen Burrowes, son of Thomas, and grandson of Edward, of Jamaica, L. I. She died August 18th, 1819, aged 70. Their children were: Stephen, born January 6th, 1769, married Elizabeth Wynkoop, of Pennsylvania, and died March, 1833, without children; Phebe, married March 17th, 1795, Jonas Addoms, of New York, whose children are: Elizabeth, wife of Samuel Kissam, Phebe R., William, married Margaretta Lawrence, Charles, married Sarah Buckley, John, married, and Henry, married, lives in Kansas; Ebenezer P. (3); and Samuel, died July 19th, 1810, aged 24, not married.

Ebenezer P. (3), son of Ebenezer (2), was an active business

*Timothy Prout, who was one of the earliest settlers of Boston, and who had a son, Ebenezer, prominent in the affairs of Watertown, which he represented in the assembly of 1693, was probably the ancestor of Ebenezer Prout, of Middlesex, Conn., whose son, Ebenezer, came to Ewing township about the year 1700, and purchased the farm still in the possession of his descendants in the sixth generation. He died October 22d, 1754, and his widow, Elizabeth, January 30th, 1759. Their children were: Elizabeth, wife of Stephen Rose; Timothy, died January 24th, 1731; Joseph, died three days after his brother; John, killed by lightning while sitting in the door-way, August 9th, 1732; Mary, wife of George Ely, died 1736; Love, wife of Captain John Moore; Rebecca, baptized at Maidenhead; and Eunice.

man, resident of Trenton, died June 21st, 1836, aged 52, having married Catharine, daughter of Dr. Jonathan Forman, of Freehold. She died September 2d, 1854, aged 66, having had children: Elizabeth W., wife of George Kissam, son of Dr. Kissam, of New York, whose children are: George F., married Julia Durant, Catharine, died aged 9, and Lillie R.; Stephen B., married Sarah T. Wykoff, of Monmouth, and removed to Utah, and had children: Charles, Anna, Kate, Harrison, and one other, died young; Jonathan Forman (4); Catharine, died aged 2; and Samuel K., married Matilda Hobensack, had one child, George K., died in infancy.

Jonathan Forman (4), son of Ebenezer (3), owned and lived on the farm transmitted from his great-great-grandfather, Ebenezer Prout, died May 21st, 1877, aged 59. He married, first, Elizabeth, daughter of Benjamin Hendrickson, (see Hendrickson family, No. 7,) and by her had children: Emma, wife of William H. Cooley; and Catharine, died at St. Mary's Hall, Burlington; second, Caroline, daughter of William Paff, of Yardleyville, Pa., whose children are: Ella; Mary L.; and Forman.

The Rozell Family.

George Rozell (1), of Lawrenceville, died 1773, having married Ruth, daughter of John Brearley, (see Brearley family, No. 1,) of that village, whose children, besides possibly others, were : Bathsheba ; John (2); and Nathaniel, married Abigail, probably no children, as he leaves by his will dated 1770, his property to his brother John's two sons, John and George, and to his kinsmen, William, James and Nathaniel Coalman.

John (2), son of George (1), died 1800, aged 64, at his home in Lawrenceville. He married Anna, daughter of John Van Cleve, (see Van Cleve family, No. 3.) She died 1786, aged 40, having had children : George, married Sarah Oxford ; John, married Mary Kerwood ; Bathsheba, wife of Waters Smith ; Catharine, married Ellett Tucker ; Ruth, wife of Israel Stevens ; and Anna, died young.

Catharine, daughter of John (2), died 1872, aged 88, married Ellett Tucker, son of William. He died 1821, aged 46. Their children were : Mary Ann, wife of James Wright ; Marcia Ellett ; George ; John R. ; William ; Cornelia ; Elizabeth ; Sarah ; Ellett ; and Louisa.

Mary Ann Tucker, daughter of Catharine Tucker, by her husband, James Wright, had children ; Cornelia, wife of Joseph Roney, whose children are : Joseph, Harry and John Hall ; Elizabeth, wife of George Conover, whose children are : Mary, James, William, Elizabeth and George ; Morrison, married Abby Morgan, and has children : Ella, Janetta and Marcia.

Marcia Ellett, daughter of Catharine Tucker, married Andrew Morrison McNeely, who died January 27th, 1849, aged 54. They had children : Robert ; Cornelia ; Mary Ann ; Morrison ; and William M., married Elizabeth, daughter of the Hon. Cornelius Dickerson, of Morris county.

Cornelia, daughter of Catharine Tucker, became the wife of Robert McNeely, and had children : John ; James ; and Charles.

NOTE.—William Tucker, brother of Samuel, was a trustee of the First Presbyterian Church. By his wife, Mercy, had children: William; Ellett; Mary, married James B. Matchett, of Trenton, and died at St. Charles, Missouri, in 1833, aged 71; her husband died in the same place and year, aged 80.

Samuel Tucker was a man of distinction in his day. He was sheriff of Hunterdon county, was president of the provincial congress that sat at Trenton from October 4th to 28th, 1775, and framed the constitution, which he officially signed July 2d, 1776. In 1768, he was a competitor of John Hart, afterwards a signer of the Declaration, for membership in the assembly of the province, and was successful, for although Mr. Hart was warmly supported by the Presbyterians, the united strength of the Methodists, Episcopalians, and Baptists, who were the favorers of Mr. Tucker, proved too much for him. Mr. Tucker left £50 to the Presbyterian Church, and £30 to the Episcopal. He married Elizabeth Gould, an English lady. They both lie buried in the little dilapidated and neglected enclosure on the hill beyond the State Lunatic Asylum, near Trenton. He died January 14th, 1789, aged 67 years, 3 months, and 19 days. She, the daughter of James and Ann Gould, died May 13th, 1787, aged 57 years and 8 months. The little run at the foot of the hill, known as Gold's run, may have taken its name from this family.

The Scudder Family.

The parliament of Great Britain, in the year 1643, for the purpose of revising the thirty-nine articles of the Church of England and of harmonizing the doctrines of the church with those of the Church of Scotland and of the Protestant churches of the continent, called together an assembly of the most able theologians and of prominent laymen of the nobility and gentry, forming, altogether, a body the most distinguished that ever held its sessions for a religious purpose on her soil. "One of the two most important synods," says Baxter, "that ever met," the other being that at Nicea. This convention met on the 1st of July, 1643, in the chapel of Henry VII., Westminster Abbey, from that circumstance known in history as the Westminster Assembly.

It was composed of ten members of the house of lords, twenty of the house of commons, six commissioners from the Presbyterian Church of Scotland—at the head of whom was the Duke of Argyle, an elder of the church—and one hundred and forty-two clergymen of England, the most eminent for their piety and learning, and of different denominations. They continued in session more than five years and a half, and the result of their labors was, besides a revision of the thirty-nine articles, the Westminster Confession of Faith and Catechism.

Among the clerical members of this venerable assembly were several who bear names not unfamiliar to our ears, and who may, without any great stretch of probability, be presumed to be of kindred families with those of corresponding names among us. Such are the following:

Rev. Jeremiah Burroughs, A. M., of Stepney; Rev. Humphrey Chambers, B. D., Claverton, Somersetshire; Rev. Thomas Coleman, M. A., Belyson; Rev. John Green, Pencomb, Herefordshire; Rev. Thomas Hill, B. D., Titchmarch, master of Trinity College, Cambridge; Rev. John Phillips, Wrentham, Suffolkshire; Rev. Henry Scudder, B. D., Colingborne, Ducis, Wiltshire; Rev. Peter Smith, D. D., Barkway; Rev. Thomas Temple, D. D., Battersea,

Surrey; Rev. John White, M. A., Dorchester; Rev. Thomas Wincop (Wyncoop), D. D., Ellesworth, Cambridge.

The above names serve, at least, to indicate the nationality of those in our midst bearing similar names.

Rev. Henry Scudder, of Colingborne, Wiltshire, England, one of these illustrious divines, graduated at Christ College, Cambridge, and was afterwards minister at Drayton, in Oxfordshire, where he was held in the highest esteem for his prudence, piety, and his excellent ministerial labors. Mr. Scudder was a constant attendant at the meetings of the assembly, and took an active part in its deliberations. He was appointed to lead the devotional exercises of the lords and commons, who sat in a room apart from the divines. He was distinguished as a preacher, and was the author of several valuable works, one of which, "The Christian's Daily Walk," has received the highest commendation from men of learning and distinction.

Thomas Scudder (1), the progenitor of most, if not all, the Scudders in America, was a near relative, if not a brother, of this Rev. Henry Scudder. He, with his family, left London, or its vicinity, and is found at Salem, Mass., as early as 1635, where he resided till his death, in 1658. He was familiarly known as "Old Goodman Scudder." In his will, dated 1657, he names his wife, Elizabeth; his sons, John (2); Thomas (3); and Henry (4); his daughter, Elizabeth; and his grandson, Thomas, son of his son William (5). His wife died in 1666. His daughter, Elizabeth, born about 1622, and died 1682, was the wife of Henry Bartholomew, a man of distinction in Massachusetts, who died 1692, aged 92; she was the mother of ten children. His son William (5) continued to live in Salem until his death, between 1651 and 1657. Thomas, son of William (5), married Sarah Maverick, and died in Boston, 1689. In his will, he calls himself a mariner, and names his wife, Sarah, but no children.

John (2), son of Thomas (1), removed, with his brothers, Thomas (3) and Henry (4), from Salem to Southold, in 1651, thence to Huntingdon, in 1657, and before 1660, John is found at Newtown, L. I., prominently engaged in its concerns. He married, about 1642, Mary, born 1623, in England, eldest daughter of William and Dorothy King, who landed, with six children, at Salem, in 1636. Their children were: Samuel (6); John (7), born 1645; Mary, baptized June 11th, 1648; Elizabeth, baptized March, 1649, married John Alburtis, son of Peter Alburtis, of English

Kills, a man of large property; and Hannah, married 1668, William Smith.

Samuel (6), son of John (2), resided in Newtown, and married Phebe, daughter of Edmund Titus, of Westbury, L. I., and died 1689, leaving a son, Samuel, who died August 31st, 1764, an old man, having had children: Samuel, twice married, without children, died 1771, Mary, married Peter Renne, Sarah, and Deborah, wife of Daniel Denton, of Elizabeth, N. J.

John (7), son of John (2), resided in Newtown, L. I., and married, in 1669, Joanna, third daughter of Capt. Richard Betts, of Newtown, a man of property and standing, and active in the concerns of the town. They had children: Richard Betts (8); John (9); and probably others.

Richard B. (8), son of John (7), the ancestor of the families of that name in Ewing and Trenton, came to this region as early, at least, as 1709, the date of his deeds. His plantation, still in the possession of his lineal descendants, was on the Delaware, near the falls known by his name. His deeds for the land were one from John Hutchinson and one from John Brierly, both to Thomas Hough, of Springfield, Burlington county, and both dated 1696. Said Thomas Hough conveyed both tracts to Richard Scudder, May, 1709. Mr. Scudder was one of the most active and influential men in the town. His name is mentioned very frequently in public instruments, charters, &c., and heads the list of grantees to whom the land on which to build a church was conveyed by Alexander Lockart, in March, 1709. He died March 14th, 1754, aged 83, twenty years after his wife, Hannah Reeder, aged 63, having had children: Hannah; Mary; Richard, died young, 1731; John (10); Abigail; Joseph (11); Samuel; Rebecca, died December 13th, 1780, aged 72; Joanna, married Mr. Pierson, and died 1778, aged 67; and Deborah, married John Hart, (see Hart family, No. 23.) Two graves in the group in the Ewing church-yard, marked "H. S., 1738," and "A. S., 1720," were, probably, Hannah and Abigail.

John (10), son of Richard (8), who died May 10th, 1748, aged 47, married Phebe, daughter of Daniel Howell, (see Howell family, No. 1.) She died January 31st, 1787, aged 89. Their children were: Daniel (12), born August 6th, 1736; Amos (13), born February 14th, 1739, and died August 11th, 1824, having married Phebe, daughter of Stephen Rose, (see Rose family, No. 1,) by whom he had several children, all of whom died young, except John (20); Prudence, born April 30th, 1738, married Joshua Jones, (see Jones family, No. 2); Jedediah (14), born 1742; Jemima, born 1744, married John Meins, lived and died in Kentucky; Ephraim, born 1747, died aged 28; and Keturah, married David Howell, (see Howell family, No. 9.)

Daniel (12), son of John (10), was a trustee of the Ewing Church, died 1811, aged 75, having married Mary Snowden, of Burlington county. She died 1798, aged 60, leaving children: Rachel, wife of Isaac Reeder; Kesiah, not married; Abner (15); and Elias (16).

Abner (15), son of Daniel (12), died 1827. By his wife, Phebe, daughter of Peter Howell, (see Howell family, No. 41), had Maria, wife of Isaac Wynkoop, who died soon after marriage, leaving a son, Edward; Rebecca, married Benjamin Moore, (see Moore family, No. 14); Sarah Ann, wife of Daniel Dougherty; and Peter Howell, married, first, a daughter of Rev. Nathaniel Snowden, of Maryland, second, Elizabeth, daughter of Joseph Huff; they removed to Ohio, where she died, and he, too, soon after marrying a third time.

Elias (16), son of Daniel (12), a trustee of the Ewing Church, died June 20th, 1811; his wife, Sarah, daughter of Jasper Smith, died 1858, aged 84. Their children were: Daniel, a lawyer, practiced his profession in Milton, Pa., married Grace, daughter of Daniel Smith, of Sunbury, Pa., had a daughter Mary, wife of Thomas Hepburn; Jasper Smith (17); John (18); and Abner, an elder in the Ewing Church, who died 1878, having married Hannah, daughter of Amos Reeder, (see Reeder family, No. 8,) and had children: Edwin, died in infancy, and Jasper Smith, who married Mary, daughter of Nathaniel Hart.

Jasper Smith (17), son of Elias (16), died October 20th, 1877, aged 80. He was the first president of the Trenton Mechanics' and Manufacturers' Bank, and for several years its cashier. He married Mary, daughter of Amos Reeder, (see Reeder family, No. 8,) and had children: Daniel, died young; Edward W. (19); and Christiana, wife of Judge William R. McIlvaine, (see McIlvaine family, No. 7.)

Judge Edward W. (19), son of Jasper S. (17), is a graduate of the College of New Jersey. He was a student under Hon. William L. Dayton, and attorney-at-law in 1844. He practiced his profession in Trenton. In 1863, he represented the county in the State Senate, and in 1865 was the president of that body. On the

23d of March, 1869, he was appointed justice of the Supreme Court of the state, was re-appointed March 23d, 1876, and again re-appointed January 15th, 1883. He received the degree of Doctor of Laws from his Alma Mater in 1880. For more than twenty years he has been a trustee of the Princeton Theological Seminary. He married Mary Louisa, daughter of Hon. George K. Drake, of Morristown, N. J., at one time a justice of the Supreme Court. Their children are: Edward D., a graduate of Princeton, married Elizabeth, daughter of Charles Hewitt, (both deceased); Henry D., married Marvina J. Davis, of Trenton; and Wallace M., married Ida Quimby, of Newark, N. J.—both were graduates of the Lehigh University, Pa.; George D., graduated by Princeton College, married H. Helen Damarin, of Portsmouth, Ohio; Mary; and Louisa.

John (18), son of Elias (16), was killed instantly by the accidental discharge of his gun in 1840. He married Nancy, daughter of James B. Green, (see Green family, No. 17,) and had children: Alfred, died 1827; Sarah, married Jesse Cook, and died 1858; Alexander, died in infancy; Catharine, became the second wife of Jesse Cook; John, married Miss Moore; and William, killed by being thrown from his carriage.

John (20), son of Amos (13), who died April 15th, 1830, aged 66, was a trustee of the Ewing Church, married Mary, daughter of Jacob Keen and Hannah Holme, who was the daughter of John Holme, and Jane, daughter of Rev. Abel Morgan, of Algock, Wales, and pastor of the Baptist Church at Pennypack from 1711 to 1722. She died 1836, aged 73. They had children: Phebe; Amos, married Abigail, daughter of John Phillips, (see Phillips family, No. 12,) and died one year after marriage, leaving a son, Amos, graduated by Princeton, a lawyer, settled at Louisville, where he died aged 28; John Holmes (21); Morgan (22); Elizabeth, wife of John Chambers, (see Chambers family, No. 7); Hannah, wife of Thomas J. Stryker; William (23); and Mary, wife of Samuel S. Stryker.

Phebe, daughter of John (20), died September 8th, 1834, aged 42, and is buried with her husband in the grounds of the Baptist Church of Trenton. She married Gershom Mott, an elder of the Baptist Church of Trenton and Lamberton, son of John Mott, a soldier of the Revolution, was captain of the Fifth Company of the Third Battalion, was before Quebec and at the battle of Trenton. Their children were: Eleanor, wife of the Rev. Dr. Hyers, a Baptist minister of Bordentown, where she died May 11th, 1848, aged

36, leaving children: Ellen, wife of Dr. Abel, Anna, wife of William Fenton, and Gershom, married Ellen Pyatt; John Scudder, married Martha, daughter of David Schenck, had children: Isabella, Garret S., and Martha; Mary Keen; Sarah Biles, wife of Samuel Hill, of Trenton; Gershom; Phebe Elizabeth, wife of Caleb Coleman; and Morgan Holmes, married Mary Morris, of Trenton.

Gershom Mott, son of Phebe Scudder and Gershom Mott, arose to high distinction in the military service of his country. When in 1846, at the beginning of the war with Mexico, a call was made by the government for volunteers, he without hesitation offered his services, and as second lieutenant in the Tenth United States Infantry, served during the entire war, distinguishing himself for his coolness in danger and courage in battle. At the close of the war, he was appointed by President Polk, collector of the port of Lamberton. With equal promptness, at the outbreak of our civil contest, he laid his services at the disposal of the government, and was made lieutenant colonel of the Fifth New Jersey Regiment of Volunteers, attached to General Hooker's Division, and was in action, first at Williamsburg, in which the Fifth held its ground for nine hours exposed to a destructive fire. For his gallantry Lieutenant Colonel Mott was promoted to the colonelcy of the Sixth. In the battle of Fair Oaks Colonel Mott was again conspicuous for his bravery, and was highly complimented by the division commander, General Hooker, in his official report of the battle of June 1st, 1862, from which we extract a few lines. "It gives me great pleasure to bear testimony to the continued good conduct of the Fifth and Sixth New Jersey Regiments. Their ranks had been greatly thinned by battle and sickness, and they had been encamped in the immediate neigborhood of troops partially demoralized from the events of the preceding day; yet, on the first indication of a renewal of the conflict, I found their lines formed, and they were as ready to meet it as though our arms had been crowned with success." Further on he says: "Especial mention is due to Colonel Gershom Mott and Lieutenant Colonel George C. Burling, of the Sixth New Jersey Regiment, for their distinguished services on this field. Here, as elsewhere, they have shown themselves to be officers of uncommon merit." In the second battle of Bull Run he was wounded, and was advanced to be brigadier-general, in command of the Second New Jersey Brigade. In the battle of Chancellorville, May 3d,

1863, the New Jersey troops, led by General Mott, were again in the thickest of the fight, where he received a severe wound that disabled him for a time. When the grand advance was made by General Grant, General Mott was placed in command of the second division of the Third Army Corps, which he held to the close of the war. In the fierce and bloody assault on Petersburg, on April 6th, 1865, General Mott, while leading his division, was for the fourth time wounded, and for his gallantry was brevetted major-general of volunteers. At the close of the war he was made full major-general, being the first soldier from New Jersey to receive the brevet, and the only Jerseyman that reached the full rank. He had been present in more than thirty-two engagements. In 1867, on the increase of the regular army, the colonelcy of the Thirty-third Infantry was offered him, which he declined. In 1875, he was appointed treasurer of New Jersey by Governor Bedle, and afterwards superintendent of the State Prison. He married Elizabeth, daughter of John E. Smith, of Trenton, and has one daughter, Kate.

John Holmes (21), son of John (20), became a merchant, residing at New York. He married, first, Sarah, daughter of Judge John Coryell, of Lambertville; second, the widow Alice Butler (Morris), by whom he had children: Alice, died young; Julia, married Charles de Cerqueria, of Lima, South America, has children: Alice, Charles and Henry; and Caroline, married Lewis Randolph Smith, and has chlldren: Mary Alice, Edward D., Holme S. and Hopeton D.

Morgan (22), son of John (20), was a trustee of the Ewing Church, died May 10th, 1868, aged 71, having married, first, Ellen, daughter of Captain Ralph Smith; second, Sally Ann, daughter of Richard Hill, (see Hill family, No. 2); third, Sarah, Lucinda, daughter of Rev. Eli F. Cooley, (see Cooley family, No. 18,) by whom he had children: Hannah, married J. Wilbur Price, whose children are: Alice, wife of Dr. Rufus H. Gilbert, son of Judge William D. Gilbert, of Caton, Steuben county, N. Y., Annie, and Elizabeth; Ellen Smith, died 1861; and Alice M., died in childhood. His fourth wife was Phebe Livensetter, of Pennsylvania.

William (23), son of John (20), was a trustee of the Ewing Church, represented the county in the legislature, died January 8th, 1852, aged 45, having married Mary M., daughter of Col. James Hay, of Monmouth, and his wife, Margaret, daughter of

Major William Montgomery.* Their children are: John Morgan; and William, died in infancy; Montgomery, married Isabella Gilbert, had children: William, Hiram, and Jennie; James, who died in 1864, having married Mary B. Savidge, whose only child was Mary Lee, wife of Harvey Edward Fisk; Mary Matilda; John Holmes, surrogate of the county for many years, married Martha, daughter of Louis Hutchinson, of Lawrence, has children: Mary Reeder and Emma Matilda; Margaret Elizabeth, wife of John W. Green; Louise Augustine, wife of William E. Green; Cornelia, died young; Wilhanna, wife of J. Scudder Hart; and Julia.

Jedediah (14), son of John (10), by his wife, Anna Roberts, had children: Richard (24); Ephraim (25); Jemima, married Jeremiah Burroughs, (see Burroughs family, No. 9); Thomas; Sarah, married, first, Samuel Green, (see Green family, No. 16,) second, Richard Hunt, (see Hunt family, No. 27); and Hannah, married Jacob Hoff, and had children: Ann, wife of Joseph Phillips, Lydia, wife of Bernard Taylor, Mary, wife of Ralph Knowles, and Scudder, married Elizabeth Phillips.

Richard (24), son of Jedediah (14), an elder in the Ewing Church, died 1838, aged 72, having married Jemima, daughter of James Burroughs, (see Burroughs family, No. 4.) She died 1837, leaving children: Charles (26); Jemima, died young; Joseph,

---

*The family of Montgomery is of great antiquity. Roger was a Frenchman of high distinction, whose son, Hugh, came over with William the Conqueror. His descendants or many generations were lairds or lords in Scotland, where they settled. The last Lord Hugh Montgomery in 1508 was created by James IV. of Scotland, Earl of Eglington; from the third son of this Hugh, first earl, was lineally descended Hugh Montgomery (1), of Bridgend, the father of William, his oldest son and heir, who emigrated to America.

William (2), son of Hugh (1), was the heir and owner of the property of Bridgend, situated about a mile from Ayr. He married Isabel, daughter of Robert Burnett, of the family of Gilbert Burnett, Bishop of Salisbury, and also one of the proprietors of East Jersey. Having lost much of his property by large and unfortunate loans he removed in 1701 with his family to New Jersey, and settled on the lands of his father-in-law, at a place to which he gave the name of Eglington, two miles from Allentown. He had sons: Robert; William (3); and James.

William (3), son of William (2), was born at Ayr, came with his father, in his ninth year, to America. He settled in Upper Freehold, where he died 1771, aged 78, having married, first, Susan, widow of John Wood, by whom he had Isabella, wife, first of John Reading, (see Reading family, No. 3); second, Mr. Baily. He married, second, Mrs. Margaret Pashall, of Philadelphia, by whom he had a son, William (4). His third wife was Mary Ellis.

Major William (4), son of William (3), born 1750, and died 1815, is buried at Crosswicks, having married Mary, daughter of Robert Rhea, of Monmouth. Their daughter, Margaret, married Col. James Hay, of Monmouth, and had children: Mary M., wife of William Scudder; Margaretta, wife of Enoch Jones; Lamar, married Miss Gary; Cornelia; and Sarah, wife of Dr. Reeder. Their daughter, Maria Matilda, married John Titus, and had children: Mary and Emma.

died young; Ann, wife of Smith Hart, (see Hart family, No. 20); Mary, died in infancy; and Sarah, wife of William S. Cook, whose children: C. Scudder, married, first, Mary Welling, second, Miss Imley, Margaret, wife of Asa Skirm, Fanny, married, first, Nicholas Connover, second, Charles Morehouse, Alfred D., married Elizabeth A. Degraw, Robert H., married Mary Boise, and Ella, died in infancy.

Charles (26), son of Richard (24), who died October 22d, 1838, aged 40, married Margaret, daughter of Uriel Titus, (see Titus family, No. 11.) She died December 7th, 1831, aged 30, having had children: Elizabeth, died in infancy; Sarah A., wife of James H. Clark; Joseph (27); and Uriel Titus, married Eliza, daughter of Joseph B. Anderson, (see Anderson family, No. 6,) their children are: Charles, and Hervey.

Joseph (27), son of Charles (26), married Amanda, daughter of William Tilton, of Burlington county, has children: Ella, married Martin Van Harlingen; Sarah, married Henry Lovett; Margaret; William; Anna; Edward; and Lilian.

Ephraim (25), son of Jedediah (14), was a trustee of the Ewing Church, married, first, Catharine Christopher, by whom he had children: Esther, married John Herron; Chatty, married John Hazard; Jesse, married Amanda Herron, whose children are: Jane, married Eseck Howell, and had by him: Sallie, Mary and Charles, died young, and Esther H., married George W. Thornley, whose children are: Albert William and Frank. By his second wife, Harriet, daughter of Nathaniel Hunt, he had children: Sarah Ann; and Mary, wife of Derrick V. Carver, of Pennsylvania.

Joseph (11), son of Richard (8), was a captain in the French war, and died January 26th, 1799, aged 93, having married, first, Hannah Reeder. She died 1741, aged 33, leaving children: Hannah; Mary; Jane, became the wife of Abraham Temple, (see Temple family, No. 2); John, born 1738, married Miss Baker, and removed to Northampton county, Pa., and there died, leaving several children. By his second wife, Mary, widow of John Carpenter, and daughter of Ralph Hart, (see Hart family, No. 1,) had one child, Joseph (28). His third wife was the widow Phillips, of Lawrence, probably another daughter of Ralph Hart. By her he had: Abigail, wife of Nathaniel Hart, (see Hart family, No. 15); Samuel, born September 14th, 1754, entered the army, was taken prisoner by the British, carried to New York, and was never afterwards heard from, was supposed to have died in the prison ship; and Rebecca, wife of Titus Hart, (see Hart family, No. 16.)

Joseph (28), son of Capt. Joseph (11), was a justice of the county; married Mary Lanning, and lived near Lawrenceville. Their children were: Samuel and John, both went West; Joseph, lived on the homestead, and married, first, Sarah, daughter of Stephen Lanning, (see Lanning family, No. 2,) and, second, the widow of Daniel Hunt; Hannah, wife of Philip Phillips, no children; Elizabeth, wife of George Bergen, formerly the husband of her deceased sister, Mercy; Sarah, wife of Daniel Hunt; Mary, not married; and Richard (29).

Richard (29), son of Joseph (28), married Mercy, daughter of James Burroughs, (see Burroughs family, No. 4,) had children: John (30); Samuel (31); Abigail, married Mr. Demount; Rebecca, wife of Mr. Yetman; Joseph (32); Mary, married Nathaniel Drake; Theophilus (33); Edward, not married; William (34); and James, married Jemima Wertz, and his children are: Horace, married Ellen Loder, Enoch, married Harriet Loder, and Lucy, married Nathan Loveless.

John (30), son of Richard (29), by his marriage with Elizabeth, daughter of David Smith, had children: Henderson G., a merchant of Trenton, married Anna Chevrier, has children: Anna Elizabeth, married Albert Scudder, Alphronzine C., married Charles H. Gillespie, Ida, Lewis C., Henderson G., and Mary R.; Joseph, married Mary Embley; William, married Mary Stout; Manning, married Lucy Embley, sister of Mary; Esther, wife of Abram Durling, of Woodsville; Sarah; Susan Ann, wife of Blackwell Hunt; and Emma, married Edward Connover.

Samuel (31), son of Richard (29), married Mary, daughter of Anthony Reed, whose children are: Jane, married James Smith; Ellen, not living; Smith L., married Parmela Blackwell; Anna, married Isaac Williamson; John.

Joseph (32), son of Richard (29), married Hannah Applegate, and has children: Richard B., married Sarah G. Stout; John P., married Elizabeth Appleton; Henry S., married Elizabeth Clendening; Mary E., married James Wentworth; Margaret A., married Cornelius De Hart; William A., a member of the Twenty-first Regiment, New Jersey Volunteers, killed at the battle of Chancellorville; Joseph, married Matilda Clendening; Julia, wife of Charles W. Biles; and Hannah.

Theophilus (33), son of Richard (29), married Hannah Reed, whose children are: Ruth; Henrietta, married Mr. Stults; Mary, married Joseph Neff; and Hale, died a young man.

William (34), son of Richard (29), married Elizabeth Embley, by whom he had children: Sarah, married Charles Lee; William B., married Elizabeth Nolan; Isabella, married William Sinclair; Alfred, died young; Amos, married Lucy Wright; and Mary.

John (9), son of John (7), changed his abode from Newtown, L. I., to that part of Elizabethtown township now Westfield, about 1698. In the year 1705 he is mentioned in the will of George Peck, of that place, whose daughter, Mary, he had married, who survived her husband many years, and died at an advanced age. He died January 15th, 1738, aged 64, having left £10 to the Presbyterian Church. Their children were: John (35); Richard (36); Samuel (37); Thomas (38); Elizabeth; Kesiah; Anna; Mary; Joanna; Phebe; and Benjamin, he is not mentioned in the will, but he was, in all probability, John's (9) son, and was, for some reason, left out, perhaps had received his share, he died April, 1743 (date of his will), having had children: Sarah, wife of Mr. Ayres, Ruth, wife of Mr. Ross, Hannah, Elizabeth, and four sons, whose names are not mentioned.

Capt. John (35), son of John (9), who died February 26th, 1777, aged 77, was a liberal benefactor to the Presbyterian Church, in the place of his residence, Westfield, to which he gave a lot of several acres, for a church and parsonage, and a wood-lot to supply its fuel. He was married at least twice, one wife being the daughter of John Davis. His wife Jane died April 10th, 1731. His wife Sarah survived him till November, 1784, aged 74. His children were: John (39); William (40); and Ephraim (41.)

John (39), son of Capt. John (35), served through the Revolutionary war, resided at Westfield. He left children: John (42); Abraham; and Phebe.

John (42), son of John (39), lived in Westfield and died April, 1848, left children: Susan, married Mr. Smith; Sarah Ann; and William (43).

William (43), son of John (42), has children: Isaac, living on the homestead, married and has one daughter; and Daniel, married, has children: George, Julia, Susan, Nancy, Mary, and Margaret.

William (40), son of Capt. John (35), was a colonel in the Revolutionary service during the whole war. He was twice married, and had children: William, a surveyor, living to an advanced age in Clintonville, Greenbrier county, W. Va.; Asa; Susan, married Mr. Spinning; and Sarah, wife of Reuben Tisdale, of Connecticut, by whom she has two sons: John H., broker, of New York, and William S., an editor.

Ephraim (41), son of Capt. John (35), died 1788, leaving children: Ephraim (44); Amos (45); Smith (46); and John, a lawyer, died unmarried.

Ephraim (44), son of Ephraim (41), who died 1849, aged 80, married Joanna Miller, of Scotch Plains, whose children were: Isaac, drowned at Savannah 1831, unmarried; Ephraim (47); Cummings, born 1799, lived in Piqua county, Ohio, married Sally Winants, of Rahway, whose children are: Ephraim, Howard, Dorcey, Sally, and Hannah; Charlotta, married Mulford Marsh; Harriet, married John Headley; Linus (48); and David, lived in Brooklyn, had sons: Samuel, Ephraim, and Fanning.

Ephraim (47), son of Ephraim (44), who died September, 1843, aged 46, married Nancy, daughter of William Hays, of Westfield, whose father, Henry, attained the extraordinary age of 110 years. Their children are: Alanson H. (49); Mary C., married William Brombush; Sarah H.; Emily; Eliza; Isaac; Anna, wife of William C. Frazee; and William H., married Louisa Russell, and moved to Sandusky, Ohio, died and left children: Arthur R., George T., Minnie, and Sarah Kate.

Alanson H. (49), son of Ephraim (47), a merchant of New York, married Abby Eliza Turner, has children: Edwin H., married Anna M. Manderville, who has a son, Alanson H.; and Frederic P.

Linus (48), son of Ephraim (44), resides in New York city, married Eliza Banta, has children: George, married Phebe Meeker, has one son, Harold; Mansfield; and Melville, married Leonora B. Lord, has children: Daisy, Hamilton, and Melville.

Amos (45), son of Ephraim (41), lived at Savannah, Ga., died June 13th, 1856, aged 78, and is buried in the Westfield Presbyterian burying-ground with his wife, Phebe, who died July 31st, 1838, aged 58, having had children: Picton, who lived and died on the homestead at Westfield, and left four sons, Mulford, John, Ephraim and George; John lived at Savannah, left one son, Henry W., who married Emma Harral, has a daughter, Mary Elizabeth; Ephraim, died unmarried at Savannah; Phebe, wife of Lewis Meeker; Emily, wife of Mulford Marsh; Mary, wife of Job Magee; Ann, married Moses Crane, has one son, Theodore; Catharine, wife of Mr. Corey, of Westfield; Matilda, married Joseph Buckner, of Savannah, Ga.; and Sarah, wife of Elias Freeland.

Smith (46), son of Ephraim (41), a lawyer, married Margaret Gaston, and had children : Isaac W., a prominent lawyer, of Jersey City, represented his district in the forty-third congress; and Mansfield, also a lawyer, died in Newark, N. J., having married Charlotte Meeker, his family settled in Chicago, had children : Mary, and William, married Mary Arnold, and died. July, 1876, leaving two sons.

Richard (36), son of John (9), who died December 24th, 1785, lived on a farm near Passaic river ; he married Rebecca, daughter of Elijah Stits, of Scotch Plains, and had children : Benjamin, a physician ; Nancy ; Stites ; Mary ; Thomas ; and Sally.

Samuel (37), son of John (9), resided at Elizabeth, died 1777, having married Apphia, daughter of Richard Miller, and had children : Samuel ; Moses ; John ; Thomas ; Matthias ; George ; Phebe ; and Hannah.

Thomas (38), son of John (9), removed to the West, and married Abigail Clark, had children : Sarah ; Jotham ; Abigail ; Ruth ; Jane ; and Daniel.

Thomas (3), son of Thomas (1), left Salem in 1651, after a residence of several years in Southhold, moved to Huntington, L. I., where he settled and became the proprietor by grant and purchase of 1000 acres of valuable land, a large portion of which is still held by his descendants of the seventh generation, Henry G., John R., and George W. He died 1690, leaving a widow, Mary, and children : Timothy (50); Benjamin (51); Mary, married Robert Arthur ; Elizabeth, married Walter Noakes ; Sarah, married Mr. Conklin ; Clemar, married Mr. Clements ; and Mercy, died unmarried.

Timothy (50), son of Thomas (3), received from his father's estate valuable landed property at Babylon, at Cow Harbor (now North Point), at Red Hook (now Vernon Valley), and at Crab Meadow. He died about 1740, having married Sarah Wood, who died 1738. Their children were : Timothy (52); Henry (53); John, died, unmarried ; and Abigail, wife of Joseph Lewis.

Timothy (52), son of Timothy (50), was born on the south side of Long Island, 1696, and married Mary, daughter of Daniel Whitehead, and died April 25th, 1778, leaving children : Jemima, born 1728, married David Roscoe ; Hannah, born 1730, married Ananias Carll ; Jerusha, born 1732, married Timothy Carll, and had one daughter, Julia, wife of Scudder Lewis, and one son, Phineas, who was the father of Dr. Selah Carll, David Carll, Platt

Carll, and Mary Carll; Timothy (54); Sarah, born 1736, married Jesse Buffet; John (55), born 1740; Henry (56), born 1743; and Joel (57), born 1746.

Timothy (54), son of Timothy (52), married Rebecca Wiser, and had children: Sarah, married Mr. Haff; Hannah, married Thomas Higby, had a daughter, who married Jesse Scidmore, and a son, Richard, married Edna Whites; Jerusha, married Peter Ruland; Jemima, married Mr. Hudson; Rebecca, died unmarried; Elizabeth, married Mr. Weeks; Timothy; and Joel, history unknown. Israel Scudder was a grandson of Timothy (54), and married Miss Burr, and died about 1830; had a son, William E., of Huntington.

John (55), son of Timothy (52), married Mary Budd; had children: John B. (58); and Mary, married Joseph Skillman.

John B. (58), son of John (55), married Hannah Scidmore, whose children are: Richard (59); Deborah, wife of Havens Kelsey; Timothy (60); Charles (61); Joseph, died unmarried; John, died unmarried; Hannah, died unmarried; and Sarah, married Joseph Lewis, whose children are: Egbert, lives at North Port, and has a large family, Joseph S., married Phebe, granddaughter of Henry Scudder (56), Henry Francis, married Ann Eliza, daughter of Harvey Bishop, and Warren B., married Fannie Higbie.

Richard (59), son of John B. (58), married Harriet Scidmore, and had one son, Richard, who married Sarah Ann White, and they have a daughter, Harriet, wife of George White, of West Hills, Long Island.

Timothy (60), son of John B. (58), married Sarah Arthur, in 1817; had children: Augustus Harley (62); Mary, wife of Mordecai Jarvis; and John B., married Miss Skinner, and has sons: Clarence, Joseph, and George B. McClellan.

Augustus (62), son of Timothy (60), married Hannah Bruce; have children: John B., married Nettie White, whose children are: Frederic B., and a daughter; Timothy, married Elizabeth Williams, and has two daughters; James Buchanan, married Mary E. Gardner; one daughter, married Mr. Covert, of New York city; one daughter, not married.

Charles (61), son of John B. (58), married Sarah Vail, and had children: Ann Eliza, married J. Amherst Woodhull, whose children are: Charles V., married Martha Leek, and Harriet, wife of E. Platt Stratton, a civil engineer, of Flushing, L. I.; Mary, married William Gardiner, whose children are: Nannie, wife of Dr.

Joseph Raymond, of Brooklyn, Mary Eliza, wife of James Bache, of Brooklyn, and Louisa, wife of Willis James, of New York city; Charles, has held many offices of trust in the town, he married a daughter of John Fleet, has one son, Charles F.; and Louisa, married Mr. Covert, of New York city, she has a son, Charles, married Ella Bruce.

Henry (56), son of Timothy (52), was a man of classical attainments. He served his country through the Revolutionary war, was aid to Gen. Nathaniel Talmage, and was distinguished for his patriotism and activity in harassing the British on Long Island. He was appointed, in 1788, to represent the county of Suffolk in the convention held at Poughkeepsie to deliberate on the adoption of the constitution of the United States. He was, for many years, a member of the state legislature. He died January 21st, 1822, having married Phebe, youngest daughter of Ananias and Hannah Carll. Their children were: Youngs Prime (63), born June 30th, 1771; Henry (64), born April 26th, 1778; Phebe, born May 21st, 1782, married Azel Lewis, whose children were: Gloriana Adeline, wife of John Bruce, of New York city, Phebe, and Henry S., left Long Island, about 1834, settling in the central part of New York state; Joel, married Charity Lewis, died 1835, no children; and Amelia, married Platt Lewis, whose children are: Phebe, born 1821, wife of Joseph S. Lewis, Gloriana, wife of Israel Carll, and Henry S., married Frances, daughter of Capt. Jonas Higby.

Youngs Prime (63), son of Henry (56), married Hannah Bryant, and had children: Mary, married Haviland Wicks, some of whose children are: Harriet, wife of Col. Amos Sawyer, of Rochester, N. Y., Elizabeth, wife of Calvin Curtis, of Stratford, Conn., and Mary, wife of Mr. Peck, of New York city; David, married in New York city, had one daughter, Amelia, wife of Mr. Lent; John, left Long Island, a young man, never heard from; Solomon, married Fannie Brush, an estimable lady of Huntington, he left four children, a son, John, has resided many years in the western states, is now living in New York, a daughter, is married, and lives West; Ophelia, married John Burdett.

Henry (64), son of Henry (56), a man of strong understanding, died near Huntington, 1863, aged 85. He married, first, Phebe, daughter of Jonah Wood, and had two daughters: Amelia, married Seabury Bryant, and had a daughter, Martha, married, and living West, and a son, Oscar, living in Illinois; and Phebe, married

Melancton Bryant, and left one daughter, Henrietta, wife of Francis Loring Blanchard. By his second wife, Elizabeth, daughter of Judge Divine Hewlett, of Cold Spring Harbor, L. I., he had Eliza Strong, born 1820, married, first, Dr. William W. Kissam, second, William W. Wood, had one son, William Wilton; Anne Cornelia, born April 26th, 1822, second wife of Henry G. Scudder (No. 86); Henry Joel (65), born September 18th, 1825; Townsend (66), born December 14th, 1829, and Hewlett, born July 25th, 1833, is a successful merchant of New York.

Henry J. (65), son of Henry (64), graduated with distinction at Trinity College, Hartford, Conn., in 1846; studied law with the late William E. Curtis; is now an eminent lawyer of New York city; in 1881, received the degree of LL. D. from Roanoke College, Va. He is a trustee of Trinity College and of Dr. William A. Muhlenberg's, at St. Johnland, and has given much attention and assistance to the cause of education. In 1872, he represented his district in the forty-second congress. His speech, as a member of the committee appointed by the house to examine into the serious disturbances agitating the State of Arkansas, was justly regarded as one of the most effective efforts of the season. He married, first, Louisa, daughter of Prof. Charles Davis, and has children: Rev. Henry Townsend, a graduate of Columbia College, assistant rector of Grace Church, Brooklyn; Charles Davies, graduate of Trinity College, Conn., and of the New York Medical College, and a student of medicine at Vienna, Austria, is now a practicing physician of New York city, married Louisa Wardner, daughter of Hon. William M. Evarts, New York; Edward Manfield, graduate of Trinity College and the New York Law School, now a member of the New York bar. By his second wife, Emma, daughter of John H. Willard, of Troy, has: Willard; Heyward; Emma; and Hewlett.

Townsend (66), son of Henry (64), lived at Northport, Long Island. He was prepared by Rev. Horace Woodruff for Trinity College, where, in 1854, he graduated with honor. He then studied and practiced law in New York city. He died 1874, having married Sarah Maria, daughter of Philomen Frost. Their children are: Philomen Halsey; Elizabeth Hewlett; Townsend; Lauren Kent; Sarah Maria; and Cornelia.

Joel (57), son of Timothy (52), married Sarah Brush and had children; Tredwell (67); Jesse (68); and Sarah, married Edward Bryant, and had children: Melancton, who married Phebe, daughter of Henry Scudder (64), Dr. Joel, married Mary A. Doty, Hannah, wife of Orlando Gardiner, and Nancy, wife of Edmund Smith.

Tredwell (67), son of Joel (57), represented his county for many terms in the state assembly and in the first congressional district of the state in the fifteenth congress. He was noted for calm, discreet judgment and great probity. He married Kesiah Oakley, whose children were: Abigail, married Silas Strong, of Comac; Hannah, married Medad Smith, her children were: Henry S. and Edgar M.; Tredwell, went to Elmira and left there sons: John and Israel O.; Richard, died, no children; Walter, living in Babylon, no children; Wilmot, lives at Riverhead, Long Island, has sons: Edward A. and Thomas; and Julia, married.

Jesse (68), son of Joel (57) married Mary Bryant, and their children were: Joel, died unmarried; Israel (69); Ruth Ann, wife of Alexander Lewis; Sarah, wife of Mr. Gould; Samuel, married Letitia Townsend and has one son, Henry K., married Alma Brush; Jesse P., died childless; and George A. (70).

Israel (69), son of Jesse (68), married Miss Sammis and left sons: William; and George, living in Huntington; and two daughters, one the wife of Steven K. Gould.

George A. (70), son of Jesse (68), resides in Huntington, has held many positions of trust. He married Mary, daughter of Judge Moses Rolph, whose children are: Reuben R., who left a son, Charles B.; and Juliette, married Mr. Hendrickson.

Henry (53), son of Timothy (50), married Bridget Gildersleeve, had children: Jonas (71); Edmund (72); and five daughters.

Jonas (71), son of Henry (53), married, first, Hannah Bunce. They had four daughters, one of whom, Bridget, married Eliphalet Arthur, had children: Jonah, married Amelia Mills; Joshua, married Miss Chikester, and left one son, Elbert, who married Margaret Scidmore; Sarah, married Timothy Scudder (60); and Mary, married Joel Scidmore, whose children are: Anna Maria, wife of John Perott, Eliphalet, died young, Jane, wife of Richard L. Fleet, has a son, John P. Fleet, and a daughter, Mary S. Fleet, Margaret, wife of Elbert Arthur, has a son, John P. Arthur, married Annie Bryant, Joel, married Laura Cheshire, and Mary. He married, second, Sarah Taylor. Of their six children, only Isaac is known to have left posterity; he married Sarah, daughter of Rev. Joshua Hart, of Huntington, and of his eight children, only one, Israel, left descendants, he married Miss Perigeau, moved to New York city, where his posterity may be found.

Edmund (72), son of Henry (53), had children: Moses (73); Stephen; Henry; Desire; Esther, died unmarried; Jemima, married Richard Holden, and removed to Connecticut fifty years ago; and Hannah, married Bethuel Sammis, her children are: Henry S., married Elizabeth Ackery, Captain Isaac, married Ann Suydam, and Mary, wife of Mr. Betts, of Brooklyn.

Moses (73), son of Edmund (72), had children: William, married Ruth Enoch; Andrus, married Hannah Hamilton; Jane, wife of Samuel Ackery.

Benjamin (51), son of Thomas (3), was a large landholder of Huntington; he received from his father's estate, lands, a grist mill and the homestead where he died 1735. He had two wives, Mary and Sarah, and children: Thomas (74); Ezekiel (75); Benjamin (76); Jacob (77); Isaac left Long Island soon after the death of his father, for Connecticut, where about 1744 he was drill-master of a troop of militia or horse, no knowledge of him after 1750; Isaiah received his inheritance in money, soon after left Long Island and is lost sight of; Moses received from his father a large landed estate, in 1751 he sold a large part of his farm to his brother Thomas (74), and died before 1754, probably leaving a son, Samuel, who settled in New York city. This is probable, as in a deed given in 1784 by a Samuel Scudder, of New York city, he appears as owner of real estate, which was probably bequeathed to Moses and left to his son Samuel; Peter left two daughters, who are lost sight of; Sarah, married Epenetus Platt; Ruth, married Mr. Rogers; and Anne, not married.

Thomas (74), son of Benjamin (51), died 1775, having married Rebecca Sammis, had children: Gilbert, died aged 20; and Thomas (78), born 1725.

Thomas (78), son of Thomas (74), married Abigail, daughter of John Sammis. They both died on the same day, February 25th, 1809, and were buried in the same grave. They had children: John, died a soldier in the Revolutionary war; Nathaniel (79); Rebecca, died unmarried; Gilbert (80), born 1764; and Thomas (81).

Nathaniel (79), son of Thomas (78), married Elizabeth, daughter of Jonathan Scudder (138), had sons: Gershom Bradley (82); Jacob (83); and others died childless or lost sight of.

Gershom B. (82), son of Nathaniel (79), born 1789, married Ruth Ketcham, left children: John Rogers (84), born 1830; Louis K., left one son, Sherwood; and Lydia Maria, not married.

John R. (84), son of Gershom B. (82), lives on the old homestead of Benjamin Scudder; he married Susan Matilda, daughter of Captain Abiatha Johnson. Their children are: Anna Cornelia; Edgar Rogers; and Susan Matilda.

Jacob (83), son of Nathaniel (79), married Elizabeth Bennet, and have children: George W., who by his wife, Phebe Bryant, has a son, George W., both father and son were born and still live on the homestead of the first Thomas, of Long Island; William, married Elizabeth Bryant; Rebecca; Charles; and Morris, not married.

Gilbert (80), son of Thomas (78), died September, 1855, having married Abigail Buffet, had children: Isaiah (85), born 1791; Hetty, married Philip Udall, died leaving two daughters; Sarah, married Joseph Lewis; Phebe, not married; Mary, married Moses Jarvis, left one daughter, Abigail, wife of Theodore Lowndes, of Connecticut; and Naomi, married Prof. Shallum B. Street, her children are: Charles R., a member of the bar, and was a member of the legislature of California, married Miss Bedford, of California, Gilbert S., a member of the legislature of Connecticut, Judge Henry C., a prominent man in the legislature of Idaho, and Mary Augusta, wife of Fayette Gould.

Isaiah (85), son of Gilbert (80), died February, 1875, having married in 1814, Rhoda, daughter of Daniel Jarvis, had one child, Henry G. (86), born May, 1818, now a retired merchant of New York, lives on his ancestral inheritance, a plantation beautifully lying along an elevation on which stands his mansion overlooking Long Island Sound. He married, first, Eleanor C. Murray, of Middletown, N. J., by whom he had children: William, settled in Ohio, married Ella Handly, and died 1881; Nora Jarvis, wife of John H. Jones, of Cold Springs Harbor, L. I.; and Henry G., is settled in Ohio, married Harriet H. Lewis, of Scranton, Pa. His second wife is Anne Cornelia, youngest daughter of Henry Scudder (64),* of Northport, L. I., by whom he has Gilbert, living at Santa Fé, New Mexico, assistant secretary of state and secretary of the bureau of immigration, married Nellie, daughter of ex-Gov. William G. Ritch, of New Mexico; and Hewlett.

Thomas (81), son of Thomas (78), married Ruth Conklin, and had: David C., who married Amelia Conklin; Thomas (87); Almeda, married Captain Philetus Jarvis, they have sons: Joseph

* Much of the information concerning the Long Island branch of the Scudder family is due to Mrs. Henry G. Scudder, of Long Island.

and Silucas; Abia, married Steven Kelsey, and left a son, Woodhull, who married Miss Tillot.

Thomas (87), son of Thomas (81), married Margaret Long, and had two sons: Thomas, who removed to Kansas thirty years ago joined the northern army in 1862, and for his valuable services was promoted to the rank of major, is now living at Topeka, Kansas, has been twice married; and James L., was skilled in the art of painting, married Lydia Kelsey, and left one son, Thomas.

Ezekiel (75), son of Benjamin (51), had children: Seth (88); John, not traced; and Joel, married, and had children: Horace, Clara, Sally, Henrietta, Lura, and Caroline.

Seth (88), son of Ezekiel (75), by his wife, Affie, had children: Ezekiel (89), born in Connecticut in 1765; Joel, married Dolly Dewey, and settled at Henrietta, Monroe county, N. Y.; Jesse, married Hannah Brooks, of Victor, Ontario county, N. Y., was killed by injuries received from a horse; Betsey, married Daniel Thayre; Isaac, went to Ohio, probably married there; Seth, lost his life in the war of 1812.

Ezekiel (89), son of Seth (88), as is said by a grandson of his, seemed to have an innate dislike for the conventionalities and monotony of life in the settled parts of the country, and a natural love for the excitements of a frontier life. In 1792, as soon as the winter had bridged the streams, he, with his young wife and infant son, and five others, started from Albany county, N. Y., for the then unbroken wilderness of the far-famed Genesee country of New York state. It required six weeks to make the journey with their ox teams, as they found great difficulty in keeping their course, and had often to chop their way through dense forests. Many of the streams they found swollen and the ice bridges broken; these troubles, with the necessity of guarding against the nightly visits of ravenous beasts, would have appalled any but the most resolute. He built his log house in what is now Victor, Ontario county. After spending thirty-five years there and seeing the wilderness change to a garden, he began to pine for the freedom of a new settlement life, and removed to Cattaraugus county, N. Y. He took part in the Revolutionary war, and died 1854. His wife, Cynthia Gould, born 1763, was a woman of undaunted courage, which was often called to the test in their early life. She died 1854. Their children were: Marvin (90), born 1791; Joel, (91), born 1793; Melania, died, aged 18; Laura, born 1796, married, first, Elisha Brace, had children: Elisha, married Mary Angle, and

Dr. Russel, of Alexandria, D. C., her second husband was Ezekiel Morse, they removed to Ohio ; Calvin (92), born 1798 ; Enos (93), born 1799 ; Betsey, born 1801, married Abram G. Bush, whose children are : Julia, Amanda, Cornelia, George, Laura, Hannah, Frank, and Henry, lawyers, of Clear Lake, Iowa, Emma, Marion, and John ; Roena, born 1803, married Jonathan Brown, whose children are : Freeman, Clara, Mary Ann, Helen, Cynthia, Eliza, Axie, and Emery ; Clarissa, born 1805, married Elijah Spaulding, whose children are : William, married Jane Brown, Fayette W., married Elizabeth Henshaw, Marion, married Wallace W. Webster, and Jane, wife of M. J. Frances ; Freeman (94), born 1808 ; and Ezekiel, died in childhood.

Marvin (90), son of Ezekiel (89), who died 1871, aged 80, was an officer in the war of 1812 ; was present at the battle of Black Rock, and the burning of Buffalo. He married Deborah, daughter of Eleazer Boughton, of Norfolk, Conn. She died 1862, aged 70. Their children were : Spencer (95), born 1814 ; Buel (96), born 1816 ; Delia, born 1818, married Rev. Dr. Calvin Kingsley, a bishop of the M. E. Church, died at Beyrout, Turkey, their children are ; Frank, Eliza, Mary, Ellen, and Martha ; Eliza C., born 1820, married Henry K. Van Renssalaer, left three daughters ; Marvin (97), born 1822 ; and Charles C., born 1827, married Margaret F. Farnam, whose children are : Irving B. and Marion G.

Spencer (95), son of Marvin (90), was a man of stern integrity and good business qualities, held many positions of trust ; he resided at Galesburg, Ill., where he died aged 64, having married, first, Caroline T. Salisbury, by whom he had Egbert M., married Kittie Hunt, died leaving seven children ; Ogden H., married Anneta Guernsey, have three children ; Ambrose S. and Adeline, died in childhood. By his second wife, Anne Souks, had A. Hamilton.

Buel (96), son of Marvin (90), resides in Cattaraugus county, N. Y., married Almira Huntington, and had children : Alvin L., married, first, Deem Fenton, second, Ada York ; Ida, married Enfield J. Leach ; and Charles B.

Marvin (97), son of Marvin (90), and his brother Charles, after several years of pioneer life in Illinois, have settled in Juniata, Nebraska. He married Sarah A. Baxter, and has children : Chapman S., married Hattie L. Maple ; Eliza, wife of W. Howard Kiddoo ; Kate L., wife of Henry H. Bartle ; and William M.

Joel (91), son of Ezekiel (89), and his wife Hannah died on the same day, and were buried together. Their children were: Polly, married, first, Hollis Marsh, by whom she had one son, Hollis; second, Nathan L. Sears, and moved to central Illinois; Ezekiel J., married and had a large family; Rosilla, married Osman Dexter; Romnia, married Henry Berry; Joel, married; Albert, married; Elizabeth, wife of Reuben E. Fenton, United States senator and ex-governor of New York; Samuel, a member of the New York legislature; Amanda Gould; Lester, married Ada Dockstader; and Dempster, killed at Fredericksburg.

Calvin (92), son of Ezekiel (89), married Mary Brace, by whom he had: James; and Mary, who married and resided at Toronto, Canada.

Enos (93), son of Ezekiel (89), left Cattaraugus county, N. Y., and settled at New Boston, Ill., where he died; he married Irena McDowell, whose children are: Laura, wife of Mr. Antrim; Lyman H., born 1829, was captain of a regiment of Illinois volunteers in the late war, receiving severe wounds, was compelled to resign his commission, he married, first, Fanny Ives, by whom he has one son, Edwin; second, Helen L. Moore; Mary, wife of Gilbert Ives; Maria, wife of Dr. Benedict; Sarah, wife of Robert Bush; and Russel S., married Elizabeth Loyd, and has children: Theodore, Ward, Jean and Fay.

Freeman (94), son of Ezekiel (89), married Jane Sample, had children: Frederick; Mary; Jane; Virginia; Dewitt; Giles; Eliza; Delia; and Estella; the sons were in the Union army.

Benjamin (76), son of Benjamin (51), born in Huntington, L. I., 1698, moved to Rahway, N. J., 1740, and bought mills of Joseph Baily. By his wife, Hannah, had children: Sarah, born 1723; Ruth, born 1724; Hannah, born 1729; Elizabeth, born 1730; Benjamin (98), born 1733; Isaac, born 1735, married Elizabeth Baldwin; Enoch (99), born 1738; and Anne, born 1742.

Benjamin (98), son of Benjamin (76), married, first, Sarah Cary, of Essex county, N. J., second, Lydia Chandler: had children: Benjamin (100), born 1762; Jesse (101), born 1766; John, died young; Anne, born 1768; Isaac (102), born 1770; and Enoch, died young.

Benjamin (100), son of Benjamin (98), sailed for the West Indies in his own vessel, and is supposed to have been lost at sea. He married Elizabeth Post, and had children: Sarah; Marion; Enoch, born 1794; Eliza; Charlotte; Abraham; and Benjamin.

Jesse (101), son of Benjamin (98), went to Butler county, Ohio, in 1816, married Kesiah Marsh, and had children : Benjamin (103), born 1789 ; Hezekiah (104); Enoch (105); and Stephen (106).

Isaac (102), son of Benjamin (98), married Elizabeth Tucker, and had children : Jacob, born 1795 ; Sarah ; Benjamin ; Joseph ; Isaac ; and Mary.

Benjamin (103), son of Jesse (101), had children : Mary ; Benjamin ; Stephen, born 1832 ; and Eliza.

Hezekiah (104), son of Jesse (101), had children : Hannah, born 1816 ; Hetty ; Jonathan H. ; William ; Charity ; Hezekiah ; Eli ; Harriet ; and Enos, was killed in the late war.

Enoch (105), son of Jesse (101), had children : Kesiah, born 1823 ; Nancy ; Aaron ; Jesse ; Mary ; Martin ; Letty ; and Amelia Ann.

Stephen (106), son of Jesse (101), had children : Elizabeth ; Hester Ann ; William M. ; Rachel ; David M. ; Kesiah ; Daniel ; Squire T. ; Sarah ; Mary ; Elizabeth ; and Hezekiah.

Enoch (99), son of Benjamin (76), and his wife, Mary, resided for a time in Westfield, N. J., then removed to the West. They had a son, John (107), born October 10th, 1770 ; and probably other children.

John (107), son of Enoch (99), returned to Westfield in his old age, died, and is buried there. He married and had children : Caleb, born 1795, was one of the first settlers of Indianapolis, he married, but no children ; Maria, born 1798 ; John (108), born 1801 ; Matthias, born 1803 ; Joseph, born 1809, moved to Missouri, where he died, leaving two or three children ; Hannah, born 1812 ; married Mr. Dalling, of Cedar Springs, Iowa ; Sarah, born 1814, married David C. Camp ; Jonathan, born 1822, died, leaving one daughter ; and Susan, born 1824.

John (108), son of John (107), married, and had children : Robert, who held the rank of lieutenant in the army of the Cumberland during the civil war, and died in 1866 ; and John, a distinguished physician of Cincinnati, professor in the Medical Eclectic College established there, author of several valuable medical works, and editor of the Eclectic Medical Journal, by his wife, Mary Hannah, has children : Mattie S., John K., Robert Paul, William B., and Henry F.

Jacob (77), son of Benjamin (51), was born November 29th, 1707, in Huntington, Long Island, where he lived 42 years, having in that time married August 5th, 1731, Abia Rowe, of the same place. She was born May 23d, 1708, and died May 5th, 1791. In

1749, Mr. Scudder sold his property of mills in Huntington, and removed with his family to the vicinity of Princeton, N. J., where he purchased November 25th of the same year, of Josiah Davinson, for £1400, a tract of land on the Millstone river of 100 acres, on which were two grist mills, a saw mill, and a fulling mill. To this tract he added another bought of John Davinson, son of the former. Mr. Scudder was an energetic man of business, of much influence, and held in high esteem. He was a man of generous spirit, a liberal contributor to the First Presbyterian Church of Princeton, in the establishment of which he took an active part, and was, says the Rev. Dr. John Woodhull, "one of its leading members." He died May 31st, 1772, leaving children: Nathaniel (109), born May 10th, 1733; Phebe, born August 2d, 1734, married Mr. Davidson, and died 1807, without children; Lucretia, born March 19th, 1737; William (110), born April 6th, 1739; Lemuel (111), born September 30th, 1741; Ruth, born October 17th, 1743, and died October 13th, 1826, having married August 18th, 1772, Major Kenneth Anderson, an officer of the Revolution, adjutant of the First Regiment of Monmouth county, of which his father, Kenneth, was colonel.

Col. Nathaniel (109), son of Jacob (77), was born in Huntington, L. I. In his 16th year, he removed with the family to the vicinity of Princeton. After due preparation, he entered the college located there, was by it graduated in 1751, and was afterwards honored, by election, to a membership in its board of trustees. After qualifying himself as a physician, he settled in Monmouth county, and soon acquired, by his skill, an extensive practice, became eminent in his profession and the instruction of others prominent in their day, as Dr. Thomas Henderson, Dr. Samuel Forman, &c. The pressing demands of his professional duties upon his time did not prevent the use of his pen and his influence in advocating, with great earnestness, ability, and effect, resistance to the arbitrary acts of Great Britain. When the day of conflict at last came, and his country called around her her ablest advisers and bravest defenders, he gave up, at once, his lucrative practice, and surrendered himself, with hearty zeal and devotion, to her service, placing, promptly, his sword at her disposal. He was immediately appointed by the legislature, lieutenant-colonel of the First Regiment of Monmouth county, and was soon after advanced to the colonelcy, on the disaffection of its former commander, Col. George Taylor. Upon the establishment of that important body of twelve known as the committee of safety, Col. Scudder was at once made a member, and continued, during its existence, to discharge its delicate duties with firmness and fidelity.

He was several times elected to a seat in the legislature, and of the assembly held at Burlington, November 30th, 1776, he was chosen the speaker. At the legislative meeting held at Princeton, November 20th, 1777, the Rev. Dr. John Witherspoon, president of the college, Dr. Scudder, Elias Boudinot, with two others, were selected to represent the state in the national congress. This Dr. Scudder continued to do till the close of 1779.

After the articles of confederation had been agreed on by congress and assented to by most of the states, three of them—New Jersey, Delaware, and Maryland—hesitated, for a time, to permit their representatives to sign them. That this permission should be promptly given by his state, Dr. Scudder urged, with great force of argument, upon the legislature, in a letter dated July 13th, 1778 (contained in New Jersey Revolutionary correspondence), addressed to the Hon. John Hart, its speaker, in the course of which he remarks: "I am of the opinion that Great Britain will never desist from her nefarious designs, nor ever consider her attempts upon our liberties vain and fruitless, until she knows that the golden knot is actually tied." This eloquent appeal had the desired effect. Consent was granted to sign the articles, which was accordingly done by Dr. Witherspoon and Dr. Scudder, on the part of New Jersey, and by February, 1781, the confederation became complete. In the conclusion of the same letter, the battle of Monmouth having just taken place, he adds: "I congratulate you on the signal success of our arms, in this neighborhood, on the 28th of June. Great plunder and devastation have been committed among my friends in this quarter, but, through the distinguishing goodness of Providence, my family and property escaped, and that in almost a miraculous manner."

Congress had taken a short recess, and Dr. Scudder, knowing that the British, on their way from Philadelphia, through New Jersey, to the seacoast, would pass near his residence, hastened home, joined the army, and was present at the battle. After the expiration of his congressional term, he was actively engaged, in conjunction with Gen. David Forman, in repelling the frequent incursions of the British and tories, for the sake of plunder and forage. On one of these occasions, when making an attack on a large force assembled at Black Point, near Shrewsbury, he was instantly killed, in the heat of battle and at the head of his command, October 16th, 1781.

Thus ended, in the vigor of his years and the midst of his usefulness, the career of a man of high classical and intellectual ability, of eminent professional attainments, and of endearing social virtues, deeply imbued with lofty Christian principle. His loss was greatly lamented through the whole land. It was said of him: "Few men have fallen, in this country, that were so useful and so generally mourned for in death." His pastor, the Rev. Dr. John Woodhull, preached his funeral sermon, from the words: "And all Judah and Jerusalem mourned for Josiah, and Jeremiah lamented for him."

Subjoined are the closing stanzas of the tribute in commemoration of his excellence, of his college classmate and life-long friend, Dr. Benjamin Youngs Prime, an eminent physician of New York and son of the Rev. Dr. Ebenezer Prime, of Huntington, L. I.

"With great applause hast thou performed thy part,
Since thy first entrance on the stage of life,
Or in the labors of the healing art,
Or in fair Liberty's important strife.
In medicine skillful, and in warfare brave,
In council steady, uncorrupt and wise,
To thee the happy lot thy Maker gave,
To no small rank in each of these to rise.
Employed in constant usefulness thy time,
And thy fine talents in exertion strong,
Thou died advanced in life, though in thy prime,
For living useful, thou hast lived long."

He was buried with all the honors of war, in the grave-yard of the old Tennent Church, of which he was an elder, and over his mortal remains is a slab of marble, covering, also, those of his wife, bearing the following inscription:

In memory of the
HON. NATHANIEL SCUDDER, who fell in defense of his country,
October 16th, 1781, aged 48 years,
and of his wife,
ISABELLA, who departed this life December 24th, 1782, aged 45.

Dr. Nathaniel married March 23d, 1752, Isabella, daughter of Colonel Kenneth Anderson,* of Monmouth county, by whom he

*Col. Kenneth Anderson was the son of the Hon. John Anderson, who emigrated from Scotland to South Amboy in the early part of the 18th century, and there lived, and in 1736 died, as a notice in an Amboy paper of March 30th testifies: "March 27th, died here in his 71st year, the Hon. John Anderson, president of his majesty's council

had children: John Anderson (112); Joseph (113); Kenneth (114); Hannah, married Colonel William Wyckoff, of Manalapan; and Lydia became the second wife of David English, of Georgetown, D. C., a graduate of Princeton College, of which he was also tutor and president of the Bank of Georgetown.

Dr. John Anderson (112), son of Colonel Nathaniel (109), was a graduate of Princeton, acquired a knowledge of medicine, and became the surgeon in 1777 of the same regiment of which his father was colonel. He was for several successive years elected to a seat in the legislature of the state, and in 1810 was chosen to represent it in the national congress. He married Elizabeth, daughter of Ezekiel Forman and Catharine Wyckoff, and removed first to Mayslick, Mason county, Kentucky; thence to Washington, Davis county, Indiana. Their children were: Charles (115); Nathaniel, died at Mayslick; Emma, married David Wood; Jacob F. (116); John (117); Henry, married Miss Beasley, has three daughters; Fenwick, married Mary Ann Hyatt, he died 1842, left one daughter; William, died, not married; Ellen, married Jesse Crabbs; and Kenneth A., a practicing physician of Indianapolis, he was for several years a member of the state legislature, and one of the commissioners who laid out the city of Indianapolis, he died 1829, aged 30, leaving a wife.

Charles (115), son of Dr. John Anderson (112), married Mary, daughter of Rhodin Horde, of Fredericksburg, Va. Having resided some years at Mayslick, Kentucky, and also at Washington, Indiana, he finally removed to St. Louis, where he died 1849. His wife died 1852. Their children are: Elizabeth, married, first, E. H. Robbins; second, Royal Farnsworth, of Lyme, N. H.; Catharine, married, first, William E. McChord; second, Henry Ames; third, Colonel Marmaduke; Mary Ellen, married; John A., president of a line of steamers to New Orleans; William H.; Charles, a proprietor of the Lindell Hotel, St. Louis; Thomas H.; and Rhodin H.

Jacob F. (116), son of Dr. John Anderson (112), married Matilda Arrell, has children: John A., a practicing physician in

---

and commander-in-chief of this province of New Jersey, a gentleman of the strictest honor and integrity, justly valued, and lamented by all." It was as president of council that he became acting governor after the death of Governor Crosby. He is buried in the old Topenhamus burying-ground, near Marlborough, not far from Freehold, where also his father-in-law, John Reed, surveyor-general of the province, is buried, whose daughter, Anne, he married, and divided his large estate among his nine children by her: John; James; Kenneth—to whom he gives also his scymetar and his gold signet ring—Jonathan; Margaret; Helena; Anna; Elizabeth; and Isabella.

Washington, Indiana, who served as surgeon of the Sixty-fifth Indiana Regiment, married Helen Van Trees, and his children are: Charles P., Matilda F., Laura G., Annie Van Trees, and David; Elizabeth F., married Rev. E. Hall; James, died aged 15; Emma; and Charles, is a physician of Davies, married Miss Baldwin.

John (117), son of Dr. John Anderson (112), was elected to the state legislature in 1851, married Alice Arrell, has children: Jacob F.; William; and one daughter.

Dr. Joseph (113), son of Colonel Nathaniel (109), was a graduate of Princeton College, became a physician, and settled in Freehold, Monmouth, where he gained an extensive and profitable practice. He died March 5th, 1843, aged 82. His wife died December 21st, 1858, aged 90. She was Maria, daughter of Colonel Philip Johnson, a gallant officer of the Revolution, who fell bravely fighting in the battle of Long Island. She was a woman, says a cotemporary, "Of no common merit, of eminent piety, intellectual, highly cultivated, of queenly dignity, and of great force of character," qualities which she largely impressed upon her children, who were: Eliza, married the Rev. William C. Schenck, of Princeton, pastor of the First Presbyterian Church there till his death in 1818, their only son, William, was a graduate of Rutgers College and Theological Seminary; and their only daughter, Margaret, married Rev. Asa S. Colton, professor of mathematics in Rutgers College; Philip Johnston (118), born July 16th, 1791; John (119), born September 3d, 1793; Maria, born October 14th, 1795, not married; Louisa, born 1797, died unmarried, 1826; William Washington, born August 7th, 1799, died 1823, was a graduate of Princeton, professor of mathematics in Dickinson College, a young man of great promise; Joseph, born July 27th, 1801, died aged 25, a graduate of Princeton College and practitioner of law in Freehold; Cornelia, born March 15th, 1803, married Rev. Jacob Fonda, D. D., of Hudson; Juliet Philip, born January 13th, 1805, married Daniel B. Ryall, a lawyer, settled at Freehold, and for several years a representative of the state in congress, whose children are: Edward, and Thomas, P. J.; Matilda, born March 5th, 1806, married Jonathan Forman, whose children are: Ellen, wife of Samuel Forman, Theodocia, wife of Lieut. Frederic Kerner, and Edward T., lieutenant of artillery in the late war; Jane, born December 19th, 1808, married Rev. Christopher Hunt, a Presbyterian clergyman of New York city, whose children are: De Witt, Joseph, Mary and Louisa; Theodocia, born January 25th, 1810, married Rev. Dr. William J. Pohlman, both of whom went as missionaries to China, where Dr. Pohlman was drowned in going from Hong Kong to Amoy in 1842, at which place Mrs. Pohlman died three years later.

Philip Johnston (118), son of Dr. Joseph (113), who died 1830, was a graduate of Princeton College; after admission to the bar practiced law at Shelbyville, Tenn., where he married, first, Elizabeth, daughter of Captain Simms, by whom he had Elizabeth, wife of Thomas Ryall, a lawyer of Trenton. By his second wife, Harriet Whitney, had James, a lieutenant of a cavalry company in the Mexican war, lost an eye in the battle of Monterey, a lawyer, was district attorney of the state, and by his marriage with Caroline Davidson became the father of Louisa, Philip, Jane, Caroline, and Jane.

Missionary John (119), son of Dr. Joseph (113), after graduating at Princeton College in 1811, studied medicine at the College of Physicians and Surgeons of New York, settled in New York city, where he gained an extensive practice. This he gave up and offered himself to the American Board of Missions as a missionary to India, whither he sailed in 1819, in company with Winslow, Spaulding and Woodward, whose wife was a granddaughter of Lucretia Scudder. He was stationed first at Tillipally, Island of Ceylon, where he remained sixteen years, and where he established and conducted a large hospital and attained a high reputation as a surgeon and physician. He was then transferred to Madras, having in the meantime studied theology and been licensed to preach. Twice during his long missionary career of thirty-six years he visited his native land to repair his failing health, and while on a visit at Wynberg, Cape of Good Hope, for the same object, he died, 1855, aged 62, having had the happiness of seeing his eight sons in the ministry, and with the exception of one who died during preparation, his fellow laborers in the missionary field, as were also his two daughters, until their marriage. Dr. Scudder was the author of several popular works on religious subjects. He married in 1816, Harriet, daughter of Gideon Waterbury, of Stamford, Conn., and sister of Dr. Jared B. Waterbury, of Boston. She died 1849, aged 54, leaving children: Henry Martin (120); William W. (121); Joseph, was a graduate of Rutgers, studied theology at the Seminary of New Brunswick, received the degree of D. D., he was obliged on account of ill-health, to leave India, whither he had gone a missionary, and became a U. S. chaplain during the late war, and was afterward appointed secretary of the American and Foreign Christian Union; he married, first, Sarah Ann, daughter of Jacob Chamberlain, of Hudson, Ohio; second, Rachel Ann De Witt, and died 1876; Samuel was graduated at Rutgers, and died in New Brunswick before completing his theological education there, preparatory to his return to India; Ezekiel (122); Jared Waterbury (123); Harriet, married William Stanes, son of James Stanes, of London; Silas D. (124); John (125); and Louisa, married Major Henry B. Sweet, of the English army.

Dr. Henry Martin (120), son of missionary John (119), a graduate of New York University, from which he received his M. D., studied theology at Union Theological Seminary, N. Y., and received the degree of D. D. from Rutgers College. He married Fanny, daughter of John Lewis, of Walpole, Mass. He was stationed at Arcot, India. With broken health, he returned to this country; was pastor, for a time, of a Presbyterian Church of San Francisco, afterward pastor of a Congregational Church in Brooklyn, and now of Plymouth Church, Chicago. Their children are: John, not living; Harriet W., married Capt. L. L. Janes; Fannie L., not living; Catharine Sophia; Henry M., married Bessie M. Scudder; John L., married Alice May Abbott; William, not living; Joseph M., not living; Doremus; and Fannie H.

Dr. William W. (121), son of missionary John (119), graduated at Princeton College in 1841, then studied theology in the seminary there. He was stationed at Vellore, India. Poor health compelled his return, and, as he has not been able to go back, has a pastorate in Glastonbury, Conn. He is honored with a D. D. He married, first, Catharine, daughter of Prof. Thomas Hastings; has one daughter, Mary Catharine. His second wife was Elizabeth, daughter of Franklin Knight, of Newark, by whom he had Lily, not living. By his third wife, Frances, daughter of Lewis Rousseau, he has: William W.; Louis R.; and Fannie A.

Dr. Ezekiel (122), son of missionary John (119), was a graduate of the Western Reserve College; studied medicine in Brooklyn and theology at New Brunswick. He is stationed at Vellore, India. He married Sarah, daughter of Myron Tracy, of Hudson, Ohio. Their children are: Ezekiel C., married Minnie E. Pitcher; Myron T.; Frank S.; Sarah W.; Harriet; Anna Edith; and Isabel.

Dr. Jared W. (123), son of missionary John (119), a graduate of Western Reserve College and of the Theological Seminary of New Brunswick, also became a physician, and is a missionary at Vellore, India. He married Julia C. Goodwin, of New Brunswick, and has children: Bessie M., married Henry M. Scudder; William Henry; Charles, not living; Julia C.; Jared W.; and Clarence G.

Dr. Silas (124), son of missionary John (119), a graduate of Rutgers and of the Theological Seminary of New Brunswick, acquired a medical education in New York, and was a missionary at Arcot, India. He returned from India in 1871, practiced medicine in Brooklyn, and died 1877. He married Marianna, daughter of Jacob Conover, of Monmouth, whose children are: Lily D.; Silas D.; Frederic J.; Ellen; and Joseph.

Dr. John (125), son of missionary John (119), was graduated at Rutgers, and studied theology at New Brunswick; is an M. D., and is a missionary, stationed at Arcot, India. He married Sophia Weld, and has children: John; Louis W.; Charles J.; Henry J.; Walter; and Ida.

Kenneth A. (114), son of Col. Nathaniel (109), was born August 21st, 1765, and died October 21st, 1843, in Homer, N. Y., whither he had removed, having, in 1801, married Elizabeth C. Neely, of Little Falls, N. Y., by whom he has children: Hannah, born October 22d, 1801, married Horatio Tyler, has a son and daughter, lives in Wisconsin; Lydia, died, aged 17; Thomas, born February 3d, 1806, married Hannah M. Neily, of Homer, and resides in Cortland, N. Y.; Mary C., born 1808, married Charles Durkee, of Homer, has a son and daughter, reside in Buffalo; Abram, born September 7th, 1812, died 1864, having married Myra M. Glass, of Fairfield, N. Y., by whom he had a son, a Methodist clergyman, residing in Honesdale, Pa., till his death, 1877; Nathaniel, born September 10th, 1814, not married; John N., born March 23d, 1816, married Elsina M. Joslyn, of Homer; Kenneth Anderson, born November 16th, 1819, married Lois Wilber, of Preble, N. Y., have, of six children, but one surviving daughter, resides in Homer; Isabella, born March 1st, 1822, married Newton Brown, of Homer, reside in Cortland, N. Y.; and two others, died young.

Hannah, daughter of Col. Nathaniel (109), who died 1834, aged 71, married Col. William Wikoff, who died 1824, aged 69. Their children were: Nathaniel S., married Ellen, daughter of Col. Elias

Conover, of Monmouth; Sarah, not married; Matilda, married John C. Smith, of Philadelphia; Ann, married Dr. John T. Woodhull, (see Woodhull family, No. 15); Charlotte, married Dr. Gilbert S. Woodhull, (see Woodhull family, No. 16); Lydia S., died in infancy; Amanda, married Rev. William H. Woodhull, (see Woodhull family, No. 17.)

Lucretia, daughter of Jacob (77), died April 13th, 1826, is buried in Princeton cemetery. She married Joseph Coward, who died 1760, aged about 50, son of Rev. John Coward, son of Capt. Hugh Coward, of London. Their children were: Elizabeth, wife of John Potts, of Imlaystown; Joseph, a member of Pulaski Legion, in the Revolution, had a daughter, Sarah, wife of Charles Parker, and other children; Ruth, married Christopher Stryker; Samuel; Jacob; John, a lieutenant in Captain Wykoff's Company, Second Regiment of Monmouth, 1777; Abiah, married Abel Middleton, by whom she had issue; Lydia, wife of Henry Woodward, who, with Drs. Winslow, Spaulding, and Scudder, formed that early and devoted band of missionaries to India, 1819, both he and his wife died there, leaving four children: Enoch, Lucretia, married Joseph Thompson, Alice, married William Leslie, Jonathan, not married, and Thomas.

Charles Parker, who married Sarah, daughter of Capt. Joseph Coward, and granddaughter of Lucretia Scudder, was a leading politician of the state. He was sheriff of Monmouth county, in which he resided, and was, for five successive years, returned to the assembly. He was afterward appointed state treasurer, an office which he filled sixteen years, living in Trenton, where he died, leaving children: Helen, first, wife of Rev. George Burrowes; Joel, a graduate of the College of New Jersey, a lawyer of Freehold, was elected to the office of governor of New Jersey for two terms, first, during the war, the affairs of which he conducted so much to the satisfaction of the people, that after an interval, he was again elected to the same office, by a majority much greater than the nominating party could furnish, and was elevated to the bench of the Supreme Court in 1880; he married Maria, daughter of Samuel R. Gummere, of Trenton, by whom he had children: Elizabeth G., Charles J., a graduate of Princeton and a lawyer, Helen, and Frederic, also a graduate of Princeton and a lawyer.

Ruth, daughter of Lucretia Scudder and Joseph Coward, married Christopher Stryker, by whom she had: Peter, married Sarah

Snowhill, of Spottswood; Samuel S.; Thomas J.; and Caroline, died in youth. Mrs. Ruth Stryker married, second, Perez Rowley; no children; died in Trenton March 15th, 1848, aged 87.

Samuel S. Stryker, grandson of Lucretia Scudder, was a resident of Trenton, a vestryman of St. Michael's Church, for a time treasurer of the state, president of the People's Fire Insurance Company, and a prosperous merchant. He died February 9th, 1875, aged 78, having married Mary, daughter of John Scudder (No. 20), and had children: Elizabeth, married Barker Gummere, a lawyer of Trenton, whose children are: Mary, Samuel R., William S., Elizabeth D., Isabella, Barker, Gertrude M., and Charles; Mary, married Henry L. Butler, a merchant of New York, whose children are: Henry L., Samuel S., J. Holmes, Edward, Albert, Mary, and Alice; Samuel S., a graduate of Princeton and of the University of Pennsylvania, is a physician of Philadelphia, married Grace M., daughter of Abner Bartlett, of New York; Sarah P., married John S. Albert, chief engineer in U. S. Navy, he died in Philadelphia July 3d, 1880, and she died August 7th, 1881, leaving children: Grace, John S., and Sarah.

Thomas J. Stryker, grandson of Lucretia Scudder, who died September 27th, 1872, aged 72, resided in Trenton, was for forty years cashier of the Trenton Banking Company, was an elder and trustee of the First Presbyterian Church for thirty-five years, a manager, from its foundation till his death, of the New Jersey Lunatic Asylum, and for a time judge of the Court of Common Pleas. He first married Hannah, daughter of John Scudder (No. 20), died March 26th, 1842, aged 37, having had children: John, died in infancy; Hannah died in 1867, aged 25; and William Scudder, a graduate of the College of New Jersey, a lawyer by profession, responded to the first call for volunteers in 1861, entered the army, and assisted in 1862 in organizing the Fourteenth Regiment of New Jersey volunteers; in 1863 was appointed major and aide-de-camp to Major-General Gillmore, and participated in the capture of Morris Island and the bloody and disastrous night attack on Fort Wagner, S. C., was afterward transferred North, on account of illness, to the pay department U. S. army, was brevetted lieutenant-colonel for meritorious services during the war, in 1867 made brigadier-general and adjutant-general of New Jersey, and was in 1874 brevetted major-general. He completed, officially, a valuable roster of Jerseymen in the Revolutionary war, and also one of the New Jersey volunteers in the war of the rebellion, and is the author of several other works of local interest. He married Helen, daughter of Lewis Atterbury, of New York, has one child, Helen B. Mr. Stryker married second, Elizabeth S., widow of John Chambers, (see Chambers family, No. 7,) and sister of his former wife. She died in Trenton December 24th, 1878.

Colonel William (110), son of Jacob (77), who died October 31st, 1793, aged 54, suddenly, of apoplexy, or by the hand of a slave; was the proprietor of a large landed estate and of several mills near Princeton, which, from his well-known patriotism and that of his brother, Colonel Nathaniel, were much damaged by the British, when passing through the state in pursuit of Washington. He was a firm patriot, and served his country during the Revolution, being lieutenant-colonel of the Third Regiment of Middlesex county, was at the battle of Monmouth. He was one of the founders and principal supporters in 1763–4 of the First Presbyterian Church of Princeton, and one of its board of trustees from 1786 to 1793. He married, first, Mary Skelton, who died a year after marriage; second, Sarah, daughter of Matthias Van Dyke, of Mapleton, by whom he had: Isaac (126); Hannah, wife of Rev. Eli F. Cooley, (see Cooley family, No. 18); Eleanor; and William, both died in infancy; William (127); and Sarah, wife of John Ross Hamilton; they removed first to Louisiana, then to Livingston, Texas, had children: Maria, William, Ellen, and perhaps others. After the death of Colonel William Scudder, his widow married Perez Rowley, by whom she had Kelsey V., a physician, who married, first, Mary Ann, daughter of John Deill; he married a second time, removed to Memphis, Tennessee, had children: Catharine, Robina, Mary, and Robert, a civil engineer, a captain in the confederate service, and was promoted to a position on General Bragg's staff; and Catharine, married Rev. Symmes C. Henry, a graduate of Princeton College and Theological Seminary, and honored with D. D. from Rutgers, was settled over the First Presbyterian Church of Cranbury, where he continued till his death, 1857, they had children: Mary, wife of Rev. Joseph G. Symmes, who at the death of Dr. Henry was called to fill his pulpit, and James Addison, a graduate of the college and theological seminary of Princeton, is pastor of the Princeton Presbyterian Church of West Philadelphia, he married Mary, daughter of Robert Steins, of Philadelphia; Mrs. Rowley died 1807. Mr. Rowley married Ruth, daughter of Lucretia Scudder and Joseph Coward, and widow of Christopher Stryker.

Isaac (126), son of Colonel William (110), born February 9th, 1786, and died February, 1833, resided on his large estate, near Cranbury, married Abigail, daughter of Colonel John Wetherill, of Cranbury. She died September 12th, 1823. Their children are: John W. (128); William (129); Henry V., married Anna, daughter of David Nevius, of Freehold, died young; Jacob G.; Sarah, married Wm. Armstead Gulick, whose children are: Symmes H., married Anna W. Ludwig, Anna G., Helen C., married John Van Dyke, Robert R., and W. Howard; Isaac (130); and Hannah, wife of John Reading Farlee, whose children are: Anna R., Robert D., Jacob S., married Mary Bell Hart, and George. His second wife was Juliana, daughter of William Beakes, by her had children; Abigail, married John Williamson Bergen, whose children are: Isaac, Elizabeth, Julia, John, Howard, William, Abiah, and Mary; Howard, married Sarah Bergen, and has children: Cora, Mary, Christopher, Henry, Laura, Julia, and Kelsey; and Kelsey, died young.

Dr. John W. (128), son of Isaac (126), a graduate of Princeton, and of the medical department of the University of Pennsylvania, and practiced in Ewing. He married Virginia, daughter of Abraham Bergen, of Cranbury, has children: Anna V.; Sarah G., wife of Rev. George L. Smith; Edwin L.; and Mary L., wife of Benjamin Hendrickson.

William (121), son of Isaac (126), lived in Lawrence, married Rebecca, daughter of Joseph Rue, of Cranbury, by whom he had children: Mary R., wife of John E. Lanning; Laura L., wife of Rev. Benjamin C. Meeker; Catharine A.; and Joseph R.

Isaac (130), son of Isaac (126), married Mary, daughter of Dr. Horace Sansbury, of Kingston, and has children: Harold T., married Elizabeth Anderson; Frank W., married Emma Van Zandt; Mary H.; and Margaret.

William (127), son of Colonel William (110), who died March 11th, 1819, aged 25, is buried in the Princeton Presbyterian grounds. He received his education at the Classical Academy of Rev. Dr. Finley, at Baskingridge, and settled near Princeton, having married Ellen, daughter of John Craig, of Monmouth, by whom he had children: James, married Ann, daughter of George Morris, of Cranbury, near which he lives, has a daughter, wife of Adrian Applegate; and William Van Dyke, a merchant of Princeton, who at the call of his country entered her service and became captain of Company E, Second Regiment New Jersey Cavalry, commanded by Colonel Joseph Kargé, now professor in Princeton College. The New Jersey regiment sometimes under the command of General Canby, sometimes of General A. Smith, and at another time united to a Missouri and Illinois regiment under General Waring, went sweeping down through the South, encountering great hardships, not so much from the skirmishes and small fights in which they were engaged, which were numerous, and often hotly contested, but from the fatigue of their long and forced marches, compelling them, at least on occasions, to keep the saddle day and night for a week together, sleeping only while their horses were feeding, so that a body of about 1200 men broke down in a short time nearly 5000 horses. This gives an idea of the severity of the service to which much of our cavalry were exposed. Captain Scudder was in the battle near Guntown, Mississippi, and at the capture of Mobile. At the close of the war he resumed his business in Princeton. He married Mary, daughter of William Conover, by whom he has children: Mary C., W. H. Newell, Helen V., and Robert L. Mrs. Ellen Scudder, after her husband's death, married Cornelius Cruser.

Lemuel (111), son of Jacob (77), who died July 9th, 1806, aged 65, owned and resided on a handsome property in the vicinity of Princeton; married a daughter of Richard Longstreet,* of the same region, and had children: Richard (131); Elias, married Jane Vanartsdalen, no children; Margaret, wife of Moses Morris; Abah, married Josiah Fithian, of Cumberland county; Jacob (132); and Elizabeth, married Mr. Dubois, and had one child, Jane, wife, first, of Mr. Nevius, second, of Mr. Lusk, a lawyer of Wilkesbarre.

Richard (131), son of Lemuel (111), who died 1840, aged 66, married, in 1796, Jane Jones, of Kingston, whose children are: William, married, and resided in Atlanta, Ga., where he died, 1874, leaving several children; Lemuel, settled near Louisville, Ky., where he died; John (133); Margaret, wife of Mr. Harris,

---

*Richard Longstreet was a man of property and standing, living in the vicinity of Princeton; was prominent among the founders of the First Presbyterian Church of that place, of which he was a ruling elder and trustee. Besides a daughter, married to Lemuel Scudder (111), he had Mary, wife of Gen. John Beatty, of Trenton; a son Richard, was in the army of the Revolution; and a son Aaron, married a Miss Vandyke, of Mapleton, whose daughter, Eleanor, married Major Cornelius Cruzer, was in the same army, and killed at Morristown.

of New York; Rebecca, wife of W. J. Parker, of Kingston; Mary, wife of Mr. Skillman; and Jane, wife of Mr. Roberts.

John (133), son of Richard (131), born November 12th, 1799, married Anna B. Hollingshead, of Princeton, and moved to Maysville, Ky., in 1846. Their children are: Ann Eliza, married Mr. Robbins, and lives near Terre Haute, Ind.; William H., lives in the same place; Henry M., a Presbyterian pastor of the church of Elizaville, Ky., for more than twenty years; Eliza V., resides in Maysville; John B., editor of Carlisle "Mercury," died June, 1876; James A., resides in Terre Haute; and Archibald L., living in Hunterdon, W. Va.

Dr. Jacob (132), son of Lemuel (111), who died 1859, aged 89, was a prominent physician; settled, first, near Richmond, Va., then on the old Longstreet homestead, near Princeton. He married Hester, daughter of Col. Alexander McLean, one of the surveyors of Mason and Dixon's line. She died February, 1860, and they are both buried in the Princeton cemetery. Their children were: Margaret, born December 29th, 1808, married Rev. John Fleming, missionary to the Indians, whose only child, Mary M., was the wife of Mr. Wilson, of Illinois; Rebecca E., married Rev. Samuel Galloway, a graduate of Princeton College and Seminary and professor of mathematics in Lafayette College, Pa., afterward resided in Belton, Texas, died of yellow fever in 1841, their children are: Charles B., of Memphis, Tenn., Elizabeth, wife of Dr. C. H. Hitchcock, of Illinois, J. S. Galloway, of Memphis, Tenn., now state senator, Mary A., married Major G. W. Davis, of Pine Bluff, Ark., Martha R., wife of Amos T. Akerman, an eminent lawyer of Georgia; John B., graduated by Princeton College, he established a classical academy at Thomasville, Ga., where he died, 1876, aged 66, having married Isabella Meldrum, of Boston, has one child, Agnes H., of South Amboy, N. J.; Samuel E. (134); Alexander McLean (135); Elias, died in childhood; Nathaniel, died, aged 19; and Robert F., received his education at Princeton, married Mary, daughter of Isaac Gulick, of Kingston, and removed to Clinton, Texas; Benjamin R., of South Amboy, N. J., married Anna, daughter of Capt. Degraw, of Princeton, whose children are: Walter E., of Troy, N. Y., William R., of Newark, Edgar, of Trenton, and Bessie D.

Samuel E. (134), son of Dr. Jacob (132), received his degree from Princeton College, became principal of the preparatory classical department of Oglethorpe University, Ga. He died 1860, having married Eunice Safford. Their children are: Margaret; Agnes, died, aged 13; Anna Maria, wife of Mr. Griffin; Gesner, died of yellow fever at Iuka, Miss., 1878; Alice; Ella E.; and Elizabeth.

Alexander M. (135), son of Dr. Jacob (132), also a graduate of Princeton College, principal of a classical academy at Athens, Ga. He died 1874, having married Susan Allen, of Northampton, Mass. Their children are: Elizabeth, married James D. Edwards, Vicksburg, Miss.; Julia, married Rev. George ———, of Milledgeville, Ga.; Caroline C., married Rev. N. Keff Smith, of Atlanta, Ga.; George Herbert, died, aged 16.

Henry (4), son of Thomas (1), removed from Salem to Southhold in 1651, thence to Huntington, in 1657, where he died, 1661, leaving a large tract of land, still held, in part, by his descendants. He married Catharine, daughter of Geoffrey Este, who moved to Southhold in 1651, and had children by her: Jonathan (136), born 1657; Moses, born 1658, died unmarried, aged 25; Rebecca; Mary; and David, who, by his wife, Mary, had children, David and Henry, not traced. Mr. Scudder's widow married a Mr. Jones, before 1680.

Jonathan (136), son of Henry (4), died before 1706, having married, November 4th, 1680, Sarah Brown, and had children: Sarah, born September 1st, 1681; Jonathan (137), born May 28th, 1683, married, and had a son, Jonathan (138); Abigail, born January, 1685; and Rebecca, born 1687.

Jonathan (138), son of Jonathan (137), who died May 12th, 1814, aged 77, married Elizabeth Sammis, whose children were: Moses (139), born March 5th, 1761; Mary, born 1764, married Gershom Bradley, of Easton, Connecticut; Elizabeth, born 1765, married Nathaniel Scudder (No. 79); and Jacob, who, with his wife, died young.

Moses (139), son of Jonathan (138), who died November 29th, 1824, aged 63, was a large farmer, and greatly respected. He married Jemima Lewis, of Northport, by whom he had: Isaac (140); Eliza, died unmarried, 1871, aged 77; Phebe, married, and died childless, 1869, aged 70; and Charity L., married Jeremiah Chichester, and removed to Troy, her children were: Caroline, wife of Henry R. Hubbell, Hannah E., wife of Rev. Birdsey G. Northrup, LL. D., Phebe, and Matilda, wife of Henry Evans, of Brooklyn.

Isaac (140), son of Moses (139), who died November, 1842,

aged 55, married Freelove, daughter of Jacob and Jerusha Townsend, of Northport, in 1811. She died February 19th, 1857, aged 67, having had children: Moses Lewis (141); Charlotte W., married Thomas Patten, of Boston, and died 1864, without children; and Henry Townsend, died unmarried, 1868, aged 49.

Moses Lewis (141), son of Isaac (142), was born November 13th, 1814; an alumnus of Wesleyan University, at Middletown, Conn.; entered the ministry of the Methodist Church, 1837; subsequently pastor of important Methodist churches in Massachusetts, New York and Connecticut; received honorary degree of D. D. by McKindree College, Ind., 1867. He married, January 1st, 1839, Sarah Ann, daughter of Caleb Pratt, of Boston, a descendant of the pilgrims. Their children are: Moses Lewis, graduated at Wesleyan University, 1863, author of works on national banking and fiction, married Clarence J. Williams, of Lake Forest, Ill., June 17th, 1873, resides at Chicago, Ill.; Henry Townsend, graduated by Wesleyan University, 1872, admitted to the bar of Wisconsin, 1876, married Minnie Kimber, June, 1876, resides at Sturgeon Bay, Wis.; Newton Pratt, also graduated by Wesleyan University, 1878, a natural scientist, sent by the Smithsonian Institution to examine the fisheries of Greenland, married Anna L. Ketcham, of Huntington, L. I., now of Smithsonian Institution, Washington, D. C.; Lucy Emily, graduated at Cooper Art School, New York, 1871; and Charles Willis, medical student, and connected with the fish commission, resides at Washington, D. C.

The Massachusetts Branch of the Scudder Family.

John Scudder (1), of Barnstable, apparently closely allied in sympathy as well as in blood to the Scudders of Salem, as indicated by the corresponding names borne by the children and other members of the respective families, was born in England, in 1619. In 1635 he came from London to America in the ship "James," in company with the family of Thomas Ewer.

He located first at Charlestown, Massachusetts, where he was admitted a freeman in 1639. From Charlestown, in 1640, he removed to Barnstable, Massachusetts, the home of his descendants, where he was admitted a freeman in 1654, and resided there until his death in 1689, leaving a wife, Hannah, and children: John (2); Sarah, baptized 1646; Elizabeth; Mary, died 1649; Hannah, baptized 1651, married, first, Joshua Bangs, of Eastham; second, Moses Hatch; and Mehitable, married John Doane.

Elizabeth Scudder, sister of John (1), removed from Boston in 1644 to Barnstable, whither her brother had preceded her. At the same time she left her church in Boston and joined Mr. Lathrop's church in Barnstable. The same year she married Samuel, son of the Rev. John Lathrop, of Barnstable. She afterwards went with her husband from Barnstable to Boston, and thence to Connecticut, where she died in 1700, leaving children: John; Samuel; Israel; Joseph; Sarah; and Elizabeth.

John (2), son of John (1), married Elizabeth, daughter of James Hamblen, in 1689. They died at Chatham, he in 1742, she 1743. Their children were: John (3), born 1690; Experience, born 1692, married Elisha Hopkins; James, born 1694; Ebenezer (4), born 1696; Reliance, born 1700; and Hannah, born 1706.

John (3), son of John (2), married Ruth Davis, and had children: Anne, born 1715, married Nathaniel March; Elizabeth, born 1717, died young; James, born 1718; John, born 1720;

Mehitable, born 1722, died young; Ebenezer, born 1724; Josiah, born 1726, was at Louisburg, 1745, in Captain Elisha Doane's company, married Sarah Phinney, whose children were: Hannah, James and Elizabeth; David, born 1727; Hannah, born 1730; Jonathan, born 1731; Nathaniel, born 1733; Benjamin, born 1736, resided for many years in Rowley, Massachusetts. Of this large family no further record has been found in Massachusetts.

Ebenezer (4), son of John (2), married Lydia Cobb, and had children: Daniel, born 1726, died aged 47; Elizabeth, born 1728; Samuel (5), born 1729; Rebecca, born 1731, married James Athorn; Ebenezer (6), born 1733; Lydia, born 1735, married James Huckins; and Eleazer (7), born 1737.

Samuel (5), son of Ebenezer (4), married, first, Rachel Lewis; second, Anne Lewis, whose children are: John; Samuel; Rachel, wife of Thomas Crocker; and Lot (8).

Ebenezer (6), son of Ebenezer (4), married Rose Delap, and had children: Ebenezer (9), born 1761; James, born 1764; Thomas, born 1766; Isaiah (10), born 1768; Asa (11), born 1771; Elizabeth, born 1773, married Morton Crocker; Josiah (12), born 1775; James D. (13), born 1779; and Thomas D., born 1782 and married, first, Huldah Hall, second, Henrietta Hallett, and had a daughter, Rose Delap, died young.

Eleazer (7), son of John (4), married Mary Lewis, whose children were: David (14), born 1763; Lydia, born 1764, married Eliphalet Loring; William (15), born 1766; Eleazer (16), born 1768; Daniel, born 1770, married Sarah Wells; and Mary, born 1772.

Lot (8), son of Samuel (5), married Sophia Goodspeed, by whom he had: Prentiss, born 1796, married Lucinda Scudder, and had one son, Prentiss W., born 1828, who married Lydia A. Davis; John W., born 1801, married Eliza Hall, whose children are: Theodore, died young, Alphonso, died 1851, aged 23, Arthur, died 1870, aged 32, and Eliza H.; Arthur F., born 1802; and Lot, born 1804, married Thankful Bearse.

Ebenezer (9), son of Ebenezer (6), married, first, Abigail Bearse, second, Betsey Lovell, whose children were: Henry, born 1791; George, born 1792; Ebenezer, born 1794; Isaac, born 1796, all died unmarried; Isaac (17); Philander, born 1800, married Jane Otis; Joseph W., born 1803, married Apphia D. Baxter; Benjamin F., born 1803, married Marcia F. Lovell; Alonzo, born 1805, married Mary D. Holmes, and has children: Elizabeth, died young; and Abigail, born 1837, wife of Arad Perkins; Abigail, born 1808, married Josiah Richardson; and Betsey, born 1812, married Andrew Phinney.

Isaiah (10), son of Ebenezer (6), married Lydia Isham, and had children: Oliver (18), born 1795; Lydia, born 1798, married Joshua Lovell; Lucy, born 1800, married Charles Phinney; Albert (19), born 1802; Mary, born 1804, married Zenas Marston; Sophia, born 1806, married Wilson Hinckley; Isaiah, born 1808; Alfred (20), born 1813; Abigail, born 1817, married, first, James P. Crowell, second, Evander White.

Asa (11), son of Ebenezer (6), married, first, Hannah; second, Lydia; third, Sarah Huckins, by whom he had children: Edward, born 1804, married Rebecca Smith, whose children are Bethia, Lydia, Asa, and Edward; Lydia, born 1806, married Nathaniel Tallent; Hannah, born 1809, married Stephen C. Nye; Nelson, born 1811, married Abigail Bassett, had two daughters, Eliza and Sarah; Daniel (21), born 1813; Sarah, born 1815, died 1841; and Caroline H., born 1819, married David Smith.

Josiah (12), son of Ebenezer (6), a man of superior intellect, and commanding the respect and confidence of those who knew him. He married Hannah Lovell. Their children were: Puella L., born 1800, married George Hinckley; Josiah (22), born 1802; Freeman L., born 1805, married Elizabeth Hinckley, whose daughter Elizabeth is the wife of Jehiel P. Hodges; Zeno, born 1807, studied law at Cambridge, was admitted to the Barnstable bar in 1836, practiced his profession in his native county, Barnstable, was a member of the Massachusetts senate in 1847, and president thereof in 1848, was a representative of his state in the thirty-second and thirty-third congress, he died unmarried; Persis, married Joseph W. Crocker; Edwin (23), born 1815; Henry A., born 1819, married Nannie B., daughter of Charles B. Tobey. In 1838 he was editor of the Barnstable "Patriot," a leading newspaper in his native county, Barnstable. He graduated at Yale College in 1842, and studied law at Cambridge, was admitted to the Suffolk bar in 1844, and practiced in Boston; he was a member of the state legislature in 1861–2–3; also of the Republican National Convention in 1864, which renominated Mr. Lincoln for the presidency. In 1869 he was appointed judge of the Superior Court of Massachusetts, which office he resigned in after years on account of ill-health. In 1882 the office of judge of the Probate Court for his native county was tendered to him, but declined.

James D. (13), son of Ebenezer (6), married Hannah Percival, and had children: Caroline, born 1806, married Prentiss Kelley; James, died young; Harvey, born 1811, married, first, Pamelia Adams, second, Mary Fifield, third, Abby F. Upshar, he had children: Harvey, James D., Isabel, Florence, and Edith; Erastus, born 1813, married Olive M. Lovell, had two children: Josephine, born 1835, wife of Francis H. West, and Zenas L., died young; Ebenezer, died young; Hannah, born 1817, married Henry Marchant; Russell, died young; Dulcy R., born 1822, married Davis P. Nye.

David (14), son of Eleazer (7), was a man of uncommon ability and distinction in his day, holding many public offices in his native town and county. He was clerk of the courts, and at one time a presidential elector. He married Desire Gage, and had children: Charles (24), born 1789; Elisha G., born 1791, married Eliza Bacon, whose children are: Rebecca, wife of Rev. Samuel P. Andrews, Elizabeth, died young, and Eliza; Alexander, born 1793, married Mary B. Crocker, and their children are: Isabel, Mary, Lucinda, and Emma; Abigail, born 1795, married Freeman Marchant; Lucinda, born 1797, married Prentiss Scudder; David, born 1800, died 1837; Horace, a successful merchant and a man of excellent repute, was born 1802, married, first, Mary Anne Bacon, second, Lydia N. Davis, had one child, Mary Anne, died young; Frederick (25), born 1804; William, died young; and Julia, born 1810, married David Crocker.

William (15), son of Eleazer (7), married Sarah Howland, whose children were: Palmer, born 1793; Irene, born 1796, married George Thacher; Daniel, born 1798; and Sarah, born 1809.

Eleazer (16), son of Eleazer (7), married Mary Lovell. Their children were: Aaron, died young; Relief, born 1800, married Isaac Chapman; Caroline, born 1803, married Hartson Hallett; and Eleazer, born 1805, married Eliza T. Lovell, and his children are: Cornelia A., wife of Lyman L. Rose, Georgiana, wife of Alexander C. Kelly, Eliza, wife of Emerson C. Rose, and Harriet J., died 1861.

Isaac (17), son of Ebenezer (9), married, first, Content Phinney, second, Susan D. Lewis, and had children: Content P., born 1834, married Freeman B. Crocker; Ebenezer, of Kalamazoo, Mich., born 1839, married Adelia Lewis, has one child, Helen G.;

Emma, born 1841, married William Howland; Cora A., born 1843, married Franklin Young; and William L., born 1845, married Mary A. Bacon, their children are: Mary R., Philander L., William L., and Isaac D.

Oliver (18), son of Isaiah (10), married Chelana Lumbert, whose children are: Frederick C., born 1819, married Henrietta H. Waitt, his children are: Charles O., born 1844, married Pauline S. Kelley, Frederick M., born 1849, married Dora M. Thayer, and Benjamin H., born 1855, married Mary A. Drinkwater; Alexander, born 1821, married Jane Bradford, whose children are: Edgar C., born 1859, Bradford A., born 1872, and Arthur A., born 1874; and Emily O., born 1831, married Noah H. Lovell.

Albert (19), son of Isaiah (10), married Asenath Richardson, whose children are: Margaret, born 1832, married Benjamin F. Handy; William R., died young; Ferdinand, born 1836, married Eliza T. Armstrong; Hannah R., born 1839; Mary J., born 1843, married Nelson G. Marchant; Albert, born 1846, married Ellen C. Wiley; and Isaiah, died young.

Alfred (20), son of Isaiah (10), born 1813, married Eliza Bearse, whose children were: Ella, born 1843, died young; and Gustavus, born 1845, married Eunice Linnel, his children are: Alice E., and Cecil G.

Daniel (21), son of Asa (11), married Bethia Smith, whose children are: Mary F., married C. H. Smith; Daniel, married Abby Crocker, has a daughter, Maude; Elizabeth, married H. H. Bangs; Ella, married E. B. Crocker.

Josiah (22), son of Josiah (12), married, first, Sophronia Hawes, second, Augusta Hinckley, had children: Rose D., married Joseph H. Parker; Isabel, married Asa E. Lovell; Sarah C., married Horace Lovell; Freeman, married Marietta F. Hinckley, whose children are: Prudence, wife of Warren Lovell, and Walter Scott; Joseph C., married Catharine Coleman; Persis, married Warren Cammet; Helen, married Henry E. Crocker; Josiah, married Bertha B. Hinckley, and has children: Oliver and Elliot; and Charles, married Rosa P. Nickerson, his children are: Augusta and Judson.

Edwin (23), son of Josiah (12), resided in Denver, Colorado, married Harriet N. Phinney, whose children are: Horace, who married Julia C. Candee, has a son, Horace; Ellen, married Daniel M. Lambert; Eliza G., married John C. Anderson.

Charles (24), son of David (14), removed to Boston, became a prosperous merchant, and was widely distinguished for his benevolence and generosity. He married Fear Sears, by whom he had: Marshall S., born 1818, a merchant, married Rebecca C. Blatchford; Charles W., born 1820, a merchant, married Alicia H. Blatchford, whose children are: Francis H., married Sarah Trufant, Henry B., married Julia Perry, Winthrop S., graduated at Harvard in 1870, Mary W., and Bessie M. By his second wife, Jane Marshall, he had: Jane M., born 1828; Eugenia I., died in infancy; Evarts, born 1833, graduated at Williams College, 1854, a clergyman, married Sarah P. Lamson, has a son, Charles L., graduated at Yale in 1882. By his third wife, Sarah L. Coit, he had David C., born 1835, graduated at Williams College, 1855, a clergyman and missionary to India, who lost his life in the midst of his usefulness, by drowning, he married Harriet L. Dutton, has a daughter, Julia D.; Samuel H., born 1837, graduated at Williams College, 1857, a naturalist, president of the Boston Society of Natural History, and editor of the journal called "Science," married Ethelinda J. Blatchford, has a son, Gardner; Horace E., born 1838, graduated at Williams College in 1858, editor of the "Riverside Magazine," and author of several literary works, he married Grace Owen, and has children: Ethel and Sylvia.

Frederick (25), son of David (14), married Cornelia Gage, and had children: Eugenia; Alice, died in infancy; William A., married Clara V. Hancock; and Elisha, married Mary E. Gale, and his children are: Prentiss G., Alice C., and Mary L.

The Slack Family.

James Slack (1), was one of the primitive settlers of Ewing. He came while quite young from Long Island, and married Elizabeth Price, of Lawrence, by whom he had children: Richard, married Mary Throckmorton, of Freehold; James, married Rebecca Chamberlain, of Amwell; Rachel, married William Bryant, of Hopewell; and Daniel (2).

Daniel (2), son of James (1), died 1811, aged 56, married Sarah Mershon, she died 1817, aged 73, having had children: James (3); Francina, died 1825, aged 54; Andrew, born 1784, having married Letitia, daughter of John Reeder, (see Reeder family, No. 6,) and had children: John, died young, Abner, and Sarah.

James (3), son of Daniel (2), died 1832, aged 63, married Nancy Carpenter, who died 1852, aged 84, having had children: Sarah, died aged 11; Amos, was the latter part of his life a teacher, died unmarried, in 1854, aged 58; Elizabeth, married Elijah Hunt, of Hopewell; Ann, a mute, died 1873; Francina, married John Howell Burroughs, (see Burroughs family, No. 27); James, married Ellen Van Winkle, resides in Brooklyn; and Daniel, removed to Ohio, where he married and had children: James, Ann, Elizabeth, Ella, Francina, and Charles Berry.

The Smith Family.

The Hon. Chief Justice or Colonel William Smith, the head of this family in America, was born in 1655, at Higham-Ferrers, Northamptonshire, England. He was a man of great wealth and influence, and for his zeal in behalf of his king, Charles I., his large estate was confiscated, and he was forced to leave the country to save his life. On the accession of Charles II. he applied to him for the restoration of his estate, but was answered by his appointment instead to the rank of colonel and as governor of Tangier, in Africa, which was a part of the dowry of his wife, Catharine, infanta of Portugal. But the Moors becoming troublesome, and his expenses greater than his revenues, he resigned his government and returned to England. Again unsuccessful in gaining possession of his property, he emigrated to this country in 1686, and after some changes settled finally at Brookhaven, Long Island. Having purchased there a large tract of land, it was by patent of Gov. Fletcher erected in 1663 into a manor, known as St. George's Manor, a part of which is still held by his descendants. The government which he held caused him to be distinguished from others of the name, as Tangier Smith. At first a merchant, he was afterwards made one of the supreme judges of the province, and finally chief justice. He was also president of the council of the province of New York till his death, February 18th, 1705, in his 51st year, at his mansion of St. George. He married Martha, daughter of Henry Tunstall, of Putney, Surrey county, England, and had by her issue : Colonel Henry, a man of talents and information, for many years a county judge, had eleven children by two of his three wives, died 1767, aged 88; William Henry (2); Gloriana ; Charles Jeffery, died young ; and Patty, wife of Col. Caleb Heathcote, an English gentleman, one of their daughters married Chief Justice De Lancey, and by him became the grandmother of Wm. Heathcote De Lancey, bishop of the Episcopal Church in New York; and his sister, the wife of James Fennimore Cooper.

Major William Henry (2), son of William (1), lived on a part of his father's place, married, first, Miss Merrit, of Boston, by whom he had a son, Merrit, who settled in Connecticut; second, Hannah Cooper, of Southampton, by whom he had children: Judge William (3); Caleb (4); Elizabeth, wife of John Woodhull, (see Woodhull family, No. 5); Martha, wife of Judge Caleb Smith, of Smithtown; Jane, died, not married; Hannah, wife of Thomas Helme, of Miller's Place; and Sarah, the wife of Rev. James Sproat, of Philadelphia, graduated by Yale, honored with the degree of D. D., by Princeton, pastor of the church at Fourth and Arch street,s Philadelphia, whose children were: John, Hannah, Olivia, Sarah, and their eldest, Major William, a gentleman of education, who served his country faithfully as an officer in the army of the Revolution, the grandfather of Harris L. Sproat, a graduate of Princeton, and member of the Philadelphia bar.

Judge William (3), married Mary, daughter of Daniel Smith, by whom he became the father of Gen. John, distinguished for his eminent abilities and for the high offices which he filled, and who married for his third wife, Elizabeth, widow of Henry Nickoll, only daughter of Gen. Nathaniel Woodhull.

Rev. Caleb (4), son of Major William Henry (2), was graduated at Yale, 1743, licensed to preach after having studied theology under the Rev. Jonathan Dickinson. He was a man of great ability, and became one of the more popular preachers of the day. He accepted the call of the Presbyterian Church of Orange, in 1748, was elected a trustee of the College of New Jersey in 1750, in behalf of which he exerted an important influence, was ever its warm and active friend, and became its president *pro tem.* after the death of President Edwards. He married, first, Martha, youngest daughter of Jonathan Dickinson, a lady of genius, refinement, and superior education. She died 1757, aged 31, leaving children: Anna, wife of George Green, (see Green family, No. 7); Elizabeth, wife of Captain John Phillips; and Jane, wife of Hon. Wm. C. Houston, (see Houston family, No. 1); his second wife was Rebecca, daughter of Hon. Major Foote, of Bramford, Connecticut, by whom he had one son, Apollos.

The Andrew Smith Family.

Andrew Smith (1), the head of one of the families of that name that found a home in Hopewell—a surveyor by profession—gave the name of Hopewell to the first purchase of land, 200 acres, made in the township by him, in 1688, from which came the name of the town. His three sons, Andrew (2), Jonathan (3), and Timothy (4), were among its earliest settlers.

Andrew (2), son of Andrew (1), by his marriage with Mrs. Mershon, had children: Charles, not married; Zebulon, died, not married; and Andrew, who married Sarah, daughter of Josiah Hart, (see Hart family, No. 6,) and had children: Benjamin, George Washington (5), Nathaniel (6).

George W. (5), son of Andrew (2), by his first wife, Mahala, daughter of Samuel Ege, had children: Benjamin; Sarah, wife of John Atchley; Mahala, married Joseph Rue Sexton, and moved West; Alfred; and Andrew Evens. By his second wife, Phebe, daughter of John Smith (7), a son, George.

Nathaniel (6), son of Andrew (2), married Eleanor, daughter of Jonathan Stout, and by her had: Jonathan; Wellington; Sarah, wife of Humphrey Hill; Andrew; Alexander; Ralph, married Catharine Baker; and Joanna.

Jonathan (3), son of Andrew (1), by his first wife, Miss Hixon, had children: John (7); Jonathan, who married Mary, daughter of Samuel Moore, (see Moore family, No. 16,) had a son, Samuel, and a daughter, married Gideon Stout; Joseph, married a daughter of John Jones, and had a daughter, Rebecca, who married John Coryell, of Lambertville; William, not married; Mary, wife of William Moore, removed to Sussex county; Anna, wife of Amos Moore, (see Moore family, No. 19.) His second wife was Abigail, daughter of Nathaniel Moore, (see Moore family, No. 6,) then the widow of Sacket Moore, (see Moore family, No. 7.)

John (7), son of Jonathan (3), was a ruling elder and trustee of the Pennington Presbyterian Church; married Sarah, daughter of Capt. John Moore, (see Moore family, No. 15); had children : Jonathan (8); Jane, wife of Theophilus Hunt; Phebe, second wife of George W. Smith (5); Sarah, wife of Creinyonce Van Cleve, (see Van Cleve family, No. 11); a daughter, married Joseph Titus; and Abigail, not married.

Jonathan (8), married Rebecca Wilson, whose children are: Jonathan, an elder in the church in Lambertville; Nathaniel; Elizabeth, wife of Aaron Moore; and Ketura, wife of Elijah Hart.

Timothy (4), son of Andrew (1), married Jane Lott, probably the daughter of Hendrick, or of his brother, Peter, of Trenton. By her he had children: Joseph; Andrew; George (9); John Berrien; Sarah, wife of James Wilson; Abigail, wife of John Vannoy; and Mary, wife of Stephen Titus, (see Titus family, No. 18.)

George (9), son of Timothy (4), died 1831, aged 65, married Mary, daughter of Ralph Hart, (see Hart family, No. 5.) She died 1856, aged 85, having had children: Ellen, wife of Morgan Scudder; Abigail, wife of Dr. John S. Mershon, their children are: Ellen Scudder and Ralph Smith; Capt. Ralph, married Harriet, daughter of Maj. Stephen Burrowes, had one son, Stephen B.

The Temple Family.

Abraham Temple (1), ancestor of the Temples of Ewing and Trenton, was of English origin, and came from Cambridge, Massachusetts, to New Jersey, in what year is not known, but he or his son was one of the town officers in 1721. By his first wife, Phebe, he had children : Abraham (2); Benjamin (3); Timothy (4); and Elizabeth. By his second wife, Rebecca, mentioned in his will, he had children : Return (5); and Joanna.

Abraham (2), son of Abraham (1), died 1777, having married Jane, daughter of Joseph Scudder, (see Scudder family, No. 11,) and had children : Daniel, who entered the army, was taken prisoner by the British, and was supposed to have died in the prison-ships April 10th, 1751, aged 27 ; and Elizabeth, married Azariah Reed, (see Reed family, No. 9.)

Benjamin (3), son of Abraham (1), died 1777, having married, first, a Miss Hart, had two daughters, who died young ; second, Sarah, daughter of Nathaniel Moore, (see Moore family, No. 6,) by whom he had : Sarah, died young ; and Joanna, wife of John Temple (6), her cousin. His third wife was the widow Horsfield, of Monmouth, no children.

Timothy (4), son of Abraham (1), who died 1751, date of will, appoints as one of his executors John Hart, "my brother," he married Sarah, daughter of Captain Edward Hart, (see Hart family, No. 2,) had children : John (6); Nathaniel (7); Joanna; wife of Benjamin Hendrickson, (see Hendrickson family, No. 4,) and Sarah, died young.

John (6), son of Timothy (4), died August 28th, 1757, having married his cousin, Joanna, daughter of Benjamin Temple (3), and had children : Asher (8); Timothy (9); William (10); Sarah, became the second wife of Asher R. Hart, (see Hart family, No. 12); Elizabeth, not married ; Joanna, died young ; and Abigail, not married.

Asher (8), son of John (6), married Mary, daughter of William Hart ; she died 1847, having had children : Nathaniel, whose wife was Eleanor Slack, and children : George and Mary Ann ; Hannah, died unmarried ; Sarah, wife of John Lanning ; Benjamin, married Catharine Peck, of Connecticut, and has children : Mary and Charlotte ; Israel, married Cornelia, daughter of Nathaniel Hunt ; John, married, first, Mahala, daughter of Andrew Phillips, she died 1844, aged 33, leaving a son, Benjamin. His second wife was Mrs. Susan Hoagland, by whom he had children : Mary, Anna, and Aurelia.

Timothy (9), son of John (6), died 1827, aged 56, married Martha, daughter of John Cornell, of Hopewell ; she died 1833, aged 60, had children : Susan, died 1842, aged 35 ; Phebe, died 1831, aged 20 ; Joanna, died 1846, aged 35 ; Nathaniel, died 1841, aged 36 ; and Hannah, died 1846, aged 33, all unmarried.

William (10), son of John (6), died September 9th, 1846, aged 71, married his cousin, Frances, daughter of Nathaniel Temple (7); she died 1846, aged 63, having had children : Joanna ; Sarah ; Timothy ; John ; Jesse ; Cornelia ; Mary Eliza, died 1847; and William, died 1841.

Nathaniel (7), son of Timothy (4), married, first, Elizabeth, daughter of Joseph Tindall, (see Tindall family, No. 1); and had children : Mary, wife of Samuel Cornell ; Sarah, wife of Benjamin Hendrickson, (see Hendrickson family, No. 7.) His second wife was Sarah, daughter of Jonathan Furman, (see Furman family, No. 2,) by whom he had : John (11); and Frances, wife of William Temple, her cousin.

John (11), son of Nathaniel (7), married Susan, daughter of Joseph Welling, (see Welling family, No. 3,) and had children : Nathaniel ; Joseph Welling, married Ann Eliza Large ; Theodore ; George, married Theodosia Dye ; John Furman, a Baptist clergyman ; Sarah Ann, wife of Nathaniel Furman ; Hannah ; William Howell married Elizabeth McClanan, whose children are Susan, Letitia, and Rev. Asher Brown, of Seneca, N. Y. ; and Charles, married Susan Johnson whose children are : Armitage, John C., Samuel J., Elizabeth, Mary, Julia and Sarah.

Return (5), son of Abraham (1), married in Massachusetts a lady by whom he had children : Abraham, who married and lived in Sussex county ; Benjamin (12); Nathaniel ; Return ; the two latter married and removed to Pennsylvania ; Rebecca, wife of Thomas Hoff, of Hopewell ; Parnel, wife of William Reese ; and John, married Rachel, daughter of Barney Vanhorne, and had children : William, Andrew, Levi and Azariah.

Benjamin (12), son of Return (5), lived in Trenton, married Sarah Burge, and had children: Asher (13); and Rebecca, wife of Asa Hart.

Asher (13), son of Benjamin (12), married Nancy Woodmansee, of Hopewell, and has children: Benjamin, married Cynthia Parker, of Union Parish, La., where he resides; John B., married Victoria, daughter of Pierson Reading, (see Reading family, No. 24); Daniel, married Louisa, daughter of Daniel Hutchinson; William, married, first, Deborah, daughter of Charles Potts; second, Mary-Jane, daughter of Benjamin Potts; Charles, married Susan, daughter of Luther Ward; Rebecca; Cornelia, married Mr. Vandergrift; Maria, married John Sanford, of New Haven, Conn,; Charlotte, married Nelson Jay, lives in Philadelphia; and Ann Elizabeth, married Westley Browne, of Princeton, lives in New York.

The Tindall Family.

Joseph Tindall (1) resided at Ewingville, died 1769, having married Mary Hart. Their children were : Joseph (2); Isabella, married John Smith ; Sarah, married John Phillips ; Elizabeth, married Nathaniel Temple, (see Temple family, No. 7.)

Joseph (2), son of Joseph (1), was a trustee for several years of the Ewing Church, died June 13th, 1819, aged 76, having married Abigail Smith, who died May 24th, 1812, aged 70, leaving children : Hannah, married Benjamin Green, (see Green family, No. 55); Elizabeth, married, first, Jacob Hendrickson, second, Benjamin Green ; William, married Christiana, daughter of John Conover ; Ralph, married Mary, daughter of Adam Lane ; Nathaniel, married Marcia, daughter of John Jones ; Thomas, married Elizabeth, daughter of Noah Howell ; Joseph, married Phebe, daughter of Thomas Hendrickson, (see Hendrickson family, No. 16.)

John Tindall (3), who lived in Clarksville, married Hannah Reeder, sister of Daniel Reeder, whose children were : Noah (4); John ; Charles ; and Rebecca, married William Biles.

Noah (4), son of John (3), married Anna Hart, and had by her John, married Phebe Petit, and resided in New York ; Enoch, married Ann, daughter of Dr. Tidd ; Nathaniel, removed to New York and there married Esther Havens ; Charles, married Mary, daughter of Henry Cook, of Lawrence ; Noah, married Phebe Greves, of New York ; Elizabeth, married Charles Reed, (see Reed family, No. 11); Sarah ; and Ruth.

The Titus Family.

Robert Titus (1), the first of the name in America, was a respectable English agriculturist, living near Stansted Abbey, Hertfordshire, England, thirty miles northeast of London, who, with his wife, Hannah, and two sons, John and Edmond, in 1635, emigrated to this country and settled at Weymouth, near Boston, Mass., and afterward, in 1644, near Providence, R. I., where were born: Samuel; Content (2); Abiel; and Susannah. The father, with his family, except John, who became the ancestor of the New England Tituses, removed, in 1654, to Oyster Bay, L. I. Samuel and Abiel, who died 1736, aged 96, settled in Huntington. Edmond died 1745, aged 85, having had eleven children, settled in Westbury, and Content (2) in Newtown, L. I.

Content (2), styled Captain, son of Robert (1), was born at Weymouth in 1643, came from Huntington to Newtown in 1672, where he remained, and became an active and valuable resident; and so vigorous were his powers at eighty, that he was elected, in 1724, to the eldership of the Presbyterian Church there. He died 1730, having married Elizabeth, daughter of Rev. John Moore, (see Moore family, No. 1,) whose children were: Robert, removed, in 1731, to New Castle county, Del.; Silas (3); John (4); Timothy (5); Hannah, died unmarried; Phebe, married Jonathan Hunt, (see Hunt family, No. 5); and Abigail, married George Furniss.

Silas (3), son of Content (2), remained in Newtown, married, in 1715, Sarah, daughter of Edward Hunt, (see Hunt family, No. 2,) and died 1748, having served both as a trustee of the town and elder of the Presbyterian Church. Their children were: Ephraim (6); Edward; John; Sarah; and Susanna.

Ephraim (6), son of Silas (3), was one of the early settlers of Hopewell, was an elder of the Presbyterian Church there, and died 1789, aged 93, having married Mary, the daughter of one of its ruling elders and principal supporters, Enoch Armitage, son of John Armitage, an emigrant from Lingate, Yorkshire, England. She died 1755, aged 74, having had children: Martha, wife of Henry Woolsey, (see Woolsey family, No. 5); Hannah; Priscilla; Lydia (?); and Ruth, who married William Phillips, (see Phillips family, No. 3,) and died 1818, aged 81.

John (4), son of Content (2), who died 1761, came early to the township of Hopewell, at least prior to 172?, as his farm is on the tax list of that year, about the same time as Timothy (5) and Ephraim (6), the three settling near each other. By his wife, Rebecca, who died 1762, he had children: Joseph (7); Andrew (8); Samuel (9); Benjamin, married a Miss Moore, and had children; John (10); Philip; Thomas, whose property was administered on 1769, by Samuel; Rebecca; Mary, wife of Josiah Hart, (see Hart family, No. 6); and Susannah, wife of Thomas Blackwell.

Joseph (7), son of John (4), an elder of the Presbyterian Church, died December 4th, 1797, aged 76. His first wife was Elizabeth, who died February 19th, 1762, aged 38; his second, Pelatiah, who died October 25th, 1773, aged 48; his third, Martha Moore, sister of Nathaniel Moore, of Hopewell, who died April 4th, 1801, aged 76. His home was on a farm near Titusville. His children were: Uriel (11); Samuel (12); Joseph (13); Hannah, died December 29th, 1802, aged 57; Rebecca, married Guild Hunt, (see Hunt family, No. 21); and Elizabeth, married Mr. Phillips.

Uriel (11), son of Joseph (7), married Hannah Ege, and had children: Elizabeth, died unmarried; Joseph (14); and Margaret, wife of Charles Scudder, (see Scudder family, No. 26.)

Joseph (14), son of Uriel (11), a ruling elder of the Pennington Church, married Eliza, daughter of Jeremiah Burroughs, (see Burroughs family, No. 9.) Their children were: Jemima, wife of John Welling, (see Welling family, No. 8); Elizabeth, wife of Benjamin Westley Titus (33); Uriel B., married, first, Ann, daughter of John Fisher Forman, son of Dr. Samuel Forman, of Freehold, children: Frank, Sarah, Joseph, and Anna, second, Anna Demarest, of Paterson; and Margaret A., married William Henry Wykoff, of Cream Ridge, she died young, leaving a son, Rev. Henry Holmes, a Presbyterian clergyman, of Sonoma, Cal.

Samuel (12), son of Joseph (7), died November 7th, 1825, aged 74, married Elizabeth, daughter of Moses Baldwin, and granddaughter of John Pruddens, of Newark. Their children were: Andrew (15); Joseph, married a daughter of Jonathan Smith; and Samuel.

Deacon Andrew (15), son of Samuel (12), married Hannah, daughter of Ephraim Woolsey, (see Woolsey family, No. 6.) They had children: Elizabeth, died young; Mary Ann, wife of Dr. Samuel Lilly, of Lambertville; George W., died young; Samuel Henry, married Elizabeth daughter of John Guild Muirheid, (see Muirheid family, No. 5,) whose children are: Mary, John, Henry, and Charles; William J., married Harriet S., daughter of Edward Hepburn; and Theodore Frelinghuysen, married Margaret Atchley.

Joseph (13), son of Joseph (7), had children: Samuel; Jonathan; Elizabeth, married Mr. Baldwin; Smith; Martha; Hannah; and Phebe, married Elijah Drake.

Andrew (8), son of John (4), died 1800, date of will, lived on his farm, near Titusville, having married Hannah, daughter of Stephen Burrowes, Sr., by his first wife, Miss Moore. Their children were: Jesse (16); John (17); and Stephen (18).

Jesse (16), son of Andrew (8), married Mary, daughter of John Phillips, whose children are: Enoch, who died November 12th, 1866, aged 80, married Phebe, daughter of Israel Davis, children are: John and Catharine; Jesse; Andrew, died 1826, not married; Lott, married Mary Everett; Abigail, wife of William Rogers; Stephen, married Nancy Mason, and moved to the West, has two sons; and Mary.

John (17), son of Andrew (8), who died 1827, married Sarah, daughter of Henry Mershon. She died January 28th, 1828, leaving children: Theodore (19); Charles, not married; Noah, not married; Theodocia, wife of Samuel Hunt, son of Jesse Hunt.

Theodore (19), son of John (17), married Catharine, daughter of Ellet Howell, (see Howell family, No. 45.) Their children were: Henry, a colonel in the Nicaraguan expedition, under Walker, he married a southern lady; Ellet; Julia, wife of Mr. Minor; Sarah, wife of Samuel Bowman; Mary; and Helen, married Mr. Provost, son of Col. Provost, of Philadelphia.

Stephen (18), son of Andrew (8), died 1825, date of will, having married Mary, daughter of Timothy Smith, (see Smith family, No. 4.) Their children were: Andrew, married Sarah, daughter of Edmund Burroughs, (see Burroughs family, No. 21); Smith, married Fanny, daughter of Richard Hunt, had a daughter, Mary; John, for many years cashier of the old Trenton Banking Company, married Matilda, daughter of Maj. William Montgomery, of Monmouth county, whose children are: Emma and Mary; George; Sarah, married John Howell, of Easton, Pa.; Aaron, married Catharine, daughter of Abner Hart, (see Hart family, No. 7); Burroughs, not married; Asa; and Charles, married Elizabeth Hoff.

Samuel (9), son of John (4), married Miss Johnson, and had children: Johnson (20); Solomon (21); Benjamin (22); Enos (23); Mary, married Elijah Hunt; Jemima, married Daniel Stout; and Rebecca, wife of Charles Merrill.

Johnson (20), son of Samuel (9), married Anna Stout, and had children: Joab (24); Noah (25); and Urie, married George Wright.

Joab (24), son of Johnson (20), an elder in the Pennington Church, married Mary Christopher, and had children: Enoch, married Frances Golden; Louisa, wife of Westley Hunt; Reuben, married Mary Golden; Amanda, wife of James Van Camp; Urie, wife of Nathaniel Cain; Theodore, married Ellen Lee; Mary, wife of John Stout.

Noah (25), son of Johnson (20), married Susan Blackwell. Their children are: John, married Sarah Cain; Johnson, married Miss Blackwell; Catharine, married Aaron Stout; Mary; Azariah, married Sarah Bunn; Noah, married Louisa Dye; and Caroline, married Simpson Van Dyke.

Solomon (21), son of Samuel (9), a deacon in Pennington Church, died December 19th, 1855, aged 76, married Susanna, daughter of Nathaniel Reed. She died January 3d, 1854, aged 93, having had children: Samuel (26); Nathaniel (27); Mary, wife of Thomas J. Blackwell; Susan, wife of Daniel Browne; Reuben (28); and Abijah (29).

Samuel (26), son of Solomon (21), married Amy, daughter of Richard Ketcham, and had children: William, died young; Angeline, married; John, married Sarah, daughter of Andrew Furman, (see Furman family, No. 7); Jane, married Mr. Wykoff; Furman, married Miss Forgeny; and Maria, married Mr. Wykoff.

Nathaniel R. (27) son of Solomon (21), married Nancy, daughter of Nathaniel Van Cleve, (see Van Cleve family, No. 7,) whose children are: Joseph, married Mary, daughter of Benjamin Phillips; William, married Frances Runkle; John, married Letitia, daughter of Benjamin Howell, (see Howell family, No. 23); Frederic, married Ann Eliza, daughter of Ephriam Woolsey, (see Woolsey family, No. 9); Rebecca; Elizabeth; and Penelope.

Reuben (28), son of Solomon (21), a deacon in Pennington

Church, married, first, Catharine, daughter of Daniel Christopher, by whom he had children: Louis, married Mary Holcomb; Daniel, married, first, Gertrude McClanahan, second, Isabella, daughter of David Wiley; Enoch, married Elizabeth, daughter of Peter Blackwell; George, married Susan Blackwell, sister of the former; William, died young; Reuben, married Abigail Waters; Benjamin, married Emma Hobensack. His second wife was Charity, daughter of Titus Hart, (see Hart family, No. 16,) by whom he had John Guild, married Emma, daughter of Westley Burroughs, (see Burroughs family, No. 24.) His third wife was Phebe Golden.

Abijah (29), son of Solomon (21), married Eliza Grey, and had children: Elizabeth, married Mr. Vermule; Sarah, died young; Juliet, died young; Hannah, married Mr. Baynor; and George, died in childhood.

Benjamin (22), son of Samuel (9), married Anna, daughter of David Lee, and had by her, issue: Randall (30); David (31); Furman, married Mary Drake, had a daughter, Adelaide, who married Mr. Blackwell; Liscomb R., a merchant of Trenton, died May 3d, 1873, aged 69, married Ida H. Schanck; Andrew (32); Benjamin Wesley (33); Nathaniel (34); Eliza, wife of Lewis Drake; Mary, wife of Williamson Updike; and Louisa, wife of Byard Drake; Sarah and Stephen, died young.

Randall (30), son of Benjamin (22), married Jane Hoagland, and had children; Harmon, married Lydia Updike; Jane, married John Van Middleworth; Benjamin, married Mary Cunningham; Stryker, married Mary Cox; Liscomb, died West; Mary Ann, married Stryker Hoagland; and Ida, married Jacob Stryker.

David (31), son of Benjamin (22), married Phebe A., daughter of Joseph M. Van Cleve, (see Van Cleve family, No. 12,) whose children are: Charity, married Oakland West; Joseph, married Caroline Hunt; James Livingston, married Harriet Hatch; and Andrew, married Jennie Cunningham.

Andrew (32), son of Benjamin (22), a deacon in the First Church of Trenton, married, first, Mary Elizabeth, daughter of Judge Stacy Potts, (see Potts family, No. 7,) by whom he had: Ella, died in infancy; Cora, married Henry Van Cleve; Stacy, died in infancy; William, married ; Gardiner, married ; and Jennie. His second wife is Juliet, daughter of Henry Phillips, (see Phillips family, No. 19,) by whom he has children: Henry; Mary; Maggie; and Andrew.

Benjamin Wesley (33), son of Benjamin (22), also a deacon in the First Church, Trenton, and a merchant of Trenton, married Elizabeth, daughter of Joseph Titus, (No. 14.) Their children are: Fernando Wood, died in childhood; Edward, died aged 19; Rev. Albert C., married Mary Whitehead; Anna, wife of Frank H. Lalor; Sarah, wife of Lewis W. Scott, a lawyer of Trenton; John Welling; Chandler W., died in infancy; and Howard, married Sarah Gladding.

Nathaniel (34), son of Benjamin, married Emeline Johnson. Their children are: Elizabeth, wife of Archibald Updike; Johnson, married Mary Updike; Furman, died a young man; Harvey, died young; Wesley, married Harriet Mapps; Ida; and Emma.

Enos (23), son of Samuel (9), was an elder in the Pennington Church. He died February 17th, 1810, aged 72, having married, first, Mary Reed, she died July 12th, 1790, by whom he had: Rebecca, wife of Henry Blackwell. By his second wife, Elizabeth Hill, he had: Charles G., married Charlotte Valentine; Stephen H., married, first, Rachel Parkes, second, Isaruah Hunt; Maria, married Joseph Bunn; Ruth Ann, married Asher Howell, (see Howell family, No. 14); Adaline Amanda, married Samuel H. Burroughs (see Burroughs family, No. 30.)

John (10) son of John (4), lived on a farm near Harbortown, is probably the one whose will is dated 1784, in which he mentions daughters: Rebecca, wife of Simeon Phillips, (see Phillips family, No. 4); Hannah, wife of Mr. Stillwell; Mary, wife of Amos Hoagland; and Anne, wife of Mr. Ege.

Timothy (5), son of Content (2), removed from Newtown, Long Island, to Hopewell, New Jersey, at an early period, at least prior to 1722, as his farm of 200 acres is on the tax list of that year. He died about 1757, the date of his will. By his wife, Mary, mentioned therein, had children: Timothy (35); Philip; Dennis; Jemima; Phebe; Mary; and Susanna, who married Edward Hunt, and had children: Timothy, John, Kesiah, wife of Elijah Hart, (see Hart family, No. 13); Mary, wife of Moore Scott, Phebe, wife of John Furman, Hannah, and Sarah.

Timothy (35), son of Timothy (5), died at an advanced age. He married, first, Miss Ketcham, by whom he had two children: Timothy (36); and Phebe, who married, first, Mr. Stout, and had children: Theophilus, Noah, and Mary, her second husband was Peter Bake, by whom she had: Timothy, Hannah, and

Rosanna. By his will, recorded 1818, he leaves property to his second wife, Tabitha, (a widow Brush,) by whom no children.

Captain Timothy (36), son of Timothy (35), who died 1831, aged 85, married Patience Hoff. She died July 13th, 1827, aged 70. Their children were: Benjamin, born October 5th, 1779; Cornelius, born January 24th, 1781, married Mary Smith, and lived in Parma, Michigan; Hannah, born November 4th, 1785, wife of Amos Hart; Elizabeth, born August 4th, 1782, married John H. Hart, (see Hart family, No. 25), and resides in Seneca county, N. Y.; Timothy, born December 3d, 1790, married Mary, daughter of George Bake, lived in Hastings, Michigan; Jane, born September 20th, 1788, wife of Gideon R. Corwine, whose children are: Cornelius, married Mary, daughter of John Hart, Rebecca, Phebe, married Isaac Farley, of Titusville, and George, married Catharine, daughter of Jeremiah Vandyke, of Hopewell.

The Tomlinson Family.

Joseph (1), first of the name in Ewing, married Phebe Baker. Their children were: Joseph (2); Samuel; Hannah, married David Fetherby; Rachel, married Nathaniel Loughbury; Lydia, not married; Margaret, married Thomas Hilbern.

Joseph (2), son of Joseph (1), married Jane Buckman, and had children: Esther, wife of John Cooper; Joseph B., married Martha, daughter of James Burroughs, (see Burroughs family, No. 19,) and had one child, James Burroughs; Phebe, married Simeon Atchley; Joshua, married Sarah, daughter of Abner Rozell, had a daughter, Mary; Samuel (3); Phineas (4); Charles; Nathaniel (5); William; Martha, married William Ribinson; James; Abner, married Prudence, daughter of Daniel Cook, had children, Elizabeth and Mary.

Samuel (3), son of Joseph (2), married Hannah Doane, and had children: Kinsey B.; William H.; Mary Jane; William, died young; Susannah; and Hannah, married William Vanpelt.

Phineas (4), son of Joseph (2), married Phebe, daughter of Azariah Reed, (see Reed family, No. 9,) and had by her: Jane Eliza, who married Daniel Cornell, and has children: Charles, John, Wesley, and Eleanor; Ellen, married John B. Reed, and had children: Phineas T., married Mary Eliza, daughter of William Wilson, George W., John Wesley, and Phebe.

Nathaniel (5), son of Joseph (2), married Elizabeth, daughter of Joshua Lanning, (see Lanning family, No. 14,) and had children: Joshua; Abner; and Simeon.

James (6), son of Joseph (2), married Eveline, daughter of Lewis Evans, and had children: Lewis; Joseph; Henry; William; Elizabeth; and John.

The Trent Family.

Our country is greatly indebted to Scotland for the high character of the early emigrants, who left her shores for our own. They were generally persons of good education, of excellent morals, of thrift and shrewdness, of industry and intelligence—and these characteristics they imparted, in no small measure, to the communities of which they became members. A man of this stamp was William Trent, a native of Inverness, who, with his brother, James, came over and cast his lot among the Friends of Penn's colony, soon after its foundation, in 1682. Mr. Trent's name appears in the index of the first book of deeds as the purchaser of several properties between 1682 and 1697, but, as the book in which the deeds are recorded is unfortunately lost, the exact date of his first purchase and probable arrival cannot now be ascertained.

In 1697, his brother, being about to return to Scotland, made, as was customary in that era of long and hazardous voyages, his will, before setting out, in which he leaves his property in the province, in London, and in Edinburgh, to his brother, William, who had already become an established and prominent merchant. His mercantile transactions, we may presume, were large and extensive, for he was both ship-owner and importer, and as such, was in partnership with Gov. William Penn and his deputy, James Logan, though his foreign operations had no very flattering results, as we may gather from a letter of Logan to Penn, dated September, 1704, in which he writes: "Thy success at sea is so very discouraging, that I should never be willing to be concerned more this way, and William Trent, who has hitherto been a partner in thy losses, almost protests against touching a vessel again where a proprietary holds part." Logan, in the same letter, commends Mr. Trent highly for his "thorough skill and insight into trade," and terms him a "successful merchant." Gov. Gookin, of Pennsylvania, in a letter to the bishop of London, styles him "a merchant of credit," and the Rev. John Talbot, rector of St.

Mary's Episcopal Church, Burlington, in a communication to the same bishop, speaks of Mrs. Trent and Mrs. Moore as "ladies of distinction and of a firm rank and quality," so that, from this united testimony, we may regard Mr. Trent as one of Philadelphia's most eminent merchants.

We may make some estimate of his prosperity from his style of living. He became, in 1703, the purchaser, at £850, of the most elegant mansion in the city, occupied, for a time, by Gov. William Penn, known as the "slate-roof house," on Second street, where the corn exchange now stands, built of brick, with a spacious lawn in the rear, extending towards the Delaware. His cultivated taste added to its attractiveness, by converting a portion of it into a beautiful garden of rare plants and exotic trees, making of it, in the words of Growdon, "a delightful *rus in urbe.*" Its comparative value and beauty, we may learn from a letter by Logan to Penn, 1709, when Judge Trent thought of returning to Europe: "William Trent, designing for England, is about selling his house, which thou lived in, with the improvement of a beautiful garden. I wish it could be made thine, as nothing in this town is so well fitting a governor. His price is £900 of our money, which it is hard thou canst not spare. I would give £20 or £30 out of my own pocket, that it were thine." But Gov. Penn never afterwards returned to his colony, nor did Judge Trent to England, permanently. In 1703, Mr. Trent was chosen a member of the governor's council, of which fact the following minute is found (Pennsylvania archives): "At a council held in Philadelphia, 9th of 12th month, February, $170\frac{3}{4}$, Mr. Trent was called to ye board, to be a member of this council, and took the oath of allegiance, and abjuration of the pope's supremacy," and of this body he continued a member during all the changes of governors, until his removal to Trenton, October 4th, 1721.

Before the year 1706, the colony had managed to conduct its domestic affairs without the intervention of a regular system of courts, but by this time, the growth of the colony and its business had so increased, that a regular and higher order of courts became imperative. Four provincial judges were deemed necessary at first.

Good policy might seem to have required them to send to England for one or more skilled in the law to place on the judicial bench, but a spirit of independence induced them to select the best material from themselves to fill positions so important.

Accordingly, although there were men of high classical attainments among them, as Loyd, a graduate of Oxford, and Logan, and lawyers of some repute, yet the business talent, the sterling good sense, and sound judgment of William Trent, pointed him out as one of the first four eminently fitted for so responsible an office.

Soon after the establishment of these courts the increasing business of the city demanded the erection of a Supreme Court for its accommodation. Of the first five supreme judges of the city of Philadelphia, Judge Trent was again selected as one. His appointment to these high offices in a government under the control of Friends, member of the Church of England as he was, strongly attests the exalted estimation in which he was held. Although not bred a lawyer, yet we find his name in the Chancellorship of Keith, among the masters in chancery, associated with such names as Logan, Dickinson, Hill, and Andrew Hamilton, men the most distinguished in the province for their talents and learning.

Judge Trent was not only for so long a term of office an expounder of the laws of the province, he was also for many years one of its law-makers. He was returned from the court to the assembly of 1710, 1715 and 1719, and was chosen to represent the city in the assembly of 1717 and 1718, of which body he was elected the speaker.

Judge Trent, amid his diversified duties and employments, was not unmindful of the interests of the church and religion. He was a zealous and active supporter and generous benefactor of the Church of England, to whose communion he belonged. Logan calls him a "noted churchman." The Rev. J. Talbot, missionary rector of Burlington Church, says of Colonel Daniel Coxe and Mr. Trent: "They have done their parts towards the society's house at Burlington;" he also remarks in a letter to the bishop of London: "I called on the Gov. [Gooken of Pa.] in company with Mr Trent, the chief man in the church, [Christ Church, Philadelphia, founded 1694 or 1696.] In addition to these evidences of his standing as a churchman and a friend of religion I may offer an epistle dedicatory, prefixed to a catechism published in London 1719, and addressed to him, presenting him to us as a man conspicuous in the church as he was in business and in public life.

"*To William Trent, Merchant of Philadelphia:*

"Sir—As your singular humanity and good will to all men, do justly recommend you to the esteem and love of all, so the instances thereof that you have applied to me particularly, require of me my thankful acknowledgment, and as such I desire of you to accept of this new and small essay for the more effectual promoting of catechetical instruction, and to vouchsafe it your patronage, for as it is designed in part for the use of our poor countrymen, who are dispersed up and down through your vast and spacious regions, so your honored and worthy name prefixed, may recommend it very much to their acceptance and use; for I know not any gentleman in all the country round about you, that is either better known and more beloved than yourself," &c.

Judge Trent invested his ample means largely in real estate and became an extensive landholder. Soon after his purchase of the slate roof house, he became also the purchaser at £850, in conjunction with Isaac Norris, of the Manse of Williamstadt, comprising 7000 acres, the property and residence of William Penn, Jr., whose extravagance and spendthrift habits compelled him to part with his homestead. The town built on a part of this land took its name from Mr. Norris. A few years later, in 1714, he purchased of Mahlon Stacy, Jr., a large body of land, consisting of 800 acres, at the Falls of the Delaware, lying on both sides of the Assanpink and along the Delaware; and four years afterwards (1718,) of Samuel Atkinson and his wife, Ruth, for £457, 200 additional acres, adjoining his former purchase and lying on the Delaware. He also bought a considerable body of land, about 28 acres, of William Burge, of Philadelphia, so that he was the proprietor at that time of most of the land on which Trenton now stands. To this place in October, 1721, he transferred his residence, it having already received in his honor the name of Trentstown. He was in the same year elected with Thomas Lambert to represent in the assembly, Burlington county, whose northern boundary at that time was the Assanpink creek, was also appointed judge of the county the same year. He received his military title at this time from Governor Burnet, who appointed him colonel of one of the regiments of Hunterdon. He was also returned for Burlington county to the assembly of 1723, of which body he was chosen speaker.

Up to this period, New Jersey had shared with New York the services of a chief justice, but the increasing prosperity and business of both provinces had rendered, at length, the duties of the office too arduous for the attention of one man, and New Jersey being the weaker of the two, her interests were, in consequence, somewhat slighted. She therefore petitioned Gov. Burnet to appoint a chief justice for herself alone, a request to which he thought proper to accede. Influenced by the great ability of Judge Trent, and his special qualifications resulting from his long experience, his choice at once fell on him, to whom accordingly belongs the honorable distinction of being the first to fill that high office in New Jersey. Gov. Burnet, in writing to the lords of trade to justify his selection, says: "The present chief justice is universally beloved, as your lordships may observe by his being chosen their speaker, and, I doubt not, will answer my expectations in executing the office."

"An honor," says Judge Richard S. Field, "that he did not long survive, as he died suddenly of apoplexy, at his mansion called Bloomsbury Court, on the 25th of December, 1724, universally beloved and lamented." "On the 29th of December of this year, 1724," says Smith (History of New Jersey), "died William Trent, Esq., chief justice of New Jersey, for several years a member, and part of that time speaker, of the assembly. He had been speaker, also, of the assembly of Pennsylvania, and bore the character of a gentleman." To the same effect is a notice from his old home, contained in the Philadelphia "Weekly Mercury," of December 29th, 1724:

"On Friday, 25th of this instant, William Trent, Esq., chief judge of the province of New Jersey, departed this life, being seized with a fit of apoplexy, at his house in Trent-town. He was one that was universally beloved and is as much lamented." Not far from the mansion which he had just built, adorned and occupied, his mortal remains found their resting place, on the bank of the Delaware, in the grave-yard of the Friends, constituting the old portion of what is now known as Riverview cemetery. Though no monument marks his grave and records his virtues, yet the State of New Jersey embalms in the name of her capital the memory of her first chief justice, a man whose purity of morals, whose probity as a judge, whose character as a Christian gentleman, and whose endearing social qualities, entitle him to be held in lasting remembrance, both by the state in whose councils he for so many years participated and whose laws he dispensed so long, from her supreme bench, and by the state, as well, on whose soil he had elected to spend the remainder of his days, and of whose Supreme Court he was the first presiding judge.

Judge Trent was twice married. His first wife was Mary Burge, daughter of widow Burge. He had by her, children: James, an active business man, to whom the legislature, "in consideration that Col. William Trent had, by his industry and application, and encouragements given by him for building—there was erected a pretty considerable town," granted the exclusive use of the river Delaware, for a ferry, two miles above and two miles below the falls, he was copartner with Thomas Lambert and John Porterfield, of Trent, and Anthony Norris, of Philadelphia, in the proprietorship of a forge, or iron works, in Nottingham, near Trenton, he was also appointed a judge of the court, by Gov. Burnet, in the latter part of his life, he lived in Philadelphia, where he became a merchant, and died 1735, probably unmarried or without children; John, appointed clerk of the Court of Common Pleas, who, at his death, 1725, was succeeded by his brother Maurice, in the same office, who died 1730, probably unmarried, as he leaves by his will, his property to his brothers, James and William, and his friend, Thomas Palmer; Mary, married Nathaniel French, merchant, of Philadelphia, whose daughter, Mary, married William Denning, merchant, of the same city. Judge Trent's second wife was Mary, daughter of Gov. William Coddington, of Rhode Island, whose widow married Anthony Norris, first mayor of Philadelphia. By her he had Thomas, died in infancy, as the following transcript from the records of baptisms and deaths of Christ Church, Philadelphia, bears witness: "Thomas, son of William and Mary, ye second wife of William Trent, born and baptized June 1st, 1711," and among the deaths, "Thomas, the son of William and Mary Trent, was buried the 29th August, 1711;" and William.

William Trent, son of Chief Justice William, born and educated in Philadelphia, engaged, as did his father, in commercial pursuits. He did not confine himself to local traffic, but extended his operations to the profitable, though distant and hazardous Indian trade in furs and peltries, a trade which in less troublous times laid the foundation of John Jacob Astor's immense fortune. He promoted this trade not only through agents and the establishment of trading-houses, but by personal visits to different and distant tribes, thus becoming acquainted with their principal chiefs, acquiring their language, and gaining over them a commanding influence, which proved of great value in after years to Pennsylvania and the neighboring colonies, and of which they not unfrequently availed themselves. There were very few of their great treaty-making assemblies at which he was not present either as counselor of one of the parties, or in some other official capacity. His introduction into public life was in the military service of Pennsylvania during what is known as King George's war (1746–7.)

The aggressions of the French and Indians upon the frontier settlements, particularly of New York, had by this time become so numerous and outrageous, that it was determined to put an end to them by carrying war into the country of the aggressors. To this end an expedition was organized against Canada, and the several colonies were called on for their respective quotas of troops; that of Pennsylvania was four companies, to a captaincy of one of which Trent was appointed by Governor Thomas. He marched with his command to Albany, and although through the inefficiency of the commanding general, the expedition failed, yet Captain Trent's company was detained six months beyond the period of enlistment, eighteen months in all. He was stationed at the advanced post near Saratoga. During this period while moving forward on one occasion to repulse an incursion of the French and their allies under St. Luc, he fell into an ambuscade, and though eight of his command fell at the first fire, he rallied his men and bravely held his ground against superior numbers until reinforcements arrived, and they were unitedly able to drive off the enemy. At the expiration of eighteen months he returned, (December, 1747,) was honorably discharged, and received the thanks of the assembly. A report to the legislature by Thomas Lawrence, in the name of council, states "That the Pennsylvania troops have during the winter in the opinion of council, contributed to the preservation of Albany and the places adjacent, and have from all accounts done very severe duty. (Col. Rec., vol. 5, p. 133.)

The services of Capt. Trent were from this time, till the close of the Revolutionary war, so frequently put into requisition to aid in councils and treaty-makings between the representatives of different Indian nations and the governments of Virginia, Pennsylvania and New York, that it is scarcely necessary to specify the occasions; scarcely was a treaty formed or an assembly held at which he was not present as a prominent and important participant.

Early in 1752 the French had so far made encroachments on

the territory north of the Ohio which the English claimed as their own, as to build a fort at Presque Isle (Erie), Le Bœuff (Waterford), and Venango (Franklin), and had broken up the trading stations by burning down the trading-houses on the whole length of the Ohio and its northern tributaries by killing or carrying off captive the traders. To remonstrate against these hostile and atrocious acts Washington had been sent; his errand was fruitless. The French were also endeavoring to win over to their interests the western tribes, of whom the Miamis were the most powerful. "They can bring into the field," wrote Governor Dinwiddie to the lords of trade, "10,000 fighting men." To confirm these in their friendship for the colonies was a matter of the first importance.

To effect this. a large appropriation was made by the English government, at the instance of Dinwiddie, to be invested in presents for this tribe. It required a man of strong courage and resolution to traverse these hundreds of miles, beset with prowling bands of hostile French and Indians, and such a man, the prudent, cautious, and self-interested Dinwiddie believed he had found in the person of Capt. Trent. He was accordingly chosen to be the bearer of these presents and conciliatory messages to Piqua, their remotest and principal town on the Miami, about 500 miles distant. This was a very perilous undertaking at this time, as it lay directly over the route along which the murders, robberies, and burnings complained of had been committed.

On the 21st of June, 1752, Capt. Trent and his party, with the Indian goods, a tempting and therefore dangerous burden, set out from the council fires of Logstown. After nine days' travel, on reaching Muskingum, 150 miles from Logstown, he heard from some white men that the town of his destination had been taken and burned by the French and Indians, the white men killed or carried off, and the Indians killed or dispersed, four days after, and 70 miles further on, below Hockhocking, this news was confirmed by a white man who had passed through from the region of Piqua. A less courageous man would have deemed it prudent to reverse his steps, but, nothing daunted, he pressed forward, merely taking a more circuitous route, as more likely to avoid any prowling hostile bands. On the 6th of July they met, at the lower Shawneestown, the only two white men that had escaped the massacre.

Taking with him, from there, a party of Indians, to rescue any that might be found at Piqua, after 13 days of further travel, he reached the place, and found it a smoking and deserted ruin. The white traders had been, one of them, killed and partly eaten, the others made captive ; the king had been killed and eaten, many of the chiefs and people killed, and the remainder compelled to seek safety in flight, and their town, of about 400 families, had been plundered and burned down. Returning to Shawneestown, he found there the king's wife and son, a chief, and a portion of the fugitives. Among these he distributed the presents, held a council, at which he warned them to be on their guard, and encouraged them to remain firm in their loyalty to the English, and returned in the early part of August, having traveled more than a thousand miles, amid dangers and alarms, that deprived them, often, of their rest, by compelling them to watch whole nights, with arms in hand, and during heat so intense that their very hunting-dogs were overpowered, and died while hunting, and having marched one day without a drop of water, a distance of 22 miles. Gov. Dinwiddie approved his course, and transmitted his journal to the lords of trade, calling their especial attention to the perils he had encountered in the discharge of his mission.

In the summer of 1753, Capt. Trent was sent by the governor of Virginia to the forks of the Ohio, to select ground suitable for the erection of a fort. This he seems to have done in the month of August, and he began work thereon soon after that time. Capt. Trent then went to Winchester, Va., where he made a treaty with the chiefs of the Picts and Shawnees, which must have been a favorable one, as he immediately returned to the forks with 100 men, whom he had organized to build the fort. Before he could finish the same, he heard from friendly Indians that the French contemplated taking possession of the forks at an early day. Seeing that no time was to be lost in getting men enlisted to garrison the fort when completed, leaving his work in charge of Lieut. Frazer, he hastened to Wills Creek, the nearest settlement, to procure a reinforcement. But before he could procure the force, the French, earlier than was expected, came down upon Lieut. Frazer with numbers nearly 1000 strong, in 300 canoes, with 20 cannon, and compelled, of course, its surrender, with its 40 effective men. The French, confirming Capt. Trent's judgment, immediately finished the fort, and enlarged it to contain their superior numbers, and called it Fort Duquesne, in compliment to the governor of Canada. Capt. Trent's company having been dispersed, he was left without a command, and Lieut.-Col. Washington, who was advancing to his aid, was driven back by the same body of French, and obliged to capitulate, after brave defence at Fort Necessity.

Capt. Trent is next found at Fort Cumberland (Wills Creek), whither he had hastened, after learning of Braddock's defeat, and lent his aid, at the request of Washington, in reorganizing the fugitive and shattered remains of the defeated army. When the savages, in the winter of 1756, were spreading death and destruction broadcast along the frontiers of Pennsylvania, Capt. Trent attempted to raise a force and go against them, but his efforts were unsuccessful, through lack of support. (Letter to Peters, Pennsylvania Archives.)

In 1757, Capt. Trent was actively engaged in various negotiations between the Indians and the governments of Virginia and Pennsylvania. On May 2d, he was at Bethlehem, Pa.; on June 16th, at Winchester, Va., and July 27th, he officiated as secretary, at Easton, Pa., at the great treaty there made between the Indians and Gov. Denny and council, on the part of Pennsylvania. October 4th, 1759, he was at another, with the Indians, at Fort Pitt, and again, in 1760, at the same place, Pittsburg, with Gen. Monckton, and on the same errand Capt. Trent's resources had become so reduced, by the repeated depredations of the Indians, that the legislature of Pennsylvania passed a bill of relief, in his behalf, which, however, was rendered of no avail, by the refusal of the king to apply his signature; but his commercial misfortunes culminated during the destructive war or conspiracy of Pontiac, when his large trading-house at Fort Pitt was plundered and destroyed, and also a great amount of goods carried by his agents into the Indian country. His financial ruin was complete. For these losses, the chiefs of the different nations, at the treaty of 1765, at the instance of Sir William Johnson, engaged to indemnify Capt. Trent and his fellow sufferers by a grant of land. When, therefore, in 1768, the great council of chiefs of the Six Nations and of the nations on the Ohio were assembled at Fort Stanwix, in the presence of the representative of England, Sir William Johnson, and of the governors of New Jersey and Pennsylvania, and the councilors of the two provinces, Capt. Trent and Wharton, were present to claim the indemnity for their losses, promised by the chiefs at the treaty before mentioned. They were ready to fulfill, with such liberality, their engagement, that Sir William was obliged to moderate their generosity. Their grant was at last so large, that the king refused to sign the deed of grant, before he had had an interview with the grantees. Capt. Trent accordingly went over to England, at the close of 1769 or beginning of 1770, and succeeded in obtaining the king's signature to the deed. To this tract thus granted, containing an area of 3,500,000 acres, lying between the Monongahela, east, and the Kenhawa, west, and between the Ohio, north, and the Laurel mountains, south, they gave the name of Indiana territory, and to the company owning it, viz., the 22 merchant traders of Philadelphia, whom Capt. Trent represented, that of the Indiana company. Capt. Trent remained several years in London, and while there, became the agent of the Grand or London Land Company, whose London head was Thomas Wampole, a member of parliament, and at one time ambassador at Munich, and whose Philadelphia principals were Benjamin Franklin, Samuel Wharton, and John Sergeant. The claims of the company conflicted with those of the Ohio Land Company, whose interests were sustained by Col. George Mercer, of Virginia, and father of the distinguished Charles Fenton Mercer, member of congress from Virginia, and gave rise to a protracted controversy between them, but the outbreak of the Revolution put an end both to their claims and the controversy.

Capt. Trent returned home in the early part of 1775, as a letter to him from the Hon. Thomas Walpole indicates, some extracts from which are here subjoined as not wholly without interest.

"May 30th, 1775.

"Dear Major—By this time I think you will have ended your voyage, and after a long and painful absence have had a meeting with your family and friends. * * * * I have observed that government and its friends, till lately, have continued to talk their old language, but I think with less confidence than before, and though they still have affected to make no doubt of prevailing in the end, they allow that it may not be done as soon as they once expected; since the account of what passed on the 19th of last month (battle of Lexington), they probably begin to think that it will not be done at all. From the accounts hitherto published, the Americans seem to have behaved with prudence and spirit in receiving the first blow and resenting it afterwards in a manner which he became. * * * Now that hostilities are begun, it is to be supposed that they will be continued, till matters are brought to some decision, and we shall receive, I doubt not, a sad account of Gen. Gage and his army. Boston too, I fear, must fall a sacrifice to the fury of England, I would say folly if that were not too mild a term for my purpose. We shall, however, I think, be beat into our senses, before it is long (the only sort of instruction, which, at present, we seem capable of receiving) and everything, in a good degree may be set right again. What should most be abhorred by both countries is separation. There are those among us, who may yet, if they are suffered to do it, prevent that common calamity.

Major Trent is again found July 6th, 1776, at Fort Pitt, in an official capacity, participating in a treaty-making with the Indians. He resided for some years at Lancaster, Pa., where his second and third children were born, for a much longer period and until 1768 he made his residence at Carlisle, and was appointed by Gov. Hamilton judge of the Court of Common Pleas of Cumberland county, where his youngest three children were born; before his visit to England he removed to Trenton, New Jersey, where his family lived during his absence, and he himself after his return until the close of 1783, as his wife is credited with the rent of the Presbyterian parsonage (Dr. Hall's History of Presbyterian Church), from 1768 to 1771, and his letters are written from Trenton, lower ferry. He was the owner of 800 acres below the falls on the Delaware, which are offered for sale in the "Trenton Gazette" of June, 1784. During this year he removed to Philadelphia, where he remained until his decease in 1787, (date of will,) engaged principally in managing the affairs of the Indiana company, of several shares of which he died possessed.

Major Trent being the grandson of a prominent lawyer, and the son of one of the most eminent merchants and distinguished judges of the colony, doubtless enjoyed in early life the best educational advantages that the city afforded, yet his tastes seem not to have led him to adopt a professional course, but rather to engage in business pursuits, to which, notwithstanding public engagements, both civil and military, he devoted himself with great activity and perseverance; yet his efforts were not crowned with the success they deserved, for such were the troublous times in which he lived, that misfortunes numerous and crushing pursued him till he was at last financially overwhelmed, from which condition, however, he partially recovered before his death.

William Trent (2), son of Chief Justice William Trent (1), married Sarah Wilkins, who died 1807, and is believed to be buried in the little grave-yard on the hill beyond the New Jersey State Lunatic Asylum, and had issue by her: William, born May 28th, 1754, at the mouth of Wills creek, and baptized by Mr. Hamilton, chaplain to the regiment, probably died young; Ann, born October 20th, 1756, at Lancaster, married Mr. Raymond; Martha, born October 24th, 1759, at Lancaster; Mary, born December 3d, 1762, at Carlisle; Sarah, born November 29th, 1768, at Carlisle; and John (3), born April 21st, 1768, at Carlisle.

Mary Trent, daughter of William (2), married Nathan Beakes, had children: Morgan, who married Hannah, daughter of George Miller, of Trenton, having one daughter; Lydia, married Gen. Zachariah Rossell, son of Hon. William Rossell, judge of the Supreme Court, who at the commencement of the war with Great Britain in 1812, entered the army, and having served his country gallantly and faithfully, retired at the end of the war to private life. He was soon after elected to the office of clerk of the Supreme Court, the duties of which he discharged with singular ability till his death; their children were: Mary Trent, married Lewis P. Higbee, son of Joseph Higbee, who died January 17th, 1859, aged 51, without issue, Nathan Beakes, William Henry, and Anna.

Nathan B. Rossell, son of Gen. Zachariah Rossell, was a major in the United States army, was brevetted and honored by a vote of the legislature for gallant conduct in the Mexican war, fell mortally wounded while bravely leading forward his men at the battle of Gaines' Mill, in the late civil contest. He married Fannie Mann, and has children: Marion Trent, wife of Baron Carl Von Langen; Clifford Beakes married Lily, daughter of Dr. Casper Wistar, of Philadelphia; Anna Morgan; and Randolph Lewis.

William Henry Rossell, son of Zachariah Rossell, was a physician, but is now a major in the United States army, he married, first, Lucinda Gayle Easton, of Alabama, and had by her: William Trent, lieutenant in engineer corps, United States army. He married, second, Margaret Dauge Martin, by whom he has Sophia Martin; Henry Dauge; and Hugh Bertram.

John Trent (3), son of William Trent (2), was a physician, resident in Charleston, South Carolina, till 1793, when he removed to Camden, South Carolina, and there remained till his decease, November 3d, 1809, of whom the following obituary notice is found in a Camden paper of that day: "Possessing as Dr. Trent did, an uncommonly acute and discriminating judgment, with a mind ardent and active in the pursuit of professional acquirements, he early proved that his abilities were not of the ordinary stamp, and by unusual success both as physician and surgeon, the utmost confidence has long been reposed in his skill; few have been more eminently useful." He married, 1798, Mary Louisa, daughter of Capt. Isaac Duhone, of Camden, South Carolina, by whom he had children: Isaac, unmarried; William Henry (4); John, died unmarried; Martha Lucretia, not married; Mary Boisseau died aged 7; Dr. Trent's widow, a very lovely and accomplished woman, married twice afterwards, by her second marriage she became the mother of the present John M. Desausure, of Camden; she died 1853, in her 71st year, after a married life of 53 years.

William Henry Trent (4), son of John (3), was of the same profession as his father. He married, first, Margaret, daughter of Nathan Loche, of Salisbury, North Carolina, son of Gen. Loche, of Rowan county, North Carolina, who represented that state in congress; his children by her were: Mary Eliza, married Rev. William Fagg, an English gentleman, and rector of the Episcopal Church at La Grange, Tenn., who died four years after marriage; without issue; Mrs. Fagg died November 5th, 1867; Martha Jane; Louisa Catharine, married 1852, James Anderson, a lawyer of Memphis, Tenn.; John, married Mary G. Anderson, niece of James Anderson, his brother-in-law, and has children: Susan C., Julia, and Mattie, he lives on the frontier of Texas, in Callahan county; Margaret Lock, married May 20th, 1863, Rev. William C. Gray, of Bolivar, and died 1874, leaving children: William Trent and Joseph Albertia. Dr. Trent had by a second marriage three children, who died young, and a son, William Henry, now living with his mother in Waco, Texas.

Louisa Catharine Trent, daughter of Dr. William Henry (4), married James Anderson, and had children: Margaret E., married T. E. Anderson, of Memphis, unrelated; John Trent lives in Callahan county, Texas; James, a lawyer of Memphis; Louisa Catharine; Mary Fagg; and William Henry.

The Van Cleve Family.

Hans. (1), pronounced Honce, a contraction, as is also Jan (Yon, for Johannes, the Latin of John) Vancleef, the first of the name in this country, emigrated with his wife, Engeltie (Angeline), from Amsterdam, Holland. He settled, at a very early period, in New Utrecht, L. I., of which he was one of the patentees, his name being mentioned in a grant by Gov. Dougan, in 1686. Benjamin Vancleef, of Freehold, was, with scarcely a doubt, a son of his, who came over from Long Island with many other Hollanders, to Monmouth county, about 1700.

Benjamin (2), son of John (1), married Hendricke Sutphen, and died 1747, date of recorded will, leaving property to his sons, John (3); Benjamin; Richard; and three daughters.

John (3), son of Benjamin (2), was twice married, first to Sarah Conwenhoven (Conover) and subsequently to Neeltic (Nellie or Cornelia), daughter of Chreynjans (Creinyonce) Van Marter. He moved to Lawrence, where he resided till his death, in 1772, aged 72; is buried there, in the old cemetery, as is also his wife, Cornelia, who died August 4th, 1782, aged 78. Their children were: Chreinyonce (4); Benjamin (5); Aaron (6); Joseph, married Elizabeth, daughter of Jacob Carle, is supposed to have had no children; Eleanor, wife of Daniel Hunt, of Lebanon; Jane, died 1809, aged 65, having married Walter Smith, who died 1829, aged 88; and Anna, died 1786, aged 40, having been the wife of John Rozell, (see Rozell family, No. 2.)

Chreinyonce (4), son of John (3), married Penelope, daughter of Philip Phillips, (see Phillips family, No. 3,) of Lawrence, and had issue: John (7); Philip (8); Ishi (9); Samuel, died unmarried; Aaron (10); Anna, wife of John Carpenter, son of John and Mary Hart, of Pennington, whose children are: John, and Elizabeth, wife of Peter Beekman, of Pennington; Catharine, wife of Stephen Keer; Elizabeth, wife of Moses Moore, (see Moore family, No. 34); and Jane, wife of Abner Hart, (see Hart family, No. 7.)

Col. John (7), son of Chreinyonce (4), a trustee of Pennington Presbyterian Church, married Elizabeth, daughter of Joseph Moore, (see Moore family, No. 17,) and had children: Chreinyonce (11); Joseph (12); Samuel (13); Charles (14); Christiana, wife of Cornelius Hoff, Jr.; Elizabeth, wife of Daniel Blackwell, of Hopewell; Nancy, wife of Nathaniel R. Titus, (see Titus family, No. 27); Martha, wife of William Phillips, (see Phillips family, No. 15); and Penelope, wife of Daniel Blackwell, of Stony Brook.

Chreinyonce (11), son of John (7), married Sarah, daughter of John Smith, (see Smith family, No. 7,) whose children were: Chreinyonce, married Miss Vanbright, of New Brunswick, had a son, Cornelius; and Ely, married Hetty, daughter of Jesse Atchley, their children are: Sarah, wife of William Quick, of Flemington, Rachel, Jane, wife of Samuel Ketcham, and Anne, wife of Liverton Mathews.

Joseph (12), son of John (7), married, first, Charity, daughter of John Stillwell; had children: Phebe Ann, wife of David L. Titus, (see Titus family, No. 31); and John Stevenson, a deacon, married Maria, daughter of Benjamin Muirheid, (see Muirheid family, No. 6); second, Sarah, sister of the former, and widow of Samuel Brown, by whom he had Elizabeth, wife of Joseph Horne.

Samuel (13), son of John (7), married Phebe, daughter of John Stillwell; had one child, Crook Stephenson, a Methodist clergyman, who married Sarah, daughter of Joshua Bunn, of Pennington, their children were: Joshua B., Wesley, and Mary.

Charles (14), son of John (7), married Sarah, daughter of John Waters, and had children: John; Samuel Ege; Charity; Mary, wife of George Beakes; Eliza, wife of Wilson Chambers; and Joseph, who was drowned.

Phillips (8), son of Chreinyonce (4), died 1843, aged 86, having married, first, Martha, only child of Henry Woolsey, (see Woolsey family, No. 5,) and had by her: Henry W., who married Esther Moore, and died 1859, aged 72, no children; Nancy, died 1841, aged 57. He married, second, Elizabeth, daughter of Capt. Samuel Hunt, (see Hunt family, No. 37.) She died 1836, aged 59, having had children: Maria; Eliza; George, married Matilda Hutchinson, whose children are: Sarah, Samuel, and George; Samuel (15); Frances, wife of Israel Blackwell, whose children are: Mary, Aaron, Robert, and Anna; Robert, married, and lives in New York.

Samuel (15), son of Phillips (8), died 1845, aged 36, having married Eleanor Hutchinson, and had children: Edward, married Gay Rockhill; E. Hutchinson, married Grace Shreve; Lizzie, wife of Dr. De Witt; and Annie, wife of Dr. McKinney.

Ishi (9), son of Chreinyonce (4), died 1827, having married Mary, daughter of Josiah Hart, (see Hart family, No. 6,) and had children: James and Eleanor, both died young; Benjamin (16); Noah, married Harriet, daughter of Hiram Woodruff, no children; and John, died young.

Benjamin (16), son of Ishi (9), married Elizabeth, daughter of Edmund Roberts, (see Roberts family, No. 2.) She died 1832, aged 48, leaving children: Eleanor, wife, first, of Ephraim Woolsey, (see Woolsey family, No. 9,) second, of James B. Green, (see Green family, No. 20); John (17); Maria, became the second wife of James B. Green; Harriet; Ann, wife of Nathaniel Blackwell; Jane, wife of James Garritson; Eliza, wife of Lemuel Anderson, son of George; and Sarah, wife, first, of Benjamin Smith, then became the second wife of Samuel Roberts.

John (17), son of Benjamin (16), died 1868, aged 56; was both an elder and trustee of the Ewing Church. He was elected to a seat in the legislature. He married Martha, daughter of James B. Green, (see Green family, No. 17,) and had by her: Benjamin, married Elizabeth, daughter of Abram Skirm; James, G., married Margaret Skirm, her sister; Henry J., married Cora, daughter of Andrew Titus, (see Titus family, No. 32); Alexander G., was graduated with distinguished honor by Princeton College, having gained the mathematical fellowship, married Matilda, daughter of Philip Hendrickson, of Princeton, (see Hendrickson family, No. 15); John S., married Harrie Warford; William G., married Kate Conner.

Aaron (10), son of Chreinyonce (4), married, first, Elizabeth, daughter of Benjamin Stevens, of Lawrence, in 1790, and removed to Batavia, N. Y., where he died at an advanced age, in 1860. She died 1811, aged 37, having had children: Hannah, died, aged 17; George, belonged to the United States Navy till 1819, and was promoted for his gallantry in the action between the Wasp and the Frolic. He is supposed to have foundered at sea. He married, and left one child, Ann Eliza; Samuel, died, aged 17; Edward, was the publisher of a paper at Lansingburgh, N. Y.; Jane, married Mr. Kinkly, lived at Pine Hill, N. Y.; Eleanor; Mary Lucy, wife of Sidney Smith, lives in Lansingburgh; and

Capt. James, of Lewiston. His second wife was Elizabeth, widow of Reuben Town. He had by her: Elizabeth, wife of Judge Taggart, of Batavia; and Ann, wife of Mr. C. M. Ganson, a banker of Detroit, Mich.

Benjamin (5), son of John (3), resided in Lawrence, and rose to distinction. He commanded a company in the battle of Long Island, and was promoted to major of the First Regiment of Hunterdon county, in 1777. He resigned on account of his election to the assembly, of which he was for several years a member, and in 1784, its speaker. He was also surrogate of the county. He died August 31st, 1817, aged 77, having married, first, Mary, daughter of Joseph Wright, who was one of the matrons dressed in white that received Washington at the bridge of Trenton. She died 1784, aged 38, having had children: John Wright (18); Phebe, married John Stevens, no children; Cornelia, married Thomas Stevens; Elizabeth, second wife of Dr. Israel Clarke, of Clarkesville, her children were: Mary, wife of Dr. Alexander Hart, of Philadelphia, son of John V. Hart, and Elizabeth; Joseph W. (19); and Benjamin, died young. He married, second, September 20th, 1786, Anna, daughter of the Rev. Caleb Smith, (see Smith family, No. 4,) of Orange, and widow of George Green, (see Green family, No. 7,) of Lawrence, she had by him, one son, died in childhood, and died 1789, aged 40.

John Wright (18), son of Benjamin (5), was a graduate of Princeton and a tutor of the college; was a lawyer, and practiced in Trenton; died 1802, having married Elizabeth, daughter of Isaac Coates, of Philadelphia, whose children are: Mary, wife of Dr. Garbett, of Georgia; Elizabeth; and Cornelia, wife of Daniel Barnes, of New York.

Joseph W. (19), son of Benjamin (5), died 1864, aged 87, having married Charity Pitney, of Morristown, and had issue: Mary, wife of Stacy Paxon, of Trenton, a merchant, and for many years treasurer of the state, she died May 26th, 1847, aged 49, having children: Henry, Capt. James, who recruited a company during the late war, and joined with it, as Company D, Forty-eighth New York Volunteers, and fell, distinguished for his bravery in the bold, but disastrous assault on Fort Wagner, Stacy, married Louisa Lathrop, of Newark, Mary, wife of Dr. Walter Walker, of Petnorth Park, Surrey, England, resided in Rochester, N. Y., and Franklin, a physician, joined the army, and is supposed to have been murdered by the Indians; Phebe, not married; Benjamin Franklin (20); and Elizabeth, died young.

Benjamin Franklin (20), son of Joseph (19), a lawyer of Trenton, married Phebe, daughter of Joshua Anderson, (see Anderson family, No. 3,) by whom he had: Frederick, member of the common council of Philadelphia; Henry; and Franklin. His widow married François Amadie Bregy, professor of French in the University of Pennsylvania.

Aaron (6), son of John (3), died 1810, aged 69, married Hannah, daughter of Jacob Carle; she died 1803, aged 52, having had issue: Elizabeth, wife of Caleb Smith Green, (see Green family, No. 28); John (21); Jacob (22); Israel, died 1803, aged 20; Cornelia, wife of the Rev. Selah Woodhull, (see Woodhull family, No. 19.)

Dr. John (21), son of Aaron (6), was a graduate of Princeton College, for a time filled the chair of chemistry in it, and was also a member of the board of trustees from 1810 till his death in 1826. He was both an elder and trustee of the First Presbyterian Church of Princeton, was an eminent physician, and won by a union of skill with exalted Christian character the confidence of the community. His children by Ann, daughter of William C. Houston, (see Houston family, No. 1,) were: Churchill Houston (23); Horatio Phillips (24); Mary Ann, wife of Mr. Gibbs, professor of oriental literature in Yale College; Louisa, wife of Camillus C. Daviess, of the United States Army, from Kentucky, by whom she had Richard Montgomery, Mary Houston, and another, her second husband was Mr. Tate, of Missouri, by whom she had Horace Phillips; John W. (25); and Margaret Fox, wife of Prof. Johnson, of New York University.

Churchill Houston (23), son of John (21), graduated by the College of New Jersey, removed to Ypsilanti, Mich., where he practiced his profession of law. He married, first, Elizabeth A. Brown, who died 1836, leaving one son, John Archer; second, Ann McKinstry, by whom he had Margaret Fox; Charles; and James Augustus.

Horatio P. (24), son of John (21), was graduated at West Point 1831, served in the army till 1836, when he resigned and engaged in civil engineering till the war broke out, when he promptly tendered his services to the governor of Minnesota, who appointed him colonelof the Second Regiment of Minnesota volunteers, and was ordered south. On the 17th and 18th of January, 1862, the advance of Gen. Thomas' army moving south from Somerset was within ten miles of the confederate lines at a place called Mills Springs. Being greatly inferior to them in number, Gen. Thomas halted for four regiments to come up, the Tenth Indiana, Ninth Ohio, Fourth Kentucky, and the Second Minnesota, Col. Van Cleve's. On the 19th the battle was fought against outnumbering foes with a bravery which would have done honor to veterans. At times so near were they to each other that their faces were burned by the powder of each other's guns. Gen. Thomas gained a signal victory, the first decisive one of the war, for which the army was publicly thanked by President Lincoln. The Second Minnesota distinguished itself for its bravery, and its colonel was promoted for gallantry brigadier-general, and assigned to the command of the Fourteenth Brigade of the Army of the Ohio. He was at the siege of Corinth in May, 1862, and in October was assigned to the command of the fifth division of the army of the Ohio, previously commanded by Gen. Crittenden. The army then started in pursuit of Breckinridge through Kentucky, overtook him at Perrysville, and on the evening of the 8th was fought the battle of Perrysville, which proved indecisive, as Gen. Bragg withdrew in the night, but the Union army continued the pursuit with frequent skirmishing. On the 31st of December, 1862, the army under Gen. Rosecrans fought the battle of Stone River, Gen. Thomas commanding the left wing, of which Gen. Van Cleve's division composed a part. Against this wing with a determination to break it, the confederates under Breckinridge threw an overwhelming force, but they stood their ground unyieldingly. Here Gen. Van Cleve's division suffered a very heavy loss, he himself was severely wounded and carried off the field, and in history is reported as having been killed. After several months' confinement he recovered, and again took command of his division, and was present on the 19th and 20th of September, 1863, at the battle of Chickamauga. The right and centre having given way, the left under Gen. Thomas sustained unflinchingly the whole brunt of the battle for hours until help arrived. Here again Gen. Van Cleve's division suffered heavily. Being now broken down in health he was appointed to the command of Murfreesborough, Tenn., which position, from the frequent assaults of the enemy, he found no sinecure. Here he continued till the close of the war, when he was mustered out of service and brevetted major-general of volunteers. In 1866 he was appointed adjutant-general of

Minnesota, which office he still holds. He married at Fort Winnebago, in 1836, Charlotte O., daughter of Capt. Clark, United States army, and by her had children : Malcolm Clark ; Anna Houston, married Mortimer Thompson, of New York, and died 1858 ; Elizabeth Archer ; Horatio Seymour ; Edward Mortimer ; Samuel Agnew ; Paul Ledyard ; and John Risley.

John W. (25), son of John (21), married Julia Hunter, of New York. They have children : William Hunter ; Mary Louisa ; Alfred Augustus ; John Woodhull ; Julia Antoinette ; Charles Eugene ; and Frank Houston, and resides in Ypsilanti, Michigan.

Jacob (22), son of Aaron (6), by his first wife, Sarah, daughter of Theophilus Phillips, of Lawrence, (see Phillips family, No. 10,) had issue : Israel ; and Cornelia. By his second, Mary, daughter of Israel Howell ; he had Andrew ; Noah and Henry, not married ; Aaron (26); Jane, married Joseph Hall, of Philadelphia ; Annie ; Alexander H. ; Mary, wife of Samuel Ogden, of Philadelphia ; and Hannah, wife of Philip Miles, of Pennsylvania.

Aaron (26), son of Jacob (22), by his first wife, Henrietta, daughter of Clark Chambers (see Chambers family), had children : Maria, Emma, married Dr. John Woolverton ; John B., graduate of Rutgers College, married Mary, daughter of Rev. Daniel Miller, a Lutheran clergyman ; Edwin ; Robert S., a graduate of Princeton, had a son, Robert S., a Presbyterian clergyman, married Catharine Spencer, of Erie, Pa. ; Aaron, died 1873, aged 28, married Ella, daughter of John Muirheid, (see Muirheid family, No. 8); Elizabeth and Henrietta, died young. His second wife was Sarah Algeo, of Philadelphia.

The John Welling Family.

John Welling (1), the ancestor of one branch of the Wellings of this region, was of Welsh origin, and came in 1727 directly from Jamaica, L. I., and purchased after a year's lease, in 1728, 223 acres in Hopewell, of Terit Lester, to whom it had been conveyed through John Muirheid and John Fitch, by John Reading and James Trent, commissioners of the loan office. He died about 1790, having married and had children: Elizabeth, born 1730, married Jacob Carle, of Ewing; and John (2).

John (2), son of John (1), was a justice of the county, died August 12th, 1832, aged 93, having married Esther, daughter of Rev. John Guild (see Guild family, No. 2); she died April 20th, 1812, aged 68. Their children were: Enoch, died young; John (3); Hannah, married John Davison; Charles (4); Asa, died unmarried, 1795, aged 16; and Isaac (5).

John (3), son of John (2), died July 5th, 1800, having married Rebecca, daughter of William Green, (see Green family, No. 41); she died March 12th, 1837, aged 63. Their children were: Enoch G., married Elizabeth, daughter of Joseph Grover, of Penn's Neck, and died June 7th, 1848, aged 50, leaving no children; John, died 1832, aged 32, having married Sarah, daughter of the same, and had children: Charles, Louis S., married a daughter of Capt. Robert Anderson, of Princeton, has children: Leroy H. and Bessie; Emily, married Mr. Lansing, and lived in Poughkeepsie; and Samuel and Elizabeth, died in childhood.

Charles (4), son of John (2), who was a trustee of the Pennington Church, and for fifty-seven years one of its ruling elders, died 1857, aged 81, having married Mary Saxon, by whom he had: Robert, married Ruth Hunt, by whom he had a daughter, Mary Elizabeth, who married Scudder Cook, son of Justice William Cook; George, died in youth; William, married Charity Spencer; Sexton, married Maria, daughter of Dr. Sansbury, of Princeton, and had by her Sarah Ellen and others, died young; Charles (6); Isaac, graduated at Princeton; Israel, married Elizabeth Thomas, and has a daughter, Florence; Asa; Elizabeth; John; last three died unmarried.

Charles (6), son of Charles (4), married, first, Elizabeth Dougherty, lives in Missouri, and has children: Mary, married Mr. Lapierre; Anna, married Mr. Medley; Bernice; Freddie, married Mr. Williams; Elizabeth; and Juliet.

Isaac (5), son of John (2), an active member of the Pennington Church, and for fifty-seven years an elder in it. He died February 29th, 1868, aged 84, having married Hannah, daughter of Louis Perrine, of Freehold, and by her had children: Henry P. (7); Elizabeth, married first, Dr. Springer, of Wilmington, Delaware; second, John Hart, son of Israel Hart; and third, David N. Wiley, son of Rev. David Wiley, of Georgetown, D. C., by whom she had: Isaac W., married Sarah Toms, Henry Martin, married Mary Willis, Isabella W., married Daniel Titus, Augusta, Harriet W., and Hannah; John (8); and Harriet S., wife of Stanhope S. Cooley, (see Cooley family No. 20.)

Dr. Henry P. (7), son of Isaac (5), was graduated by the College of New Jersey and by the medical department of the University of Pennsylvania, practiced his profession in Pennington; by his marriage with Louisa A., daughter of Peter V. Schenck, of Pennsylvania, he had one child, Edward Livingston, also a graduate of Princeton, of the Medical College of Chicago, and of the medical department of the University of Pennsylvania. At the commencement of the war he offered his services to the government, and was appointed in 1861 assistant surgeon of the Third Regiment of New Jersey volunteers, was with McClellan through the campaign of the Peninsula, was advanced to be full surgeon of the Eleventh New Jersey, was made division surgeon under General Sickles of the Army of the Potomac, was appointed medical director of the Third Army Corps hospitals, was afterwards made brigade surgeon of M'Allister's brigade, Mott's division, and was finally advanced to the post of division hospital surgeon of Mott's division, and in it remained till the close of the war, having been engaged in every battle of the army of the Potomac. His rank is now that of surgeon-in-chief of the National Guard of New Jersey, and is secretary of the society of the Third Army Corps. He married Alice Dick, of Belvidere, and has children: Louisa and Henry Livingston.

John (8), son of Isaac (5), was a deacon in the Pennington Church, and elder in the church of Titusville, where he resided.

He married Jemima, daughter of Joseph Titus, (see Titus family, No. 14,) and had by her: John Calvin, who married Charlotte, daughter of Theodore Paul, of Belvidere, and had children: Bessie and John Paul; Joseph Titus, married Helen, daughter of Frederick Kingman, a lawyer of Trenton, and had children: Frederick and Susie; Isaac Henry, married Carrie Surles, of Scranton, and has children: Jared, Margaret and Fanny.

The William Welling Family.

William Welling (1), the ancestor of the Ewing family, married Miss Snowden, and had children: John (2); Joseph (3); Elizabeth, married Nathaniel Furman, (see Furman family, No. 6); Abigail, married William Napton, of Princeton, and by her became the father of John, whose son, Barclay N., was a graduate of Princeton College, studied law, removed to Missouri, and became one of its supreme judges.

John (2), son of William (1), an elder of the Trenton and Lamberton Baptist Church, in which grave-yard he and his wife are buried, died November 7th, 1834, aged 77; married Mary, daughter of Samuel Hart, (see Hart family, No. 4.) She died November 1st, 1859, aged 99, having had children: William (4); John (5); Elias (6); Sarah, married Ralph Green, (see Green family, No. 57); and Hannah.

William (4), son of John (2), who died in 1848, aged 67, and is buried in the Baptist ground of South Trenton, married Jane, daughter of Smith Hill. She died 1860, aged 74, having had children: Louisa, married David Eastburn, of Pennsylvania, and had a daughter, Louisa; Sarah, married Samuel Hill, of Hamilton; James C., married Genevieve Garnet, of Richmond, Va., resides in Washington, D. C., is the proprietor of the "Intelligencer," has a daughter, Genevieve.

John (5), son of John (2), married, first, Elizabeth, daughter of Jesse Hunt, of Hopewell, by whom he had children: William B.; Charles H., a merchant of New York, married Catharine Greer, of Providence, R. I., had children: William Brinton, Richard, Catharine, and Emily. His second wife was Ann, daughter of Enoch Smith, of Philadelphia, and had one daughter, Elizabeth, who married William Wilson, and resides in Philadelphia.

Elias (6), son of John (2), married Rebecca, daughter of Elijah Hendrickson, (see Hendrickson family, No. 8,) and had children: Elias, married Rebecca, daughter of John Stout, had one son, Alden; Elizabeth, married Benjamin Ogden, of Springfield, Mass., a physician of Trenton, where he died about two years after marriage, leaving a daughter, Emily, who married Dr. Giddings, of Connecticut.

Joseph (3), son of William (1), died 1814, aged 64; married Hannah, daughter of Isaac Howell, (see Howell family, No. 4.) She died 1821, aged 56, and left children: Joseph Carter, a physician, graduated at Jefferson Medical College, Philadelphia, died 1837, aged 31, having married Sarah, daughter of Dr. Simeon Dillingham, of Philadelphia, and leaving one son, Simeon, a physician of Des Moines, Iowa; Robinson, died young; Elizabeth, married Daniel Laning, of Lawrence; Susan, married John Temple, (see Temple family, No. 11); Charity, not married, died 1837, aged 48; Abigail, who died September 5th, 1861, aged 71, married Stephen Closson, of Trenton, who died June 9th, 1837, aged 42; Mary Ann, married Nathaniel Bunn, of Trenton; William, married Rachel Potter, of Shrewsbury, and has children: Joseph, a lawyer of Wayne county, N. Y., and James.

The White Family.

Abraham (1) and Mahitable White, ancestors of the families of this name of Lawrence and Trenton, were residents of Shrewsbury, Monmouth county, N. J. Their son, John (2), changed his residence to Lawrence, and there married, first, Catharine, daughter of James Olden, of Stony Brook, by whom he had Job, died unmarried; Nancy, died unmarried; and James (3). His second wife was Mary, daughter of John and Hannah Smith. Their children were: Catharine, married Giles W. Olden; Benjamin C., married Ann Paxson; and Jonathan, died unmarried.

James (3), son of John (2), a thriving and estimable man, lived on a valuable farm, in the vicinity of Lawrenceville. He died in 1851, aged 73, having married Martha, daughter of Philip Hendrickson, (see Hendrickson family, No. 5.) She died 1848, aged 77. They had children: Job (4); Robert, died 1857, aged 57, having married, first, Elizabeth, daughter of Daniel Cook, and had by her, one child, Samuel, died, aged 13, second wife was Ruth Hunt, widow of Robert Welling; William (5); George (6); and John.

Job (4), son of James (3), married Mary C., daughter of Noah Howell, (see Howell family, No. 15), and had children: Elizabeth, wife of Charles Henry Skirm; Martha Ann, died young; Jane, died young; and Benjamin C., married Mary, daughter of William Rouse, and has daughters, Elizabeth, wife of Alonzo Howell, and Martha.

William (5), son of James (3), was a merchant of Philadelphia for many years, and a part of the time associated with that eminent business man, Matthew Newkirk. After his retirement from the active pursuits of trade, he removed to Trenton, where he lived till his death. By his marriage with Hannah Haines, he had children: Ephraim, died young; George; Anna; Elizabeth, died young; James, died in youth; and Maria Elizabeth.

Dr. George (6), son of James (3), studied and practiced his

profession in Lawrenceville. He married Mary C., daughter of Peter Z. Schenck, of Pennington, by whom he had children: Louisa A.; James E., died in childhood; Catharine Olden; George Schenck; and Robert, a physician, settled at Riverton, Pa., died young.

The Woodhull Family.

Richard Woodhull (1), descended from illustrious ancestors through a long line, which has been preserved with great care from the Norman Conquest, 1060, was the son of Lawrence, and grandson of Baron Nicholas Woodhull, and he was born 1620, in Thenford, Northampton county, England. Having taken the side of liberty he emigrated to this country a little before the accession of Charles II. He is known to have been on Long Island as early as 1648, and being possessed of ample means, purchased in 1665, 103,000 acres, now the site of Brookhaven, to which town he made over his purchases, and is numbered the first one on its list of residents in 1655. In 1666 he was made justice of the Court of Assizes, and is known in history as Justice Woodhull. He died in 1690, leaving by his wife, Deborah, children: Richard (2); Nathaniel, died unmarried, 1680; and Deborah, who died 1742, aged 83, having married Capt. John Lawrence, of Newtown, Long Island, son of Major Thomas Lawrence, and grandson of Thomas Lawrence, who emigrated from Great St. Albans, Hertfordshire, England, about 1635.

Richard (2), son of Richard (1), died October 13th, 1699, aged 50, married Temperance, daughter of Rev. Josiah Fordham, pastor of Southampton, (Setauket,) and granddaughter of Rev. Robert Fordham, of England, and had children by her; Richard (3); and Nathaniel, who died 1760, having married Sarah, daughter of Richard Smith, of Smithtown, by whom he had twelve children. One was the brave and distinguished Gen. Nathaniel Woodhull, who, after having filled many high civil and military offices, fell at last in the battle of Long Island, August 27th, 1776, and died of his wounds, and of his subsequent sufferings in the horrible prison ships into which he was cruelly thrust. His last act was one of great generosity. He requested his wife to bring him all his money that she could; this he then caused her to distribute among his fellow sufferers. His wife was Ruth, daughter of Nicholl Floyd, and sister of Gen. William Floyd, one of the signers of the Declaration of Independence on the part of New York. She died 1822, aged 90, having had one child, Elizabeth, the wife, first, of Henry Nicholl, second, Gen. John Smith.

Richard (3), son of Richard (2), died 1767, aged 76, married Mary, daughter of John Homan, of Long Island. She died 1768, aged 75, having had children: Richard (4); Mary, wife of Jonathan Thompson; John (5); Nathan (6); Stephen; Henry; and Phebe.

Richard (4), son of Richard (3), died 1788, aged 76, was a judge of the Court of Common Pleas. He married Margaret, daughter of Edmund Smith, of Long Island, and had children: Richard (7); Abraham, judge of Common Pleas; and others.

Richard (7), son of Richard (4), died 1774, aged 33, was graduated by Yale College, was a judge of the Court of Common Pleas, married Sarah, daughter of Richard Miller, of Miller's Place, L. I., and had children: Richard (8); Sarah; Dorothy; and Julia.

Richard (8), son of Richard (7), died 1815, married Marion, daughter of James Horner Maxwell, had by her: Maxwell (9); and Marion, wife of Henry Cheeseborough.

Maxwell (9), son of Richard (8), was a commander in the United States Navy. His death was a most melancholy one. While accompanying a presidential party on a visit to Fortress Monroe, he stepped before the mouth of a cannon that was firing a salute, at the moment of discharge, was cut in two and blown from the parapet. His wife was Ellen F., daughter of Moses Poor, of Washington, D. C.; by her he had: Maxwell Van Gands Woodhull, brevet brigadier-general of the United States Army.

John (5), son of Richard (3), a gentleman of wealth, probity, and distinction, resided at Miller's Place, Suffolk county, L. I., died 1794, aged 75, having married, first, Elizabeth, daughter of Major William Henry Smith, (see Smith family, No. 2); she died 1794, aged 43, had children: William (10), born December 3d, 1741; John (11); Caleb; Merrit Smith; Henry; James (12); Elizabeth; Gilbert; and Geoffrey Amherst. By his second wife, Elizabeth Hedges, had Temperance; and Mary. His third wife was Hannah Davis.

Dr. William (10), son of John (5), a Presbyterian clergyman, was graduated at Princeton, and settled in Chester, Morris county, where he died 1824, aged 83. He not only preached but practiced patriotism, for he represented his congregation in the provincial congress, and was a member of the congress that formed the first constitution of New Jersey. He married Elizabeth, daughter of William Hedges, of East Hampton, L. I., and by her had children: William; John; Jeremiah; Henry H. (13); Caleb Gilbert; Temperance; Sophia; Hannah; Mehitable; and Elizabeth.

Henry H. (13), son of Dr. William (10), married first, Nancy, daughter of William Kirkpatrick, of Monmouth, whose children were: Mary Ann; and Nancy K.; second, Catharine Eoff, and had by her: Wm. Henry, a graduate of Princeton, and a lawyer; and Sarah Forman, wife of John Grandon Reading, (see Reading family, No. 11.)

Rev. Dr. John (11), son of John (5), was graduated at Princeton College, of which he was one of the trustees from 1780 till his death, 1824, aged 80. He was honored by Yale with the degree of D. D., was one of the eminent clergymen of his day, a faithful pastor of high intellectual endowments, and distinguished for his active zeal and patriotism during the war, and was for most of his life pastor of the Presbyterian Church of Freehold. He married Sarah, only daughter of Capt. George Spafford, of Philadelphia, and step-daughter of Rev. Gilbert Tennent; had children: William Henry, a merchant; Sarah, wife of Major William Gordon Forman, of Shrewsbury; George Spafford (14); John Tennent (15); and Gilbert Smith (16.)

Rev. George Spafford (14), son of John (11), was graduated at Princeton, 1790, studied theology, was settled over the Presbyterian Church of Cranbury from 1798 to 1820, over the First Church of Princeton the succeeding twelve years, and over the church at Matawan two years, where he died 1834, aged 61, having had by his wife, Gertrude, daughter of Col. John Neilson, of New Brunswick: Wm. Henry (17); Cornelia, died young; Alfred Alexander (18); John Neilson, a graduate of Princeton, and of the medical department of the University of Pennsylvania, settled in Princeton, where he gained a large and lucrative practice, and died in 1867, unmarried, leaving $40,000 to establish a professorship in the college.

Rev. William Henry (17), son of George Spafford (14), a graduate of Princeton College and Seminary, pastor of the First Presbyterian Church of Upper Freehold, died 1835, leaving by his wife Amanda, daughter of Col. William Wykoff, of Freehold, children: William W.; Spafford Eugene; John N.; and Cornelia N.

Dr. Alfred Alexander (18), son of George Spafford (14), a

graduate of Princeton, a physician and a trustee of the Presbyterian Church, was a man of piety, and died in 1836, in his prime. In his last illness, when conscious that he was about to enter into the "rest that remaineth for the people of God," he dictated the following beautiful stanzas, worthy of preservation:

"Traveler! dost thou hear the tidings
Borne unto thy weary ear,
Soft as angels' gentlest whispers
Breathing from the upper sphere,
Sweetly telling,
Thy redemption now is near?

"In the desert's gloomy terrors,
'Mid the tempest's booming roar,
Hark! the still, small voice of mercy
Breaking from yon peaceful shore,
Sweetly telling,
All thy toil will soon be o'er.

"Mourner! when the tear of sorrow
Wells from up thy stricken breast,
Raise thy streaming eyes to mansions
Where the weary are at rest,
Sweetly telling,
Here thou'lt be a welcome guest.

"Mortal! when death's viewless arrow
Quivers in thy fluttering heart,
Lift thy lapsing thoughts to Jesus,
Who disarms the fatal dart,
Sweetly telling,
I to thee my peace impart."

He married Maria, daughter of Dr. Dirck G. Solomons, and Susan, daughter of the Rev. Dr. Samuel Stanhope Smith, by whom he had one son, Albert A., graduated by Princeton and by the medical department of the Pennsylvania University. He is a surgeon in the army, and inspector-general of the medical department of the United States Army, and is married to Margaret Ellicott, of Baltimore, Md.

Dr. John T. (15), son of John (11), received his degree of M. D. from the University of Pennsylvania, practiced in Freehold, and there married Anna, daughter of Colonel William Wyckoff and Hannah Scudder, and had children: George Spafford, a graduate of Princeton College, a lawyer and judge of the Supreme Court, resident of Camden, married Caroline, daughter of G. B. Vroom, of New York, has seven children: Matilda, wife of Joseph Combs, son of Elijah, a graduate of Princeton, and judge of the Court of

Errors; Julia, wife of Rev. James Clark, D. D., of Philadelphia; Wm. Wyckoff, a graduate of Princeton College, of which he was tutor, and Ph. D., married Ellen C., daughter of Nathaniel Scudder Wyckoff, of Freehold; Maria Scudder, married Gilbert Combs, son of Elijah, a Princeton graduate and lawyer; Charles Frederic, graduated by Princeton; Hannah W.; Gilbert Tennent, a graduate of Princeton College and Seminary, pastor of the Presbyterian Church at Fishkill Landing, and professor of languages in Lincoln University, married Elizabeth, daughter of William B. Waldo, of Fishkill; and Addison Waddell, a graduate of Princeton, and of the Medical University of New York, married Emma, daughter of Dr. Daniel E. Taylor, of Freehold, and is settled at Newark.

Dr. Gilbert Smith (16), son of John (11), was graduated by the Medical College of New York, and practiced in Freehold till his death in 1844, having married Charlotte, daughter of Colonel William Wyckoff and Hannah Scudder, and had by her: Henry William Beck, a graduate of Princeton College, and of the Medical College of New York, and married Azelia, daughter of Joseph Girard, of New York; Sarah, wife of Barbarie Throckmorton, merchant of New York; Anna Matilda; and Charlotte Gilberta.

James (12), son of John (5), died 1798, aged 46, resided in New York, married Keturah, daughter of Judge Selah Strong, of New York. She died 1831, aged 74, having had children: Selah Strong (19); and Elizabeth, wife of George Griswold, a wealthy and eminent East India merchant of New York, and by him had Maria, wife of Woodward Havens, and Sarah, wife of John C. Green, (see Green family, No. 31.)

Rev. Dr. Selah Strong (19), son of James (12), a graduate of Yale College, from which he received the degree of D. D., was professor of ecclesiastical history and pastoral theology in the Theological Seminary of New Brunswick, and professor of mental philosophy in Rutgers College, died 1826, aged 40, having married Cornelia, daughter of Aaron Van Cleve, (see Van Cleve family, No. 6,) by whom he had Eliza Ketura, wife of Jonathan B. Condit, D. D., professor in Auburn Theological Seminary; Matilda Griswold, wife of James G. Nutman; Sarah Strong, became the second wife of her brother-in-law, Jonathan B. Condit; Cornelia Van Cleve, wife of Josiah L. Packard; and Jane Green.

Capt. Nathan (6), son of Richard (3), married Joanna, daughter of Isaac Mills, by whom he had the Rev. Nathan Woodhull, pastor of the Presbyterian Church of Newtown; Ellen, wife of Rev. Dr. John Goldsmith; Sarah, wife of Rev. Richard Storrs, D. D.; Martha, wife of Hon. Lewis Condit, M. D., of New Jersey.

The Woodruff Family.

Elias (1), ancestor of one of the families of that name in Trenton and Ewing, resided in the eastern part of the state, at Elizabethtown. He married Mary Joline, of that city, and had issue: Aaron Dickinson (2); George (3); Elizabeth, wife of Rev. Thomas Howe, an Episcopal clergyman; Susan, wife of John Dowers; Maria, wife of Robert C. Thomson, of Warren county; Abner, resided at Perth Amboy, was graduated at Princeton, was connected with the United States Navy for a time, afterward became a merchant, and died, 1842, having married, first, Miss Austin, second, sister of the former, and third, Miss Brown.

Aaron D. (2), son of Elias (1), was a man highly esteemed for his abilities and probity; was born at Elizabeth, in 1762; was graduated with honor by the College of New Jersey, in 1799, having been appointed valedictorian of the class. He was admitted to the bar in 1784; made attorney-general in 1793, an office which he filled for twenty-four years, with high distinction, till his death, in 1817, having won, by his uncompromising integrity, the confidence of all. He served for a time in the legislature, and was a trustee of the First Church of Trenton. He married Grace, daughter of Thomas Lowry, of Alexandria, N. J., who died 1815, aged 49, and by her had children: Elias Decou (4); Thomas L. (5); Susan, wife of George Thomson, whose children are: Maria, Elias D., and George; Hetty, married Rev. John Smith, for some years pastor of the First Church of Trenton; and Aaron D., died in youth.

Elias D. (4), son of Aaron (2), was a graduate of Princeton, became a member of the bar, and died September 19th, 1824, aged 38, having married Abigail Whitall, by whom he had children: Aaron D., a physician, settled at Haddonfield, married Anne Davidson, of Georgetown, D. C.; Sarah, wife of Isaac Jones, of Philadelphia, has children: Woodruff and Thomas; Elizabeth, married Richard Dale, a merchant of Philadelphia; and Anna, wife of Rev. George Richards, of Boston.

Dr. Thomas L. (5), son of Aaron (2), graduated at Princeton, studied medicine, and died March 8th, 1851, aged 61, having married Anna, daughter of Israel Carle,* who died February 10th, 1849, aged 54. Their children were: Israel Carle (6); Aaron P. (7); Thomas; Lydia; and George.

Gen. Carle (6), son of Dr. Thomas (5), was educated at West Point; was colonel of engineers and brigadier-general in the United States Army, married Caroline Mayhew, of Buffalo. Their children are: Col. Carle A., of United States Army, married Effie Haywood, of North Carolina, is stationed at Newport, Ky.; Elise, married George W. Dix, of Staten Island; Virginia S., married Maj. William R. King, of the United States Army, stationed at Chattanooga, Tenn.; Thomas M., of the United States Army, married Annie Sampson, of Ohio, stationed at Fort Keogh; Edward L., a civil engineer and architect, married May Bateman, and resides on Staten Island; and Isabella.

Aaron D. (7), son of Dr. Thomas (5), married Eliza Anthony, and had children: Anna, wife of William Hay; William; Dickinson, married Ruth Wooley; Mary; Julia; Thomas; and Caroline.

George (3), son of Elias (1), a man of high moral excellence, was graduated by the College of New Jersey, studied and practiced law in Georgia, was appointed district attorney by President Adams, and died at his residence, near Trenton, September 3d, 1846, aged 82, having married Jean Houstoun, of Savannah, who died March, 1848, aged 73. She was the daughter of George Houstoun, son of Sir Patrick Houstoun, whose son, John, was governor of Georgia. Their children were: George H., a graduate of Princeton, took orders in the Episcopal Church, and died at Carlisle, 1822, aged 25; Elias, died in England; Houstoun, married Louisa C. Johnston, of Georgia, who died a few months after the birth of her only child, Louisa C.; Robert I., also a graduate of Princeton, married, first, Mary, daughter of Rue Baker, who

---

*Jacob Carle, probably of Huguenot descent, who was an elder in the Ewing Presbyterian Church, 1771, and who died November 23d, 1800, aged 73, on his farm in Ewing, married Elizabeth, daughter of John Welling, (see Welling family, No. 1,) who died May 22d, 1801, aged 73, and by her had children: Hannah, wife of Aaron Van Cleve, (see Van Cleve family, No. 6); Elizabeth, wife of John Vanmarter; Anna, died 1776, aged 22; and Israel, who, at his death, in July, 1822, aged 65, left £100 to the trustees of the Presbyterian Church, he married, first, Eliza Stevens, who died March 12th, 1790, aged 29, by his marriage with his second wife, Lydia, daughter of William Green, (see Green family, No. 41,) who died August 23d, 1828, aged 56, he had a daughter, Anna, who married Dr. Thomas L. Woodruff (5).

died soon after marriage, he moved to Princeton, Ill., and married, second, Isabella Swift, has children: Mary and Susan; T. Moody, moved to Princeton, Ill., married Eliza Swift, has children: George and William; Mary, wife of Dr. Charles L. Pearson, of Trenton, has sons: Charles and George; and Dickinson, was educated at Princeton, studied law, and practiced in St. Louis, joined the United States Army, and is now colonel in the service.

The Woolsey Family.

George Woolsey (1), son of Benjamin, son of Thomas, grandfather of the first settler of that name, in Hopewell, came from England to Manhattan Island in 1623 or 1635, and resided for a time among the Hollanders; thence he removed, in 1665, to Jamaica, where he died, August 17th, 1698, aged 86. He had at least three children: Capt. George (2); Thomas; and John.

Capt. George (2) had sons: George (3); and Rev. Benjamin, whose grandson is Theodore D. Woolsey, president of Yale College.

George (3), son of George (2) came to Hopewell from Long Island with his son, Jeremiah (4), about 1700. The deed of their farm bears date of that year. In 1727, he was appointed by Gov. Burnet, captain in Col. John Reading's Regiment, of Hunterdon. He had also children: Daniel, who had a son, Benjamin, that lived in Trenton, and was the father of Henry and Nancy; Henry (5); Joseph, married Miss Montgomery, and removed to Maryland; and Jemima, wife of Ralph Hart, (see Hart family, No. 5.)

Jeremiah (4), son of George (3), died April 14th, 1801, aged 82; married Mary, daughter of Joseph Hart, (see Hart family, No. 2.) She died October 14th, 1808, aged 82. Both are buried in the Presbyterian church-yard of Pennington. Their children are: Hannah, died unmarried: Ephraim (6), born 1757; Mary, born 1759, wife of Louis Perrine, of Freehold, and had by him: Henry, Jeremiah W., married Mary Blackwell, John, married Azubah Hunt, Hannah, wife of Isaac Welling, (see Welling family, No. 5,) Mary, wife of Samuel Green, (see Green family, No. 44,) and Abigail, wife of William Clark; Jemima, died unmarried; Susannah, died unmarried; and Jeremiah (7).

Henry (5), son of George (3), lived in Pennington; married Martha, daughter of Ephraim Titus, (see Titus family, No. 6); had one child, Martha, who became the wife of Philip Van Cleve, (see Van Cleve family, No. 8.)

Ephraim (6), son of Jeremiah (4), who died 1817, aged 60, married Anna Johnson, of Montgomery county, Pa. She died 1835, aged 78, and is buried with her husband, in the Pennington grave-yard. They had: George (8); Ephraim (9); Hannah, wife of Deacon Andrew Titus, (see Titus family, No. 15); Mary, wife of Philemon Blackwell, son of Jacob; and Eliza.

George (8), son of Ephraim (6), a deacon in Pennington church, and for three years a member of the legislative council of New Jersey, married Elizabeth, daughter of George Muirheid, (see Muirheid family, No. 4,) and had by her: Theodore, who married Sarah Ann, daughter of John S. Hunt, and has children: George S., Charles N., Elizabeth M., Henry Harrison, and Edgar; Charity M., married Joseph A. Pittenger, has children: George W., Henry M., and Ella W.; Mary Ann, married Jesse Atchley, has children: Elizabeth W., Andrew Titus, Caroline A., Anna V., Minnie, Charles, and Frank; and Ellen V., married David Baldwin, has children: Henry L. and Elizabeth W.

Ephraim (9), son of Ephraim (6), married Eleanor, daughter of Benjamin Van Cleve, (see Van Cleve family, No. 16,) and had by her: Noah, married Martha Martindale; Ann Eliza, married Frederic Titus, son of Nathaniel, (see Titus family, No. 27); and Henry Harrison, was a graduate of Princeton, was admitted to the bar, and laid aside his practice to take up arms as captain of a company in defence of the Union, having distinguished himself by his gallantry in several battles, especially that of Gettysburg, where he commanded his regiment. He fell at last, mortally wounded, before Petersburg, Va., June 18th, 1864. His last words were, "I die in a glorious cause, and feel that I have not lived in vain, for this world or the world to come." His wife, Thirza, daughter of George A. Hutchinson, of Trenton, died just before him.

Jeremiah (7), son of Jeremiah (4), was a physician, and practiced his profession, for some years, in Allentown and Trenton. About 1812, he removed to Cincinnati, where he died, 1834, aged 65. His wife was Martha, daughter of Alexander Montgomery, of Allentown; died 1832. By her he had Catharine; William, a druggist of Evansville, Ind.; Sarah; Samuel; Daniel, a druggist of Evansville, Ind.; and Susan.

The Yard Family.

By a well-authenticated and carefully-preserved genealogy brought over by its first emigrants to this country, the family of Yard appears to have been of Norman origin, its earliest ancestor having accompanied William the Conqueror. The name was first spelled De Yarde, but after a time the "De" was dropped; the terminal "e," however, is still retained by the English members.

The annals of Devonshire make honorable mention of many individuals of this family and of their estates.

William and Joseph Yard, brothers, about the year 1688, emigrated from near Exeter, Devonshire, England, and with their families landed at Philadelphia, where Joseph remained, but about 1700 William, with two of his sons and his daughters, transferred his residence to Trenton, and at the time of his death, 1742, five of his sons were living there. Mr. Yard purchased of Mahlon Stacy, in 1712, two acres on Second, now State, street, extending to the Assanpink, and between Greene and Warren streets; on Front street he built his residence. He was a purchaser of other large portions of land and property, so that when a name was to be given to the town, it was a question for a time whether it should be Yard's-town or Trent's-town. Mr. Yard was active and prominent in the affairs of the town, and a zealous supporter of the Presbyterian Church. By his wife, Mary Peace, he had: Joseph (2); William (3); John (4); Benjamin (5); Jethro, who left by his will dated 1767, £7 to the poor of the Presbyterian Church, and the remainder of his considerable property to his relatives, probably; if married, he had no children; Mary, married Henry Mershon, and had William, Joseph, Benjamin, and perhaps others; Elizabeth, wife of Morris Justice, by whom she had Elizabeth, Mary, Joseph, William, and John, married Rebecca Osburn, of Philadelphia.

Joseph (2), son of William (1), was clerk of the Court of Common Pleas, a member of the king's council, a man of worth and prominence, and a friend both of the church and education. He gave a part of the ground on which the First Presbyterian Church stands, and his name is found among the seven corporators of the Presbyterian Church, incorporated in 1756, in the trusteeship of which he continued till his decease. He manifested his friendship for the cause of education by leaving to the College of New Jersey £100. His death occurred 1763, having married Anne, daughter of John Dagworthy, of Lawrence, by whom he had Joseph (6); Archibald William (7); Jethro, died young, without children; and Mary Ann.

Joseph (6), son of Joseph (2), married, and had children: James, who went abroad when quite young, when he returned, about 1790, he became a shipping merchant of great enterprise, in Philadelphia, where he died, 1835, aged 75, and is buried in the St. Peter's Episcopal church-yard, having married Elizabeth Kortright, of Santa Cruz, she died April 12th, 1824, aged 59, and is buried in St. Peter's church-yard; Furman, died young, unmarried; Anne, became the second wife of Gen. Frelinghuysen, by whom she had a daughter, died young, and Elizabeth, wife of Dr. Elmendorf, of Millstone.

Archibald W. (7), son of Joseph (2), who died March 10th, 1810, aged 78. By his first wife, Margaret, he had Mary, born January 5th, 1775, and died, aged 90, married Andrew Mershon, of Lawrence, had a son, Edward, died unmarried, 1840, aged 50, and a daughter, Sarah; Margaret, born January 12th, 1757, married Mr. Ashmore, and died, aged 34, leaving a son, Jabish, and six or seven other children; Joseph, born August 9th, 1758, died at Mt. Pleasant, N. Y., unmarried; William, born October 5th, 1759, married Sarah, daughter of Manuel Eyre, of Philadelphia, had a daughter, Mary; Capt. Edward (8); Archibald, born April, 1762, supposed to have been killed in the battle of the Nile; Jethro, born January 4th, 1763, died unmarried; Jethro, born January 4th, 1765, died young. He married for his second wife, Catherine Pearson, who died November 9th, 1791, having had: Thomas, born January 2d, 1769, married, and had children; Jethro, born October 20th, 1770, married Ruth Potter, whose children were: Joseph, Jethro, Archibald, and Ann; Robert, born October 18th, 1772, lived in Tennessee; Anna, born January 4th, 1775, wife of Daniel Phillips, of Trenton, (see Phillips family, No. 23); Sarah, born April 23d, 1777, died January 4th, 1840, married Jacob Keen, son of Jacob, lived in Harrison, Ohio, where he died, December 9th, 1831, aged 57; Elizabeth, born December

10th, 1779, married Joseph Taylor, whose children were: Morris, William, Catherine, and Pearson; Theodocia, born April 12th, 1782, died unmarried; Rachel, born October 3d, 1783, wife of Benjamin Stephens, lived in Batavia, N. Y., and has one daughter; and Pearson, born October 12th, 1788, married Ann Cook, and has children: William, married Mary Morgan Champion, of Philadelphia, and Catherine, wife of John R. Dill, of Trenton, no children.

Capt. Edward (8), son of Archibald (7), died May 8th, 1839, aged 78. He devoted himself, early in life, to the marine service; was captured by the British Maidstone frigate, during a voyage from Philadelphia to Madeira, and was detained a prisoner till 1782, when he escaped from Plymouth to London, and came over in the fleet of Admiral Digby. He afterwards commanded ships engaged in the trade to India and China, and withdrew from the sea during the embargo, in 1808. He retired, on a farm near Pennington; was twice returned to the legislature from his county. He married Abigail, daughter of Col. Joseph Phillips, (see Phillips family, No. 33.) His children are: Maria A.; Elizabeth; Frances; and Edward, a captain in the United States naval service, married Josephine, daughter of Oliver Olmsby, a merchant of Pittsburg, who died soon after marriage, leaving one daughter, Josephine, married Lieut. James B. Breese, of the marine corps, son of Sidney Breese, chief justice of Illinois, and nephew of Commodore Breese.

William (3), son of William (1), married, and had children: Isaiah (9); Elijah; Mary, married, first, Mr. Tennent, by whom she had a son, William, second, Mr. Emmerson, having by him: Richard, John, Samuel, and others.

Isaiah (9), son of William (3), was captain of a company of the First Regiment of Hunterdon county, 1777, married Helena Jones, of Philadelphia, by whom he had: John, unmarried; Charles Jacob, married Eliza Bayard, of Philadelphia, where he resided and died, having had by her a daughter, wife of Thomas Wallace Evans, a merchant of Philadelphia, whose store was one of the ornaments of Chestnut street; Isabella, wife of Seth Roberts; and Mary, married Henry Thornton.

John (4), son of William (1), died 1763, had by his first wife: Isaac (10); and William, unmarried; and by his second wife, Hannah Oakley, Daniel (11); Benjamin (12); Achsa, who died October 2d, 1823, aged 79, married Samuel Bellerjeau, their children were: Henry, Benjamin, John, Samuel, Thomas, Daniel, Hannah, married Mr. Gee, and Sarah.

Isaac (10), son of John (4), married Mary, sister of George Ely, of Trenton, and had children: Isaac (13); Benjamin (14); William; Jane, wife in succession of James Kelly and Gilbert Brown; John, married Effie Dippolt; and Prudence, wife of James Bond.

Isaac (13), son of Isaac (10), married Mary Margerum, and had children: Rebecca, married Wilson Margerum; John, married; and George, married Ann Fine, of Easton, where he resides and has children.

Benjamin (14), son of Isaac (10), died September 9th, 1832, aged 64, having married Priscella, daughter of Jacob Keen, she died December 28th, 1852, aged 82, having had children: Isaac, died unmarried 1821, aged 30; Edmund J. (15); Jacob, married widow of Stephen Gay; John (16); Charles C., a man much respected, and for many years elected to the common council, and died unmarried, September 18th, 1866, aged 66; Joseph A. (17); William K., married, and died 1850, aged 40, leaving three children: Benjamin, a lieutenant in the United States service, died at Metamoras, Mexico, October 22d, 1847, having married Mary Davis, of Easton, she died January 11th, 1844, aged 32, leaving children: Elizabeth F. and Alexander G.; Mary D., wife of Henry B. James, by whom she had: Rev. James H., Mary P., Anna E., and Charles M.; and Wilson, died young.

Edmund J., (15), son of Benjamin (14), married Jane McCurdy, resided in Philadelphia. Their children are: Benjamin F., editor of "Temperance Visitor," married Helen Park; and Edmund S., married Emeline F. Carriger.

John (16), son of Benjamin (14), married Eliza Walter, of Philadelphia, has children: Hannah M., married Robert McCurdy; Charles, married Mary Letherman; and Ann Eliza, wife of Rush Heentzelman.

Joseph A. (17), son of Benjamin (14), died October 17th, 1878, aged 76, and was captain of "Jersey Blues," in the Mexican war, and also commander of a company of volunteers, raised in Trenton during the war for the Union, married Mary W., daughter of Wesley and Ann Sterling, died November 14th, 1863, aged 59, and had by her: James S., married Addie Swift; Anna Mary, wife of Alfred S. Sly; Rev. Robert B., married, first, Hannah Wilkins, of Mt. Holly; and second, Sarah Purdieu, of Haverstraw; Caroline, wife of Dr. H. S. Desonges, of New York; Wesley S., married Sarah Jordan; Thomas S., a physician, died September 26th, 1879, aged 42; Alexander A.; Stephen A.; Benjamin F.; Henry H.; and John Tyler.

Daniel (11), son of John (4), died November 28th, 1849, aged 94, having married Mary Boden, and had children: Achsa, died, aged 22; Theodocia, died, aged 20; Hannah, died March 9th, 1859, aged 71, having married Elias Kennedy, and had children: Theodocia, John, Daniel, and Rosanna, married William Eldree; and Daniel, married, and died in New Orleans, was captain of a company of volunteers, in 1812, has children.

Benjamin (12), son of John (4), married Elizabeth Kortright, daughter of an English gentleman of Santa Cruz, where he died, August 21st, 1787, having by her: Cornelius, died 1803, aged 19, buried in St. Peter's grounds, Philadelphia; Samuel, died young; Eliza, wife of Charles Kuhn, a wealthy merchant of Philadelphia. Mr. Yard's widow married James Yard, son of Joseph Yard (6).

Benjamin (5), son of William (1), in the early days of Trenton, was active and zealous in promoting the several interests of the community. He is recorded in the minutes of the trustees of the Presbyterian Church as having been elected by the congregation, in 1765, one of the first two directors of their school-house. In the same year, he was also appointed an elder of the church. He died 1808, aged 94, having married Ann Pierson, and having had children: James (18); John (19); George (20); Nahor (21); Samuel; Benjamin; Mary; and Elizabeth—the last four not married.

James (18), son of Benjamin (5), married Nancy Mounttier, whose children are: Anna, married, successively, Mr. Tunie, of Philadelphia, and Alexander Campbell; William, married Miss Brittain; James C., not married; Benjamin, married Ellen Loyd: and John.

John (19), son of Benjamin (5), died 1807, having married Mary Stillman, and had: Mary, died young; Theodocia, wife of William McKee, and they had children: James, John, and Amanda, married George Miller.

George (20), son of Benjamin (5), married Catherine Stout, and by her had: Benjamin; Anna, wife of Josiah Robinson; John, married Elizabeth, daughter of Joseph Wall; Elizabeth, wife of John Dillenbush; Catherine, wife of Nicholas Dillenbush; Margaret, married Thomas Ford, and had: William, married

Miss Hutchinson, Catherine, married Furman Hutchinson, Mary Ann, wife of Alexander Thompson, Margaret, wife of Daniel Stryker, Thomas, married Louisa West, George, married Catherine Dilts, and Benjamin, married Sarah Dorsett.

Benjamin (22), son of George (20), married Sarah, daughter of John Reed, whose children are: Stout; Charles; George; Ann; and Catherine, who married Mr. Paul.

Nahor (21), son of Benjamin (5), died September 18th, 1791, married March 23d, 1787, Elizabeth, daughter of Thomas Biggs, of England, (who came over about 1750, settled in Pennsylvania, and married Sarah, daughter of Alexander Biles, son of Stephen.) They had children: Sarah, died in childhood; Anna, wife of Ely Hutchinson; and Joseph (23).

Joseph (23), son of Nahor (21), died 1872, aged 83, having married Elizabeth Brinley, by whom he had: Nahor B., an early settler of Galveston, Texas, married Caroline Nichols, has children: Elizabeth C., Edward J., and George N.; Jacob S., married Angeline C. Brenlinger, has children: Henry H. and Elyanta H.; Joseph, married Sarah Ann Neal, has children: Emery N. and J. Herbert; William S. (24); George, a justice, married Melicent Wilgus, has children: Nahor B., Laura E.. and Anna M.; Jane Elizabeth, died aged 17; and Herbert, married Margaret Mason, has a child, Frederick B.

William S. (24), son of Joseph (23), a member of the legislature and judge of the Court of Common Pleas, Mercer county, N. J., married Mary M., daughter of Samuel Hamilton, of Lancaster, Pa., had by her: Mary Elizabeth, wife of James H. Clark; Caroline, wife of J. Vanwart Schenck, a Presbyterian clergyman; William H.; Jane F.; George Brown; and Edward Scudder.

Errata.

The following errors were discovered after this work was printed. All these mistakes in names appear in the original manuscript. In reference thereto, attention is respectfully called to the last paragraphs of the publisher's preface. All who have had any experience in compiling volumes of this character, know how difficult it is to make them perfectly accurate. Great care has, however, been taken to have the proofs corrected by some one having personal knowledge of each family. It is suggested that any person particularly interested in any one family, interleave the pages of that family genealogy with thin paper, and note, from time to time, additions or corrections:

Page 6, line 2, Margaret L. should be Margaret F.
" 18, " 30, John Stephens should be John Stevens.
" 18, " 31, Miss Vanzant should be Sarah Margerum.
" 18, " 32, Miss Golder should be Christine Golden.
" 18, " 33, John V. Raum should be John O. Raum.
" 66, " 1, paternal should be maternal.
" 75, " 3, Ezekiel (10) should be Ezekiel (11).
" 83, " 11, John Thomas should be John Fletcher.
" 83, " 21, John Kennedy should be James Kennedy.
" 83, " 22, Virginia should be omitted.
" 98, " 35, No. omitted—should be Joseph (2).
" 132, " 5, Ezekiel (17) should be Joseph (18).
" 132, " 37, No. 18 should be No. 14.
" 136, " 6, Peter (42) should be Peter (41).
" 142, " 4, Peter Z. Schenck should be Peter S. Schenck.
" 157, " 18, Ralph (33) should be Ralph (32).
" 157, " 22, William (34) should be William (33).
" 208, " 15, Edward (9) should be Edward (10).
" 220, " 27, 1836 should be 1839.
" 220, " 40, Rev. Dr. Hyers should be Rev. Dr. Hires.
" 221, " 1, Dr. Abel should be Dr. Abell.
" 222, " 23, Charles de Cerqueria of Lima should be Charles de Cerqueria Lema.
" 222, " 41, James Hay should be James N. Hay.
" 231, " 16, 1872 should be 1875.
" 231, " 17, forty-second should be forty-third.
" 231, " 21, Charles Davis should be Charles Davies.
" 231, " 27, Manfield should be Mansfield.
" 236, " 41, Joel (9) should be Joel (91).
" 239, " 21, Col. Nathaniel (108) should be Col. Nathaniel (109).
" 242, " 24, Horde should be Hord.
" 242, " 29, William McChord should be William McCloud.
" 250, " 26, William (121) should be William (129).
" 252, " 27, Amos T. Akerman, an eminent lawyer of Georgia, should be Amos T. Akerman, attorney-general of the United States and a member of President Grant's cabinet.
" 253, " 4, Elizabeth should be omitted.
" 300, " 21, Peter V. Schenck should be Peter S. Schenck.
" 305, " 2, Peter Z. Schenck should be Peter S. Schenck.

Index of Families.

Index of Names.